MW01204830

Rocky Mountain Flowers

PLATE 1

OCKY MOUNTAIN FLOWERS

AN ILLUSTRATED GUIDE FOR PLANT-LOVERS AND PLANTERS

WITH TWENTY-FIVE PLATES IN COLOR AND TWENTY-TWO PLATES IN BLACK AND WHITE

PLATE 1

BUTTERCUP FAMILY

1. Aconitum columbianum: Monkshood
2. Aquilegia coerulea: Blue Columbine
3. Aquilegia canadensis: Red Columbine
4. Delphinium scopulorum: Larkspur

D.

MINNESOTA, AND STATE BOTANIST,
ALPINE LABORATORY

AND

CLEMENTS, Ph. D.

UNIVERSITY OF MINNESOTA AND IN THE
ALPINE LABORATORY

THE H. W. WILSON COMPANY
WHITE PLAINS, N. Y. AND NEW YORK CITY
1914

ROCKY MOUNTAIN FLOWERS

AN ILLUSTRATED GUIDE FOR PLANT-LOVERS AND PLANT-USERS

WITH TWENTY-FIVE PLATES IN COLOR AND
TWENTY-TWO PLATES IN BLACK AND WHITE

FREDERIC EDWARD CLEMENTS, PH. D.

HEAD OF THE DEPARTMENT OF BOTANY IN THE UNIVERSITY OF MINNESOTA, AND STATE BOTANIST;
DIRECTOR OF THE PIKE'S PEAK ALPINE LABORATORY

AND

EDITH SCHWARTZ CLEMENTS, PH. D.

INSTRUCTOR IN BOTANY IN THE UNIVERSITY OF MINNESOTA AND IN THE
PIKE'S PEAK ALPINE LABORATORY

THE H. W. WILSON COMPANY
WHITE PLAINS, N. Y. AND NEW YORK CITY
1914

PREFACE

The present book is an endeavor to present the materials of the Rocky Mountain flora in preliminary form from the standpoint of the experimental ecologist. The latter is concerned primarily with the relationships of "species" and their subdivisions as an organic expression or measure of habitat differences, and of the competitive relations of the various formations. Whatever the taxonomic value of the numerous segregates of the last decade or two, the fact that the binomial form conceals the relationship to the original species, and that the segregate itself is based not at all or only slightly upon habitat relations, makes them of little value to the ecologist. This condition is emphasized by the extreme difficulty of their field determination and recognition. No attempt has been made to pass upon the merits of segregates as such, but similarity and relationship have been taken as determining the units used, with the conviction that the differences will appear all the more clearly when habitat and formation have been thoroughly studied experimentally. To the ecologist, it seems certain that such experimental analysis of the unit must carry with it the regular use of the trinomial, leaving binomials only for the unit as a whole, whether capable of analysis or not.

In spite of some quantitative study of the origin of new forms by adaptation to the habitat, and some statistical study of variation from habitat to habitat, during the past decade, the authors recognize clearly the tentative nature of the units employed. While the latter agree in the main with the "species" of Linné, and of Gray and the earlier American botanists, the initial test of continuous variation or discontinuous adaptation has merged a considerable number of these, and must be expected to unite still more. The questions of a species, its inherited constancy, etc., have not been raised, as this seems futile without continued experiment. The units employed may be "species" or not, but at present they mean nothing more than that the individuals or groups of individuals in a unit are more nearly related to each other than to any other group. In fact, whenever the curve of variation is continuous, it is felt that a unit is indicated, regardless of the height of the modes.

iii

The book is a forerunner of one on the vegetation of the Rocky Mountains, which has been under way since 1899. The latter is planned not only to outline the structure and development of the vegetation, but it is hoped also that it will be of practical value to the forester and others who touch the habitat and formation in their daily work. Such a book can be of practical use only when the units with which it deals can be recognized with some readiness and certainty. The opportunity for such recognition is materially increased by using relationship to determine the units. This is enhanced by the number of units illustrated, 175 in color and 355 in line. In addition, the illustrations make possible the recognition of a number of common plants by the plant-lover without botanical training. Furthermore, to the botanist the present book will serve to summarize the first results of the quantitative study of the origin of new forms, and to indicate the basis of the work under way in the experimental and statistical study of variation and adaptation.

The descriptions of several hundred units were written in the field from a large number of individuals, whenever possible under different conditions. It was early found that full descriptions would make the book unwieldy, and they were dropped, in so far as the units were concerned. It is felt that the generic descriptions and the full keys in the larger genera will be sufficient in practically all cases of doubt. For the same reason, no synonyms are given under the units. In fact, the value of synonyms is slight until much fuller experimental and statistical studies have been made. In general, the synonyms given by Nelson have been accepted, usually after the scrutiny of co-types. In other cases, the union of segregates is clearly indicated by the key. While the nomenclature conforms in general with the American code, no compunction has been felt in correcting improperly formed names, or in using short and significant names in preference to long ones without meaning. In the matter of measurements, the smaller units of the metric system have been used below an inch as a rule, in preference to lines or fractions.

Constant use has been made of Rydberg's "Flora of Colorado," Nelson's "New Manual of Rocky Mountain Botany," Coulter's "Manual of Rocky Mountain Botany," Britton and Brown's "Illustrated Flora," and Gray's "New Manual of Botany," as well as the original papers of Eastwood, Greene, Nelson, Rydberg and others, for which grateful acknowledgment is made. In determining the relationship of recent segregates, as well as of earlier "species," and in confirming the field and experimental results, Torrey and Gray's "Flora of North America" and Gray's "Synoptical

Flora" in particular have been invaluable. The Besseyan system of classification has been employed with a few slight modifications. The sequence in the text is from buttercups to mints, then from roses to asters, and from arrowheads to orchids and grasses. The pines are placed at the end and quite frankly out of their proper position for reasons of convenience.

The color illustrations have been made in the field with few exceptions. The line drawings are largely from herbarium material. In both cases, drawings have been made natural size throughout, except in case of small parts such as fruits, spikelets, perigynia, etc.

The range of the book is essentially that of Coulter-Nelson's "Manual," namely, Colorado, Wyoming, most of Montana, Northern New Mexico, Eastern Utah, and Western North and South Dakota, Nebraska and Kansas. The layman will find the book useful over a much wider area, since the majority of the species in color occur from the Canadian Rockies to California or Arizona.

FREDERIC E. CLEMENTS,
EDITH S. CLEMENTS.

Minnehaha-on-Ruxton,
Manitou, Colorado.
July 22, 1913.

CONTENTS

vii

CONTENTS

LIST OF PLATES

THE FLOWER CHART

The flower chart (Plate 2) is an attempt to express in concise graphic form the general lines of the evolution of flowering plants from the ancestral ferns, and to indicate the relationships of the various groups. By following two or three simple rules which will be given later, the chart also serves as a key to determining the group to which a flower belongs.

A "flower," as the term is generally understood, is made up of four different sets of parts, arranged in concentric circles at the tip of a stem or flower-stalk. The outer circle is composed of green, leaf-like structures known as sepals or calyx. The next circle of white or colored parts consists of petals, which form the corolla. Within this row, or sometimes fastened to the petals, are the pollen-bearing organs or stamens, made up of little sacks which contain the pollen and are attached to slender stalks or filaments. In the center of the flower are found the pistils or a single pistil. Each usually has a swollen or enlarged part at the base, the ovary, which contains the ovules or young seeds, a slender stalk or style arising from the ovary, and a roughened or branched end to the style, called the stigma.

The simplest flowers occur among the families of cone-bearing trees and shrubs, and among the buttercups. The flowers of the former are made up of cones of pollen-bearing and of seed-bearing scales, and lack both calyx and corolla. The flowers of the buttercups, on the other hand, possess calyx or corolla, or both, as well as stamens and pistils, and are regarded as the most primitive or the simplest flowers, among what are popularly known as "flowering plants." In detail, one of these primitive or simple flowers is made up of a large number of separate stamens and pistils, and a variable number of separate similar petals and separate similar sepals. The flower parts are arranged, as indicated above, in concentric circles on the end of the flower stalk or "receptacle" and at practically the same level. A simple flower of this sort may become advanced or specialized by one or more of the following changes: (1) reduction in number of parts, (2) union of parts among themselves or with each other,

(3) elevation of corolla or stamens or of both, (4) change of form and arrangement, producing irregularity. The sepals may be united to each other into a cup-shaped calyx, as in the Pinks or Gentians (Plate 18), and this may in turn be united or grown to the ovary, as in the Evening Primroses and Mentzelias (Plate 32). They may become irregular in shape and brightly colored, as in the Buttercups (Plate 1), or they may be reduced in number. The petals may become united to each other, either partly or entirely, as in the Morning Glories and Phloxes (Plate 19). They may grow up and on the ovary as in the Bluebells and Parsleys (Plate 36). They may become either one or all irregular in shape, as in the Irises and Orchids (Plate 43), or the Snapdragons (Plate 22), the Pentstemons (Plate 23), and the Mints (Plate 24), or they may be reduced in number or even lost entirely, as in the Willows (Plate 12). So also the stamens may grow together, in whole or in part, the union taking place either by the filaments or the pollen-sacks. They may grow together with the petals, thus becoming attached to them. They may be reduced in number and even be lacking in the pistillate flowers of a monoecious or dioecious species. Finally the pistils may become united into a several to many-celled compound pistil, or the cross-walls may disappear between the cells, leaving a 1-celled compound pistil. The number of simple, separate pistils may vary from many to one, but there is never more than one compound pistil in any one flower. Of the utmost importance is the union of the simple pistils and the number of cells in the compounded pistil. It will be seen by reference to the chart, that this union is the first step of advance above the Buttercups.

The setting apart of flowering plants in orders and families is based upon the kind and degree of change apparent in the structure of the flowers. Moreover, a study of flowers in the field will convince one that the above changes have been brought about as a result of the visits of bees, butterflies and other insects in search of nectar and pollen. Since insects are attracted to flowers largely by color, the corolla is the part most directly affected. For example, uniting the separate petals into a continuous corolla makes a broader and hence more attractive expanse of colored surface. Raising the corolla, which occurs when the petals grow from the top of the ovary, makes it more conspicuous, as does also any irregularity in shape. It will be seen from the chart that three of the four steps of advance, which distinguish the higher from the lower groups, affect the corolla. It may also be noted by referring to the flower formulas that these changes in the corolla are almost invariably accompanied by changes in the stamens and sepals. When the corolla is united, as shown by the parenthesis about the number of petals, it will be seen that the calyx also shows this union, and that the stamens are attached to the corolla tube, as indicated by placing the symbol above that for the corolla. Practically every flower with a united corolla possesses a united calyx and stamens fastened to the corolla tube. When there is a change in the position of the corolla from the end of the flower-stalk to the top of the ovary, the calyx-lobes and stamens are found at the same level. When the corolla becomes irregular in shape, the calyx usually shows irregularity also. The number characteristic of any flower is usually the same for calyx and corolla, and frequently for the stamens. Thus, in studying any particular flower, the number, position and character of the petals is of more importance than variations in other parts, except the pistil. As noted above, the great change in the latter is the union of simple pistils into a compound ovary and the reduction in the number of cells.

To sum up, the changes which occur in the evolution of the higher or more specialized forms of flowers from the lower or simpler ones, in order of their importance, are (1) union of pistils, (2) elevation of corolla, (3) union of corolla and (4) irregularity of corolla. The color-lines on the chart indicate at what points in the three main lines of development these different changes occur. The buttercup-aster line of development shows all four of the possible changes and thus asters are considered the most highly developed group of the entire plant kingdom. The other two lines—from buttercups to orchids, and from buttercups to mints—have each emphasized one of the four possible changes and have as yet made regular use of but three. In the buttercup-orchid line there is no union of petals except in occasional instances, while in the buttercup-mint line there is no elevation of the petals except in rare cases. Both of these lines, however, possess at the upper ends examples of the most irregular flowers known.

Taking up the steps of advance as they occur in order in the three lines of evolution, it will be noticed that the arrowhead family, nearest the buttercups in the buttercup-orchid line, are merely buttercups with flower parts in threes. They show no distinct step of advance, but like other members of this line, often called monocotyledons, have parallel-veined leaves and a single seed-leaf. The number three is thereafter characteristic of all the families of this line of development, and the other changes are additional to it. For instance, the lilies show an advance over the arrowheads in having reduced the pistils to three and having united them into a compound ovary with three cells. In most lilies, the sepals have become brightly colored like the petals, and this similarity is thereafter characteristic of the higher types in the same line of advance. The irises have gone one step farther than the lilies by raising the colored perianth of petals and sepals upon the ovary, making the latter inferior.

The orchids have the compound ovary of the lilies, and the raised corolla of the irises, but have gone a step farther by developing a very irregular corolla, one petal usually taking the form of a lip or sack.

In advancing from the buttercups to the mints, the first change noticed is the union of the simple pistils into a compound one. The poppies still show a close connection with the buttercups in the numerous stamens, while in the other families of the mustard and higher orders, reduction in number is apparent. The number of sepals and petals becomes regularly 5, with 4 frequent, while 6, 7, 8 and 9 are very rare. The number of stamens and of cells of the ovary varies somewhat more widely but is often constant for the different groups. Thus the mallows are characterized by many stamens grown together in a tube at the base; the geraniums, flaxes and oxalises have always a 5-celled ovary, while the pinks have a 1-celled ovary, which is made up of a varying number of carpels as shown by the styles. All these groups between the buttercups and primroses possess but the one step of advance over the buttercups, i. e., the union of several simple pistils into a compound one. The characteristics which separate the different families from one another in this region are minor ones of differences of number in stamens or cells of the ovary, or other differences, not apparent in a flower-formula. The primrose group is marked off from the preceding by the added union of the petals with each other into a bell-shaped or tube-shaped corolla. From the pinks onward in this line of development, all flowers must possess the two steps of advance, i. e. united pistils, or a compound ovary, and united petals. The two most highly developed groups, the snapdragons and mints, have added to these the third step of irregularity of corolla, and this organ is characteristically a 2-lipped or variously irregular tube. Thus the buttercup-mint line terminates its development, as the buttercup-orchid line has, in a highly specialized form of corolla, but differs from it in having united the petals instead of elevating them upon the ovary. The two have arrived at much the same stage of development but by different methods.

Turning to the buttercup-aster line, it will be seen that all the methods possible have been made use of in this line of development. The right-hand and left-hand lines have taken the same initial step, that of uniting the simple pistils unto a common ovary. The middle line shows elevation of the petals upon the calyx or ovary as the first step, though the second step of uniting the simple pistils follows very quickly. The rose order exhibits among its many families all variations from separate pistils on the same level and separate pistils below the corolla, to compound pistils at the normal level and compound pistils below the corolla. The orders and families just above the roses however, are characterized by the compound ovary with the petals elevated upon it. The petals themselves show no change in the direction of union in the families between the roses and the honeysuckles, this step of advance being apparent first only in the latter group and in the bluebells. As in the other two lines of development, the final change in the buttercup-aster line affects the shape of the corolla. The change often appears in different form, however, for instead of specializing the shape of each separate flower, the aster group is characterized by the collecting together of the separate flowers into a close head of flowers, and only the outer row or rows of these possess an irregular corolla. In the aster or daisy, what seems to the casual observer a single large star-like flower is in reality a whole cluster of flowers. Certain ones of these, i. e. the yellow ones in the center, are specialized for seed-production while those on the outer edge, which are commonly but wrongly called "petals," are set apart for insect-attraction by means of their long, ribbon-like corollas. Not only are the asters, or composites, considered the mostly highly developed group in the plant kingdom, because of the fact that they have taken the four steps of advance, but also because of this community arrangement of the single flowers, the specialization of the different flowers to different tasks, and the consequent greater efficiency of the group in the matter of seed-production.

Use of the Chart as a Key to Orders

In using the chart as a key for determining the group to which a flower belongs, it is absolutely essential for satisfactory results that the structure of the flower in question be correctly determined. This is recorded in the form of the flower-formula. The next point is to note what steps of advance this structure indicates and hence which of the three lines is to be followed. Having once determined the proper line of development, this should be followed just as far as the steps of advance indicate, as shown by the colored lines, taking these strictly in order. If there are several groups in the region thus finally arrived at, the flower in question should be assigned to the one which it most closely resembles in structure as indicated by the flower-formula. The practical working out of the above rules may best be shown by taking a few flowers and "running them down" in this way. A knowledge of the meaning of such terms as "petals," "sepals," "corolla," "calyx," "pistils," "ovary," "compound ovary" and "stamens" is absolutely essential to the use of even the simplest key to flowering plants. These are all defined in the glossary, but are most readily recognizable from the color plates.

A knowledge of how to express flower structure in the symbols of a flower-formula is also essential. In this, the symbols are as follows: Ca—

calyx; Co—corolla; S—stamens; P—pistils; Sc—scales. The pappus or calyx of the aster family is written Ca^p. The number immediately following the symbol in each case denotes the number of sepals in the calyx, of petals in the corolla, of stamens in the flower, simple pistils or of cells in a compound one, etc. Union of any part is indicated by a ( ) around the figure denoting the number of parts. Elevation of the petals and sepals on the ovary, as well as the attachment of stamens to the tube of the corolla in those flowers with united petals, is shown by a horizontal line below the parts elevated. Irregularity of the corolla is indicated by separating the petals into groups, i. e. the characteristically 2-lipped corolla of the mints and snapdragons, in which there are 2 petals in one lip and 3 in the other, is written Co$^{(3+2)}$. The corolla of the pea, which consists of 2 wings, 2 petals united into the keel, and the standard, is written Co^{2+2+1}; the characteristic lip-like petal of the orchids is indicated as Co^{2+1}.

In order of importance in determining flower relationship and hence classification, the step of advance which affects the pistil comes first, i. e., union of simple pistils into a compound one; and the elevation of the corolla on the ovary, second. The other two changes affect the corolla also, and of these the uniting of the petals into a bell or tube is of most importance, while the change in shape is of the least weight in determining flower relationships. This is because irregularity of corolla, though characteristic of all the highest groups, may occur occasionally in almost any group, even the buttercups. For this reason, the steps of advance must be followed in the order in which they occur, across any of the three lines of development, and no one can be "skipped" in order to reach a farther one. This will become clear in the examples given below. Since the ovary is the keynote to the family relationships, one must be very careful to determine with certainty whether it is simple or compound, and if the latter, exactly how many cells it possesses. This must be done by a cross-section of as mature an ovary as possible, and determined not from one specimen alone but from several. It is well to study the other parts from several specimens also, as variations from the normal may occur in any one and so spoil results.

Let us now take a flower with 5 sepals, 5 petals, 10 stamens and a compound pistil with 5 cells. The formula for this would be Ca^5 Co^5 S^{10} P$^{(5)}$, and the steps of advance thus indicated would be only that of a united pistil. Now, looking at the chart, one sees two directions in which one may follow up a line possessing united pistils, the left-hand one and the right-hand one. But, the former comprises only those flowers with a number-plan of 3, while the right-hand line is composed of 4 and 5-plans. This starts us along the buttercup-mint line. Since the flower in question shows but one step of advance, we must place it in the groups between the first and second cross-lines of advance, or in those between buttercups and primroses. By looking these over, it is quickly seen that the formula is exactly similar to that of the geranium family, so we conclude the flower belongs to that order. A flower with the formula $\frac{Ca^3\ Co^3\ S^3}{P_{(3)}}$ has two steps of advance, one that of a united or compound pistil and the other an elevated corolla. The united pistil and the 3-plan of flower start us along the left-hand line and the two steps of advance place the flower between the second and third cross-lines, or in the iris group. The flower-formula for still a third flower is $\frac{S^5}{\frac{\overline{Ca_{(5)}\ Co_{(5)}}}{P_{(3)}}}$ The steps of advance indicated are united pistils, raised calyx and corolla, and united corolla. The raised corolla and the number 5 start the flower along the middle line, while the three steps of advance bring it well towards the top of the line above the line indicating union of corolla, where it is seen to belong to the bluebells. These are clear-cut types, however, and for the sake of illustrating those which are not so distinct, let us take a few other flowers and follow them up. If we have a flower with three separate pistils, many stamens, an irregular calyx of 5 parts and only 2 petals, the formula would be $Ca^{2+2+1}\ Co^2\ S^\infty\ P^3$. The only step of advance apparent in this formula is that of the irregular corolla. The rule is that one must start at the bottom of the chart and proceed upwards, taking the cross-lines of advance in order and skipping none. Now, since the step of advance indicated here is the fourth step in order, there is nothing to do but stop right at the beginning in the buttercups, since the flower is the monkshood (Pl. 1, fig. 1), one of the irregular buttercups. Irregular flowers may occur in any group, but if the other steps of advance are always considered first in order of occurrence, this fourth one will not be of determining value except when it occurs as a third or fourth step, according to the line of development. If one discovers a lily with a united corolla, the fact that the flower has the plan of three and not the fact that it possesses union will be the determining factor which places it on the left-hand line, where union of petals occurs as an exception. If the beginner starts with clear-cut types, such as many of those in the color-plates, he will soon acquire the ability of recognizing members of the same group with facility and derive a great deal of pleasure from so doing, as this ability is of use wherever flowers grow. The general types are similar all over the world and only the minor points which determine the smaller groups differ.

NAMES OF PLANTS

The name of a plant consists as a rule of two parts or words, as for example, *Aquilegia coerulea, Calochortus Gunnisonii, Lilium philadelphicum,* etc. The first word indicates the *genus,* and is always capitalized. The second word indicates the *species,* or kind, and is capitalized only when it is the genitive of a personal name. The meaning of the terms *genus* (plural, *genera*) and *species* (plural, *species*) may be clearly illustrated by the columbines and violets. The blue columbine and the red columbine are different kinds or species of the *genus* of columbines, *Aquilegia,* each one designated by a species name, *coerulea* and *canadensis,* respectively. The blue violet, yellow violet and white violet are different species of the violet genus, *Viola;* they are designated by the respective species names, *pedatifida, biflora,* and *blanda.* Genera which are related to each other are placed in the same family, for example, the columbines, larkspurs, monks-hoods, anemones and buttercups in the buttercup family, *Ranunculaceae;* the asters, sunflowers, goldenrods, cone flowers, daisies, black-eyed Susans, etc., in the aster family, *Asteraceae.* The ending *-aceae,* which is always used to denote a family, is the feminine plural of the Latin suffix, *-aceus,* meaning *like* or *related to.* The family name, *Asteraceae,* is really an adjective agreeing with *plantae,* plants, and meaning "plants related to the aster." Related families are themselves grouped into orders which also bear a distinctive ending, e. g., *Asterales, Ranales.* This ending is likewise in the feminine plural, and the meaning of the name is "plant families related to the aster family," etc. Orders are further arranged into larger groups, such as *Monocotyledons,* flowering plants with a single seed-leaf, scattered bundles in the stem, parallel-veined leaves, and a flower-plan of 3, and *Dicotyledons,* with 2 seed-leaves, ringed bundles, netted-veined leaves and a flower-plan of 5 or 4. These two groups form the *Angiosperms,* with closed pistils and usually with sepals and petals, which are contrasted with the *Gymnosperms,* with open pistils and no sepals or petals.

HOW TO USE THE KEY

The method of finding the name of a plant by means of the key to families (page XX) may be illustrated by an example. In the case of the Mariposa Lily, which has 3 petals and 3 sepals, the first choice is made between "I. Petals present" and "II. Petals absent." Since the petals are present, the second choice is ignored, and the next decision rests between "1. Flowers in heads" and "2. Flowers single or in clusters." As the flowers are single, the latter is chosen, and the next choice lies between "a. Petals separate" and "b. Petals united." The petals are found to be separate, and the next choice is between the subdivisions "(1) Petals 1-3," "(2) Petals 4," and "(3) Petals 5 or more." The plant in hand falls under the first, where the decision rests between "(a) Petal 1," "(b) Petals 2" and "(c) Petals 3." The latter is the proper number, and the next choice is between "x. Sepals green, unlike the petals," and "y. Sepals and petals more or less alike in color." Beneath the former are two possibilities, "(x) Leaves grass-like; flower withering in a few hours," and "(y) Leaves not grass-like; flower persistent." While the leaves are somewhat grass-like, the flower is persistent, and the choice must fall upon "(y)." Under the latter, the decision lies between "m. Pistils 6-many, distinct; water-plants," and "n. Pistil 1, compound, with 3 cells; land-plants." A cross-section of the single pistil shows that it has 3 cells, and the plant is clearly a land-plant. It is thus seen to belong to the Lily Family, Liliaceae, page 304. The next step is to read the family description in order to see that the plant is in essential agreement, and then it is traced through the key to genera in the manner already indicated. The first choice lies between "1. Styles distinct" and "2. Styles united." Under the latter, the choice is between "a. Flowers axillary, solitary or 1-few in a cluster" and "b. Flowers terminal." The latter is true, and the next choice rests between "(1) Flowers on a leafy stem," and "(2) Plants stemless." Under the former, the color of the flower determines upon "(a) Flowers white or whitish to lilac" instead of "(b) Flowers yellow to orange or purple." Under "(a)," the choice falls upon "y" rather than "x," since the flowers are usually 1-2. The next choice is between "(x) Flowers nodding; leaves ovate to lance-oblong" and "(y) Flowers erect; leaves linear, grass-like." The latter is chosen, and the final decision lies between "m. Flowers 1-3 in. wide; petals fringed at base" and "n. Flowers 1-2 cm. wide; petals not fringed." The name of the genus of the Mariposa Lily is thus found to be "Calochortus," and the name of the species is found by turning to page 308. The plant should first be compared with the description, after which the species is obtained by deciding between "1" and "2". Since the gland is oblong and transverse, and the anthers acute, the species concerned is "Calochortus Gunnisonii."

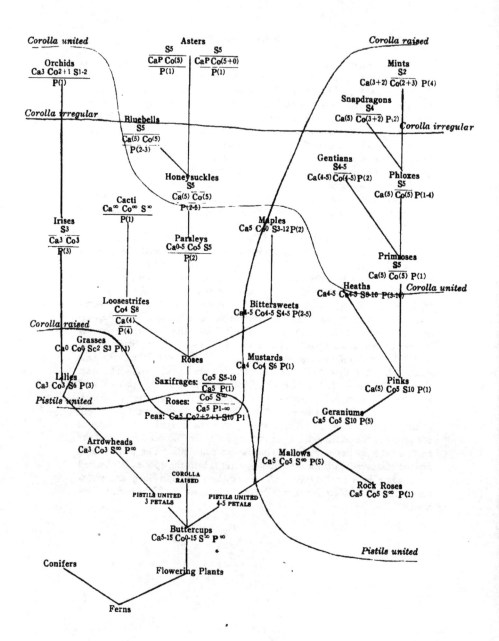

KEY TO FAMILIES

I. Petals present
  1. Flowers in heads, as in the aster and clover
    a. Ovary superior   TRIFOLIUM IN FABACEAE 186

    b. Ovary inferior
      (1) Petals separate; style simple; upper leaves in a whorl of 4-6   CORNACEAE 222
      (2) Petals united; style 2-cleft; leaves rarely whorled   ASTERACEAE 243
  2. Flowers single or in clusters
    a. Petals separate
      (1) Petals 1-3
        (a) Petal 1; stamens 10; shrub   AMORPHA IN FABACEAE 170

        (b) Petals 2
          x. Ovary superior, smooth
            (x) Water plants; stamens 2-3   ELATINACEAE 42
            (y) Land plants; stamen 1   CALYPTRIDIUM IN PORTULACACEAE 49

          y. Ovary inferior, bristly-hairy   CIRCAEA IN ONAGRACEAE 201

        (c) Petals 3
          x. Sepals green, unlike the petals
            (x) Leaves grass-like; flower withering in a few hours   COMMELINACEAE 304

            (y) Leaves usually broad; flower persistent
              m. Pistils 6-many, distinct; water plants   ALISMACEAE 299
              n. Pistil 1, compound, with 3 cells; land plants   LILIACEAE 304
          y. Sepals and petals more or less alike in color
            (x) Flowers regular

  r. Stamens 4–5   SAXIFRAGACEAE 191
  s. Stamens 3   PORTULACACEAE 48
y. Stamens 6   BRASSICACEAE 16
z. Stamens more than 6
 (x) Leaves compound
  m. Style 5-lobed; leaves pinnate   LIMNANTHACEAE 37
  n. Style entire or 2-lobed
   (m) Leaves digitate, of 3–5 leaflets CAPPARIDACEAE 13
   (n) Leaves 2-3-ternate   ACTAEA IN RANUN-
                CULACEAE 2

 (y) Leaves simple
  m. Sepals 2; leaves fleshy   PORTULACACEAE 48
  n. Sepals 4–5; leaves not fleshy
   (m) Shrubs
    r. Flowers white
     (r) Leaves alternate, evergreen LEDUM IN ERICA-
                 CEAE 86

     (s) Leaves opposite, not ever-
       green   SAXIFRAGACEAE 191
    s. Flowers purplish-yellow; leaves
      linear, strong-scented   THAMNOSMA IN
                 RUTACEAE 40

   (n) Herbs
    r. Pistils superior
     (r) Stamens 8   SAXIFRAGACEAE 191
     (s) Stamens many   PAPAVERACEAE 9
    s. Pistil inferior; stamens 8   ONAGRACEAE 199
 (b) Flowers irregular
  x. Flowers spurred or hooded; leaves
   deeply cut or compound
   (x) Stamens many; pistils 2-3   RANUNCULACEAE 1
   (y) Stamens 6; pistil 1   FUMARIACEAE 12
  y. Flowers not spurred; leaves simple   ONAGRACEAE 199
(3) Petals 5 or more
 (a) Flowers regular
  x. Pistils simple, 1-many
   (x) Pistils few-many
    m. Stamens and petals coming off with
     the calyx   ROSACEAE 150

n. Stamens and petals entirely free
    from the calyx   RANUNCULACEAE 1
(y) Pistil 1
  m. Stamens 5-12
    (m) Petals 6; shrubs   BERBERIDACEAE 8
    (n) Petals 5; herbs   MIMOSACEAE 167
  n. Stamens many
    (m) Woody plants   PRUNACEAE 165
    (n) Herbs   RANUNCULACEAE 1
y. Pistil compound
  (x) Woody plants
    m. Vines with tendrils   VITACEAE 211 ·
    n. Trees or shrubs
      (m) Leaves simple
        r. Style 1   ERICACEAE 83
        s. Styles 2
          (r) Ovary superior
          h. Ovary deeply 2-divided,
             winged   ACERACEAE 217
          i. Fruit a 1-celled capsule FRANKENIACEAE 42
          (s) Ovary inferior; woody
             plants   SAXIFRAGACEAE 191
        t. Styles 3-5
          (r) Flowers white or pink MALACEAE 163
          (s) Flowers greenish   RHAMNACEAE 212
      (n) Leaves compound
        r. Leaves opposite, pinnate ZYGOPHYLLACEAE 41
        s. Leaves alternate
          (r) Flowers greenish; plants
             often poisonous to the
             touch   ANACARDIACEAE 220
          (s) Flowers white or whitish
          h. Leaflets 3; fruit winged RUTACEAE 40
          i. Leaflets many; fruit fleshy MALACEAE 163
  (y) Herbs
    m. Plants fleshy
      (m) Plants leafless, spiny; petals
        many   CACTACEAE 207
      (n) Stems leafy, not spiny; petals
        4-5   CRASSULACEAE 188

.n. Plants not fleshy

  (m) Ovary many-celled

    r. Stamen filaments united into a tube   MALVACEAE 31

    s. Stamen filaments not united into a tube

      (r) Aquatic plants with simple floating leaves   NYMPHAEACEAE 9

      (s) Land plants with pinnate leaves   ZYGOPHYLLACEAE 41

  (n) Ovary 5-celled

    r. Ovary superior

      (r) Leaves simple or none

        h. Leaves none; plants not green   MONOTROPACEAE 82

        i. Leaves present; plants green

          (h) Leaves evergreen; petals persistent   PIROLACEAE 78

          (i) Leaves not evergreen; petals falling in a few hours   LINACEAE 40

      (s) Leaves deeply cut or compound

        h. Leaves deeply cut   GERANIACEAE 37

        i. Leaves of 3 leaflets   OXALIDACEAE 39

    s. Ovary inferior   ARALIACEAE 222

  (o) Ovary 1-4-celled

    r. Ovary 2-4-celled

      (r) Ovary superior

        h. Leaves simple

          (h) Ovary 2-celled   SAXIFRAGACEAE 191

          (i) Ovary 3-celled   EUPHORBIACEAE 34

        i. Leaves compound

          (h) Leaves of 3 leaflets   MENYANTHACEAE 99

          (i) Leaves pinnate   LIMNANTHACEAE 37

      (s) Ovary inferior

        h. Calyx tube not grown to the ovary; capsule many-seeded   LYTHRACEAE 199

        i. Calyx tube grown to the
           ovary; fruit 2-seeded   APIACEAE 223
    s. Ovary 1-celled
     (r) Sepals 5
      h. Ovary superior
       (h) Styles 2
         k. Pistils 2 at top, open-
           ing on the inner
           face   SAXIFRAGACEAE 191
         l. Capsule opening by 4
           teeth   CARYOPHYLLACEAE
                          43
       (i) Styles 3-5
         k. Stamens usually twice
           as m a n y as the
           petals   CARYOPHYLLACEAE
                          43
         l. Stamens numerous   HYPERICACEAE 42
      i. Ovary ;inferior; stamens
        many   LOASACEAE 209
     (s) Sepals 2
      h. Stamens 3-20   PORTULACACEAE 48
      i. Stamens many   PAPAVERACEAE 9
  (b) Flowers irregular
    x. Flowers spurred or hooded
     (x) Sepals green   VIOLACEAE 29
     (y) Sepals petal-like   RANUNCULACEAE 1
    y. Flowers not spurred
     (x) Petals of 3 shapes   FABACEAE 168
     (y) Petals somewhat irregular CASSIACEAE 167
b. Petals united
  (1) Ovary superior
   (a) Low, usually evergreen shrubs   ERICACEAE 83
   (b) Herbs
    x. Ovary 1-celled
     (x) Carpels 2
      m. Leaves entire, opposite
       (m) Flowers irregular   MARTYNIACEAE 141
       (n) Flowers regular   GENTIANACEAE 93
      n. Leaves toothed, lobed or compound

(m) Petals very hairy on the upper
          face   MENYANTHACEAE
                                              99

(n) Petals smooth
    r. Flowers regular; terrestrial   HYDROPHYLLACEAE
                                              116

      s. Flowers irregular; aquatic   PINGUICULACEAE 139
(y) Carpels 5   PRIMULACEAE 88
y. Ovary 2-celled, 2-divided or 4-lobed
  (x) Ovary 2-celled or 2-divided
    m. Leafless herbs; plants not green
      (m) Stems twining; flowers regu-
                lar   CUSCUTACEAE 109
      (n) Stems not twining; flowers ir-
                regular   OROBANCHACEAE 140
    n. Leafy herbs
      (m) Stamens 5
        r. Ovary 2-lobed or pistils 2 and
                separate
          (r) Stamens distinct, around a
                  crown   ASCLEPIADACEAE 101
          (s) Stamens united; crown
                  none   APOCYNACEAE 100
        s. Ovary 1, 2-celled, not 2-lobed
          (r) Seeds 2-several; mostly
                  climbing or trailing   CONVOLVULACEAE
                                              108
          (s) Seeds many   SOLANACEAE 110
      (n) Stamens 4
        r. Corolla brightly colored, the
                lobes usually 5
          (r) Fruit a 2-celled capsule   SCROPHULARIACEAE
                                              125
          (s) Fruit 2 or 4 1-seeded nut-
                  lets   VERBENACEAE 142
        s. Corolla papery, the lobes 4   PLANTAGINACEAE 92
  (y) Ovary 4-lobed or divided
    m. Flowers usually irregular; leaves
          opposite   LAMIACEAE 143

n. Flowers usually regular; leaves
  mostly alternate   BORAGINACEAE 118
z. Ovary 3-5-celled
 m. Stems green, leafy
  (m) Stems trailing or climbing   CONVOLVULACEAE
               108
  (n) Stems not trailing or climbing POLEMONIACEAE 103
 n. Stems not green, the leaves re-
   duced to scales   MONOTROPACEAE 82
(2) Ovary inferior
 (a) Woody plants
  x. Stamens 5   CAPRIFOLIACEAE 237
  y. Stamens 8-10   VACCINIACEAE 87
 (b) Herbs
  x. Stamens 3
   (x) Stems erect; fruit with a feathery
     pappus   VALERIANACEAE 243
   (y) Stems trailing or climbing; fruit
     fleshy   CUCURBITACEAE 210
  y. Stamens 4-5
   (x) Sap milky as a rule; herbs with
     large flowers   CAMPANULACEAE
               241
   (y) Sap not milky
    m. Shrubs   CAPRIFOLIACEAE 237
    n. Herbs   RUBIACEAE 237
  z. Stamens 8-12   ADOXACEAE 241
II. Petals absent
 1. Sepals present, rarely very minute
  a. Woody plants
   (1) Vines; petals falling quickly   VITACEAE 211
   (2) Shrubs or trees
    (a) Flowers in catkins, at least the staminate FAGACEAE 221
    (b) Flowers not in catkins
     x. Style 1; stigma 1 or slightly 2-cleft
      (x) Trees with compound leaves   OLEACEAE 99
      (y) Shrubs with simple leaves
       m. Leaves silvery-scurfy   ELAEAGNACEAE 213
       n. Leaves green   ROSACEAE 150
     y. Styles or long sessile stigmas 2

        (x) Leaves deeply cut or compound   Aceraceae 217

        (y) Leaves simple, not deeply cut   Urticaceae 33

b. Herbs

    (1) Nearly colorless herbs, parasitic on trees   Loranthaceae 216

    (2) Plants grass-like, sometimes leafless; sepals
        6

        (a) Ovaries 3-6, separating at least when ripe   Juncaginaceae 303

        (b) Ovary 1, of 3 carpels   Juncaceae 312

    (3) Plants with broad green leaves

        (a) Pistils several-many   Ranunculaceae 1

        (b) Pistil 1, at least the ovary

          x. Stamens as many as the sepals or fewer

           (x) Ovary superior

             m. Flowers and bracts papery, not
                withering   Amarantaceae 67

             n. Flowers and bracts not papery and
                not persistent

               (m) Flowers in small involucres, or
                   the stems with papery
                   sheaths at the joints   Polygonaceae 51

               (n) Flowers not in involucres, and
                   stems without papery
                   sheaths

                r. Style and stigma 1, or 2: if the
                  latter, the leaves digitate or
                  digitately lobed   Urticaceae 33

                s. Styles 2-5, the leaves simple or
                  pinnatifid

                 (r) Styles 2-3; leaves typically
                   alternate   Chenopodiaceae 59

                 (s) Styles 3-5; leaves opposite   Aizoaceae 50

           (y) Ovary half-inferior; style and
              stigma 1   Santalaceae 216

           (z) Ovary inferior

             m. Leaves alternate   Apiaceae 223

             n. Leaves opposite   Nyctaginaceae 68

         y. Stamens more numerous than the sepals

           (x) Ovary superior

             m. Sepals 4

               (m) Stamens 6; style and stigma 1 Brassicaceae 16

(n) Stamens usually 8; style and
 stigma 2   SAXIFRAGACEAE 191
n. Sepals 5
  (m) Stamens numerous; styles 3   EUPHORBIACEAE 34
  (n) Stamens 6-8; stigmas 2-3   POLYGONACEAE 51
  (y) Ovary inferior; aquatic herbs   GUNNERACEAE 206
2. Sepals absent, or occasionally very minute
a. Woody plants
  (1) Leaves scale-like or needle-like, usually
      evergreen
    (a) Stems jointed, low and shrubby; scales
        papery   GNETACEAE 369
    (b) Stems not jointed, mostly trees; leaves
        green, usually needle-like   PINACEAE 364
  (2) Leaves not scale-like or needle-like, de-
      ciduous
    (a) Leaves simple, alternate
      x. Fruit with many hairy seeds; flowers
         dioecious   SALICACEAE 72
      y. Fruit 1-seeded; flowers usually monoe-
         cious   BETULACEAE 220
    (b) Leaves compound, opposite   OLEACEAE 99
b. Herbs
  (1) Flowers in heads, surrounded by 5 petal-
      like glands   EUPHORBIACEAE 34
  (2) Flowers not in heads with petal-like glands
    (a) Flowers in spikelets with papery scales;
        leaves grass-like
      x. Flower enclosed in 2 scales; stem hol-
         low, round   POACEAE 335
      y. Flower with a single scale; stems solid,
         mostly triangular   CYPERACEAE 324
    (b) Flowers not in spikelets with papery
        scales
      x. Plants small floating leaf-like disks   LEMNACEAE 315
      y. Plants with leafy stems
        (x) Leaves in whorls of 6-8   CERATOPHYLLACEAE
                                              9
        (y) Leaves not in whorls of 6-8
        m. Leaves parallel-veined

RANALES   BUTTERCUP ORDER

RANUNCULACEAE   BUTTERCUP FAMILY

Sepals 3-15, separate, often petal-like, petals 3-20, or none, separate, stamens many, pistils many, few or none, the ovary 1-celled, fruit an achene, follicle or berry, 1-many-seeded; flowers regular, sometimes irregular, usually clustered; annual or perennial herbs, rarely woody shrubs or climbers, with simple or compound leaves.

I. Flowers regular
  1. Petals and sepals both clearly present
    a. Petals spurred   AQUILEGIA
    b. Petals not spurred
      (1) Pistils several to many in each flower
        (a) Flowers greenish, tiny   MYOSURUS
        (b) Flowers yellow or white   RANUNCULUS
      (2) Pistil 1   ACTAEA
  2. Petals lacking, sepals often petal-like
    a. Sepals petal-like, white or colored
      (1) Leaves opposite; often climbing or trailing CLEMATIS
      (2) Leaves alternate
        (a) Stem with a whorl of leaves, i. e., an involucre, below the flower
          x. Flowers 1-4 cm. wide; styles short, not plumy   ANEMONE
          y. Flowers 4-8 cm. wide; styles long and plumy   PULSATILLA
        (b) Stems leafy, without an involucre
          x. Leaves simple, toothed   CALTHA
          y. Leaves deeply cleft or divided   TROLLIUS
    b. Sepals green or greenish-white, small   THALICTRUM
II. Flowers irregular
  1. Upper sepal spurred   DELPHINIUM
  2. Upper sepal hood- or helmet-like   ACONITUM

ACONÍTUM Linné 1753   ACONITE, MONKSHOOD

(Gr. *akoniton*, monkshood, perhaps from its mountain habit)

Pl. 1, fig. 1.

Sepals 5, petal-like, blue to yellowish-white, the upper larger, helmet- or hood-shaped; petals 2-5, small or minute when 2, hidden in the helmet; stamens many, usually about 30, pistils 1-5, usually 3, fruit a several-seeded follicle; flowers irregular, in a raceme or panicle; leaves 3-7-cleft or divided; poisonous perennials.

Flowers 2.5-3.5 cm. long; sepals of 3 kinds; petals 2,
  hidden   *A. columbiánum*

ACTAÉA Linné 1753   BANEBERRY

(Gr. *aktea*, elder, perhaps from resemblance of the leaves)

Sepals 4-5, petal-like, white, falling as the flower opens, petals 4-10, small, white, spatulate, stamens many, pistil 1, the ovary 1-celled with sessile stigma, fruit a poisonous berry; flowers regular, in a spike-like raceme; leaves thrice compound, leaflets coarsely toothed or lobed; perennial.

Berries red, white or purple-black   *A. spicáta*

ANEMÓNE Linné 1753   ANEMONE, WINDFLOWER

(Gr. *anemone*, shaken by the wind, hence windflower)

Pl. 3, fig. 1.

Sepals 4-20, petal-like, white, pink, red or purple, separate, petals none, stamens many, pistils many, fruits 1-seeded usually hairy achenes in a dense head or spike; flowers regular, single or few in a cluster; leaves usually 3-5-divided, the upper usually sessile and forming an-involucre below the flower; perennial.

1. Fruits many, woolly
  a. Stem branched; flowers 2-several
    (1) Head of fruit cylindric   *A. cylindrica*
    (2) Head of fruit round or nearly so   *A. multifida*
  b. Stem not branched; flowers single
    (1) Sepals usually 10 or more   *A. decapétala*
    (2) Sepals 5-6   *A. parviflóra*
2. Fruits usually less than 25, somewhat hairy, or
    smooth
  a. Fruits somewhat hairy; flowers white or pink-
    ish

(1) Stem branched, hairy; flowers 3-6 cm.
wide *A. dichótoma*
(2) Stem simple, smooth; flowers 2-3 cm. wide *A. nemorósa*
b. Fruits smooth; flowers usually yellowish *A. narcissiflóra*

AQUILÉGIA Linné 1753   COLUMBINE

(Lat. *aquilegia,* perhaps from Lat. *aquila,* eagle, in allusion to the resemblance of the spurs to an eagle's talons)

Pl. 1, fig. 2-3.

Sepals 5, petal-like, petals 5, spurred, red, yellow, blue or white,
stamens many, some often petal- or scale-like, pistils 5, the ovules many,
2-rowed, fruit a follicle; flowers regular, single or in clusters; leaves usually twice ternately compound; perennial.

1. Flowers red to yellow
   a. Flowers red and yellow; spur 1-2 cm. long   *A. canadénsis*
   b. Flowers yellow; spur 3-6 cm. long   *A. chrysántha*
2. Flowers blue, rarely white
   a. Flower stalk leafy
      (1) Flower large, 5-6 cm. wide   *A. caerúlea*
      (2) Flower small, 2-3 cm. wide   *A. brevístyla*
   b. Flower stalk leafless; leaflets crowded   *A. Jónesii*

CÁLTHA Linné 1753   MARSH MARIGOLD
(The Latin name of the true marigold)

Sepals 6-10, petal-like, white or yellow, falling away, petals none,
stamens many, pistils 3-10, fruit a beaked many-seeded follicle; flowers
regular, mostly single, or few in a cluster; leaves simple, elliptic to rounded;
fleshy perennials.

Leaves heart-shaped at base, wavy-toothed; flowers
2-5 cm. wide   *C. leptosépala*

CLÉMATIS Linné 1753   CLEMATIS, VIRGIN'S BOWER
(Gr. *klematis,* a climbing plant)

(Atragene Linné)

Pl. 3, fig. 2.

Sepals 4-5, petal-like, white to purple, petals 0, or merely broadened
stamens, stamens many, the outer often like tiny petals, pistils many, fruit

PLATE 3.

an achene with a long plumy style; flowers regular, solitary or clustered; leaves opposite, usually pinnate or pinnatifid, sometimes entire; stems perennial, climbing by the leaf stalks, trailing or erect.

1. Stems climbing; flowers small, white   *C. ligusticifólia*
2. Stems trailing or erect; flower large, blue to violet
     a. Stems trailing, rarely climbing; leaves ternate
         (1) Leaves 3-foliate   *C. occidentális*
         (2) Leaves twice-ternate   *C. álpina*
     b. Stems erect; leaves pinnatifid   *C. Douglásii*

DELPHÍNIUM Linné 1753   LARKSPUR

(Gr. *delphinion,* larkspur, from *delphis,* dolphin, perhaps in allusion to the irregular form)

Pl. 1, fig. 4.

Sepals 5, petal-like, the back one spurred, blue, white or red, petals 2 or 4, the back ones spurred, the lateral small or lacking, stamens many, pistils 1-several, usually 3, fruit a many-seeded follicle; flowers irregular, in a raceme, often spike-like, or sometimes in a panicle; leaves palmately cleft or divided; stems from a caudex or from tuberous roots; ours poisonous perennials.

1. Stem and leaves, or at least the flower cluster, glandular and sticky   *D. occidentále*
2. Stem and leaves not sticky glandular
     a. Roots thickened, more or less tuberous; plants usually .5-3 ft. high
         (1) Stems mostly closely and densely grayhairy; flowers often whitish   *D. caroliniánum*
         (2) Stems smooth or with loose spreading hairs above   *D. Menziésii*
     b. Roots woody and branched, scarcely tuberous; plants 3-8 ft. high   *D. scópulorum*

MYOSÚRUS Linné 1753   MOUSE-TAIL

(Gr. *myouros,* mouse-tail, from the tail-like spike of fruits)

Sepals 5, somewhat petal-like, spurred, petals 5, tiny, or none, stamens many, pistils many, fruits achenes, forming a spike; flowers regular, single, on leafless stalks; leaves basal, linear, entire; low annuals.

  1. Fruiting spike bristly from the long-beaked
     achenes   *M. aristátus*
  2. Fruiting spike smooth, the achenes short-beaked *M. minimus*

PULSATÍLLA Adanson 1753   PASQUE FLOWER
(Lat. diminutive of *pulsatus*, shaken, hence wind-flower)

Pl. 3, fig. 5.

Sepals 5-7, usually 6, petal-like, blue, purple or whitish, petals none, stamens many, pistils many, fruits 1-seeded achenes, the styles long and plumy in fruit; flowers regular, single; leaves 3-divided and cleft; perennial.

Flowers cup-shaped, then expanded; fruiting styles
   2.5-4 cm. long   *P. hirsutíssima*

RANÚNCULUS Linné 1753   BUTTERCUP, CROWFOOT
(Lat. *rana*, frog, *-unculus*, little, from the amphibious habitat of some)

Pl. 3, fig. 3, 6.

Sepals 5, green or petal-like, petals regularly 5, yellow or white, rarely red, with a nectary at the base, stamens many, pistils many, achenes compressed, rarely cylindric, 1-seeded; flowers regular, single or somewhat racemose; leaves various, simple and entire to lobed and dissected, or compound; annual or perennial.

I. Petals yellow or yellowish; land plants, rarely sub-
      merged
   1. Leaves simple, entire to divided or dissected
      a. Leaves entire, at most finely toothed   *R. flámmula*
         (1) Plants erect   *alismifólius*
         (2) Plants creeping   *réptans*
      b. Leaves, or at least some of them, coarsely
         toothed, lobed or divided
         (1) Achenes nerved lengthwise   *R. cymbalária*
         (2) Achenes not nerved lengthwise
            (a) Some of the leaves entire   *R. ellípticus*
            (b) All the leaves lobed or cleft, or at least
                  coarsely toothed
               x. Pedicels and sepals densely brown-hairy *R. Macáuleyi*
               y. Pedicels and sepals not densely brown-
                     hairy

2. Stems spineless; leaves compound
   a. Low, 1-3 dm. high, usually trailing; leaflets 3-
      11, many-toothed   *B. répens*
   b. Taller, 1-2 m. high, erect; leaflets 3-7, few-
      toothed   *B. Frémontii*

CERATOPHYLLACEAE   HORNWORT FAMILY

Sepals many, united, petals none, stamens 10-20, ovary 1-celled, style 1, fruit a beaked achene; stamens and pistils in different flowers, the latter solitary in the leaf axils; submerged aquatics, with finely cut leaves in whorls of 5-12.

CERATOPHÝLLUM Linné 1753 HORNWORT
(Gr. *keras, keratos,* horn, *phyllon,* leaf)

Characters of the family.
Stems 2-5 ft. long; leaf lobes thread-like; fruit ellipsoid *C. demérsum*

NYMPHAEÁCEAE   WATER LILY FAMILY

Represented by the following genus:

NYMPHÁEA Linné 1753   YELLOW POND LILY
(Gr. *nymphaea,* water nymph)

Pl. 3, fig. 4.

Sepals 5-12, yellow, petal-like, petals many, small, stamen-like, stamens many, pistils many, united, the 8-24 stigmas forming a wheel-like disk; flowers large, single; aquatic herbs with large roundish heart-shaped floating leaves.
Flowers 3-5 in. wide; sepals 9-12; leaves 4-15 in. long *N. polysépala*

BRASSICALES   MUSTARD ORDER
PAPAVERÁCEAE   POPPY FAMILY

Sepals 2 or 3, usually falling as the bud opens, petals 4-6, separate, stamens many, pistil 1, stigmas one or several, united into a spreading disk, ovary 1-celled or incompletely several-celled, fruit a capsule; flowers single or clustered; herbs with alternate pinnatifid or pinnate leaves and milky or orange-yellow juice.

1. Stem leafless, 1-flowered; leaves not prickly   PAPAVER
2. Stem leafy, several-flowered; leaves prickly   ARGEMONE

PAPÁVER Linné 1753   POPPY
(Lat. *papaver*, poppy)

Sepals 2, brown-hairy, petals 4, yellow or red, stamens many, ovary 1-celled, stigma lobes 5-7, capsule bristly-hairy, opening by pores beneath the stigma disk; flowers solitary, bud nodding; leaves basal, pinnatifid; sap white-milky; perennial.

Stems hairy, 2-3 inches high; leaf outline lance-ovate;
    flowers 1-3 in. wide   *P. álpinum*

ARGEMÓNE Linné 1753   PRICKLY POPPY
(Gr. *argemone*, a kind of poppy used for eye troubles)

Sepals usually 3, sometimes 2, prickly, petals 4-6, white or yellow, stamens many, ovary 1-celled, stigma lobes 3-6, capsule prickly, oblong, opening by 4 slits or valves; flowers solitary, large, 2-5 in. wide, buds erect; leaves on the stem, pinnatifid to bipinnate, with stout prickles or sometimes nearly smooth; stem prickly and glaucous, prickly and bristly-hairy, or nearly smooth; sap white to yellow; perennial.

   1. Petals white   *A. platýceras*
   2. Petals yellow, rarely white   *A. mexicána*

FUMARIÁCEAE   BLEEDING HEART FAMILY

Sepals 2, small and scale-like, and easily overlooked, petals 4, paired, irregular, touching and somewhat grown together, one or both of the outer pair sack-like or spurred at the base, stamens 6, in groups of 3, ovary 1-celled, stigma entire or 2-4-lobed, fruit linear to oblong, splitting into 2 valves, or remaining closed; flowers in racemes; herbs with alternate compound leaves; sap clear.

   1. Both of the outer petals spurred or sac-like;
       flower pinkish, solitary   BICUCULLA
   2. One of the outer petals spurred
     a. Flowers yellow; pods oblong, splitting   CAPNOIDES
     b. Flowers purplish; pods globose, closed   FUMARIA

BICUCÚLLA Adanson 1763   BLEEDING HEART
(Lat. *bi-*, two, *cuculla*, cowl, hood, from the sack-like petals)

Sepals 2, petals 4, the outer sack-like, pinkish, ovary 1-celled, stigma 2-lobed, capsule oblong, swollen, splitting into 2 valves; flowers solitary; leaves basal, pinnate, the leaflets pinnatifid; perennial.

Stems 2-6 in. high; leaves solitary; flowers pinkish   *B. uniflóra*

CAPNOÍDES Adanson 1763   CAPNOIDES

(Gr. *kapnodes*, like smoke, from the odor of some species)

(Corydalis Medicus)

Pl. 5, fig. 6.

Sepals 2, petals 4, one of the outer spurred, golden-yellow, cream, or white, ovary 1-celled, stigma entire or lobed, capsule linear, splitting into 2 valves; flowers in a raceme; leaves compound; annual or perennial.

1. Flowers golden; pods long, linear; leaves finely
   cut   *C. áureum*
2. Flowers white or cream; pods short, ellipsoid;
   leaflets large, ovoid   *C. Brandégei*

FUMÁRIA Linné 1753   FUMITORY

(Lat. *fumarius*, smoky, said to be from the smell of some species)

Sepals 2, petals 4, one of the outer pair spurred, purplish, ovary 1-celled, stigma entire or lobed, fruit 1-seeded, globose, remaining closed; flowers in a raceme; leaves finely cut.

Stems more or less spreading; flowers 4-5 mm. long *F. officinális*

CAPPARIDÁCEAE   CAPER FAMILY

Sepals 4, persistent or deciduous, petals 4, separate, stamens 4-many, pistil 1, ovary 1-celled, often stalked, seeds on the wall, i. e., parietal, style short, stigma entire, fruit a pod, or capsule but without cross wall, splitting into 2 parts when ripe; flowers solitary or in racemes; herbs or shrubs with alternate simple or digitate leaves, the sap often biting.

1. Petals cut-fringed, unequal in size   CRISTATELLA
2. Petals entire to 3-toothed, not cut-fringed, equal
   a. Pods flat, rhomboid   CLEOMELLA
   b. Pod linear-oblong, more or less cylindric
      (1) Stamens 4-6; pods stalked   CLEOME
      (2) Stamens 9-24; pods sessile or nearly so POLANISIA

CRISTATÉLLA Nuttall 1834   FRINGED CAPER

(Lat. *cristatus*, crested, fringed, *-ellus*, small, from the fringed petals)

Sepals 4, petals 4, 2 smaller, cream-colored or whitish, with a stalk or claw, fringed above, stamens 6-12, pod linear-oblong, stalked, beaked, many-seeded; flowers in racemes, occasionally solitary; leaves of 3 leaflets, digitate, sticky; annual.

PLATE 5.

Leaflets 3, linear to oblong; flowers whitish to yellowish, 3-6 mm. long   *C. Jámesii*

Cleomélla De Candolle 1824   Cleomella
(Diminutive of Cleome)

Sepals 4, petals 4, yellow, stalkless, stamens 6, pod rhomboid, short,
somewhat inflated, long-stalked, 4-10-seeded; flowers in racemes; leaves
of 3 entire leaflets, digitate, smooth; annual.
  1. Style none; stalk 1-2 times as long as its pod   *C. angustifólia*
  2. Style evident; stalk 3 or more times as long as the
      pod   *C. oocárpa*

Cléome Linné 1753   Cleome, Rocky Mountain Bee-Plant
(Of uncertain origin)
Pl. 5, fig. 3.

Sepals 4, petals 4, pink, white or yellow, usually stalked, stamens 6
or 4, pod linear-oblong to oblong, roundish in section, beaked, stalked, 6-30-
seeded; flowers in corymbs or racemes; leaves of 3-5-leaflets, digitate,
smooth; annual.
  1. Flowers pink to white; leaflets 3
    a. Leaflets lanceolate; petals 8-12 mm. long; pods
        10-30-seeded   *C. serruláta*
    b. Leaflets linear; petals 4 mm. long; pods 6-8-
        seeded   *C. sonórae*
  2. Flowers yellow; leaflets mostly 5   *C. lútea*

Polanísia Rafinesque 1819   Polanisia
(Gr. *polys*, many, *anisos*, unequal, from the stamens)

Sepals 4, purplish, petals 4, whitish to yellowish, stalked, notched,
stamens 8-24, unequal, pod oblong, elongated, roundish or somewhat compressed, stalkless or nearly so, many-seeded; flowers in racemes; leaves of
3 entire leaflets, digitate, sticky; annual.
  1. Stamens about twice as long as the petals; flow-
      ers 7-12 mm. long   *P. trachyspérma*
  2. Stamens hardly if at all longer than the petals;
      flowers 4-6 mm. long   *P. gravéolens*

BRASSICACEAE   MUSTARD FAMILY

Sepals 4, petals 4, rarely none, separate, usually with a claw, stamens usually 6, 2 shorter, rarely 1-4, ovary 2-celled, style 1, stigma entire or 2-lobed, fruit a pod, usually 2-celled and many-seeded; flowers in racemes or corymbs; herbs with alternate simple, rarely compound leaves.

I. Pod round, globose or triangular to short-oblong
   1. Pods flattened
      a. Pods of 2 round halves, resembling spectacles DITHYREA
      b. Pods round to ovoid or oblong
         (1) Seeds single in each half; pods round to
             short-oblong   LEPIDIUM
         (2) Seeds 2-many in each half
           (a) Pods round, winged or margined
              x. Pods winged all around; flowers white
                 or purplish   THLASPI
              y. Pods margined above; flowers yellow-
                 ish   ALYSSUM
           (b) Pods ovoid to elliptic or oblong, not
              winged
              x. Leaves pinnatifid; seeds several in each
                 cell
                (x) Flowers 1-2 mm. wide; pods 3-4 HUTCHINSIA
                    mm. long
                (y) Flowers 5-8 mm. wide; pods 6-12
                    mm. long   SMELOWSKIA
              y. Leaves entire or toothed; seeds many in
                 each cell   DRABA
      c. Pods triangular, not winged; leaves pinnatifid BURSA
   2. Pods round in section or inflated, not flattened
      a. Submerged aquatic; leaves awl-shaped   SUBULARIA
      b. Terrestrial
         (1) Pods of 2 inflated cells   PHYSARIA
         (2) Pods globose to pear-shaped or oblong, not
             inflated
           (a) Leaves pinnatifid   RORIPA
           (b) Leaves entire
               x. Leaves gray with star-shaped hairs;
                 pods globose to oblong   LESQUERELLA
              y. Leaves green, not stellate-hairy; pods
                 pear-shaped   CAMELINA

II. Pods oblong to linear, more than twice as long as
    wide
  1. Pods strongly flattened
    a. Weeds with cream or yellowish flowers and
       pinnatifid leaves   SISYMBRIUM
    b. Natives with white to pink flowers, if yellow
       the leaves not pinnatifid
      (1) Anthers arrow-shaped at base; leaves usu-
          ally clasping   STREPTANTHUS
      (2) Anthers not arrow-shaped
        (a) Pods less than 2 cm. long   DRABA
        (b) Pods 2-8 cm. long
          x. Pods 1-nerved on each face   ARABIS
          y. Pods without a distinct nerve or rib on
             each face   CARDAMINE
  2. Pods 4-angled or round in section
    a. Pods round in section
      (1) Pods closed when ripe; weed   RAPHANUS
      (2) Pods splitting when ripe
        (a) Pods distinctly stalked in or above the
           calyx
          x. Stamens long-exserted   STANLEYA
          y. Stamens included
            (x) Petals flat   THELYPODIUM
            (y) Petals wavy-margined   CAULANTHUS
        (b) Pods not stalked above the calyx
          x. Pods with a beak 3-15 mm. long BRASSICA
          y. Pods not beaked
            (x) Seeds few   SMELOWSKIA
            (y) Seeds many
              m. Leaves finely dissected   SOPHIA
              n. Leaves pinnatifid, but not finely
                dissected
               (m) Seeds in 1 row in each half of
                  the pod   SISYMBRIUM
               (n) Seeds in 2 rows in each half RORIPA
    b. Pods 4-angled
      (1) Pods stalked in or above the calyx THELYPODIUM
      (2) Pods not stalked
        (a) Flowers white or cream-colored

x. Flowers cream-colored; pods 2-4 in.
    long   Conringia
y. Flowers white; pods 2-3 cm. long   Stenophragma
(b) Flowers yellow to orange, rarely deep
    red-purple
   x. Pods with a beak 3-15 mm. long   Brassica
   y. Pods beakless or nearly so
    (x) Leaves entire or toothed   Erysimum
    (y) Leaves pinnatifid   Barbarea

Alýssum Linné 1753   Yellow Alyssum
(Gr. *alysson,* a plant used to check hiccup)

Pl. 6, fig. 7.

Sepals 4, petals 4, yellowish or whitish, stamens 6, pod round, flattened, winged, 4-seeded, notched, style short; flowers in dense racemes; leaves spatulate to oblong, densely gray stellate-hairy; low annual.

Stems several from the base, hairy; flowers tiny   *A. calycínum*

Árabis Linné 1753   Rockcress
(Named for Arabia)

Pl. 6, fig. 41-42.

Sepals 4, petals 4, white to purple, rarely yellowish, stamens 6, pod long, linear, flat, seeds in 1 or 2 rows, style short; flowers in racemes or corymbs; leaves entire to pinnatifid; annual, biennial or perennial.

1. Pods erect or spreading
  a. All or nearly all the stem leaves smooth
    (1) Lower part of the stem and basal leaves
       hairy or shaggy   *A. glábra*
    (2) Stem and basal leaves smooth, often
       glaucous   *A. Drummóndii*
  b. Stem and leaves usually hairy or ciliate
    throughout   *A. hirsúta*
2. Pods recurved or hanging   *A. Holbóellii*

Barbaréa Linné 1753   Wintercress
(Named for St. Barbara)

Pl. 6, fig. 30.

Sepals 4, petals 4, yellow, stamens 6, pod linear, 4-angled, seeds in

1 row, style short, forming a short beak; flowers in racemes; leaves pinnatifid; biennial or perennial.

1. Segments of the leaf 3-9   *B. vulgáris*
2. Segments of the leaf 9-17   *B. praécox*

BRÁSSICA Linné 1753   MUSTARD

(The Latin name of the cabbage)

(Sinapis Linné)

Pl. 6, fig. 33-35

Sepals 4, petals 4, yellow, stamens 6, pods linear, or lanceolate, round or 4-sided in section, often constricted, seeds in 1 row, style long, broadening below into a long often 1-seeded beak; flowers in racemes; basal leaves pinnatifid, stem leaves often merely toothed or entire; annual, biennial or perennial.

1. Beak cylindric or conic
   a. Pods distinctly and suddenly narrowed into the
       slender beak
      (1) Pods 1-2.5 cm. long; beak 2-3 mm. long   *B. nigra*
      (2) Pods 3-5 cm. long; beak 7-12 mm. long   *B. júncea*
   b. Pods tapering gradually into the stout beak,
      3-4 cm. long; beak 6-12 mm. long   *B. arvénsis*
2. Beak flattened, as long as the pod   *B. álba*

BÚRSA Weber 1780   SHEPHERD'S PURSE

(Lat. *bursa*, purse, from the pod)

(Capsella Medicus)

Pl. 6, fig. 3.

Sepals 4, petals 4, white, stamens 6, pod triangular wedge-shaped, flattened at right angles to the partition, notched, several-seeded, style short; flowers in racemes; leaves pinnatifid, with forked hairs; annual or biennial.

Stems erect from a rosette; stem leaves lanceolate,
eared   *B. bursa-pastóris*

CAMÉLINA Crantz 1762   FALSE FLAX

(Gr. *chamae*, on the ground, *linon*, flax, from its growing in flax fields)

Pl. 6, fig. 8.

Sepals 4, petals 4, yellow, stamens 6, pod pear-shaped, somewhat flattened, seeds several to many in 2 rows, style slender; leaves entire or toothed; annual.

Upper leaves clasping, arrow-like; pod margined   *C. sativa*

CARDÁMINE Linné 1753   BITTERCRESS
(Gr. *kardamine*, a cress-like herb)
Pl. 6, fig. 39.

Sepals 4, petals 4, white or purple, stamens 6 or 4, pod long, linear, flat, seeds in 1 row, style short or none; flowers mostly in corymbs; leaves entire, lobed or pinnate; mostly perennial.

1. Leaves simple, wavy-toothed or entire, smooth
    or hairy   *C. cordifólia*
2. Leaves pinnatifid or pinnate
    a. Lateral leaflets oblong to linear   *C. pennsilvánica*
    b. Lateral leaflets round to broadly obovoid   *C. Bréweri*

CAULÁNTHUS Watson 1871
(Gr. *kaulos*, stem, *anthos*, flower)
Pl. 6, fig. 38.

Sepals 4, usually purplish, petals 4, greenish-yellow, stamens 6, pod linear, long, nearly round in section, seeds in 1 row, style short; flowers in racemes; leaves entire, toothed or lobed; perennial.

Stem usually fleshy and hollow; flowers ascending to
  reflexed   *C. crassicaúlis*

CONRÍNGIA Heister   HARE'S-EAR MUSTARD
(Named for Professor Conring)
Pl. 6, fig. 27.

Sepals 4, petals 4, white or cream-colored, stamens 6, pod linear, long, 4-sided, seeds in 1 row in each half, beaked; flowers in loose corymbs; leaves entire or wavy, clasping; annual.

Leaves oblong to elliptic, glaucous; pods 2-4 in. long *C. orientális*

DITHÝREA Harvey 1845
(Gr. *di-*, two, *thyra*, door, valve, from the pod)
Pl. 6, fig. 17.

Sepals 4, petals 4, yellow to purple, stamens 6, pod of two roundish flattened 1-seeded disks, resembling eye-glasses, style stout; flowers in dense corymbs or racemes; leaves gray-hairy, wavy-toothed or lobed; perennial.

Stems erect, densely white-hairy; leaves ovate to
lanceolate   *D. Wislizénii*

DRÁBA Linné 1753   DRABA
·   (Gr. *drabe*, a plant of the mustard family)
Pl. 5, fig. 5; pl. 6, fig. 18-20.

Sepals 4, petals 4, yellow, yellowish or white, stamens 6, pod ovoid to oblong or linear-oblong, flat, few-many-seeded, style usually short; flowers in racemes or corymbs; leaves simple, entire or toothed; annual, biennial or perennial.

1. Annuals
   a. Flowers white
      (1) Pods in an umbel-like cluster; leaves entire   *D. caroliniána*
      (2) Pods in a raceme; leaves usually toothed *D. cuneifólia*
   b. Flowers yellow or white
      (1) Plant low, 5-10 cm. high, smooth; leaves basal   *D. crassifólia*
      (2) Plant 10-30 cm. high, hairy; stem leafy, at least below   *D. nemorósa*
2. Perennials, as shown by the rootstock or the old stem or leaf bases
   a. Flowering stems leafless, tufted; flowers yellow to white
      (1) Leaves ovoid to spatulate; pods oblong   *D. ventósa*
      (2) Leaves linear to linear oblong; pods ovoid *D. oligospérma*
   b. Flowering stems leafy
      (1) Flowers white   *D. incána*
      (2) Flowers yellow
         (a) Pods smooth, straight   *D. chrysántha*
         (b) Pods hairy, twisted
            x. Stem and leaves with long spreading hairs   *D. streptocárpa*
            y. Stem and leaves gray with close hairs *D. aúrea*

ERÝSIMUM Linné 1753   ERYSIMUM, WALLFLOWER
(Gr. *erysimon*, hedge-mustard, transferred from another plant)
Pl. 5, fig. 4; pl. 6, fig. 28-29.
Sepals 4, petals 4, yellow, orange or purple, pod linear, 4-sided, seeds

PLATE 6

MUSTARD FAMILY

1. Lepidium Fremontii
2. Lepidium virginicum
3. Bursa bursa-pastoris.
4. Hutchinsia procumbens
5. Thlaspi arvense
6. Thlaspi alpestre
7. Alyssum calycinum
8. Camelina sativa
9. Lesquerella argentea
10. Lesquerella montana
11. Subularia aquatica
12-13. Roripa palustre
14. Roripa curvisiliqua
15-16. Physaria didymocarpa
17. Dithyrea Wislizeni
18. Draba oligosperma
19. Draba caroliniana
20. Draba aurea
21-22. Smelowskia calycina
23-25. Sisymbrium incisum
26. Sisymbrium linifolium
27. Conringia orientalis
28. Erysimum asperum
29. Erysimum cheiranthoides
30. Barbarea vulgaris
31. Thelypodium aureum
32. Thelypodium integrifolium
33. Brassica juncea
34. Brassica arvensis
35. Brassica nigra
36. Raphanus raphanistrum
37. Stanleya pinnatifida
38. Caulanthus crassicaulis
39. Cardamine Breweri
40. Stenophragma virgatum
41. Arabis Drummondii
42. Arabis Holboellii
43. Streptanthus cordatus

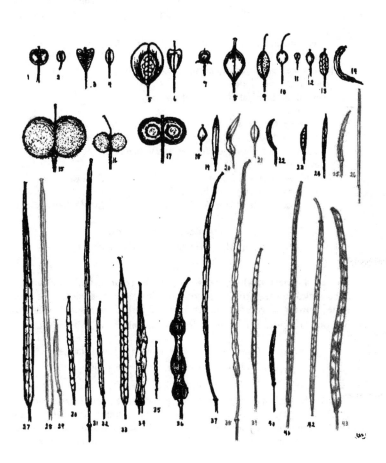

in 1 row, style stoutish, stigma 2-lobed; flowers in racemes or corymbs; leaves entire, sinuate-toothed or lobed, often gray-hairy; annual, biennial or perennial.

1. Flowers small, petals 3-6 mm. long; pods 1-2.5
cm. long   *E. cheiranthoides*
2. Flowers medium to large, petals 6-20 mm. long;
pods 3-20 cm. long
    a. Annual or biennial, i. e., no old woody stems
present
        (1) Petals 6-10 mm. long; pods 3-8 cm. long *E. parviflorum*
        (2) Petals 12-20 mm. long; pods 5-20 cm. long *E. asperum*
    b. Perennials, i. e., bases of former stems usually
evident
        (1) Flowers yellow; plant low, 2-6 in. high   *E. nivale*
        (2) Flowers orange to brownish-orange, or
rose-purple; plant 6-16 in. high   *E. Wheeleri*

HUTCHÍNSIA Robert Brown 1812
(Named for Miss Hutchins, an Irish botanist)
Pl. 6, fig. 4.

Sepals 4, petals 4, white, stamens 6, pod more or less elliptic, flattened at right angles to the partition, slightly notched, several-seeded, style short or none; flowers in racemes; lower leaves 3-forked or pinnatifid; annual. Stems low, branched, spreading, hairy, 3-8 in. tall   *H. procúmbens*

LEPÍDIUM Linné 1753   PEPPERWEED, PEPPERGRASS
(Gr. *lepidion*, little scale, from the pods)
Pl. 6, fig. 1-2.

Sepals 4, petals 4 or none, white or greenish, stamens 2 or 6, rarely 4, style short or none, pod more or less circular, much flattened, usually notched at the top, often winged; flowers in dense often spike-like racemes; leaves entire to pinnatifid, especially the basal; annual, biennial or perennial.

1. Stamens 6
    a. Leaves entire or toothed, oblong-ovate   *L. draba*
    b. Leaves pinnatifid, or narrow when entire
        (1) Some or all the leaves narrow and entire,
the basal ones usually pinnatifid
            (a) Pods broadly rounded   *L. Fremóntii*
            (b) Pods ovoid   *L. alyssoides*

(2) All or nearly all the leaves pinnatifid; pods
    ovoid   ·   *L. montánum*

2. Stamens 2, rarely 4
  a. Pods hairy   *L. lasiocárpum*
  b. Pods smooth or nearly so
    (1) Petals typically present   *L. virgínicum*
    (2) Petals tiny or none   *L. apétalum*

· LESQUERÉLLA Watson 1888   BLADDER POD

(Named for Lesquereux, an American botanist)

Pl. 6, fig. 9-10.

Sepals 4, petals 4, yellow, stamens 6, pod globose to ovoid or oblong, slightly inflated, hairy or smooth, few-seeded, style long, persistent; flowers densely corymbose; leaves densely gray-stellate hairy, entire; biennial or perennial.

1. Pods hairy
  a. Pods globose; leaves linear to spatulate or
    obovate   *L. argéntea*
  b. Pods ovoid to oblong
    (1) Plant tufted, 1-3 in. high; leaves usually
       linear   *L. alpina*
    (2) Plant spreading, stems 3-10 in. long;
       leaves spatulate to obovate   *L. montána*
2. Pods smooth, globose; leaves linear, lanceolate,
  spatulate·or ovate   *L. Féndleri*

PHYSÁRIA Gray 1871   BLADDER POD

(Gr. *physa*, pair of bellows, bubble, from the pods)

Pl. 5, fig. 7; pl. 6, fig. 15-16.

Sepals 4, greenish yellow, petals 4, yellow, rarely cream-colored, stamens 6, pod inflated into two globoid halves, often large and bladder-like, each 1-2-seeded, style long, slender, persistent; flowers in dense corymbs; leaves thickish, gray-hairy or densely gray-felted, the basal in a dense rosette, spatulate, ovoid, rhombic, or fiddle-shaped, entire or lobed, stem leaves lanceolate to lance-ovate or spatulate; rosette perennials.

Stems few to many, prostrate; pod halves 5-15 mm.
  diam.   *P. didymocárpa*

Ráphanus Linné 1753   Radish

(Gr. *rha-,* quick, *phanos,* appearing, from its quick germination)

Pl. 6, fig. 36.

Sepals 4, petals 4, pink, white or yellow, stamens 6, pod lance-linear, round in section, usually constricted, beaked, 2-10-seeded, remaining closed on ripening, style slender; flowers in racemes or corymbs; leaves usually pinnatifid; annual or biennial.

1. Flowers yellow, fading to white; pod 4-10-seeded *R. raphanistrum*
2. Flowers pink or white; pod 2-3-seeded   *R. sativus*

Róripa Scopoli 1760   Watercress

(Name of unknown origin and meaning)

Pl. 6, fig. 12-14.

Sepals 4, petals 4, yellow or white, stamens 1-6, pod oblong to cylindric, rarely globoid, round in section, occasionally 1-celled, seeds typically in 2 rows, style mostly short; flowers in racemes; leaves pinnatifid to pinnate-dissected, rarely entire; annual, biennial or perennial, some aquatic.

1. Flowers white
   - a. Floating or creeping; leaves of 3-9 leaflets   *R. nastúrtium*
   - b. Erect; leaves pinnatifid   *R. trachycárpa*
2. Flowers yellow
   - a. Annuals or biennials
     - (1) Pods usually curved, oblong   *R. curvisiliqua*
     - (2) Pods and pedicels rarely curved
       - (a) Plant erect, 1-4 ft. high, smooth to hispid hairy; pods globoid to oblong *R. palústris*
       - (b) Plant diffuse, .5-1 ft. high, spreading, usually smooth; pods globoid to oblong *R. obtúsa* ·
   - b. Perennials, with a horizontal rootstock, low and spreading   *R. sinuáta*

Sisýmbrium Linné 1753   Tansy, Mustard

(Gr. *sisymbrion,* name of some aromatic plant)

(Sophia Adanson, Schoenocrambe Greene)

Pl. 6, fig. 23-26.

Sepals 4, petals 4, yellow or yellowish, stamens 6, pods linear, round or flat in section, seeds in 1 or 2 rows, style distinct; flowers in racemes; leaves entire, pinnatifid or pinnate; annual, biennial or perennial.

1. Leaves pinnate to bipinnate
   a. Seeds in 1 row in each half of the pod   *S. incísum*
   b. Seeds in 2 rows   *S. pinnátum*
2. Leaves pinnatifid or entire
   a. Leaves pinnatifid, the segments broad; weeds *S. officinále*
   b. Leaves mostly entire, leaves or segments linear; .
     native   *S. linifólium*

SMELÓWSKIA C. A. Meyer 1831

(Named for Smelowski, a Russian botanist)

Pl. 6, fig. 21-22.

Sepals 4, petals 4, white or pink, stamens 6, pods lance-oblong, flattened at right angles to the partition, but appearing 4-angled, few-seeded, style short or none; flowers in corymbs or racemes; leaves pinnatifid, hairy, often hoary; tufted perennials.

Stems 2-8 in. high; leaves mostly basal, leaflets linear
   to ovoid   *S. calycína*

STÁNLEYA Nuttall 1818   STANLEYA

(Named for Lord Stanley)

Pl. 6, fig. 37.

Sepals 4, yellow or yellowish, petals 4, yellow to creamy or greenish, stamens 6, pod long, linear, roundish in section, long-stalked; flowers in long racemes; leaves extremely variable, from entire to pinnatifid or even pinnate; perennial.

Leaves entire to pinnatifid or pinnate, smooth or
   hairy; flowers yellow to creamy or greenish-yellow *S. pinnatífida*

STENOPHRÁGMA Celakovsky 1877

(Gr. *stenos*, narrow, *phragma*, partition)

Pl. 6, fig. 40.

Sepals 4, petals 4, white, stamens 6, pod linear, somewhat 4-angled, seeds in 1 or 2 rows, style short, stout; flowers in racemes; leaves toothed or entire; rosette biennial.

Stems hairy; stem leaves clasping, entire, rosette
   leaves toothed   *S. virgátum*

STREPTÁNTHUS Nuttall 1838
(Gr. *streptos,* twisted, bent, *anthos,* flower)
(Euklisia Rydberg)
Pl. 6, fig. 43.

Sepals 4, petals 4, white, yellow or purple, stamens 6, pod linear or linear-oblong, flat, sometimes beaked, seeds in 1 row; flowers in racemes; leaves simple to pinnatifid, often clasping; annual, biennial or perennial.

1. Stem leaves clasping, ovoid to oblong, usually
   entire; pods blunt, ascending or spreading   *S. cordátus*
2. Lower stem leaves not clasping, often petioled,
   lance-oblong, pinnatifid; pods beaked, reflexed *S. longiróstris*

SUBULÁRIA Linné 1753   AWLWORT
(Lat. *subula,* an awl, from the shape of the leaves)
Pl. 6, fig. 11.

Sepals 4, petals 4, white, stamens 6, pod oblong to elliptic, short-stalked, seeds few, in 2 rows in each half, style none; flowers few in a raceme; leaves basal, awlshaped: annual submerged aquatic.

Plants tufted in shallow water or in mud, 1-3 in. high *S. aquática*

THELYPÓDIUM Endlicher 1842
(Gr. *thelys,* female, *podion,* little foot, from the stalked ovary)
Pl. 6, fig. 31, 32.

Sepals 4, petals 4, white to purple or yellow, stamens 6, pod linear, long, round or 4-angled in section, sometimes with a short base or stalk, style short; flowers in dense corymbs or racemes; leaves usually entire, sometimes toothed or lobed; annual, biennial or perennial.

1. Flowers white or purple
   a. Stem leaves clasping by an eared base   *T. sagittátum*
   b. Stem leaves not clasping
      (1) Stem leaves distinctly petioled, broad,
          toothed or lobed   *T. Wrightii*
      (2) Stem leaves sessile or nearly so, narrow
          and entire   *T. integrifólium*
2. Flowers yellow; leaves clasping   *T. aúreum*

THLÁSPI Linné 1753   PENNYCRESS
Pl. 6, fig. 5-6.

Sepals 4, petals 4, white, stamens 6, style sometimes very short, pod circular to ovoid, broadly or narrowly winged, much flattened, more or less notched at the top; flowers in racemes; leaves oblong to ovoid, sessile, entire or toothed, often glaucous; annual or perennial.

1. Pods large, round, broadly winged; leaves coarsely toothed; weed in waste places   *T. arvénse*
2. Pods small or medium, slightly winged; leaves usually entire; native from 5-14000 ft.   *T. alpéstre*

VIOLÁCEAE   VIOLET FAMILY

Sepals 5, often unequal, petals 5, separate, irregular, the lower one larger or spurred, stamens 5, ovary 1-celled, with 3 seed rows (placentae) on the wall, stigma 1, fruit a capsule, splitting into three parts; flowers solitary or clustered; low stemless or stemmed herbs with simple entire to parted leaves with stipules.

1. Flowers large, 10-25 mm. long; petals of 2 lengths, lower spurred   VIOLA
2. Flowers small, 4-6 mm. long; petals of 3 lengths, lower merely swollen at base   CALCEOLARIA

VÍOLA Linné 1753   VIOLET, PANSY
(Lat. *viola*, violet)
Pl. 5, fig. 1-2.

Sepals 5, petals 5, blue, purple, yellow, cream-color or white, sometimes with blue or purple veins or dots; flowers solitary, rarely 2; leaves lanceolate to ovate and round, sometimes deeply cut or parted, often all basal; perennial, rarely annual.

1. Stemless, flower- and leaf-stalks arising from the base
  a. Flowers pale lilac to white; rootstock slender, creeping, bearing stolons
    (1) Petals pale lilac, rarely white, somewhat bearded   *V. palústris*
    (2) Petals white, purple-veined, beardless   *V. blánda*
  b. Flowers blue to purple, rarely pale; rootstock thick, without stolons
    (1) Leaves deeply parted into linear lobes   *V. pedatífida*
    (2) Leaves merely wavy-toothed, heart-shaped   *V. oblíqua*
2. Leafy-stemmed, leaves and flowers from a visible stem

a. Flowers yellow or cream-colored
  (1) Stipules at base of leaf stalks small, not
    conspicuous, leaf-like and lobed
    (a) Stems short at flowering; leaves lance-
      linear to ovoid, rarely heart-shaped at
      base   *V. Nuttállii*
    (b) Stems long, weak; leaves broadly round
      or kidney-shaped, heart-shaped at base *V. bicolor*
  (2) Stipules conspicuous, leaf-like and lobed
    or cut; some petals often bluish   *V. tenélla*
b. Flowers blue, purple or white
  (1) Flowers blue to purple; stipules cut or
    fringed; plants smooth or rough   *V. canína*
  (2) Flowers white; stipules entire   *V. canadénsis*

CALCEOLÁRIA Loefling 1758

(Lat. *calceolus*, little shoe, from the corolla)

Sepals 5, somewhat unequal, petals 5, white, the lower largest, swollen at base, the two lateral ones larger than the upper; flowers solitary, nodding; leaves alternate or opposite, linear to oblanceolate; perennial.

Stems 3-12 in. high from a woody base; leaves entire *C. lineáris*

POLYGALÁCEAE   MILKWORT FAMILY

Sepals 5, irregular, the two lateral petal-like, petals 3, united into a tube somewhat attached to the stamens, stamens 6 or 8, united below into 1, or into 2 sets, ovary 2-celled, 2-seeded, style simple, fruit a capsule; flowers in racemes, spikes or heads; herbs or shrubs with alternate, opposite or whorled leaves.

POLÝGALA Linné 1753   MILKWORT

(Gr. *polys*, much, *gala*, milk, from its supposed virtue as pasturage)

Characters of the family; flowers white, purple, yellow or greenish.

1. Plants herbaceous; corolla with a fringed crest
  a. Leaves in whorls of 4 or 5   *P. verticilláta*
  b. Leaves alternate   *P. álba*
2. Plants more or less shrubby and spiny; corolla
    without a fringed crest
  a. Plant 2-3 ft. high; flowers 3-4 mm. long   *P. acanthóclada*
  b. Plant 2-8 in. high; flowers 7-10 mm. long   *P. subspinósa*

MALVALES   MALLOW ORDER
MALVACEAE   MALLOW FAMILY

Sepals 5, somewhat united, petals 5, stamens many, the filaments grown into a column and united at base with the petals, ovary 5-20-celled, entire or lobed, styles or stigmas 5-20, fruit a 5-celled capsule splitting when mature, or breaking into 5-20 nutlike segments; flowers solitary, or in racemes or spikes; herbs or shrubs with alternate, simple, entire or divided leaves.

1. Stigmas linear, along inner side of styles
  a. Fruit divisions 1-seeded
    (1) Involucre of 3 bracts; stamens in one tube
      (a) Petals broadly notched; fruits not beaked MALVA
      (b) Petals straight across; fruits beaked CALLIRRHOE
    (2) Involucre none
      (a) Stamens in a double series or tube SIDALCEA
      (b) Stamens in one series CALLIRRHOE
  b. Fruit divisions 3-several-seeded; involucre none ABUTILON
2. Stigmas capitate, at tips of styles
  a. Flowers yellow SIDA
  b. Flowers white to red or vermilion
    (1) Fruit divisions 1-seeded; flowers vermilion MALVASTRUM
    (2) Fruit divisions 2-3-seeded; flowers white to
      purple or red SPHAERALCEA

ABÚTILON Gaertner 1791   VELVET LEAF
(The Arabic name)

Sepals 5, united, without accessory bracts, petals 5, yellow, anthers at the top of the stamen column, ovary with 5-many cavities, stigmas at the tip of the styles, fruits or carpels 2-valved, falling away after ripening; flowers single, axillary; leaves entire or toothed, rarely lobed, heart-shaped at base; annual.

1. Flowers 1-2 cm. wide; carpels 12-15, 2-beaked *A. Avicénnae*
2. Flowers less than 1 cm.; carpels 5, not beaked *A. párvulum*

CALLÍRRHOE Nuttall 1821   POPPY MALLOW
(Gr. *kallirrhoe*, beautiful flowing, a famous spring at Athens)
Pl. 7, fig. 8.

Sepals 5, united at base, bracts none or 3, petals 5, white to pink or rose-purple, truncate, anthers at the top of the stamen column, ovary with 10-20 cavities, stigmas along the inner side of the styles, fruits or carpels

10-20 in a circle, beaked, closed or splitting, 1-seeded; flowers solitary or
few in a terminal cluster; leaves lobed or divided; perennial.

1. Flowers white to pink, 1 in. wide; no bracts below;
   sepals none   *C. alceoídes*
2. Flowers rose-purple, 1-3 in. wide; bracts 3   *C. involucráta*

MÁLVA Linné 1753   MALLOW
(Gr. *malache,* Lat. *malva,* mallow, from its mucilage)

Sepals 5, united, usually with 3 leaf-like bracts just below, petals 5,
white to pink or red, anthers at the top of the stamen column, ovary with
10-20 cavities, stigmas along the inner side of the styles, fruits or carpels
10-20 in a circle, beaked, closed, 1-seeded; flowers solitary or clustered;
leaves lobed or divided; annual, biennial or perennial.

Stems creeping; leaves rounded, 5-9-lobed; flowers
   whitish   *M. rotundifólia*

· MALVÁSTRUM   Gray 1848   MALVASTRUM
(Lat. *malva,* mallow, *-astrum,* like, from the resemblance)
Pl. 7, fig. 7.

Sepals 5, united, petals 5, yellow to orange or red, anthers at the top
of the stamen column, ovary with 5-many cavities, stigmas at the tip of
the styles, fruits or carpels 5-many in a circle, beaked, closed or splitting;
flowers solitary or in a spike-like raceme; leaves entire, toothed or divided;
annual or perennial.

1. Leaves 3-5-divided, gray with star-shaped hairs   *M. coccineum*
2. Leaves 3-parted, silvery with shield-shaped hairs *M. leptophýllum*

SÍDA Linné 1753
(Greek name of a plant)

Sepals 5, united, without bracts beneath, petals 5, yellow, anthers at the
top of the stamen column, ovary with 5-many cavities, stigmas at the tip
of the styles, fruits or carpels 5-many, 1-seeded, mostly closed; flowers
solitary or clustered; leaves toothed or lobed; annual or perennial.

Stem and leaves silvery-scaly; leaves arrow-shaped   *S. lepidóta*

SIDÁLCEA   Gray 1848   SIDALCEA
(Gr. *sida,* and *alkea,* mallow)
Pl. 7, fig. 3.

Sepals 5, united, without bracts beneath, petals 5, rose, purple or white,
stamens united in 2 rows, ovary with 5-9 cavities, stigmas along the inner

side of the styles, fruits or carpels 5-9, 1-seeded, beakless, mostly closed; flowers in spike-like racemes; leaves lobed or divided; perennial.

1. Flowers white or creamy   *S. cándida*
2. Flowers rose or rose-purple   *S. neo-mexicána*

SPHAERÁLCEA St. Hilaire 1825   GLOBE-MALLOW
(Gr. *sphaira*, ball, *alkea*, mallow)

Sepals 5, united, with 3 leaf-like bracts below, petals 5, white, purple or red, anthers at the top of the stamen column, ovary with 5-many cavities, stigmas at the tip of the style branches, fruits or carpels 5-many, splitting; flowers in spike-like racemes; leaves entire to lobed, often gray-silvery; perennial.

1. Leaves large, deeply lobed, maple-like; petals
    white or purplish, 2-4 cm. long   *S. rivuláris*
2. Leaves smaller, entire or with shallow round
    lobes; petals rose-purple to red, 1-2 cm. long
    a. Leaves oblong to lanceolate   *S. cuspidáta*
    b. Leaves ovoid or rounded, heart-shaped at base   *S. margináta*

URTICÁCEAE   NETTLE FAMILY

Sepals 2-9, often united, petals none, stamens 2-9, ovary 1-celled, styles 1-2, fruit an achene or a nut-like drupe; flowers often imperfect, the stamens and pistils in different flowers; herbs, or trees with alternate or opposite simple leaves.

1. Trees   CELTIS
2. Herbs
    a. Climbers, with opposite 3-7-lobed leaves   HUMULUS
    b. Erect herbs, with entire or toothed leaves
       (1) Low annuals, smooth; leaves entire   PARIETARIA
       (2) Perennials with stinging hairs; leaves
          toothed   URTICA

CÉLTIS Linné 1753   HACKBERRY
(Lat. *celtis*, lotus tree)
Pl. 4, fig. 4.

Sepals 4-6, sometimes united, petals none, stamens 4-6, ovary 1-celled, stigmas 2, fruit a drupe, the outer coat pulpy, the inner stony; leaves alternate in 2 rows, simple, serrate or entire; stamen flowers in a raceme, pistil flowers solitary; trees.

Leaves ovate or lance-ovate, 3-nerved at base; fruit
globose, blackish, persisting   *C. occidentális*

Húmulus Linné 1753   Hop
(Lat. *humus*, ground, perhaps from its trailing habit)

Sepals 5 in the stamen flowers, 1 in the pistil flowers, petals none,
stamens 5, ovary 1-celled, stigmas 2, fruit an achene, the latter forming a
cone-like cluster when mature; stamen flowers in panicles, pistil flowers in
spikes; leaves opposite 3-7-lobed; climbing herbs.

Stems twining or clambering, rough-hairy   *H. lúpulus*

Parietária Linné 1753   Pellitory
(Lat. *paries*, wall, from the habitat of some species)

Sepals 4, often united, petals none, stamens 4, ovary 1-celled, stigma
tufted, fruit an achene enclosed in the withered calyx; stamen and pistil
flowers clustered in the leaf axils; leaves alternate, entire; smooth annuals.

Plants 6-14 in. high; leaves lanceolate, 3-nerved, 1-3
in. long   *P. pennsilvánica*

Urtíca Linné 1753   Nettle
(Lat. *urtica*, nettle, from *uro*, burn, from the stinging hairs)

Sepals 4, somewhat united, petals none, stamens 4, ovary 1-celled,
stigma tufted, fruit an achene enclosed by the calyx; flowers of two sorts,
stamen and pistil-bearing, in long axillary clusters; leaves opposite, serrate;
stinging perennials.

1. Leaf bases heart-shaped; leaves broadly ovate   *U. dioéca*
2. Leaf bases rounded or tapering; leaves lance-
    oblong to lance-ovate   *U. grácilis*

EUPHORBIÁCEAE   SPURGE FAMILY

Sepals 3-10, united, or 1 and very minute, petals 3-5, small, or none,
stamens 4-16, or 1, ovary usually with 3 cavities, ovules 1-2 in each cavity,
styles 3, fruit a 3-lobed capsule splitting when ripe; flowers with stamens
and pistils separate, mostly single or in racemes, or in minute flower-like
heads; herbs with opposite, alternate or whorled mostly simple entire or
toothed leaves.

1. Plant silvery-gray with star-shaped hairs; sta-
    mens 10   Croton
2. Plant not gray-stellate; stamens mostly 1-5

a. Stems and leaves with stinging hairs   TRAGIA

b. Stems and leaves without stinging hairs
- (1) Flowers separate   DITAXIS
- (2) Stamen and pistil flowers in a calyx-like cup, often bordered by petal-like glands EUPHORBIA

CRÓTON Linné 1753   CROTON
(Gr. *kroton*, name of the castor-oil plant)

Stamen flowers with 4-6 united sepals, tiny petals and 5-10 stamens; pistil flowers with 5-10 united sepals, no petals and a 3-celled ovary with 1 ovule in each cell, styles branched, fruit splitting into 2 parts; flowers monoecious, in small clusters; leaves more or less silvery-gray with star-shaped hairs; annual.

Leaves oblong-ovate to lance-oblong, entire, silvery   *C. texénsis*

DITÁXIS Vahl 1824
(Gr. *di-*, two, *taxis*, row, from the stamens)

Stamen flowers with 4-5 united sepals, 4-5 petals, and 4-15 stamens united into a column; pistil flowers similar as to sepals and petals, ovary 3-celled, 1 ovule in each cell, styles branched, fruit splitting into 3 parts; flowers monoecious, in small clusters; leaves entire; perennial.

Plant 4-10 in. high; leaves ovate to oblong, 1-3 cm.
long, petioled, hairy   *D. húmilis*

TRÁGIA Linné 1753   TRAGIA
(Named for Tragus or Bock, one of the earliest herbalists)

Stamen flowers with 3-5 united sepals, no petals, and mostly 1-3 stamens; pistil flowers with 3-8 united sepals, 3-celled ovary, 1 ovule in each cell, styles simple; flowers in racemes; leaves toothed, with stinging hairs; perennial.

Plant 4-10 in. high; leaves lance-ovate, 1-5 cm. long *T. ramósa*

EUPHÓRBIA Linné 1753   SPURGE
(Named for the physician Euphorbus)
Pl. 7, fig. 4.

The apparent flower is really a cluster or involucre, containing several tiny flowers, consisting of one stamen each and a single scale, and one pistil flower, with the characteristic 3-lobed ovary; the 3-lobed fruit projects from the involucre on a stalk; leaves opposite, alternate or whorled, entire, toothed or lobed, typically with a milky juice; annual, biennial, or perennial.

1. Leaves opposite, at least most of them
   a. Leaves wholly entire
      (1) Leaves with the sides unequal at base
         (a) Plant smooth
            x. Seeds smooth
               (x) Stems prostrate, leaves rounded to
                   ovoid, 3-7 mm. long; appendages
                   tiny   *E. sérpens*
               (y) Stems erect or ascending; leaves
                   linear to oblong, 1-3 cm. long; ap-
                   pendages large, white, petal-like *E. petaloídea*
            y. Seeds wrinkled crosswise
               (x) Appendages of the involucre large
                   and petal-like, usually white   *E. albomargináta*
               (y) Appendages small and inconspicu-
                   ous   *E. Féndleri*
         (b) Plant hairy; leaves lance-ovoid, very
             unequal at base   *E. láta*
      (2) Leaves with the sides equal at base, linear
          to lanceolate, smooth; plant erect   *E. hexágona*
   b. Leaves variously toothed, often but slightly
      (1) Leaves small, about 1 cm. or less long,
          ovoid to oblong, unequal at base
         (a) Plant smooth
            x. Seeds wrinkled crosswise   *E. glyptospérma*
            y. Seeds pitted, scarcely or not at all
               wrinkled   *E. serpyllifólia*
         (b) Plant hairy   *E. stictóspora*
      (2) Leaves larger, mostly more than 3 cm.
          long, equal at base   *E. dentáta*
2. Leaves alternate
   a. Upper leaves white or white-margined; ap-
      pendages large and petal-like   *E. margináta*
   b. Upper leaves green; appendages none or in-
      conspicuous
      (1) Leaves toothed, spatulate to broadly ob-
          lanceolate; capsule warted   *E. dictyospérma*
      (2) Leaves entire
         (a) Leaves linear; capsule warted   *E. cyparíssias*
         (b) Leaves broadly oblong to ovoid or
             rounded; capsule smooth   *E. montána*

LIMNANTHÁCEAE   FALSE MERMAID FAMILY

Sepals 2-5, slightly united at base, petals 2-3, separate, alternating with 2-3 glands, stamens 4-6, pistils 2-3, partly united, stigmas 2-3, fruit deeply 2-3-lobed, or the carpels separate, fleshy, not splitting; flowers solitary, axillary, perfect, white to pink; annual herbs with alternate, pinnately-divided leaves.

FLOÉRKEA   Willdenow 1801

(Named for Floerke, a German botanist)

Characters of the family.

Stems weak, 4-15 in. long; leaves .5-3 in. long; flow-
　ers 2-3 mm. wide　　　　　　●　　　　*F. proserpinacoídes*

CALLITRICHÁCEAE   CALLITRICHE FAMILY

Sepals none, petals none, stamens 1, pistil 1, ovary 4-celled, styles 2, fruit flattened, lobed, the lobes more or less winged, separating at maturity into 4 1-seeded carpels; flowers solitary, axillary, perfect or monoecious; aquatic herbs with slender stems and opposite entire spatulate or linear leaves.

CALLÍTRICHE   Linné 1753   WATER STARWORT

(Gr. *kalli-*, beautiful, *thrix*, hair, from the hair-like stems)

Characters of the family.

1. Submerged; all leaves linear to oblong; bracts
　　none　　　　　　　　　　　　　　*C. bifida*
2. Amphibious; air leaves spatulate or obovate;
　　bracts present　　　　　　　　　　*C. palústris*

GERANIALES   GERANIUM ORDER

GERANIÁCEAE   GERANIUM FAMILY

Sepals 5, petals 5, stamens 5-10, ovary 5-celled, lobed, ovules 1 or 2 in each chamber, stigmas 5, fruit a capsule splitting into 5 nut-like parts; flowers solitary or clustered; annual, biennial or perennial herbs with alternate or opposite divided or compound leaves.

1. Stamens with anthers 5; leaves pinnate　　　ERODIUM
2. Stamens with anthers 10; leaves palmately divided
　　　　　　　　　　　　　　　　　　GERANIUM

PLATE 7.

ERÓDIUM   L'Héritier 1807   STORKSBILL, ALFILARIA

(Gr. *erodios,* heron, from the form of the fruit)

Pl. 7, fig. 5.

Sepals 5, petals 5, pink or rose-purple, the upper 2 smaller, stamens 5, alternating with 5 sterile filaments, ovary 5-lobed, stigmas 5, lobes of the fruit 1-seeded, separating, styles hairy on the inner side; flowers in umbels; leaves pinnate, the leaflets finely cut; annual.

Stems spreading, 2-8 in. high; flowers 6-12 mm.
broad.   *E. cicutárium*

GERÁNIUM   Linné 1753   GERANIUM, CRANESBILL

(Gr. *geranos,* crane, from the form of the fruit)

Pl. 7, fig. 6.

Sepals 5, petals 5, white to red or purple, stamens 10, in 2 rows, ovary 5-lobed, stigmas 5, lobes of the fruit 1-seeded, remaining united by the tips of the styles, the latter not hairy on the inner side; flowers solitary or clustered; leaves palmately 3-9-divided.

1. Petals bright pink, red or purple; plant more
   or less glandular hairy; typically in moist soil   *G. caespitósum*
2. Petals white or pinkish; plant more or less
   glandular hairy; typically in dry soil   *G. Richardsónii*

OXALIDÁCEAE   WOOD SORREL FAMILY

Sepals 5, petals 5, yellow, rose-purple or white, stamens 10, in two lengths, united at base, ovary 5-celled, styles 5, fruit a capsule, splitting lengthwise, flowers in cymes; leaves alternate, often basal, of three leaflets; annual or perennial, often stemless, herbs with an acid sap.

ÓXALIS   Linné 1753   WOOD SORREL

(Gr. *oxalis,* sorrel, from *oxys,* sour, from the sap)

Pl. 7, fig. 2.

Characters of the family.

1. Flowers yellow; stems leafy, 1-12 in. high; fruit
   cylindric   *O. strícta*
2. Flowers rose-purple, or whitish; stems leafless,
   3-10 in. high; fruit ovoid   *O. violácea*

RUTÁCEAE   RUE FAMILY

Sepals 4-5, often united, petals 4-5, stamens 4-8, ovary 2-celled, style 1, fruit a 2-lobed capsule, or a winged samara; flowers solitary or in terminal clusters; shrubs or trees with simple or palmately compound leaves.

1. Leaves palmate, consisting of 3 leaflets; fruit
   winged   PTELEA
2. Leaves simple; fruit 2-lobed, not winged   THAMNOSMA

PTÉLEA Linné 1753.   HOPTREE
(Greek name of the elm)
Pl. 4, fig. 5.

Sepals 4-5, united, petals 4-5, greenish white, stamens 4-5, ovary 2-celled, style 1, fruit round, broadly winged, 1-seeded; flowers in terminal clusters; leaves of 3 lance-ovate to obovate leaflets; shrubs or low trees.
Shrub 5-20 ft. high; leaflets 1-3 in. long; fruit 12-20
        mm. wide   *P. trifoliáta*

THAMNÓSMA Torrey 1858
(Gr. *thamnos*, bush, *osme*, odor)
Pl. 4, fig. 6.

Sepals 4, petals 4, yellow or tinged with purple, stamens 8, ovary 2-celled, style 1, fruit a 2-lobed capsule, with 4-6 seeds in each lobe; flowers solitary; leaves simple, linear, heavy-scented; low shrubs.
Stems branched at base, 3-12 in. high; leaves 1-2 cm.
        long   *T. texána*

LINÁCEAE   FLAX FAMILY

Sepals 5, petals 5, yellow or blue, falling after a few hours, stamens 5, united below, ovary 4-5-celled, or 8-10-celled by new partitions, styles 5, fruit a capsule opening by 5-10 valves; flowers in cymes or racemes; annual or perennial herbs with alternate, opposite or whorled simple entire leaves.

LÍNUM Linné 1753   FLAX
(Gr. *linon*, Lat. *linum*, flax)
Pl. 7, fig. 1.

Characters of the family.
1. Flowers blue
   a. Petals 3-4 times, fruit 2-3 times, longer than
      the obtuse sepals   *L. perénne*

b. Petals 2 times longer, fruit hardly longer, than
    the sepals   *L. usitatissimum*
2. Flowers yellow; plant glabrous or finely hairy   *L. rigidum*

ZYGOPHYLLÁCEAE   CALTROP FAMILY

Sepals 5, petals 5, stamens 10, ovary 5-12-celled, style 1, fruit splitting into 5-12 nut-like divisions; flowers solitary; herbs or shrubs with opposite compound leaves.

1. Leaflets 2; shrub   Covillea
2. Leaflets 6-10; herb   Kallstroemia

Covíllea Vail 1895   Creosote Bush
(Named for the American botanist, Çoville)

Pl. 4, fig. 7.

Sepals 5, petals 5, yellow, stamens 10, ovary 5-celled, style 1, fruit long-hairy, splitting into 5 nut-like divisions; flowers solitary; leaves of 2 leaflets, evergreen, heavy-scented; shrubs.

Branched shrub 3-10 ft. high; leaflets unequal, oblong,
    curved   *C. tridentáta*

Kallstróemia Scopoli 1777   Caltrop
(Named for Kallstroem)

Sepals 5, petals 5, yellow, deciduous, stamens 10, ovary 10-12-celled, style 1, fruit splitting into 10-12 divisions; flowers solitary; leaves pinnate, of 6-10 leaflets; annual.

Plants spreading, hairy, 3-15 in. high; fruit beaked
    warted   *K. máxima*

CISTALES   ROCKROSE ORDER

CISTÁCEAE   ROCKROSE FAMILY

Sepals 3-5, unequal, petals 5, 3 or none, yellow, stamens many, ovary 1-several-celled, style 1, stigma 1, sometimes 3-lobed, fruit a capsule; flowers of two sorts, petal-bearing and petal-less, in racemes or panicles; woody herbs with alternate simple entire leaves.

Heliánthemum Persoon 1807   Frostweed
(Gr. *helios*, sun, *anthemon*, flower, from the golden petals)

Characters of the family.

Leaves lance-oblong to oblanceolate; petal flowers
  terminal   *H. május*

HYPERICÁCEAE   ST. JOHN'S WORT FAMILY

Sepals 5, petals 5, yellow, stamens many, often in clusters, ovary 3-5-celled or 1-celled, with 3-5 seed rows on the wall, styles 3-6, fruit a 1-6-celled capsule; flowers in cymes; annual or perennial herbs with opposite simple entire dotted leaves.

HYPÉRICUM Linné 1753   ST. JOHN'S WORT

(Gr. *hyperikon*, St. John's wort)

Characters of the family.

1. Petals twice the length of the sepals or longer   *H. formósum*
2. Petals little if at all longer than the sepals   *H. május*

ELATINÁCEAE   WATERWORT FAMILY

Sepals 2-4, petals 2-4, stamens 2-8, ovary 2-4-celled, styles 2-4, fruit a globose many-seeded capsule opening by 2-4 valves; flowers tiny, solitary in the leaf axils; aquatic or marsh herbs with opposite or whorled simple leaves.

ELATÍNE Linné 1753   WATERWORT

(Gr. *elatine*, a kind of toad-flax)

Characters of the family.

1. Flowers in 2's; leaves obovate   *E. americána*
2. Flowers usually in 3's; leaves oblong or oblance-
    olate   *E. triándra*

FRANKENIÁCEAE   FRANKENIA FAMILY

Sepals 5, united, petals 5, white, stamens 5, or more, ovary 1-celled, with 2-3 seed rows on the wall, styles 2-4, fruit a capsule enclosed by the persistent calyx; flowers solitary or clustered in the axils; perennial herbs with opposite or clustered simple leaves.

FRANKÉNIA Linné 1753

(Named for Franken, a Swedish physician)

Stems woody at base; leaves clustered, linear, 5-6 mm.
  long   *F. Jámesii*

CARYOPHYLLALES   PINK ORDER
CARYOPHYLLACEAE   PINK FAMILY

Sepals 4-5, separate or united into a tube, petals 4-5 or none, separate, the lower half often claw-like, stamens 10, rarely 3-8, ovary mostly 1-celled, rarely 3-5-celled, styles 2-5, fruit typically a capsule with several to many seeds; flowers solitary or variously clustered; annual or perennial herbs with opposite simple entire leaves.

1. Sepals united into a tube
   a. Styles 2   Saponaria
   b. Styles 3, rarely 4   Silene
   c. Styles 5
      (1) Calyx lobes long and leaf-like   Agrostemma
      (2) Calyx lobes not long and leaf-like Lychnis
2. Sepals separate, or at least not forming a tube
   a. Petals present
      (1) Petals deeply notched or 2-cleft
         (a) Styles 3, rarely 4   ·   Stellaria
         (b) Styles 5   Cerastium
      (2) Petals entire or nearly so
         (a) Styles 3
            x. Leaves with papery stipules at base   Spergularia
            y. Leaves without papery stipules, mostly
               linear and sharp-tipped   Arenaria
         (b) Styles 5   Sagina
   b. Petals absent; leaves with papery stipules   Paronychia

Agrostémma Linné 1753   Corn Cockle
(Gr. *agros*, field, *stemma*, garland)
Pl. 9, fig. 3.

Sepals 5, united into a 10-ribbed tube, the lobes long, narrow and leaf-like, petals 5, red, with a claw-like base, stamens 10, ovary 1-celled, styles 5, fruit a capsule; flowers solitary on long stalks; leaves opposite, simple, entire; annual.

Leaves lance-linear; flowers 2-3 in. wide   *A. githágo*

Arenária Linné 1753   Sandwort
(Lat. *arena*, sand, from the habitat of many species)
(Moehringia Linné)
Pl. 9, fig. 4-5.

Sepals 5, separate, petals 5, white, entire or nearly so, rarely wanting, stamens 10, ovary 1-celled, styles usually 3, rarely 2-5, fruit splitting usu-

PLATE 8

PINK ORDER

1. Allionia linearis
2. Mirabilis multiflora: Four O'Clock
3. Chenopodium capitatum: Goosefoot
4. Polygonum pennsilvanicum: Heart's-ease
5. Eriogonum Jamesii
6. Silene acaulis: Alpine Pink
7. Saponaria vaccaria: Cow-pink
8. Rumex venosus: Dock

PLATE 8.

ally into 3-6 valves; flowers in terminal clusters or solitary; leaves opposite, simple, entire; annual or perennial.

1. Leaves needle-shaped, the tips often sharp
   a. Sepals lanceolate, long-pointed; leaves sharp-
      pointed
      (1) Flowers in an open branching cluster
          (a) Leaves rigid and pungent, 1-2 cm. long *A. púngens*
          (b) Leaves softer and less pungent, 2-10 cm. *A. Féndleri*
      (2) Flowers in a dense head-like cluster   *A. Hoókeri*
   b. Sepals oblong to lance-ovate, obtuse or short-
      pointed; leaves not sharp-pointed; dwarf
      alpine plants
      (1) Flowers 8-15 mm. wide; petals much
          longer than sepals   *A. biflóra*
      (2) Flowers 3-6 mm. wide; petals about as
          long as sepals   *A. vérna*
2. Leaves much broader, lanceolate to ovate
   a. Petals about twice as long as sepals   *A. lateriflóra*
   b. Petals shorter to a little longer than sepals
      (1) Leaves 2-6 cm. long   *A. macrophýlla*
      (2) Leaves .5-1.5 cm. long   *A. saxósa*

CERÁSTIUM Linné 1753   CHICKWEED
(Gr. *kerastion*, little horn, from the form of the pod)
Pl. 9, fig. 7-8.

Sepals 5, rarely 4, separate, petals 5, or 4, white, notched or cleft, rarely wanting, stamens usually 10, styles usually 5, or 4, ovary 1-celled, styles 5, or 3-4, fruit opening by 10, rarely 8, apical teeth; flowers in terminal clusters, or solitary; leaves opposite, simple, entire; annual or perennial.

1. Perennials, shown by the presence of rootstocks
   or old stems, smooth or hairy; flowers 10-15
   mm. wide; pods little longer than calyx   *C. arvénse*
2. Annuals, sticky-hairy; flowers 4-6 mm. wide;
   pods 2-3 times longer than calyx   *C. nútans*

LÝCHNIS Linné 1753   LYCHNIS
(Gr. *lychnos*, lamp, from the use of a woolly species for wicking)
Pl. 9, fig. 2.

Sepals 5, united into a tube, petals 5, entire, cleft or fringed at the tip, with a claw-like base, rarely wanting, white to red, stamens 10, ovary mostly 1-celled, styles mostly 5, fruit splitting by 5-10 valves; flowers solitary or clustered; leaves opposite, simple, entire; biennial or perennial.

1. Alpine dwarf, 2-5 in. high; stems 1-flowered;
   petals exserted or included *L. áffinis*
2. Stems 1-2 ft. high, several-flowered; petals usually included *L. Drummóndii*

Paronýchia Adanson 1763   Paronychia

(Gr. *paronychia,* swelling about a nail, and hence used of the healing plant)

Pl. 9, fig. 9-10.

Sepals 5, somewhat united, bristly-tipped, petals none, stamens 5, sometimes with 5 sterile ones also, ovary 1-celled, style 2-cleft, fruit small, bag-like, 1-seeded; flowers solitary or clustered; leaves opposite, simple, entire; perennial.

1. Plants densely cushion-like; flowers mostly solitary and terminal
   a. Leaves oblong, obtuse; stipules entire *P. pulvináta*
   b. Leaves needle-like, sharp-pointed; stipules 2-
      cleft *P. sessiliflóra*
2. Plants tufted, but rarely densely cushion-like;
   flowers in clusters; leaves awl-shaped, bristle-
   pointed *P. Jámesii*

Sagína Linné 1753   Pearlwort

(Lat. *sagina,* food, from its early use for pasturage)

Sepals 4-5, separate, petals 4-5, or none, whitish, stamens 4, rarely 5, ovary 1-celled, styles 4-5, fruit splitting to the base into 4-5 valves; flowers solitary, leaves minute, awl-shaped; low annuals or perennials.

1. Petals shorter than the green sepals *S. saginoídes*
2. Petals longer than the purplish sepals *S. niválís*

Saponária Linné 1753   Soapwort; Cow-herb
(Lat. *saponaria,* soap-like, from the soapy sap)
Pl. 8, fig. 7.

Sepals 5, united into a tube, petals 5, white, pink or red, with a claw, stamens 10, ovary 1-celled or imperfectly several-celled, styles 2, fruit a capsule opening by 4 apical teeth; flowers in corymbs or corymb-like clusters; annual or perennial.

1. Flowers 2-3 cm. wide, in a dense cluster; calyx
tubular *S. officinális*
2. Flowers about 1.5 cm. wide, on slender stalks;
calyx becoming 5-angled and inflated in fruit *S. vaccária*

SILÉNE Linné 1753   CATCHFLY, CAMPION

(Probably from Gr. *sialos*, saliva, from the sticky stems)

Pl. 8, fig. 6; Pl. 9, fig. 1.

Sepals 5, united into a tube, petals 5, white or pink, yellowish or purplish, the lower part narrow and claw-like, stamens 10, ovary 1-celled, or
somewhat 2-4-celled, styles 3, rarely 4, fruit opening by 6 or 3 apical teeth;
flowers solitary or clustered; leaves opposite, simple, entire; annual or
perennial.

1. Stemless alpine mat plants; flowers pink   *S. acaúlis*
2. Leafy-stemmed; flowers white to purplish or
pink
   a. Calyx swollen and bladdery; weed   *S. vulgáris*
   b. Calyx not swollen and bladdery
      (1) Annual weeds
         (a) Stems sticky-hairy; flowers white,
             night-blooming, fragrant   *S. noctiflóra*
         (b) Stems smooth, the upper joints sticky;
             flowers pink, day-blooming   *S. antirrhína*
      (2) Perennials, natives
         (a) Flowers in spreading forked clusters;
             leaves broad, thin   *S. Menziésii*
         (b). Flowers in a long narrow cluster; leaves
             narrow, thick   *S. Scoúleri*

SPERGULÁRIA Persoon 1805   SAND SPURRY

(Lat. *spergo*, to scatter; *spergula*, a little weed)

(Tissa Adanson)

Sepals 5, separate, petals 5 to none, white to purplish or lilac, entire,
stamens 10, or fewer, ovary 1-celled, styles 3, capsule opening by 3 valves;
flowers solitary or clustered; leaves linear, opposite and entire; annual or
perennial.

Flowers violet, solitary; low branching annual   *S. sparsiflóra*

Stellária Linné 1753   Starwort
(Lat. *stellaria*, star-like, from the flower)
(Alsine Linné)
Pl. 9, fig. 6.

Sepals 5, rarely 4, separate, petals 5, or 4, or rarely none, white, notched or 2-cleft, stamens usually 10, ovary 1-celled, styles usually 3, rarely 4-5, fruit splitting usually into 6 valves; flowers in terminal clusters or solitary; leaves opposite, simple, entire; annual or perennial.

1. Leaves ovate, the lower distinctly petioled;
   weeds   *S. média*
2. Leaves mostly lanceolate or linear, without petiole
   a. Petals absent
      (1) Flowers in a terminal umbel-like cluster
          with small papery scales   *S. umbelláta*
      (2) Flowers mostly lateral in the axils of leaves
          (a) Leaves lanceolate; stems erect   *S. boreális*
          (b) Leaves ovate; stems prostrate   *S. obtúsa*
   b. Petals present
      (1) Smooth or hairy, but not sticky
          (a) Floral leaves mostly small papery scales   *S. longifólia*
          (b) Floral leaves mostly leaf-like   *S. boreális*
      (2) Sticky-hairy   *S. jamesiána*

PORTULACÁCEAE   PURSLANE FAMILY

Sepals 2, rarely 4-8, separate, petals 5, rarely 3-16, white to red or yellow, separate, stamens 2-many, ovary 1-celled, style 1, 2-3-cleft, fruit a capsule opening by a cap or by 3 valves; flowers solitary or clustered; annual or perennial herbs with fleshy, alternate or opposite, usually entire, leaves.

1. Sepals 2, rarely 3
   a. Stigmas 3; flowers rose or white, rarely yellow
      (1) Sepals falling away   Talinum
      (2) Sepals persistent
          (a) Stamens 5   Claytonia
          (b) Stamens more than 5   Oreobroma
   b. Stigmas 2; flowers rose

(1) Petals 2; stamen 1   CALYPTRIDIUM
(2) Petals 4; stamens 3   SPRAGUEA
  c. Stigmas 4-6; flowers yellow   PORTULACA
2. Sepals 4-8   LEWISIA

CALYPTRÍDIUM Nuttall 1838
(Gr. *kalyptra,* cap, *-idium,* little)

Sepals 2, usually persistent, petals 2, rose, minute, stamens 1, ovary 1-celled, stigmas 2, capsule 2-valved; flowers in axillary or terminal spikes; leaves alternate; annual.

Stems weak, 2-5 in. long; leaves oblong-spatulate   *C. róseum*

CLAYTÓNIA Linné 1753 SPRING BEAUTY
(Named for Clayton, an American botanist)
Pl. 9, fig. 11-12.

Sepals 2, persistent, petals 5, white. rose or yellow, stamens 5, on the petal bases, ovary 1-celled, stigmas 3, capsule 3-valved; flowers in terminal clusters; leaves opposite or alternate; annual or perennial.

1. Basal leaves spatulate in a dense rosette, from a
    fleshy tap root; at 10-14000 ft.   *C. megarrhiza*
2. Basal leaves few, single or none, linear to lance-
    oblong; at 5-9000 ft.
    a. Stems from a bulb-like corm   *C. lanceoláta*
    b. Stems not arising from a corm, often with
       runners or rooting at the joints   *C. Chamissoi*

LEWÍSIA Pursh 1814 BITTER-ROOT
(Named for Lewis, of the Lewis and Clarke expedition)

Sepals 4-8, unequal, persistent, petals 8-16, rose to white, stamens many, ovary 1-celled, style deeply 3-8-cleft, capsule splitting circularly; flowers single; leaves in a dense rosette; perennial.

Stemless; leaves linear to spatulate, 1-3 cm. long;
flowers 1-2 in. wide   *L. redivíva*

OREOBRÓMA Howell 1893 OREOBROMA
(Gr. *oreos,* mountain, *broma,* food)
Pl. 9, fig. 13.

Sepals 2, persistent. petals 5-10, red, pink or white, stamens more than 5, ovary 1-celled, style 3-7-cleft, capsule opening circularly; flowers solitary or few in a cluster; leaves linear to spatulate; perennial.

1. Leaves basal in a rosette, from a tap root; stem
   leaves mere scales
     a. Petals rose-red; sepals toothed   *O. pygmaéa*
     b. Petals white; sepals entire   *O. nevadénsis*
2. Stem leaves 2-3, basal leaves none, from a bulb-
   like corm   *O. triphýlla*

PORTULÁCA Linné 1753   PURSLANE

(Lat. *portulacus*, purgative)

Sepals 2, united below and partly grown together with the ovary, petals usually 5, yellow or red as a rule, stamens 7-many, ovary 1-celled, partly inferior, style deeply 3-9-cleft; flowers solitary, usually terminal; leaves alternate, obovate, spatulate or cylindric; annual.

Prostrate-spreading; flowers 4-6 mm. wide, opening
only in sunshine   *P. olerácea*

SPRÁGUEA Torrey 1853

(Named for Sprague, a botanical artist)

Sepals 2, unequal, petals 4, rose, stamens 3, ovary 1-celled, stigmas 2, capsule 2-valved; flowers in dense spikes, grouped in an umbel: leaves mostly basal, spatulate; biennial.

Stems 2-10 in. high; sepals papery, as long as petals   *S. múlticeps*

TALÍNUM Adanson 1763   TALÍNUM

(Of unknown meaning)

Pl. 9, fig. 14.

Sepals 2, petals 5, pink to white, disappearing, stamens 5-10, ovary 1-celled, stigmas 3, capsule 3-valved; flowers in open clusters; leaves alternate, linear-cylindric; perennial.

Stems 3-10 in. high; leaves basal; flowers pink   *T. parviflórum*

AIZOACEAE CARPET-WEED FAMILY

Sepals 4-5, united, petals none, stamens 3-5, ovary 3-5-celled, styles 3-5, fruit a capsule; flowers perfect, solitary or clustered; annual herbs with opposite or whorled simple entire leaves.

1. Leaves opposite, fleshy   SESUVIUM
2. Leaves whorled, not fleshy   MOLLUGO

Sesúvium Linné 1753   Sea Purslane
(Of doubtful meaning)

Sepals 5, united, pink or purplish, petals none, stamens 5-60, ovary 3-5-celled, styles 3-5, warted along the inner side, capsule 3-5-celled oblong, splitting circularly; flowers solitary or clustered in the axils; leaves opposite; fleshy annual.

Stems spreading, 3-12 in. long; flowers 2 mm. wide   *S. maritimum*

Mollúgo Linné 1753   Carpet-weed
(Lat. *mollis*, soft)

Sepals 5, greenish-white, united, petals none, stamens 3-5, ovary 3-celled, globose or ovoid, capsule 3-celled, 3-valved; flowers small, axillary; leaves in whorls; annual.

Stems prostrate; leaves 1-3 cm. long; flowers 2 mm.
wide   *M. verticilláta*

POLYGONÁCEAE   BUCKWHEAT FAMILY

Sepals 2-6, united, greenish or petal-like, often winged in fruit, petals none, stamens 2-9, ovary 1-celled, style 2-3-cleft, fruit an achene, usually 3-angled; flowers small, greenish or colored, perfect, monoecious or dioecious, in spikes, heads, racemes or panicles; herbs or twining vines with alternate rarely opposite or whorled simple leaves, and usually with boot-like papery stipules or sheaths at the joints of the stem.

1. Flower clusters with a toothed involucre; stamens 9; stems without papery sheaths   Eriogonum
2. Flower clusters without involucre; stamens 4-8; stem with papery sheaths at the joints
   a. Calyx 6-parted; the 3 inner sepals usually winged; stigmas tufted   Rumex
   b. Calyx 4-5-parted
     (1) Stigmas tufted; achene winged   Oxyria
     (2) Stigmas globose; achenes not winged   Polygonum

Erióganum Michaux 1803   Eriogonum
(Gr. *erion*, wool, *gonu*, knee, from the woolly jointed stems)
Pl. 8, fig. 5.

Sepals 6, united, petal-like, white, pink, or yellow to orange-red, petals none, stamens 9, ovary 1-celled, style 3-parted, stigmas capitate, fruit a 3-angled achene; flowers in a 5-8-toothed top-shaped to cylindric involucre, the involucres in racemes, panicles, or heads; leaves simple, usually entire, alternate, opposite, whorled or basal; annual or perennial.

1. Flowers white or pink
   a. Flower involucres in dense heads or head-like clusters
   (1) Heads single on leafless stalks
      (a) Leaves ovoid to elliptic, densely white-woolly   *E. ovalifólium*
      (b) Leaves oblanceolate or linear
      x. Leaves oblanceolate, densely white-woolly   *E. múlticeps*
      y. Leaves linear, green, usually smooth   *E. pauciflórum*
   (2) Heads many in forking leafy clusters; leaves oblanceolate, woolly   *E. Jámesii*
   b. Flower involucres in forking cymes or in a long spike-like cluster
   (1) Flowers in forking cymes
      (a) Stems leafy
      x. Perennials, the stems woody at base, and branched
         (x) Leaves ovate to elliptic; branches few   *E. Jónesi*
         (y) Leaves linear to oblong; branches several to many
         m. Stamens and styles included   *E. effúsum*
         n. Stamens and styles exserted   *E. corymbósum*
      y. Annuals, the stems simple at base, densely white woolly   *E. ánnuum*
      (b) Leaves basal
      x. Leaves linear to oblanceolate, greenish above, white-woolly below   *E. Símpsoni*
      y. Leaves ovoid to orbicular
         (x) Flower involucres hanging   *E. cérnuum*
         (y) Flower involucres erect or ascending
         m. Annual; stems single; leaves 1-5 cm. long, green   *E. Górdoni*
         n. Perennial; stems tufted; leaves 5-15 cm. long. densely white-woolly   *E. tenéllum*

(2) Flowers in a long narrow spike-like
    cluster; leaves basal, ovate to lanceolate,
    white-woolly below   *E. racemósum*
2. Flowers yellow, yellowish or cream-colored
  a. Flower involucres in dense heads or head-like
    . clusters
    (1) Heads single on a leafless stalk
      x. Heads with leaf-like bracts beneath   *E. flávum*
      y. Heads with inconspicuous bracts
        (x) Flower stalks 1-2 cm. high; leaves
          3-5 mm. long   *E. acaúle*
        (y) Flower stalks 5-30 cm. high; leaves
          5-30 mm. long
          m. Leaves ovate to elliptic   *E. ovalifólium*
          n. Leaves oblong to spatulate   *E. caespitósum*
    (2) Heads in umbels or in forking cymes
      x. Heads in umbels, the latter sometimes
        compound
        (x) Leaves linear or narrowly oblanceo-
          late   *E. chrysocéphalum*
        (y) Leaves oblong, spatulate, obovate or
          rounded
          m. Calyx hairy; leaves mostly spatulate,
            woolly   *E. flávum*
          n. Calyx smooth
            (m) Flower stalk with a ring of
              leaves near the middle   *E. heracleoídes*
            (n) Flower stalk without a median
              ring of leaves   *E. umbellátum*
      y. Heads in 2-4-forked clusters
        (x) Calyx tapering into its stalk   *E. Bákeri*
        (y) Calyx abruptly passing into its stalk *E. lachnógynum*
  b. Flower involucres in open much-branched
    clusters
    (1) Stems leafy, not inflated; leaves oblanceo-
      late to spatulate
      (a) Stems bristly-hairy, perennial, 2-6 ft.
        high; achenes winged   *E. alátum*
      (b) Stems smooth, annual, 2-6 in. high;
        achenes not winged   *E. salsuginósum*

PLATE 9

PINKS—AMARANTHS

PINK FAMILY

1. Silene Hallii: Catchfly
2. Lychnis Drummondii
3. Agrostemma githago: Corn Cockle
4. Arenaria biflora: Sandwort
5. Arenaria Fendleri
6. Stellaria longipes: Starwort
7. Cerastium arvense: Chickweed
8. Cerastium nutans
9. Paronychia Jamesii
10. Paronychia pulvinata

PURSLANE FAMILY

11. Claytonia chamissoi: Spring Beauty
12. Claytonia megarrhiza: leaf and flower stalk
13. Oreobroma pygmaea
14. Talinum teretifolium

FOUR O'CLOCK FAMILY

15. Abronia fragrans: a, leaf; b, cluster and fruit
16. Abronia micrantha: fruit

BUCKWHEAT FAMILY

17. Polygonum bistorta: Bistort
18. Oxyria digyna: Mountain Sorrel; fruit cluster

AMARANTH FAMILY

19. Froelichia floridana
20. Acnida tamarischina: Water-hemp
21. Amarantus hybridus: Amaranth
22. Amarantus graecizans

(2) Stems leafy at base only, often inflated
   (a) Stems top-like, inflated, bluish; leaves
       smooth, ovate to round   *E. inflátum*
   (b) Stems solid; leaves woolly, oblanceo-
       late to spatulate   *E. campanulátum*

OXÝRIA Hill 1765° MOUNTAIN SORREL
(Gr. *oxys,* sour)
Pl. 9, fig. 18.

Sepals 4, united, green; petals none, stamens 6, ovary 1-celled, style short, 2-parted, stigmas fringed, persistent on the wings of the fruiting calyx, fruit an ovate, lens-shaped achene; flowers small, perfect, in terminal panicles; leaves mostly basal, long-petioled, kidney-shaped, round, or heart-shaped; perennial.

Stems 2-15 in. high; leaves 1-4 cm, wide   *O. digyna*

POLÝGONUM Linné 1753 SMARTWEED, KNOTWEED, BINDWEED
(Gr. *polys,* many, *gonu,* knee, from the jointed stems)
Pl. 8, fig. 4; pl. 9, fig. 17.

Sepals 4-5, united, green, white, pink or purple, petals none, stamens 5-0, ovary 1-celled, style 2-3-parted, stigmas globose, fruit a flattened or 3-angled (rarely 4-angled) achene; flowers small in terminal or axillary clusters; leaves alternate, entire with funnel-form sheaths at the base; annual or perennial, terrestrial or aquatic.

  1. Flowers in a single (rarely 2) terminal spike-
     like cluster or raceme, white to rose-red
   a. Flowers usually white; stems from a thick
      often bent rootstock; at altitudes of 7-14000
      ft.; bistorts
     (1) Raceme oblong, 1-5 cm. long, 1-2 cm.
        wide; stems 2-10 dm. high   *P. bistórta*
     (2) Raceme cylindric, 3-10 cm. long, .5-1 cm.
        wide; stems 1-2 dm. high   *P. vivíparum*
   b. Flowers rose-red or pinkish, sometimes white
      to greenish; at altitudes of 3-7000 feet;
      water or mud plants; hearts-ease, smartweeds
     (a) Racemes 1-3 cm. long; leaves elliptic-
        oblong, obtuse or acute   *P. amphíbium*
     (b) Racemes 3-10 cm. long; leaves lance-
        ovate, long-pointed   *P. emérsum*

2. Flowers in several to many axillary or terminal
   racemes or clusters
   a. Flowers in large axillary and terminal racemes
   (1) Stems twining or trailing; leaves ovate-
       arrow-shaped or heart-shaped; bindweeds
       (a) Leaves ovate to lance-arrow-shaped;
           stems .5-4 ft. long; sepals not winged
           in fruit   *P. convólvulus*
       (b) Leaves ovate-heart-shaped; stems 3-10
           ft. long; sepals broadly winged in fruit *P. scándens*
   (2) Stems erect, not twining; leaves not ar-
       row-shaped, or heart-shaped
       (a) Papery sheaths at the swollen stem joints
           fringed with bristles
           x. Racemes erect
              (x) Racemes oblong, dense   *P. persicária*
              (y) Racemes cylindric, narrow, often
                  interrupted
                  m. Sepals covered with waxy dots *P. punctátum*
                  n. Sepals without waxy dots   *P. hydropiperoídes*
           y. Racemes nodding; flowers greenish;
              juice sharp   *P. hydropíper*
       (b) Papery sheaths not fringed with bristles
           x. Racemes nodding, lance-cylindric, nar-
              row; stamens 6   *P. lapathifólium*
           y. Racemes erect, oblong, broad; stamens
              usually 8   *P. pennsilvánicum*
   b. Flowers mostly in small axillary clusters, the
      ends of the branches in some raceme-like;
      knotweeds
      (1) Clusters all axillary, the stems leafy
          throughout
          (a) Plants prostrate, or nearly so; leaves
              small; stamens mostly 8   *P. aviculáre*
          (b) Plants erect; leaves large; stamens 5-6 *P. eréctum*
      (2) Clusters axillary, but the upper leaves in-
          conspicuous
          (a) Flowers and fruits erect
              x. Achenes projecting beyond the calyx
                 for half its length or more   *P. exsértum*

    y. Achenes enclosed in the calyx or near-
      ly so
      (x) Stems branched throughout; sta-
          mens 3-6   *P. ramosíssimum*
      (y) Stems branched from the base; sta-
          mens 8   *P. ténue*
   (b) Flowers and fruits hanging   *P. Dóuglasi*
 (3) Clusters really axillary but forming a
     terminal spike-like cluster by the re-
     duction of the upper leaves or the ag-
     gregation of the flowers
   (a) Raceme long, slender and interrupted *P. spergularifórme*
   (b) Raceme short and crowded, head-like
    x. Plants mostly 1-10 cm. high; floral
      leaves broadly white-margined; sta-
      mens 8   *P. polygaloídes*
    y. Plants mostly 10-20 cm. high; floral
      leaves green; stamens 3-5   *P. Wátsoni*

Rúmex Linné 1753   Sorrel, Dock
(Lat. name of the sorrel)
Pl. 8, fig. 8.

    Sepals 6, the 3 inner mostly developed into wings in fruit, green, petals none, stamens 6, ovary 1-celled, style 3-parted, stigmas shield-shaped, tufted, fruit a 3-angled achene with wings, either entire, or with bristle-like teeth, flowers perfect, dioecious or polygamo-monoecious, whorled on jointed stalks in racemes or panicles; leaves entire or wavy-margined, the sheaths cylindric, brittle and disappearing; perennial or annual.

1. Leaves arrowshaped, sour; flowers dioecious   *R. acetosélla*
2. Leaves not arrowshaped
  a. Leaves sour; flowers dioecious   *R. paucifólius*
  b. Leaves not sour; flowers mostly perfect
    (1) Valves of the fruit, i. e. the 3 inner en-
      larged sepals, 10-30 cm. wide, usually
      reddish
     (a) Valves 15-30 mm. wide   *R. venósus*
     (b) Valves 10-15 mm. wide
      x. Valves ovate; achene 5-6 mm. long *R. hymenosépalus*
      y. Valves reniform; achene 10 mm. long *R. salínus*
    (2) Valves of the fruit less than 10 mm. wide

(a) One or more of the valves with a swelling on the midvein
  x. Edge of the valves fringe-toothed
    (x) One of the valves warted; lower leaves heart-shaped at base   *R. obtusifólius*
    (y) All the valves warted; lower leaves tapering at base   *R. persicáris*
  y. Edge of valves entire, not fringe-toothed
    (x) All three valves warted
      m. Leaves curly at edge   *R. críspus*
      n. Leaves flat, not curly at edge   *R. brittánica*
    (y) One valve only warted
      m. Pedicels about the length of the valves   *R. altíssimus*
      n. Pedicels 2-4 times as long as the valves   *R. patiéntia*
(b) All valves without warts, the edge often toothed   *R. occidentális*

CHENOPODIÁCEAE   GOOSEFOOT FAMILY

Sepals 2-5, united, sometimes none, rarely 1, petals none, stamens 2-5, rarely 1, ovary 1-celled, styles 1-3, fruit a 1-seeded utricle; flowers small, green or greenish, rarely colored, perfect, monoecious or dioecious, usually in dense clusters; annual or perennial herbs, rarely shrubs, with alternate rarely opposite simple entire to lobed often fleshy leaves.

1. Leaves present; stem not jointed
  a. Leaves fleshy, linear, terete or nearly so, entire
    (1) Shrub; flowers monoecious; fruit winged   SARCOBATUS
    (2) Herbs; flowers perfect
      (a) Fruit winged; leaves spiny-tipped   SALSOLA
      (b) Fruit wingless; leaves not spiny
        x. Calyx white-hairy   KOCHIA
        y. Calyx smooth, greenish   DONDIA
  b. Leaves hardly fleshy, flat, toothed or entire
    (1) Flowers or most of them with both stamens and pistils
      (a) Fruit horizontally winged   CYCLOLOMA ·
      (b) Fruit not winged

 x. Calyx of 1 sepal

  (x) Leaves arrow-shaped, 3-lobed Monolepis

  (y) Leaves linear, entire   Corispermum

 y. Calyx of 2-5 united sepals

  (x) Leaves thread-like, entire   Kochia

  (y) Leaves linear-oblong to ovoid,
   mostly toothed or lobed   Chenopodium

 (2) Flowers with stamens or pistils alone

  (a) Fruits densely long-silky   Eurotia

  (b) Fruits not long-silky

  x. Fruiting bracts flat, united by the edges
   at their bases to beyond the middle Atriplex

  y. Fruiting bracts folded, completely united by the edges into a sack

   (x) Leaves entire; sack entire, ovoid
    to round   Grayia

   (y) Leaves wavy-toothed; sack hastate,
    2-toothed at tip   Suckleya

2. Leaves none; stems jointed   Salicornia

Átriplex Linné 1753 Saltbush

(The Latin name)

Pl. 10, fig. 1-5.

 Sepals 3-5, united in the stamen flowers, none in the pistil flowers, petals none, stamens 3-5, ovary 1-celled, stigmas 2, fruit 1-seeded, enclosed in two scales or bracts, which are often winged, crested or warted; flowers of two sorts, in spikes or head-like clusters; leaves alternate, simple, often silvery-scurfy; annual or perennial, the latter usually shrubby.

 1. Plants shrubby, at least the base woody and persistent

 a. Fruits with broad wings; shrubs 1-5 ft. high

  (1) Bracts of the fruit with 4 toothed wings;
   leaves oblong to oblanceolate *A. canéscens*

  (2) Bracts extended above the fruit in a broad
   wing; leaves ovoid to obovoid *A. confertifólia*

 b. Fruits not winged, the bracts crested, warty
  or lobed; low shrubs 1-2 ft. high

  (1) Bracts covered with crests or warts *A. Nuttállii*

  (2) Bracts lobed at apex, but not crested or
   warted   *A. pabuláris*

2. Plants herbaceous, annual
  a. Bracts of the fruit united only at the base
    (1) Bracts ovoid or orbicular, thin, the fruit
        appearing broadly winged   *A. horténsis*
    (2) Bracts triangular, thick, often warted   *A. pátula*
  b. Bracts united beyond the middle
    (1) Fruiting bracts 3-4 mm. long
        (a) Bracts horned and warted   *A. argéntea*
        (b) Bracts smooth, toothed   *A. truncáta*
    (2) Fruiting bracts 1-2 mm. long
        (a) Bracts entire, united at the edges *A. ováta*
        (b) Bracts 3-toothed, free at the edges *A. Wólfii*

CHENOPÓDIUM Linné 1753   GOOSEFOOT, LAMB'S QUARTERS

(Gr. *chen*, goose, *podion*, little foot, from the leaf)

Pl. 8, fig. 3.

Sepals 2-5, somewhat united, somewhat fleshy, occasionally colored, petals none, stamens 1-5, ovary 1-celled, styles 2-3, fruit 1-seeded, enclosed in the calyx; flowers perfect, usually in spikes or heads; leaves alternate, simple, usually toothed or lobed; mostly annual.

1. Leaves silvery-mealy, at least below
  a. Leaves coarsely toothed or lobed, lance-ovate
     to ovoid
    (1) Plants low and spreading, much branched
        at the base, 2-15 in. high
        (a) Leaves oblong or lance-oblong, each
            edge sharply 3-5-toothed   *C. gláucum*
        (b) Leaves triangular-ovate, mostly 3-lobed *C. incánum*
    (2) Plants tall, erect, 2-8 ft. high; leaves
        ovoid, toothed or lobed   *C. álbum*
  b. Leaves entire, or nearly so, linear to lance-
     oblong   *C. leptophýllum*
2. Leaves green, not silvery-mealy
  a. Leaves pinnatifid, sticky-hairy
    (1) Flowers single, 5 mm. wide, on forking
        branches   *C. cornútum*
    (2) Flowers densely clustered, 1-1.5 mm. wide,
        on spike-like stems   *C. bótrys*
  b. Leaves smooth

PLATE 10

GOOSEFOOT FAMILY

1-2. Atriplex canescens: Salt Bush; 1, fruiting branch; 2, staminate flower cluster
  3. Atriplex Nuttallii
  4. Atriplex confertifolia
  5. Atriplex pabularis
6-8. Sarcobatus vermiculatus: Greasewood; 6, fruits; 7, staminate cluster; 8, spine
  9. Kochia americana
 10. Eurotia lanata
 11. Grayia Brandegei
 12. Grayia spinosa
 13. Corispermum hyssopifolium: Bugseed
 14. Dondia depressa: Salt Blite
 15. Monolepis nuttalliana
 16. Cycloloma atriplicifolium: Tumble Weed
 17. Salsola kali: Saltwort, Russian Thistle
 18. Salicornia herbacea: Glasswort

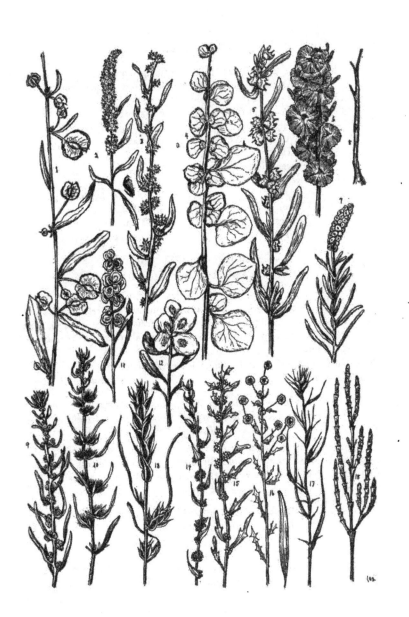

(1) Flowers in ball-like heads, forming an
open spike, usually pink or red in fruit *C. capitátum*
(2) Flowers in more open clusters, greenish
  (a) Leaves 2-lobed, broadly arrow-shaped,
rarely toothed, very thin   *C. Fremóntii*
  (b) Leaves sharply several-toothed or lobed,
thicker
    x. Flower clusters much branched, leaf-
less; leaves 2-4 inches long; stems 2-8
ft. high   ·   *C. hýbridum*
    y. Flower clusters little branched, leafy;
leaves .5-2 in. long; stems 1-3 ft.
high   ·   *C. rúbrum*

CORISPÉRMUM Linné 1753   BUGSEED
(Gr. *koris*, bug, *sperma*, seed)
Pl. 10, fig. 13.

Sepals 1 (rarely 2) green, petals none, stamens 1-3, rarely more, ovary
1-celled, ovoid, styles 2, fruit 1-seeded, with an acute or winged margin;
flowers small, solitary in the upper axils; leaves alternate, entire, narrow,
1-nerved; annual.

Stem much branched, .5-2 ft. high; leaves 2-5 cm.
long, 2-4 mm. wide   *C. hyssopifólium*

CYCLOLÓMA Moquin 1840   TUMBLE WEED
(Gr. *kyklos*, circle, *loma*, fringe, from the calyx wing)
Pl. 10, fig. 16.

Sepals 5, united, green, petals none, stamens 5, ovary 1-celled, styles
2-3, fruit 1-seeded, partly enclosed by the winged calyx, flowers small, sessile, in panicled spikes; leaves alternate, petioled, toothed; annual.

Bush-like, 1-3 ft. high; leaves 1-4 in. long   *C. atriplicifólium*

DÓNDIA Adanson 1763   SALT BLITE
(Named for Dondi, an Italian naturalist)
(Sueda Forskal)
Pl. 10, fig. 14.

Sepals 5, united, green, petals none, stamens 5, ovary 1-celled, styles 2,
fruit 1-seeded, enclosed by the ridged or slightly winged calyx; flowers
perfect or polygamous, solitary or clustered in the upper axils; leaves
alternate, narrow, thick, entire, sessile; annual or perennial.

1. One or more sepals strongly ribbed or keeled;
   stems erect or spreading   *D. depréssa*
2. Sepals not ribbed or keeled
   a. Woody perennial   *D. Móquini*
   b. Annual herb   *D. diffúsa*

EURÓTIA Adanson 1763   EUROTIA
(Gr. *eurotios,* mouldy, from the dense hairiness)
Pl. 10, fig. 10.

Sepals 4 in the stamen flowers, united, bracts none, stamens 4, exserted, sepals none in the pistil flowers, bracts 2, united, densely covered with long, silky hairs, ovary 1-celled, ovoid, hairy, styles 2, exserted, fruit 1-seeded; flowers monoecious or dioecious, in heads or spikes in the axils of the leaves; leaves alternate, entire, narrow, perennial.

Stems .5-3 ft. high; leaves revolute, .5-2 in. long   *E. lanáta*

GRÁYIA Hooker and Arnott 1841   GRAYIA
(Named for the American botanist Gray)
Pl. 10, fig. 11-12.

Sepals 4-5, united, petals none, stamens 4-5, ovary 1-celled, style jointed at base, stigmas 2, fruit compressed, round winged; flowers dioecious, in racemes or spikes; leaves alternate or clustered, entire; spiny shrubs.

1. Leaves spatulate to obovate; fruit 8-10 mm. wide *G. spinósa*
2. Leaves linear-spatulate; fruit 4-5 mm. wide   *G. Brandégei*

KÓCHIA Roth 1799   KOCHIA
(Named for Koch, a German botanist)
Pl. 10, fig. 9.

Sepals 5, united, petals none, stamens 3-5, ovary 1-celled, style 1, stigmas 2, fruit oblong, 1-seeded, enclosed by the calyx; flowers perfect or pistillate, clustered in the axils; leaves alternate, sessile, narrow, entire; perennial or annual.

Stems .5-1.5 ft. high, long-hairy to smooth   *K. americána*

MONÓLEPIS Schrader 1830   MONOLEPIS
(Gr. *monos,* one, *lepis,* scale, from the single sepal)
Pl. 10, fig. 15.

Sepals 1, petals none, stamens 1, ovary 1-celled, styles 2, slender, fruit

1-seeded, flat; flowers polygamous or perfect in small axillary clusters; leaves small, narrow, alternate, entire, toothed or lobed; annual.

Stems 3-10 in. high; leaves usually 3-lobed or hastate,

1-5 cm. long   *M. nuttalliána*

SALICÓRNIA Linné 1753   GLASSWORT

(Lat. *sal*, salt, *cornu*, horn, from its home and form)

Pl. 10, fig. 18.

Sepals 3-4, united, petals none, stamens 2, or 1, ovary 1-celled, styles 2, fruit enclosed by the spongy calyx; flowers in clusters of 3-7, mostly hidden beneath the opposite scale-like leaves; annual or perennial fleshy herbs with round apparently leafless branches.

Stems forked, 3-18 in. high; fruiting spikes 1-3 in.

long, 2-4 mm. wide   *S. herbácea*

SÁLSOLA Linné 1753   SALTWORT, RUSSIAN THISTLE

(Lat. *salsus*, salty, *-ola*, little, from its original home)

Pl. 10, fig. 17.

Sepals 5, united, petals none, stamens 5, ovary 1-celled, styles 2, fruit 1-seeded, flattened, enclosed by the winged calyx, flowers small, solitary in the axils or sometimes several; leaves stiff, prickle-pointed; annual or perennial bushy herbs.

Stems much branched, 1-3 ft. high; leaves 1-5 cm.

long   *S. káli*

SARCOBÁTUS Nees 1839   GREASEWOOD

(Gr. *sarkos*, fleshy, *batos*, thorn, from the fleshy leaves and thorny stems)

Pl. 10, fig. 6-8.

Sepals lacking in stamen flowers, petals none, stamens 2-5 together, under shield-shaped, spirally arranged scales; sepals 2, united in the pistil flowers, fused with the bases of the stigmas, and with a border which expands into a leathery horizontal wing in fruit, ovary 1-celled, stigmas 2, awl-shaped, roughened, fruit 1-seeded; flowers monoecious or dioecious, the stamen-flowers in terminal spikes, the pistil-flowers solitary in the axils, or rarely several together; leaves alternate, linear, fleshy, entire, sessile, branches spiny; shrubs.

Stems 1-10 ft. high; leaves 2-5 cm. long, 2-4 cm. wide   *S. vermiculátus*

SÚCKLEYA Gray 1875   SUCKLEYA

(Named for the American naturalist, Suckley)

Sepals 4-5, united, petals none, stamens 4-5, ovary 1-celled, fruit with crested margin and 2-toothed tip; flowers monoecious, in axillary clusters; leaves roundish, toothed; annual.

Stems spreading, 8-12 in. long; leaves 1-3 cm. long   *S. petioláris*

AMARANTÁCEAE   AMARANTH FAMILY

Sepals 3-5, often united, rarely none, petals none, stamens 3-5, ovary 1-celled, style 1 or none, stigmas 1-3, fruit a 1-seeded utricle or achene; flowers greenish, or purplish, with papery bracts, in dense terminal or axillary clusters; mostly annual herbs with alternate or opposite simple leaves.

  1. Leaves alternate; plants green
    a. Calyx always present   AMARANTUS
    b. Calyx none in the pistil flowers   ACNIDA
  2. Leaves opposite; plant gray-woolly or gray-hairy
    a. Flowers in terminal spikes, densely woolly   FROELICHIA
    b. Flowers in small axillary clusters   CLADOTHRIX

AMARÁNTUS Linné 1753   AMARANTH, PIGWEED

(Gr. *a-*, not, *marantos*, withered, from the papery bracts)

Pl. 9, fig. 21-22.

Sepals 3-5, separate, greenish or purplish, petals none, stamens 3-5, ovary 1-celled, stigmas 2-3, fruit a utricle splitting circularly or remaining closed, 2-3-beaked; flowers usually with 3 bracts, in dense terminal spikes or in axillary clusters; leaves alternate, simple, entire or wavy; annual.

  1. Flowers in terminal spikes 1-6 in. long
    a. Leaf axils with 2 spines   *A. spinósus*
    b. Leaf axils not spiny
      (1) Spikes stout, 1-3 cm. thick   *A. retrofléxus*
      (2) Spikes slender, .5-1 cm. thick
        (a) Top of fruit falling off like a lid
          x. Bracts beneath the flower 3   *A. hýbridus*
          y. Bract single   *A. Powélli*
        (b) Fruit remaining closed
          x. Bracts spiny, twice as long as the sepals *A. Pálmeri*
          y. Bracts not spiny, about as long as the
            sepals   *A. Tórreyi*

2. Flowers in small axillary clusters
    a. Stems prostrate; sepals 4-5   *A. blitoídes*
    b. Stems erect; sepals 3   *A. graecízans*

ACNÍDA Linné 1753   ACNIDA, WATER-HEMP
(Gr. *a-*, without, *knide*, nettle, from its lack of spines)
Pl. 9, fig. 20.

   Sepals 5, in the stamen flowers, green, papery, erect, longer than the bracts, petals none, stamens 5; sepals and petals lacking in the pistil flowers, ovary 1-celled, ovoid, stigmas 2-5, warted or plumy, fruit 1-seeded, flowers small, 1-3-bracted, in terminal and axillary spikes, or clustered in the axils; leaves alternate, petioled, thin; annual.
Stems 1-8 ft. high; leaves lanceolate or lance-ovate   *A. tamariscina*

CLADÓTHRIX Nuttall 1849
(Gr. *klados*, branch. *thrix*, hair, from the star-shaped hairs)

   Sepals 5, united, petals none, stamens 5, ovary 1-celled, globose, style short, stigma globose or 2-lobed, fruit 1-celled, 1-seeded, flowers small, solitary or clustered in the axils; leaves opposite, entire; annual or perennial.
Stems prostrate or spreading, 4-12 in. long; leaves
ovate to round   *C. lanuginósa*

FROELÍCHIA Moench 1794   FROELICHIA
(Named for Froelich, a German botanist)
Pl. 9, fig. 19.

   Sepals 5, united, densely woolly, petals none, stamens 5, united, ovary 1-celled, stigma 1, globose or tufted, fruit enclosed in the winged or crested calyx; flowers perfect, in dense spikes; leaves opposite sessile entire or wavy; woolly annuals.
   1. Stems 1.5-4 ft. high; spikes opposite   *F. floridána*
   2. Stems .5-1.5 ft. high; spikes mostly alternate   *F. grácilis*

NYCTAGINÁCEAE   FOUR-O'CLOCK FAMILY
   Sepals 4-5, corolla-like, united into a bell-shaped, tubular or salverform calyx, petals none, stamens 3-5, ovary 1-celled, 1-ovuled, style 1, stigma globose, fruit grooved or winged; flowers in terminal or axillary clusters in an involucre of separate or united bracts; leaves simple entire.
   1. Leaves below the flowers, i. e. involucral bracts,
      separate   ABRONIA

2. Leaves below the flowers united and calyx-like
  a. Stamens 5; involucre bell-shaped; fruit not ribbed   MIRABILIS
  b. Stamens 3; involucre saucer-shaped
    (1) Fruit smooth, not ribbed   ALLIONIELLA
    (2) Fruit hairy, ribbed or warted   ALLIONIA

ABRÓNIA Jussieu 1774   ABRONIA

(Gr. *abros*, pretty, from the flowers)

Pl. 9, fig. 15-16.

Sepals 5, united into an elongated, tubular or funnelform calyx, white to pink, petals none, stamens 3-5, ovary 1-celled, style slender, fruit dry, 1-5 winged, with netted veins; flowers in many-flowered involucres, solitary or clustered on long axillary stalks; leaves opposite, petioled, thick, entire; annual or perennial.

1. Flowers white or greenish-white; fruits narrowly winged; perennials
  a. Flowers white, 2-3 cm. long; wings 2-5   *A. frágrans*
  b. Flowers greenish, 1.5-2 cm. long; wings mostly 5   *A. ellíptica*
2. Flowers pinkish to reddish; fruits broadly winged; annuals
  a. Flowers 4-5 mm. wide, 1.5-2 cm. long, reddish-green   *A. micrántha*
  b. Flowers 8-10 mm. wide, 3-4 cm. long, pinkish   *A. cyclóptera*

ALLIÓNIA Loefling 1788   ALLIONIA

(Named for Allioni, an Italian botanist)

Pl. 8, fig. 1.

Sepals 5 united into a bell-shaped calyx, corolla-like, rose-purple, petals none, stamens 3-5, ovary 1-celled, fruit 1-seeded, club-shaped, strongly ribbed, fine-hairy; flowers in loose terminal panicles, involucre of 3-5 partially united bracts, 3-5-flowered, becoming enlarged and net-veined after flowering; leaves opposite.

1. Involucre 5-lobed; fruit wingless
  a. Stem with long shaggy hairs   *A. hirsúta*
  b. Stem smooth, at least not shaggy
    (1) Leaves linear to lanceolate   *A. lineáris*

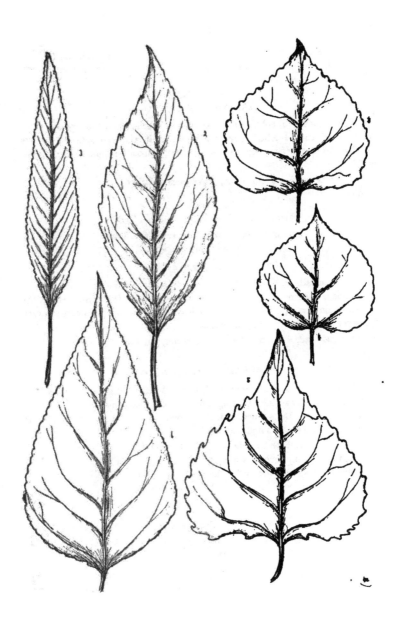

(2) Leaves ovate   *A. nyctagínea*
2. Involucre 3-lobed; fruit winged   .   *A. incarnáta*

Allioniélla Rydberg 1902
(Diminutive of Allionia)

Sepals mostly 5, corolla-like, united into a bellshaped tube, petals none, stamens 3, ovary 1-celled, stigma globose, fruit a ribbed achene; flowers usually 3 in a saucer-shaped involucre; leaves opposite simple entire; perennial.

Flowers rose-purple, 1 cm. long; leaves heart-shaped,
    sticky   *A. oxybaphoídes*

Mirábilis Linné 1753   Four-o'clock
(Lat. *mirabilis*, wonderful, from the flowers)
(Quamoclidion DC.)
Pl. 8, fig. 2.

Sepals mostly 5, corolla-like, united into a funnelform tube, rose-purple, petals none, stamens 5, ovary 1-celled, stigma globose, fruit an achene without ribs; flowers usually 5-6 in a bellshaped calyx-like involucre; leaves opposite, simple and entire; perennial.

Flowers rose-red, 4-5 cm. long; leaves ovate, smooth *M. multiflóra*

SALICACEAE   WILLOW FAMILY

Sepals 0, petals 0, stamens 1-60, ovary 1-celled, stigmas 2, often 2-4-cleft, fruit a small capsule, splitting into 2-4 parts, seeds many, tiny, cottony; flowers in catkins, the stamen and pistil flowers on different trees; trees or shrubs with alternate simple leaves.

1. Trees, mostly with rounded or ovate leaves; buds
    covered with several scales   Populus
2. Shrubs, or sometimes trees, mostly with lanceo-
    late or lance-oblong leaves; buds covered with
    a single scale   Salix

Pópulus Linné 1753   Poplar, Cottonwood, Aspen
(L. *populus*, poplar, probably from the root *pal, to shake)
Plate 11.

Sepals and petals none, but the disk often cup-like, stamens 6-60, ovary 1-celled, stigmas 2-4, entire or lobed, fruit 2-4-valved, smooth or hairy;

flowers appearing before the leaves in red-brown or yellowish hanging cat-kins with fringed scales; leaves alternate simple, usually broad; trees.

1. Leaves with much flattened petioles
    a. Leaves rounded, short-pointed, entire or finely
        toothed   *P. tremuloídes*:
                           aspen.
    b. Leaves broadly triangular, long-pointed,
        coarsely toothed   *P. deltoídes*:
                           cottonwood
2. Leaves with round or roundish petioles
    a. Leaves broadly ovate or rounded, whitish be-
        neath   *P. balsamífera*
    b. Leaves lanceolate to lance-ovate, green be-
        neath
        (1) Leaves blunt or acute, 5-15 cm. long, 1-4
            cm. wide   *P. angustifólia*
        (2) Leaves long-pointed, 5-10 cm. long, 2-5
            cm. wide   *P. acumináta*

Sálix Linné 1753 Willow

(L. *salix*, willow, or sallow, the old English name of the willow)

Plates 12-13.

Sepals and petals none, stamens 1-10, usually 2, ovary 1-celled, stigmas 2, fruit 2-valved, smooth or hairy; flowers appearing before the leaves in gray, greenish or yellow catkins, with entire usually hairy scales; leaves alternate, simple, mostly narrow; ours mostly shrubs.

1. Stems low and creeping, mat-like, 1-4 in. high   *S. reticuláta*
2. Stems taller, 1-50 feet high
    a. Leaves smooth or nearly so on both sides when
        mature
        (1) Leaves linear, linear-oblong or lance-
            linear   *S. fluviátilis*
        (2) Leaves broader, lanceolate to obovate
            (a) Shrubs
                x. Young twigs with a bluish bloom
                y. Young twigs without a bluish bloom;
                    leaves oblong lanceolate   *S. irroráta*
                (x) Leaves entire, or mostly so
                    m. Leaves lanceolate to lance-ovate *S. chlorophýlla*
                    n. Leaves obovoid   *S. Nuttállii*

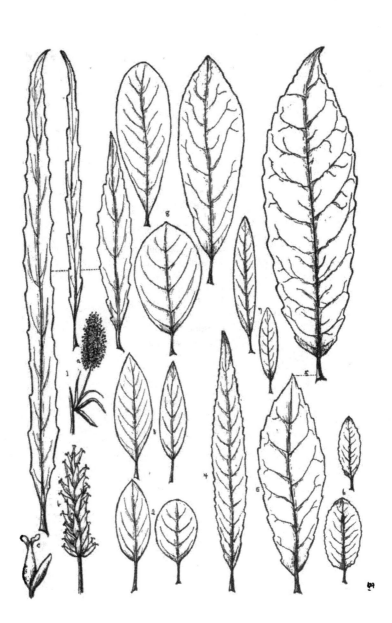

PLATE 13

WILLOWS

1. Salix glaucops
2. Salix geyeriana
3. Salix rostrata
4. Salix nigra
5. Salix amygdaloides
6. Salix cordata
7. Salix candida
8. Salix lasiandra

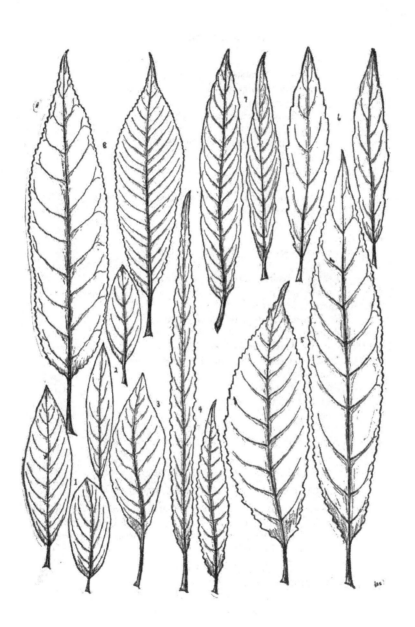

(y) Leaves toothed

  m. Leaves lanceolate

    (m) Fruits hairy   *S. discolor*

    (n) Fruits smooth

      h. Stipules small and glandular, or none,   *S. lasiándra*

      i. Stipules large, scarcely glandular   *S. cordáta*

  n. Leaves oblanceolate or elliptic to obovoid

    (m) Leaves smooth beneath, acute   *S. montícola*

    (n) Leaves hairy beneath, blunt as a rule   *S. Nuttállii*

 (b) Trees

  x. Leaves narrowly lanceolate, short-petioled   *S. nígra*

  y. Leaves broadly lanceolate, or lance-ovate, long-petioled   *S. amygdaloídes*

b. Leaves persistently hairy

 (1) Twigs densely white-hairy; leaves linear-oblong   *S. cándida*

 (2) Twigs not densely white-hairy

  (a) Fruits densely white-woolly; leaves lanceolate to ovoid   *S. gláucops*

  (b) Fruits merely hairy

    x. Leaves narrowly lanceolate to oblanceolate   *S. geyeriána*

    y. Leaves lance-oblong to obovoid   *S. rostráta*

  (c) Fruits smooth   *S. Wólfii*

ERICALES   HEATH ORDER

PIROLÁCEAE   WINTERGREEN FAMILY

Sepals 4-5, united, petals 4-5, separate, stamens 8-10, ovary 4-5-celled, style short or slender, often turned downward, stigma 5-lobed, or 5-crenate, fruit a capsule; flowers solitary or in racemes or corymbs; evergreen perennials with simple, entire petioled leaves.

PÍROLA Linné 1753   WINTERGREEN
(Lat. *pirum*, pear, *ola*, little, from the leaves)
Pl. 14, fig. 1-4; pl. 16, fig. 7.

Sepals 5, petals 5, concave, sessile, white, yellowish, pink or purple, stamens 10, ovary 5-celled, style straight, or declined, slender or thickened at the summit, stigma 5-lobed, capsule subglobose, 5-lobed, 5-celled, 5-valved from the base; flowers nodding, in terminal racemes; leaves basal; perennial.

1. Flowers pink or rose-purple; leaves roundish,
   often heart-shaped at base   *P. uliginósa*
2. Flowers greenish to white, rarely pinkish
   a. Style curved
      (1) Leaves mottled with gray below   *P. pícta*
      (2) Leaves not mottled
         (a) Leaf blades shorter than the petioles *P. chloróntha*
         (b) Leaf blades longer than the petioles   *P. ellíptica*
   b. Style straight
      (1) Style enclosed in corolla; leaves rounded *P. mínor*
      (2) Style projecting beyond corolla; leaves
         ovate   *P. secúnda*

Monéses Salisbury 1821   Monéses

(Gr. *monos*, one, *hesis*, joy, from the single flower)

Pl. 14, fig. 5.

Sepals 4-5, petals 4-5, white or pink, stamens 8 or 10, ovary 4-5-celled, globose, style straight, club-shaped at summit, stigma 4-5-lobed, capsule subglobose, 4-5-celled, 4-5-valved from the summit; flowers terminal, solitary; leaves petioled, fine-toothed, opposite or whorled in 3's; perennial.

Stems 1-8 in. high; leaves ovate to round, .5-3 cm. long;
flowers nodding, 1-2 cm. wide   *M. uniflóra*

Chimáphila Pursh 1814   Pipsissewa

(Gr. *cheima*, winter, *philos*, loving)

Pl. 14, fig. 6.

Sepals 5, petals 5, white or purplish, stamens 10, ovary 5-celled, 5-lobed, globose, style very short, obconic, stigma large, round, 5-crenate, capsule erect, globose, 5-lobed, 5-celled, 5-valved from the top; flowers spreading or nodding in terminal corymbs; leaves opposite, or whorled, evergreen, short-petioled, toothed; perennial.

Stems 3-10 in. high; leaves lanceolate to ovate, 1-3 in.
long; flowers 1-2 cm. wide   *C. umbelláta*

PLATE 14

WINTERGREENS AND INDIAN PIPES

WINTERGREEN FAMILY

1. Pirola elliptica: Wintergreen
2. Pirola chlorantha
3. Pirola minor
4. Pirola secunda
5. Moneses uniflora
6. Chimaphila umbellata: Pipsissewa

INDIAN PIPE FAMILY

7. Monotropa uniflora: Indian Pipe
8. Pterospora andromedea: Pine Drops
9. Hypopitys multiflora: Pinesap

MONOTROPÁCEAE   INDIAN PIPE FAMILY

Sepals 2-6, united at the base, deciduous, petals 3-6, united or separate, stamens 6-12, ovary 1-6-celled, 4-6-lobed, stigma globose or shield-shaped, capsule 4-6-lobed, or terete, 1-6-celled, 4-6-valved; flowers terminal, solitary or clustered; leaves reduced to scales or lacking; humus-plants or saprophytes.

1. Flower solitary, nodding   MONOTROPA
2. Flowers clustered
   a. Cluster 1-4 in. long; petals separate, falling
      away   HYPOPITYS
   b. Cluster 6-20 in. long; petals united, persistent PTEROSPORA

MONÓTROPA Linné 1753   INDIAN PIPE
(Gr. *monos,* one, *tropa,* turn, from the nodding stem)
Pl. 14, fig. 7.

Sepals 2-4, deciduous, petals 5-6, white, separate, stamens 10-12, ovary 5-celled, style 1, short, thick, stigma funnelform, capsule 5-celled, 5-valved, erect; flowers solitary, nodding; bracts yellowish or red; succulent herb.
Stems white to reddish, 2-15 in. high; flowers .5-1
   in. long   *M. uniflóra*

HYPÓPITYS Adanson 1763   PINESAP
(Gr. *hypo,* beneath, *pitys,* fir, from its habitat)
Pl. 14, fig. 9.

Sepals 3-5, petals 3-5, white, yellowish or red, stamens 6-10, ovary 3-5-celled, style slender, stigma funnelform, capsule 3-5-celled, 3-5-valved, erect; flowers in a terminal, nodding one-sided raceme which soon becomes erect.
Stems usually clustered, 4-12 in. high; flowers 8-15
   mm. long   *H. multiflóra*

PTERÓSPORA Nuttall 1818   PINE DROPS
(Gr. *pteron,* wing, *spora,* seed)
Pl. 14, fig. 8.

Sepals 5, united, petals 5, united, reddish, stamens 10, included, ovary sub-globose, 5-lobed, 5-celled, style short columnar, stigma globose, 5-lobed, capsule globose, 5-lobed, 5-celled, 5-valved; flowers nodding in racemes.
Stems red-brown, 1-5 ft. high; flowers 5-10 mm.
   wide   *P. andromedéa*

ERICÁCEAE   HEATH FAMILY

Sepals 4-5, separate or united, petals 4-5, separate or united, stamens 4-10, ovary 2-5-celled, stigma globose or shield-shaped, fruit a capsule, berry or drupe; flowers solitary or clustered; shrubs, or perennial herbs with simple leaves.

1. Petals separate   LEDUM
2. Petals united
   a. Leaves in 4 rows, overlapping, blunt awl-
      shaped   CASSIOPE
   b. Leaves alternate, flat, spreading
     (1) Corolla flat, saucer-shaped   KALMIA
     (2) Corolla bell- or urn-shaped
       (a) Flowers 4-parted; stamens 8   MENZIESIA
       (b) Flowers 5-parted; stamens 10
         x. Low erect shrubs with linear leaves   PHYLLODOCE
         y. Creeping shrubs with broad leaves
           (x) Leaves entire; flowers in terminal
              clusters   ARCTOSTAPHYLUS
           (y) Leaves toothed; flowers solitary,
              àxillary   GAULTHERIA

ARCTOSTÁPHYLUS Adanson 1763   BEARBERRY, KINNIKINNIC

(Gr. *arktos*, bear, *staphyle*, grape)

Pl. 16, fig. 10.

Sepals 4-5, united at base, petals 4-5, white or pink, united, stamens 8-10, included, ovary 4-10-celled, style slender, fruit a drupe, with 4-10 seed-like nutlets coherent into a solid stone; flowers nodding, stalked, in terminal racemes, panicles or clusters; leaves alternate, petioled, firm, persistent, evergreen; creeping shrub.

Stems creeping; leaves oblong to spatulate, 1-3 cm.
  long; flowers 7-10 mm. long   *A. uva-úrsi*

CASSÍOPE Don 1834   CASSIOPE

(Named for Cassiope)

Pl. 15, fig. 5.

Sepals 4-5, petals 4-5, white or pink, united, stamens 8-10, included, ovary 4-5-celled, style 1, stigma simple, capsule globose or ovoid, 4-5-valved, each valve 2-cleft at the apex; flowers with stalks, solitary, nodding,

terminal or axillary; leaves small, sessile, densely crowded, entire; low tufted branching heath-like evergreen shrubs.

Stems tufted, moss-like, 1-5 in. high; leaves 2-5 mm.
long; flowers 6-8 mm. wide   *C. hypnoídes*

GAULTHÉRIA Linné 1753

(Named for Gaultier, a Canadian botanist)

Pl. 15, fig. 6.

Sepals 5, petals 5, white, red or pink, united into an urn- or bell-shaped corolla, stamens 10, included, stigma obtuse, entire, ovary 5-celled, 5-lobed, calyx becoming fleshy and at length surrounding the capsule, forming a berry-like fruit; flowers axillary, solitary or in racemes; leaves alternate, leathery, persistent, evergreen; shrubs.

Stems creeping, flower branches 1-4 in. high; leaves
oval to roundish, 12-15 mm. long   *G. humifúsa*

KÁLMIA Linné 1753   KALMIA

(Named for Kalm, a Swedish botanist)

Pl. 15, fig. 2.

Sepals 5, petals 5, lilac-purple, united into a saucer-shaped corolla, stamens 10, shorter than the corolla, ovary 5-celled, style slender, stigma depressed globose, capsule subglobose, obscurely 5-lobed, 5-celled, 5-valved from the summit; flowers in umbels or corymbs or solitary, or 2-3 together in the axils; leaves entire, evergreen, leathery, alternate, opposite, or whorled in 3's; shrubs.

Stems .5-2 ft. high; leaves oblong .5-2 in long; flowers 10-20 mm. wide   *K. glaúca*

LÉDUM Linné 1753   LABRADOR TEA

(Greek name of a plant)

Pl. 15, fig. 3.

Sepals 5, petals 5, white, stamens 5 or 10, exserted, ovary ovoid, scaly, 5-celled, style slender, stigma 5-lobed, capsule oblong, 5-celled, 5-valved from the base; flowers numerous in terminal umbels or corymbs; leaves alternate, thick, short-petioled, oblong or linear, rolled back at the margins, fragrant when crushed; evergreen and resinous shrubs.

Stems 2-5 ft. high; leaves 1-2 in. long   *L. glandulósum*

MENZIÉSIA Smith 1791   MENZIESIA

(Named for Menzies, an English naturalist)

Pl. 15, fig. 1.

Sepals 4, petals 4, greenish purple, united into an urn-shaped or globose corolla, stamens 8, included, ovary mostly 4-celled, style slender, stigma 4-lobed or 4-toothed, capsule subglobose or ovoid, 4-celled, 4-valved; flowers solitary; leaves alternate, entire, deciduous; shrubs.

Stems 2-6 ft. high; leaves oblong to elliptic, somewhat rusty   *M. ferruginea*

PHYLLÓDOCE Salisbury 1806   MOUNTAIN HEATH

(The name of a sea-nymph)

Pl. 15, fig. 4.

Sepals 5, petals 5, pink, blue or purple, sometimes yellow, united into a bell-shaped corolla, constricted at the throat, stamens 10, included, ovary 5-celled, style slender, included, stigma obscurely 5-lobed or globose, capsule subglobose, or globose-oblong, 5-valved to about the middle; flowers long-stalked, nodding, in terminal umbels; leaves small, crowded, linear, obtuse, leathery, evergreen; low branching shrubs.

1. Corolla rose-red, 5-10 mm. long   *P. empetrifórmis*
2. Corolla yellowish, 3-5 mm. long   *P. glanduliflóra*

VACCINIACEAE   BLUEBERRY FAMILY

Sepals 4-5, united, petals 4-5, united (rarely separate) into a globose, urn-, bell-shaped, or tubular corolla, deciduous, stamens 8-10, upon the ovary or at the base of the corolla, ovary inferior, 2-10-celled, style slender, stigma simple, or minutely 4-5-lobed or 4-5-toothed, ovules solitary or several in each cavity, fruit a berry or drupe, globose, cells 1-several-seeded, or the drupe containing several nutlets; flowers clustered or solitary; leaves alternate simple; shrubs or small trees.

VACCÍNIUM Linné 1753   BLUEBERRY, CRANBERRY

(The Latin name)

Pl. 15, fig. 7-9.

Sepals 4-5, united into a globose, hemispheric, or top-shaped tube, not angled, united to the ovary, persistent, petals 4-5, white, pink or red, united into an urn-shaped, bell-shaped or cylindric corolla, stamens 8-10, ovary 4-5-celled, or 8-10-celled by false partitions, style straight, stigma small, fruit a many-seeded berry; flowers in terminal or lateral racemes or clusters, or rarely solitary in the axils; leaves alternate, often leathery; shrubs or small trees.

  1. Flowers solitary; corolla 5-lobed
    a. Branches with line-like angles
      (1) Stems 2-15 in. high; berries black to red   *V. myrtillus*
      (2) Stems 1-3 ft. high; berries black   *V. membranáceum*
    b. Branches round, not angled   *V. caespitósum*
  2. Flowers 2-4 in a cluster; corolla 4-lobed   *V. occidentále*

PRIMULALES   PRIMROSE ORDER

PRIMULACEAE   PRIMROSE FAMILY

Sepals 4-9 (usually 5), united, petals 4-9, (usually 5), united, stamens as many as the petals, and attached to them, ovary 1-celled, style 1, stigma 1, globose, fruit a 2-6-valved capsule; flowers terminal or axillary, solitary or clustered; annual or perennial herbs with alternate or opposite, mostly simple, leaves.

  1. Petals present
    a. Flowers white, pink or rose-purple, never bright yellow
      (1) Flowering stems leafy only at base
        (a) Corolla lobes reflexed; flowers usually hanging   DODECATHEON
        (b) Corolla lobes not reflexed; flowers erect or ascending
          x. Flowers pink, lilac or rose-purple
            (x) Corolla lobes notched or cleft; fruits many-seeded   PRIMULA
            (y) Corolla lobes entire; fruits 1-2-seeded   DOUGLASIA
          y. Flowers white, rarely yellowish or pinkish   ANDROSACE
      (2) Flowering stems leafy throughout; flowers white, in racemes   SAMOLUS
    b. Flowers bright yellow
      (1) Flowers solitary   STEIRONEMA
      (2) Flowers in spikes   NAUMBERGIA
  2. Petals absent, the calyx white, pink or purplish   GLAUX

ANDRÓSACE Linné 1753   ANDROSACE

(Gr. *androsakes,* a kind of plant)

Pl. 16, fig. 5.

Sepals 5, united, petals 5, white, rarely yellowish or pinkish, united into a salver- or funnel-form corolla, the tube not longer than the calyx, stamens 5, included, ovary 1-celled, style 1, stigma globose, capsule top-shaped, ovoid, or globose, 5-valved from the apex; flowers in terminal umbels with basal involucre; leaves small, simple, basal; low annual or perennial.

1. Corolla 5-10 mm. wide, white to pinkish or yellow; perennial, the rosettes connected   *A. chamaejásme*
2. Corolla 2-4 mm. wide, white
  a. Fruiting calyx top-shaped, the teeth lanceo-
    late, longer than the capsule
    (1) Bracts of the involucre ovate to oblong   *A. occidentális*
    (2) Bracts of the involucre lanceolate to
      linear; plant very variable, dwarf ros-
      ettes or tall and diffuse   *A. septentrionális*
  b. Fruiting calyx globose, the teeth ovate-triang-
    ular, shorter than the capsule   *A. filifórmis*

DOUGLÁSIA Lindley 1828

(Named from Douglas, an English botanist)

Pl. 16, fig. 9.

Sepals 5, united, petals 5, red to purple, united in a tube, stamens 5, ovary 1-celled, style slender, capsule top-shaped, 1-2-seeded; flowers solitary or 2-3 in a terminal cluster; leaves small, crowded, entire, linear or awl-shaped; perennial.

Stems tufted; leaves 5-12 mm. long; flowers 1-3   *D. montána*

GLÁUX Linné 1753   SEAWORT

(Gr. *glaukos,* sea-green)

Pl. 16, fig. 8.

Sepals 5, united, pink or white, petals none, stamens 5, ovary 1-celled, style slender, stigma globose, capsule globose-ovoid, beaked, 5-valved, at the top; flowers minute, nearly sessile, axillary; leaves opposite, entire, obtuse, small, fleshy; succulent perennial.

Stems spreading or erect, 1-8 in. high; leaves linear
  to oblong, 3-15 mm. long   *G. marítima*

PLATE 16.

NAUMBÚRGIA Moench 1802 LOOSESTRIFE

(Named for Naumburg, a German botanist)

Sepals 5-7, petals 5-7, yellow, united, the tube exceedingly short, stamens 5-7, exserted, ovary 1-celled, style slender, stigma capitate, capsule 5-7-valved, flowers in axillary spike-like racemes or heads; leaves opposite, sessile, lance-shaped, entire; perennial.

Stems 1-3 ft. high; leaves lanceolate, 2-4 in. long; flowers 4-6 mm. wide *N. thyrsiflóra*

DODECÁTHEON Linné 1753 SHOOTING STAR

(Gr. *dodeka*, twelve, *theoi*, gods)

Pl. 16, fig. 4.

Sepals 5, united, petals 5, united at base, pink, or rose-purple to white, strongly reflexed, stamens 5, an exserted cone on the throat of the corolla, ovary 1-celled, style slender, exserted, stigma globose, capsule oblong or cylindric, erect, 5-6-valved at the apex or splitting to the base; flowers nodding, in terminal umbels; leaves basal, simple; perennial.

Stems 2 in.-3 ft. high; leaves usually oblanceolate to obovate, 2-10 in. long; flowers 1.5-3 cm. long *D. meádia*

PRÍMULA Linné 1753 PRIMROSE, COWSLIP

(Lat. *primus*, spring, *-ula*, small, from the time of blooming)

Pl. 16, fig. 1, 3, 6.

Sepals 5, united, petals 5, pink, lilac or rose-purple, united into a funnel- or salver-form corolla, the tube longer than the calyx, the lobes sometimes notched or 2-cleft, stamens 5, included, ovary 1-celled, style slender, stigma globose, capsule oblong-ovoid, or globose, 5-valved at the summit; flowers in terminal umbels, or racemes, sometimes single; leaves basal, simple; perennial.

1. Leaves densely white mealy below; corolla lobes deeply cleft *P. farinósa*
2. Leaves green on both sides; corolla lobes merely notched
   a. Plant low, 1-5 in.; leaves .5-2 in. long; flowers 1-few, 1-2 cm. long *P. angustifólia*
   b. Plant tall, 6-25 in.; leaves 3-10 in. long; flowers several to many, 2-3 cm. long *P. Párryi*

SÁMOLUS   Linné 1753   BROOKWEED
(The ancient name)

Sepals 5, united, petals 5, white, united, bell-shaped, stamens 5, ovary 1-celled, capsule globose or ovoid, 5-valved from the summit; flowers in terminal racemes or panicles; leaves alternate, entire; perennial.

Stems .5 1.5 ft. high; leaves obovate, 1-3 in. long; flowers 1-2 mm. wide   *S. floribúndus*

STEIRONÉMA   Rafinesque 1820   LOOSESTRIFE
(Gr. *steiros*, sterile, *nema*, thread, from the sterile stamens)
Pl. 16, fig. 2.

Sepals 5, petals 5, yellow, stamens 5, sterile stamens 5, ovary 1-celled, globose, capsule 5-valved, flowers axillary on slender stalks; leaves opposite or whorled, simple, entire; perennial.

Stems 1-4 ft. high; leaves ovate to lance-ovate, 2-5 in. long; flowers 1-2.5 cm. wide   *S. ciliátum*

PLANTAGINÁCEAE   PLANTAIN FAMILY

Sepals 4, united, petals 4, united, papery, stamens 4 or 2, inserted on the tube or throat of the corolla, ovary 1-2-celled, or falsely 3-4-celled, style slender, simple, ovules 1-several in each cell, fruit a pod or capsule opening by a lid, or a nutlet, seeds 1-several in each cavity; flowers small, perfect, polygamous or monoecious, in dense terminal spikes or heads, or rarely solitary; annual or perennial stemless or short-stemmed herbs with basal, opposite or alternate leaves.

PLANTÁGO   Linné 1753   PLANTAIN
(Lat. *planta*, sole, *-ago*, like, from the shape of the leaf)
Pl. 20. fig. 1.

Sepals 4, united, petals 4, greenish or purplish, united into a salverform corolla, the tube cylindric or constricted at the throat, stamens 4 or 2, ovary 2-celled or falsely 3-4-celled, ovules 1-several in each cell, fruit opening by a lid; flowers in terminal spikes or heads; leaves basal or alternate; stemless or short-stemmed herbs.

1. Leaves linear, 1-5 mm. wide
    a. Leaves 3-6 mm. wide, gray woolly; spikes 5-6
       mm. wide; stamens 4   *P. Púrshii*
    b. Leaves .5-1 mm. wide, minutely hairy; spikes
       2 mm. wide; stamens 2   *P. elongáta*

2. Leaves lanceolate to ovate, 1-10 cm. wide
   a. Leaf bases in a mass of red-brown wool   *P. eriópoda*
   b. Leaf bases without red-brown wool
      (1) Leaves lanceolate
         (a) Spike oblong, 1-3 cm. long   *P. lanceoláta*
         (b) Spike cylindric, 3-6 cm. long   *P. Tweédyi*
      (2) Leaves ovate to round
         (a) Pod ovoid, splitting circularly about the
            middle   *P. májor*
         (b) Pod oblong splitting circularly near the
            base   *P. Rugélii*

GENTIANALES   GENTIAN ORDER

GENTIANÁCEAE   GENTIAN FAMILY

Sepals 4-7, united, petals 4-7, united into a funnel-, bell-, club-, or saucer-shaped corolla, stems 4-14, ovary 1-2-celled, style simple or none, stigma entire or 2-lobed or 2-cleft, capsule mostly splitting by 2 valves; flowers in terminal or axillary clusters, or solitary at the ends of stems or branches; herbs with opposite, entire, rarely whorled leaves.

1. Style short and persistent, or none
   a. Corolla flat, saucer-shaped
      (1) Flowers green; leaves 3-6 in a whorl; stem
         2-5 ft. high   FRASERA
      (2) Flowers purple, blue or white; leaves op-
         posite; stems .5-2 ft. high
         (a) Petals with a fringed nectary at base   SWERTIA
         (b) Petals without fringed nectaries   PLEUROGYNE
   b. Corolla tubular or bell-shaped   GENTIANA
2. Style slender, thread-like, falling away at maturity
   a. Corolla bell-shaped   EUSTOMA
   b. Corolla salver-shaped   ERYTHRAEA

ERYTHRAÉA Necker 1790 CENTAURY

(Gr. *erythraios*, red, from the color)

Sepals 4-5 united, petals 4-5, pink, white or yellow, united into a sal-verform corolla, stamens 4-5, ovary 1-celled, style slender, stigma 2-lobed,

capsule oblong-ovoid, or spindle-shaped, 2-valved; flowers in cymes or spikes; leaves sessile, or clasping the stem; annual or biennial.

Stems 4-12 in. high; leaves oblong to lance-linear   *E. arizónica*

EUSTÓMA   Salisbury 1806   EUSTOMA
(Gr. *eu-*, good, true, *stoma*, mouth, from the open corolla)
Pl. 18, fig. 5.

Sepals 5-6, united, petals 5-6, blue, purple or white, united into a broad, bell-shaped corolla, stamens 5-6, ovary 1-celled, style slender, stigma 2-cleft, capsule oblong or ovoid, 2-valved; flowers long-stalked, axillary and terminal, solitary or in panicles; leaves opposite, sessile or clasping; annual.

Stems 4-15 in. high; leaves oblong to elliptic, 1-2 in.
long   *E. Andréwsii*

FRÁSERA   Walter 1788   FRASERA, GREEN GENTIAN
(Named for Fraser, a botanical collecter)
Pl. 18, fig. 3.

Sepals 4, united, petals 4, greenish, each bearing 1-2 fringed glands, united into a saucer-shaped corolla, stamens 4, ovary ovoid, 1-celled, style slender or short, but distinct, stigma 2-lobed or nearly entire, capsule ovoid, leathery, somewhat compressed, 2-valved; flowers in terminal open or crowded panicles; leaves opposite or whorled; perennial or biennial.

Stems 1-5 ft. high; leaves linear to obovate, 4-12 in.
long   *F. speciósa*

GENTIÁNA   Linné 1753   GENTIAN
(Named for Gentius, king of Illyria)
Pl. 18, figs. 1-2, 4, 6.

Sepals 4-7 (usually 5), united, petals 4-7, blue, purple, yellow or white, united into a tube-, bell-, salver-, or funnel-shaped corolla, stamens 8-14, on the corolla, included, ovary 1-celled, style short or none, stigma 2-cleft, capsule 2-valved; flowers solitary or clustered, terminal or axillary; leaves opposite (rarely whorled) entire, sessile or short-petioled; perennial.

1. Corolla with a shorter lobe or fold between the
     main lobes
   a. Plants low, .5-3 in. high; flowers small, .5-1
        cm. long; leaves tiny
      (1) Flowers white or whitish; fruit stalked;
           at 7-10000 ft.   *G. húmilis*

(2) Flowers bright blue; fruit scarcely stalked;
at 10-14000 ft.   *G. prostráta*

b. Plants .5-2 ft. high; flowers large, 2-5 cm. long
  (1) Corolla greenish-yellow, purple dotted; at
  10-14000 ft.   *G. frígida*
  (2) Corolla blue or purple
    (a) Corolla open
      x. Corolla widely open, 3-5 cm. long,
        mostly 1.5-2 cm. wide   *G. calycósa*
      y. Corolla narrowly open, 2-3 cm. long, 1
        cm. or less wide   *G. áffinis*
    (b) Corolla nearly or completely closed   *G. Andréwsii*

2. Corolla without lobes or folds between the main
  lobes, the latter fringed at the margin or at the
  base
  a. Lobes fringed along the margin; flowers 1-2
    in. long
    (1) Flowers on long leafless stalks; corolla
      lobes obovoid, dark blue   *G. serráta*
    (2) Flowers on short stalks, enclosed in 2
      leaves; corolla lobes oblong, light blue *G. barbelláta*
  b. Lobes usually entire at margin, but fringed at
    base; flowers .5-2 cm. long
    (1) Flowers single on long slender stems bear-
      ing a few small leaves; rare   *G. tenélla*
    (2) Flowers usually many on short stalks from
      leafy stems; common   *G. amarélla*

PLEURÓGYNE Eschscholtz 1825

(Gr. *pleuron*, side, *gyne*, female, from the lateral stigmas)

Sepals 4-5, united at the base, petals 4-5 white to blue, with a pair of narrow appendages at the base of each, united into a saucer-shaped corolla, stamens 4-5, ovary 1-celled, style none, stigma running down the ovary, capsule 2-valved; flowers in terminal narrow racemes or panicles, or solitary at the ends of the slender stalks, leaves opposite; annual.

Stems 4-15 in. high; leaves linear, 2-3 cm. long; flowers 12-25 mm. wide   *P. rotáta*

SWÉRTIA Linné 1753 SWERTIA
(Named for Swert, a Dutch botanist)
Pl. 18, fig. 7.

Sepals 4-5, united, petals 4-5, blue, purple, or white, united into a

PLATE 18

GENTIAN FAMILY

1. Gentiana amarella: Gentian
2. Gentiana serrata: Fringed Gentian
3. Frasera speciosa: Green Gentian
4. Gentiana barbellata: Fringed Gentian
5. Eustoma Andrewsii
6. Gentiana Calycosa: Gentian
7. Swertia perennis

PLATE 18.

saucer-shaped corolla, stamens 4-5, ovary 1-celled, stigma 2-lobed, or divided, capsule ovate; flowers in a compact panicle; leaves alternate, simple, the lower with margined petioles; perennial.

Stems 3-20 in. high; leaves 1-5 in. long; flowers in
open to dense clusters, 1-3 cm. wide; petals 4 or 5   *S. perénnis*

MENYANTHÁCEAE   BUCKBEAN FAMILY

Sepals 5, united, petals 5, united into a funnelform, or saucer-shaped corolla, stamens 5, on the corolla, ovary 1-celled, fruit a capsule or closed; flowers regular and perfect, in clusters; perennial aquatic or marsh herbs with basal or alternate entire crenate or 3-foliate leaves.

MENYÁNTHES Linné 1753 BUCKBEAN
(Gr. *men*, month, *anthos*, flower)
Pl. 17, fig. 3.

Sepals 5, united, petals 5, white or purplish, united into a short funnelform corolla, fringed or bearded within, stamens 5, on the tube of the corolla, disk of 5 glands below the ovary, ovary 1-celled, style awl-shaped, stigma of 2 flat plates, capsule oval; flowers in racemes or panicles on long lateral stalks; leaves alternate, long-petioled, 3-foliate, basal; perennial marsh herb with creeping root-stocks.

Leaflets oblong to obovate, 1.5-3 in. long; flowers 10-
12 mm. long   *M. trifoliáta*

OLEÁCEAE   OLIVE FAMILY

Sepals 2-4 (or none) united into a calyx, petals 2-4 (or none) separate or united, stamens 2-4, on the corolla, ovary 2-celled, fruit a capsule, sometimes a winged fruit (samara), drupe, or berry; flowers perfect, polygamous or dioecious, in terminal or axillary panicles, cymes or clusters, trees or shrubs with opposite or alternate, simple or pinnate, entire or dentate leaves.

1. Leaves pinnate; fruits winged   FRAXINUS
2. Leaves simple; fruits berry-like   ADELIA

FRÁXINUS Linné 1753 ASH
(The Latin name)
Pl. 17, fig. 1.

Sepals 4 (or none) united, petals none or 2-4, separate or united in pairs at the base, greenish, stamens 2 (rarely 3 or 4), ovary 2-celled, with

2 ovules in each cavity, stigma 2-cleft, fruit a flat samara, winged at the apex only or all around, usually 1-seeded; flowers small, dioecious or polygamous, rarely perfect, clustered, appearing before or with the leaves; leaves odd-pinnate; trees.

1. Tree 20-50 ft. high; leaflets lanceolate, 3-8 in.
   long   *F. lanceoláta*
2. Shrub 8-20 ft. high; leaflets round to ovate, 1-2
   in. wide   *F. anómala*

Adélia   P. Brown 1756

(Gr. *adelos*, inconspicuous, from the flowers)

Pl. 17, fig. 2.

Sepals 4 or none, united, petals none or 1 or 2, small, deciduous, yellow or greenish, stamens 2-4, ovary 2-celled, ovules 2 in each cell, style slender, stigma 2-lobed, fruit an oblong or subglobose drupe with 1 or rarely 2 seeds; flowers small, dioecious or polygamous, in clusters, short racemes or panicles from scaly buds produced at the leaf-axils of the preceding season, appearing before or with the leaves; leaves opposite, simple, toothed or entire; shrubs.

Stems 3-10 ft. high; leaves 2-3 cm. long   *A. neo-mexicána*

APOCYNACEAE   DOGBANE FAMILY

Sepals 5, united into a tube, petals 5, united, stamens 5, inserted on the corolla tube, ovary of 2 distinct carpels, style and stigma 1, fruit of 2 long follicles; flowers solitary or clustered; perennial herbs with alternate or opposite simple, usually entire leaves.

1. Leaves opposite   Apocynum
2. Leaves alternate   Amsonia

Amsónia   Walter 1788   Amsonia

(Named for Amson, an American physician)

Sepals 5, united, petals 5, blue or bluish, united, stamens 5, in the throat of the corolla, ovary of 2 carpels connected above by the style, fruit of 2 erect, cylindrical several-seeded follicles; flowers in cymes; leaves alternate, entire; perennial.

Stems .5-2 ft. high; leaves linear to oblong, 1-2 in.
   long; flowers 1-2 cm. long   *A. texána*

APÓCYNUM Linné 1753 DOGBANE

(Gr. name of the dogbane; *apo*, from, *kyon, kynos*, dog)

Pl. 17, fig. 4.

Sepals 5, united, petals 5, white to pink, united into a bell-shaped tube, bearing 5 triangular scales, alternating with the 5 stamens, ovary of 2 carpels, stigma obscurely 2-lobed, fruit of 2 long terete follicles, seeds with a hairy apex; flowers in terminal and axillary cymes; leaves opposite, entire; perennial.

1. Corolla pink or pinkish, rarely white, with tube
   longer than calyx and lobes turned back   *A. androsaemifólium*
2. Corolla white or greenish, tube shorter than calyx
   and lobes erect   *A. cannábinum*

ASCLEPIADÁCEAE   MILKWEED FAMILY

Sepals 5, united, petals 5, united into a bell-, urn-, saucer-, or funnel-shaped corolla, a 5-lobed or 5-parted crown between the corolla and the stamens and united to one or the other, stamens 5, inserted on the corolla, usually near its base, filaments short, stout, ovary of 2 carpels, styles 2, short, connected at the summit by the shield-shaped stigma, fruit 2 follicles, flowers perfect, regular, in umbels; perennial herbs, vines or shrubs, mostly with milky juice and opposite, alternate or whorled leaves.

1. Hoods of the crown without horn or crest   ACERATES
2. Hoods with horn or crest within
   a. Leaves mostly opposite or whorled; hoods with
      an incurved horn   ASCLEPIAS
   b. Leaves alternate; hoods with a crest   ASCLEPIODORA

ACERÁTES Elliott 1817 ACERATES

(Gr. *a-*, without, *keras*, horn, from the hornless hoods)

Pl. 17, fig. 5.

Sepals 5, united, petals 5, green or purplish, united, turned back, crown-column very short, crown of 5 somewhat pitcher-shaped hoods, stamens 5, pollen masses solitary in each sac, oblong, hanging, stigma 5-lobed; flowers in umbels, terminal or short-stalked, leaves thick, alternate or opposite; perennial herbs.

1. Flower clusters on stalks 1-5 cm. long; leaves
   very long and narrow   *A. auriculáta*
2. Flower clusters stalkless or nearly so
   a. Hoods 3-toothed at tip; leaves elongated, linear *A. angustifólia*

b. Hoods entire at tip; leaves ovate to lance-
linear   *A. viridiflóra*

ASCLÉPIAS Linné 1753 MILKWEED
(Named for Asklepios, the Greek god of medicine)
Pl. 17, fig. 6-10.

Sepals 5, united, petals 5, greenish-white to pink or purple, united,
turned back, crown-column generally present, crown of 5 concave erect
or spreading hoods, each bearing within a slender or awl-shaped incurved
horn, stamens 5, pollen-masses solitary in each sac, hanging, stigma nearly
flat, 5-angled or 5-lobed, follicles usually thick, taper-pointed; flowers in
terminal or axillary umbels; leaves opposite, whorled or rarely alternate,
entire; perennial.

1. Leaves opposite or mostly so
   a. Leaves linear, 5-10 mm. wide   *A. brachystéphana*
   b. Leaves broader, lanceolate to round
      (1) Flowers red; leaves lanceolate, 1.5-4 cm.
          wide   *A. incarnáta*
      (2) Flowers greenish, white, yellowish or
          purplish; leaves lance-ovate to round
          (a) Leaves lance-ovate, usually velvety-
              hairy, rather acute   *A. Hállii*
          (b) Leaves broadly ovate to round
             x. Leaves smooth when mature
                (x) Petals 1-1.5 cm. long; horns con-
                    cealed in hoods   *A. cryptóceras*
                (y) Petals 5-7 mm. long; horns ex-
                    serted   *A. latifólia*
             y. Leaves velvety-hairy
                (x) Hoods long-pointed, 10-15 mm.
                    long; leaves pointed   *A. speciósa*
                (y) Hoods blunt, 4-5 mm. long; leaves
                    retuse   *A. arenária*
2. Leaves alternate or scattered
   a. Flowers orange; leaves lanceolate to oblong,
      hairy   *A. tuberósa*
   b. Flowers greenish-white; leaves long linear,
      smooth
      (1) Plants 2-8 in. high; leaves densely crowded *A. púmila*
      (2) Plants 1-2 ft. high; leaves in whorls

(a) Hoods entire   *A. verticilláta*
(b) Hoods arrow-shaped   *A. galioídes*

ASCLEPIODÓRA Gray 1876 MILKWEED

(Gr. *Asklepios; doron*, gift)

Pl. 17, fig. 11.

Sepals 5, lance-shaped, petals 5, united into a wheel-shaped corolla, hoods oblong, inserted over the whole of the very short crown-column, curved upward, obtuse, crested within, at least in the upper part, slightly longer than the anther, at the clefts between the hoods a small lobe or appendage, alternating with the anther wings and resembling an inner crown, anthers 5, pollen masses hanging, pear-shaped, follicles ovoid or oblong, erect or ascending on the curved or twice-bent fruiting stalks; flowers in terminal, solitary or clustered umbels; leaves alternate or opposite, entire; perennial herbs.

Stems ascending, .5-2 ft. high; leaves lanceolate, 3-8
in. long; flowers 1.5-2 cm. wide   *A. decúmbens*

POLEMONIALES PHLOX ORDER

POLEMONIÁCEAE PHLOX FAMILY

Sepals 5, united into a tube, petals 5, united into a regular, funnel-form to saucer-shaped corolla, stamens 5, on the tube of the corolla and alternate with its lobes, ovary 3-celled, stigmas 3, fruit a 3-valved capsule; flowers mostly in panicles and cymes, rarely solitary; annual or perennial herbs with alternate or opposite, simple and entire or lobed to pinnate leaves.

1. Leaves opposite and entire   PHLOX
2. Leaves usually alternate, mostly pinnatifid to
    pinnate
    a. Leaves pinnate; corolla bell-shaped   POLEMONIUM
    b. Leaves entire to pinnatifid; corolla tubular to
        salverform
        (1) Leaves entire
            (a) Ovule one in each cavity   COLLOMIA
            (b) Ovules 2-many in each cavity   GILIA
        (2) Leaves pinnatifid
            (a) Leaves with rigid needle-like lobes   NAVARRETIA
            (b) Leaves with soft spineless lobes   GILIA

COLLÓMIA Nuttall 1818 COLLOMIA

(Gr. *kolla,* glue, from the wetted seeds)

Pl. 19, fig. 7.

Sepals 5, united into a cup-shaped or obpyramidal calyx, petals 5, purple, white or reddish, united into a tubular-funnelform or salverform corolla, stamens 5, on the tube of the corolla, ovary 3-celled, ovules 1-few in each cavity, capsule oval to obovoid; flowers in heads or cymes; leaves alternate, mostly entire; annual or rarely perennial.

Stems 2 in. to 3 ft. high; leaves lance-linear to lance-
oblong; flowers 10-15 mm. long   *C. lineáris*

GÍLIA Ruiz and Pavon 1794 GILIA

(Named for Gil, a Spanish botanist)

Pl. 19, fig. 3; pl. 20, fig. 5-6.

Sepals 5, united into a bell-shaped or tube-shaped calyx, petals 6, white, red, pink, violet or blue, united into a funnelform or tubular, bell-shaped or rarely salverform corolla, stamens 5, on the corolla, ovary 3-celled, ovules solitary or several in each cell, capsule ovoid or oblong, 3-celled; flowers solitary or clustered; leaves opposite or alternate, entire, or pinnately or palmately cut or dissected; annual, biennial or perennial.

1. Flowers in a panicle, often much branched
   a. Leaves regularly alternate
     (1) Flowers more than 1 cm. long, often 3-5 cm.
       (a) Leaves mostly entire and basal   *G. subnúda*
       (b) Leaves pinnatifid, the stems leafy
         x. Corolla lobes narrow, lance-ovate. acute; fruit and calyx nearly equal; flowers red to white   *G. aggregáta*
         y. Corolla lobes broad, ovate to round; fruit twice as long as calyx; flowers white
           (x) Corolla 3-5 cm. long, the lobes round   *G. longiflóra*
           (y) Corolla 1.5-3 cm. long, the lobes somewhat acute   *G. laxiflóra*
     (2) Flowers 4-12 mm. long
       (a) Stamens exserted
         x. Corolla white, dotted, 10-12 mm. long *G. polyántha*

y. Corolla pale blue or purplish, 4-6 mm.
　　long　　　　　　　　　　　　　　　*G. pinnatífida*
(b) Stamens included
　x. Corolla 4-5 mm. long; seeds unchanged
　　when wet　　　　　　　　　　　　*G. leptoméria*
　y. Corolla 5-10 mm. long; seeds with
　　spirals when wet　　　　　　　　　*G. inconspícua*
b. Leaves regularly opposite
　(1) Stamens hairy　　　　　　　　　　*G. pharnaceoídes*
　(2) Stamens smooth　　　　　　　　　*G. Harknéssii*
2. Flowers in a dense spike or head
　a. Flowers in an oblong spike 2-8 in. long; leaves
　　linear, mostly entire　　　　　　　*G. spicáta*
　b. Flowers in a roundish head
　　(1) Stems naked, except for the 2 persistent
　　　seed leaves, 1-4 in. high; head with an
　　　involucre of 4-5 leaves　　　　　*G. nudicaúlis*
　　(2) Stems leafy; heads not involucrate
　　　(a) Corolla tube equalling calyx lobes; heads
　　　　dense　　　　　　　　　　　　*G. congésta*
　　　(b) Corolla tube twice as long as calyx;
　　　　heads loose　　　　　　　　　*G. púmila*
3. Flowers solitary, or in open corymbs
　a. Flowers 1-2 cm. long
　　(1) Leaves needle-pointed
　　　(a) Leaves alternate, at least above; flowers
　　　　solitary　　　　　　　　　　*G. púngens*
　　　(b) Leaves opposite　　　　　　*G. Wátsoni*
　　(2) Leaves not needle-pointed; flowers in
　　　corymbs　　　　　　　　　　　*G. Nuttállii*
　b. Flowers 2-4 mm. long
　　(1) Corolla twice as long as the calyx　*G. tenérrima*
　　(2) Corolla little longer than the calyx
　　　(a) Stamens equally exserted　　*G. minutiflóra*
　　　(b) Stamens unequally exserted　*G. micrántha*

NAVARRÉTIA　Ruiz and Pavon 1794
(Named for Navarrete, a Spanish botanist)

Sepals 5, united into a prism-shaped or pyramid-shaped calyx, spiny-tipped, petals 5, white or yellow, united into a tubular funnelform or sal-verform corolla, stamens 5 on or below the throat of the corolla, ovary

PLATE 19

MORNING GLORIES—PHLOXES

POTATO FAMILY

1. Quincula lobata: Purple Ground-cherry
4. Solanum rostratum: Buffalo Bur

MORNING GLORY FAMILY

2. Ipomoea leptophylla: Bush Morning Glory

PHLOX FAMILY

3. Gilia aggregata
5. Polemonium speciosum
6. Polemonium pulchellum
7. Collomia linearis

PLATE 19.

2-3-celled, capsule 1-3-celled; flowers in dense terminal bracted clusters; leaves alternate, spiny and pinnately cut, or the lowest entire; annual.

1. Corolla yellow; leaves sticky   *N. Bréweri* '
2. Corolla white; leaves not sticky
    ɑ. Corolla 5-6 mm. long   *N. intertéxta*
    ɔ. Corolla 2-3 mm. long   *N. mínima*

PHLÓX Linné 1753 PHLOX
(Gr. phlox, flame, name of a red plant)
Pl. 20, fig. 2-4.

Sepals 5, united into a tubular or bell-shaped calyx, petals 5, blue, purple, red or white, united into a salverform corolla, with narrow tube, stamens 5, on the corolla tube, ovary 3-celled, style usually slender, ovules 1-4 in each cavity, fruit an ovoid 3-valved capsule, flowers in terminal cymes or cyme-like panicles; leaves opposite, entire or some of the upper ones alternate; annual or perennial.

1. Leaves densely to sparsely woolly; cushion plants
    a. Corolla tube much longer than calyx
        (1) Leaves awl-shaped, prickly, sparsely woolly   *P. canéscens*
        (2) Leaves ovate, scarcely prickly, densely woolly   *P. bryoídes*
    b. Corolla tube about the length of the calyx   *P. Hoódii*
2. Leaves not woolly, but smooth, hairy, or the edge ciliate
    a. Leaves ciliate at the edge, sometimes glandular also; cushion plants
        (1) Leaves less than 1 cm. long; corolla about 1 cm. wide   *P. caespitósa*
        (2) Leaves 1-2 cm. long; corolla 1-2 cm. wide   *P. Kélseyi*
    b. Leaves little or not at all ciliate, but smooth, hairy or glandular
        (1) Leaves 1-2 cm. long; stems tufted, somewhat woolly, 1-4 in. high   *P. Douglásii*
        (2) Leaves 2-5 cm. long; stems rarely tufted, 4-15 in. high, often glandular   *P. longifólia*

POLEMÓNIUM Linné 1753 POLEMONIUM
(The Greek name of a plant)
Pl. 19, fig. 5-6.

Sepals 5, united into a bell-shaped calyx, petals 5, blue, white or yellow, united into a bell-shaped, or funnelform corolla, rarely wheel-shaped, stamens 5, inserted near the base of the corolla, ovary ovoid, capsule ovoid, obtuse, 3-valved; flowers in open or close cyme-like panicles; leaves alternate, pinnate; perennials or rarely annuals.

1. Corolla funnelform, 2-3 cm. long, its tube longer
    than calyx or limb
  a. Leaflets whorled, crowded
    (1) Flowers blue in a dense cluster   *P. confértum*
    (2) Flowers yellowish in an open often interrupted cluster   *P. c. mellitum*
  b. Leaflets two-rowed, often paired   *P. speciósum*
2. Corolla bell-shaped, 1-2 cm. long, its tube about
    the length of the calyx, and shorter than the
    limb
  a. Stems spreading, clustered, 1-12 in. high; stem
    leaves few   *P. pulchéllum*
  b. Stems erect, usually single, 2-4 ft. high, leafy *P. caerúleum*

CONVOLVULÁCEAE   MORNING GLORY FAMILY

Sepals 5, united, petals 5, united into a funnelform, salverform, or bell-shaped corolla, stamens 5, inserted low down on the tube of the corolla, ovary 2-3-celled with 2 ovules in each cell, or falsely 4-6-celled with a single ovule in each cell, entire or 2-4-divided, styles 1-3, fruit a 2-4-valved capsule or of 2-4 distinct carpels; flowers solitary or in axillary cymes; herbs with twining, trailing or erect stems, and alternate, entire to lobed or dissected leaves.

1. Low silvery-silky herb; styles 2, 2-forked   EVOLVULUS
2. Stems twining or trailing, or bushy and shrub-
    like; style 1
  a. Stigmas globose; flowers mostly blue to red IPOMOEA
  b. Stigmas oblong to linear; flowers white or
    pinkish   CONVOLVULUS

CONVÓLVULUS Linné 1753 BINDWEED
(Lat. *convolvo*, twine around)

Sepals 5, united, petals 5, pink, purple or white, united into a funnel- or bell-shaped corolla, stamens 5, inserted on the tube of the corolla, included, ovary with 1-2 cavities, ovules 4, style slender, stigmas 2, threadlike, oblong or ovoid, capsule globose or nearly so, 2-4-valved; flowers axillary, solitary or clustered; leaves 'entire, toothed or lobed, mostly heart- or arrow-shaped and stalked; perennial with trailing, twining or erect stems.

1. Base of the flower enclosed in 2 sepal-like bracts
   a. Leaves smooth, the basal lobes spreading   *C. sépium*
   b. Leaves hairy, basal lobes not spreading   *C. répens*
2. Base of the flower without sepal-like bracts.
   a. Leaves smooth, entire   *C. arvénsis*
   b. Leaves gray-hairy, more or less lobed   *C. incánus*

EVÓLVULUS Linné 1762 EVOLVULUS
(Lat. *e-*, not, *volvulus*, twining)

Sepals 5, united, petals 5, blue, pink or white, united into a funnel-form, bell-shaped or saucer-shaped corolla, stamens 5, on the corolla, ovary with 2 cavities, style 2-divided to the base or near it, each division deeply 2-cleft, stigmas thread-like, capsule globose to ovoid, 2-4-valved, 1-4-seeded; flowers axillary, solitary or in clusters; leaves small, usually entire; annual or perennial.

Stems 4-12 in. high; leaves oblong to spatulate, 5-20
  mm. long; flowers 6-12 mm. wide   *E. argénteus*

IPOMÓEA Linné 1753 MORNING GLORY
(Gr. *ips, ipos*, worm, *homoios*, like)
Pl. 19, fig. 2.

Sepals 5, united, petals 5, pink, red, blue, purple or white, united into a funnel- or bell-shaped corolla with a more or less plaited tube, stamens 5 on the tube of the corolla, included, ovary with 2-4 cavities and 4-6 ovules, style thread-like, included, stigmas 1 or 2, globose, capsule globose or ovoid, 2-4-valved; flowers axillary, solitary or clustered; leaves entire, heart-shaped or lobed; annual or perennial.

1. Plant bushy, 2-5 ft. high; leaves linear; flowers
   pink to red   *I. leptophýlla*
2. Plant trailing or climbing; flowers blue to purple
   or white
   a. Leaves entire, heart-shaped at base   *I. purpúrea*
   b. Leaves 3-lobed   *I. hederácea*

CUSCUTÁCEAE DODDER FAMILY

Sepals 5, separate or united, petals 5, united into a bell-shaped to cylindric tube, the latter usually containing fringed scales alternate with the lobes, stamens 5, alternate with the corolla lobes, ovary 2-celled, ovules

4, styles 2, rarely united below, capsule splitting or remaining closed; flowers usually in dense clusters; thread-like parasites with minute scales in place of leaves, twining about herbs or shrubs.

Cúscuta Linné 1753 Dodder

(Probably of Arabic origin)

Pl. 20, fig. 16.

Characters of the family.

1. Scales within the corolla projecting beyond the
    tube   ·   *C. umbelláta*
2. Scales included in the corolla
    a. Stigmas thread-like; fruit opening circularly *C. grácilis*
    b. Stigmas shield- or ball-like; fruit remaining
        closed
        (1) Sepals separate, with similar bracts below
            them
            (a) Flowers stalked, in loose clusters; bracts
                entire   *C. cuspidáta*
            (b) Flowers sessile, in dense rope-like clus-
                ters; bracts finely toothed   *C. glomeráta*
        (2) Sepals united
            (a) Flowers sessile or nearly so
                x. Scales within corolla tube ovate, fringed *C. arvénsis*
                y. Scales none or much reduced   *C. polygonórum*
            (b) Flowers stalked
                x. Tips of corolla lobes inflexed
                    (x) Fruit enclosed by the corolla   *C. indecóra*
                    (y) Fruit capped by the corolla   · *C. córyli*
                y. Tips of corolla lobes not inflexed
                    (x) Scales shorter than corolla-tube,
                        finely fringed all around   *C. cephalánthi*
                    (y) Scales equaling or exceeding the
                        corolla-tube, long-fringed at the
                        top   *C. Gronóvii*

SOLANÁCEAE   POTATO FAMILY

Sepals 5, united, petals 5, united into a saucer-, bell-, funnel-, salver-, or tube-shaped corolla, stamens 5, inserted on the tube and alternate with the lobes of the corolla, ovary with 2 cavities, ovules numerous, style slender, stigma terminal, fruit a berry or capsule; flowers solitary or

clustered; herbs, shrubs or vines with alternate or rarely opposite, entire,
toothed, lobed or dissected leaves.

1. Herbs
   a. Calyx inflated and balloon-like in fruit
      (1) Flowers purple, bell-shaped, erect   QUINCULA
      (2) Flowers yellow or yellowish, saucer-
              shaped, nodding   PHYSALIS
   b. Calyx not balloon-like in fruit
      (1) Corolla saucer-shaped
         (a) Fruiting calyx enclosing the fruit   CHAMAESARACHA
         (b) Fruiting calyx not enclosing the fruit SOLANUM
      (2) Corolla funnelform or salverform
         (a) Corolla lobes irregular, tube short   HYOSCYAMUS
         (b) Corolla lobes regular, tube long .
            x. Fruit prickly   DATURA
            y. Fruit smooth   NICOTIANA
2. Shrubs   .   LYCIUM

CHAMAESÁRACHA Gray 1876 GROUND SARACHA
(A hybrid, meaning ground Saracha)

Sepals 5, united into a bell-shaped calyx, somewhat enlarged in fruit
but not inflated, close-fitting to the berry, not exceeding the berry, petals
5, white or cream-colored, often tinged with purple, united into a saucer-
shaped corolla, stamens 5, inserted near the base of the corolla, style
slender, somewhat bent, stigma minutely 2-cleft, fruit a berry; flowers
solitary or in groups of 2-4 in the axils; leaves entire to pinnately cut,
the blade running down on the leaf-stalk; perennial.

Leaves lance-linear to obovate, entire to lobed, vari-
    ously **hairy**   *C. corónopus*

DATÚRA Linné 1753 THORN-APPLE, JIMSON WEED
(The Hindoo name)

Sepals 5, united into a long tube splitting circularly near the base
which is persistent below the prickly capsule, petals 5, white, purple or
violet, united into a funnel-shaped corolla, stamens 5, included or little
exserted, filaments thread-like, very long, inserted at or below the middle
of the corolla tube, ovary with 2 cavities or 4 by false partitions, style
thread-like, stigma slightly 2-lobed, capsule 4-valved from the top or
bursting irregularly; flowers solitary, erect, on short stalks; leaves alternate, stalked, entire, wavy-toothed or lobed; annual or perennial.

PLATE 20

PHLOXES—SNAPDRAGONS

PLANTAIN FAMILY

1. Plantago Purshii: Plantain

PHLOX FAMILY

2. Phlox bryoides
3. Phlox Kelseyi
4. Phlox longifolia
5. Gilia pungens
6. Giliá pinnatifida

WATERLEAF FAMILY

7. Hydrophyllum Fendleri: Waterleaf
8. Hydrophyllum capitatum

BORAGE FAMILY

9. Lappula texana
10. Lappula floribunda: Stickseed
11. Krynitzkia glomerata
12. Krynitzkia virgata
13. Krynitzkia sericea
14. Krynitzkia crassisepala

POTATO FAMILY

15. Physalis lanceolata: Ground Cherry

DODDER FAMILY

16. Cuscuta cuspidata: Dodder

SNAPDRAGON FAMILY

17. Chionophila Jamesii
18. Besseya plantaginea

1. Flowers white
   a. Flowers 3-4.5 in. long; pod nodding, bursting
      irregularly   *D. meteloídes*
   b. Flowers 6-8 in. long; pod erect, 4-valved   *D. stramónium*
2. Flowers violet; pod erect, 4-valved   *D. tátula*

HYOSCYÁMUS Linné 1753 HOG-BEAN
(Gr. *hyos*, hog, *kyamos*, bean)

Sepals 5, united into an urn- or narrowly bell-shaped calyx, with slender longitudinal grooves or channels, enlarged and enclosing the capsule in fruit, petals 5, greenish yellow with purple veins, united into a funnel-shaped corolla with unequal more or less spreading lobes, stamens 5, on the tube of the corolla, mostly exserted, ovary with 2 cavities, style slender, stigma globose, capsule splitting circularly above the middle; lower flowers solitary in the axils, the upper in a more or less 1-sided spike or raceme; leaves alternate, mostly lobed or pinnately cut; annual, biennial or perennial.

Stems 1-3 ft. high; leaves oblong to ovate in outline,
3-7 in. wide; flowers 1-2 in. wide   *H. níger*

LÝCIUM Linné 1753
(Named for the country Lycia)

Sepals 3-5, united into a bell-shaped calyx, persisting at base of the berry, petals 5, greenish to purple, united into a bell-shaped or funnel form corolla, stamens usually 5, ovary 2-celled, stigma globose or 2-lobed, fruit a globose to oblong berry; flowers solitary or clustered, axillary or terminal; leaves alternate, entire; shrub or woody vine, often spiny.

Stems 1-3 ft. high; leaves oblong to oblanceolate, 1-2 ·
in. long   *L. pállida*

NICOTIÁNA Linné 1753 TOBACCO
(Named for a French ambassador, Nicot)

Sepals 5, united into a tube-, or bell-shaped calyx, petals 5, white, yellow, greenish or purplish, united into a funnel-, salver-, or nearly tube-shaped corolla, the tube usually longer than the spreading lobes, stamens 5, inserted on the tube of the corolla, ovary with 2 (rarely 4) cavities, style slender, stigma globose, capsule 2-valved or sometimes 4-valved at the top; flowers in terminal racemes or panicles; leaves alternate entire or slightly wavy; annual or perennial.

1. Flowers day-blooming; leaves clasping   *N. trigonophýlla*
2. Flowers night-blooming; leaves stalked   *N. attenuáta*

PHYSÁLIS Linné 1753 GROUND CHERRY
(Gr. *physalis*, bubble, from the inflated calyx)
Pl. 20, fig. 15.

Sepals 5, united into a bell-shaped calyx, enlarged and bladdery-inflated in fruit, membranous, 5-angled or prominently 10-ribbed and netted-veined, wholly enclosing the pulpy berry, petals 5, yellowish or whitish, often with a darker brownish or purplish center, united into an open bell-shaped or rarely saucer-shaped corolla, stamens 5, inserted near the base of the corolla, ovary with 2 cavities, style slender, stigma minutely 2-cleft, fruit a berry; flowers solitary; leaves entire or wavy-toothed; annual or perennial.

1. Perennial, as shown by underground stems and
   buds
   a. Leaves sticky-hairy   *P. heterophýlla*
   b. Leaves smooth or hairy, but not sticky
      (1) Leaves smooth   *P. longifólia*
      (2) Leaves hairy
          (a) Hairs simple, not branched or star-
              shaped
              x. Fruiting calyx pyramidal, 5-angled and
                 base deeply sunken   *P. virginiána*
              y. Fruiting calyx ovoid, scarcely angled or
                 sunken at base ·   *P. lanceoláta*
          (b) Hairs branched or star-shaped
              x. Hairs branched on the lower surface *P. púmila*
              y. Hairs star-shaped   *P. Féndleri*
2. Annual; fruiting calyx sharply 5-angled; hairy
   or sticky   *P. pruinósa*

QUÍNCULA Rafinesque 1832 PURPLE GROUND-CHERRY
(Name unexplained, probably from *quinque*, five)·
Pl. 19, fig. 1.

Sepals 5, united into a bell-shaped calyx inflated in fruit, sharply 5-angled and netted-veined, enclosing the fruit, petals 5, purplish or violet, united into a flat corolla, 5-sided in outline, veiny, stamens 5, ovary with 2 cavities, fruit a berry; flowers on stalks, most commonly in pairs from the axils, sometimes solitary or in clusters of 3-5; leaves from wavy-margined to pinnately cut, somewhat fleshy; perennial.

Stems spreading or flat, 2-8 in. high; leaves spatulate
   to ovate, 1-3 in. long; flowers 2-3 cm. wide   *Q. lobáta*

SOLÁNUM   Linné 1753   NIGHTSHADE, BUFFALO BUR
(Lat. *sola*, solace, perhaps from use as medicine)
Pl. 19, fig. 4.

Sepals 5, united into a bell- or saucer-shaped calyx, petals 5, white, blue, purple or yellow, united into a saucer-shaped corolla, the lobes plaited, the tube very short, stamens 5, inserted on the throat of the corolla, ovary usually with 2 cavities, stigma small, berry mostly globose, the calyx either persistent at the base or enclosing it; flowers clustered; leaves entire, toothed or pinnately cut; annual or perennial.

1. Flowers white; plants not prickly
  a. Leaves entire to pinnatifid, annuals
    (1) Leaves entire to toothed; berries black *S. nigrum*
    (2) Leaves pinnatifid; berries green *S. triflórum*
  b. Leaves pinnate, of 7-9 leaflets; perennial from
    tubers *S. Jámesii*
2. Flowers yellow or blue; plants prickly
  a. Flowers yellow; fruit prickly; leaves pinnatifid *S. rostrátum*
  b. Flowers blue or violet, rarely white
    (1) Fruit prickly; leaves pinnatifid *S. heterodóxum*
    (2) Fruit smooth; leaves entire or toothed *S. elaeagnifólium*

HYDROPHYLLÁCEAE   WATERLEAF FAMILY

Sepals 5, united, petals 5, united into a funnelform, salverform, bell-shaped or saucer-shaped corolla, stamens 5, on the tube or base of the corolla, ovary 2-celled, or 1-celled with 2 placentae, styles 2, separate or partly united, capsule 1-2-celled; flowers in curved cymes, spikes or racemes, or rarely solitary; herbs with alternate or basal, rarely opposite leaves.

1. Styles 2; flowers solitary in the forks of the stem NAMA
2. Style 1, 2-cleft
  a. Flowers solitary; leaves opposite, at least the
    lower
    (1) Calyx with bracts between the sepals, not
      greatly enlarged in fruit NEMOPHILA
    (2) Calyx without alternating bracts, greatly
      enlarged in fruit MACROCALYX
  b. Flowers in clusters
    (1) Corolla lobes imbricate before the flower
      opens PHACELIA
    (2) Corolla lobes convolute HYDROPHYLLUM

HYDROPHYLLUM Linné 1753 WATERLEAF

(Gr. *hydro-*, water, *phyllon*, leaf, from the splotches on the leaf)

Pl. 20, fig. 7-8.

Sepals 5, united, petals 5, white, blue or purple, united into a tubular to bell-shaped corolla, each lobe with a linear appendage within, which extends to the base of the corolla, stamens 5, exserted, filaments hairy below or at the base, ovary 1-celled, hairy, styles united nearly to the summit, capsule 2-valved, seeds 1-4; flowers in terminal or lateral more or less curved cymes; leaves lobed, pinnately cut or divided; perennial or biennial.

1. Edge of leaflets toothed; flower stalks longer
    than leaf stalks   *H. Féndleri*
2. Edge of leaflets entire; flower stalks much short-
    er than leaf stalks   *H. capitátum*

MACROCÁLYX Trew 1761

(Gr. *makros*, large, *kalyx*, cup, calyx)

Sepals 5, united, much enlarged in fruit, petals 5, white or bluish, united into a bell-shaped or nearly cylindric corolla, usually with 5 minute appendages on the tube within, stamens 5, included, ovary 1-celled, styles united below, ovules 2-4 on each of the placentae; flowers solitary or in racemes; leaves opposite or alternate, pinnately divided or 1-3 pinnate; annual.

Stems hairy, 3-10 in. high; leaves pinnately divided;
    flowers white or bluish   *M. nyctélea*

NÁMA Linné 1753 NAMA

(Gr. *nama*, brook, referring to the habitat of some species)

Sepals 5, distinct, petals 5, white or blue, united into a shallow bell-shaped corolla, stamens 5, on the base of the corolla, ovary 2-celled (rarely 3-celled), style 2 (rarely 3) slender, stigma globose, capsule globose or ovoid; flowers in cyme-like clusters or racemes; leaves alternate, entire, sometimes with spines in their axils; perennial.

Stem 3-8 in. high, hairy; leaves linear; flowers small *N. angustifólium*

NEMÓPHILA Nuttall 1822 NEMOPHILA

(Gr. *nemos*, wood, *philos*, loving)

Sepals 5, united, with a turned-back or spreading appendage in each groove, petals 5, white, blue or variegated, united into a bell-shaped corolla. usually with 10 small appendages within at the base, stamens 5, included, ovary 1-celled, styles partly united, capsules 2-valved, seeds 1-4; flowers solitary, stalked, lateral or terminal; leaves alternate or opposite, mostly pinnately cleft or lobed; annuals.

Stems spreading or trailing; leaves lobed or divided;
　　flower whitish　　　　　　　　　　　　　　　　　*N. parviflóra*

PHACÉLIA　Jussieu 1789　PHACELIA

(Gr. *phacelos,* cluster)

Pl. 21, fig. 6.

Sepals 5, united, somewhat enlarging in fruit, petals 5, blue, purple, violet, or white, united into a bell-shaped, tubular or funnelform corolla, stamens 5, attached near the base of the corolla, ovary 1-celled, styles united below, capsule 1-celled, or falsely nearly 2-celled, 2-valved; flowers in terminal curved cymes or racemes; leaves alternate, entire, toothed lobed, pinnately cut or dissected, the lowest rarely opposite; annual or perennial.

　1. Leaves or some of them entire
　　a. Leaves oblanceolate to ovate, entire; perennial *P. heterophýlla*
　　b. Leaves linear to oblong, often lobed; annual *P. lineáris*
　2. Leaves coarsely toothed to pinnatifid
　　a. Leaves coarsely toothed　　　　　　　　　*P. integrifólia*
　　b. Leaves divided, often to the midrib
　　　(1) Flowers typically in 1-sided curved cymes;
　　　　　sticky annuals　　　　　　　　　　*P. glandulósa*
　　　(2) Flowers in an oblong spike; silky-hairy
　　　　　perennials　　　　　　　　　　　　*P. serícea*

BORAGINÁCEAE　BORAGE FAMILY

Sepals 5, united, petals 5, united, stamens 5, inserted on the tube or throat of the corolla and alternate with the lobes, ovary of 2 2-ovuled carpels, entire or the carpels commonly deeply 2-lobed, making it appear as of 4 1-ovuled carpels, style simple, entire or 2-cleft, fruit mostly of 4 1-seeded nutlets or of 2 2-seeded carpels; flowers in 1-sided spikes, racemes, flat-topped clusters or sometimes scattered; annual, biennial or perennial herbs or shrubs, with alternate, rarely opposite or whorled entire, usually rough or hairy leaves.

　1. Fruits bur-like, with hooked prickles; flowers
　　white to light blue　　　　　　　　　　　　LAPPULA

2. Fruits smooth or merely toothed
   a. Ovary of 4 nutlets
     (1) Flowers blue or bluish
       (a) Dwarf, 1-5 cm. high, with densely white
           woolly stems and basal leaves   ERITRICHIUM
       (b) Taller, 1-10 dm. high, not densely white
           woolly
         x. Nutlets attached laterally to a cone-like
           receptacle; very common   MERTENSIA
         y. Nutlets attached at their bases; rare MYOSOTIS
     (2) Flowers white to yellow or greenish
       (a) Corolla funnelform or salverform, the
           lobes spreading; style included
         x. Flowers mostly bright yellow to orange;
           nutlets attached at their bases   LITHOSPERMUM
         y. Flowers mostly white or greenish, rare-
           ly yellow; nutlets attached laterally KRYNITZKIA
       (b) Corolla tubular, lobes straight; style long
           exserted   ONOSMODIUM
   b. Ovary entire, not divided into 4 nutlets; flow-
     ers white
     (1) Style 2-cleft; stems repeatedly 2-forked COLDENIA
     (2) Style entire or none; stems not 2-forked HELIOTROPIUM

COLDÉNIA Linné 1753 COLDENIA

(Named for Colden, an English botanist)

Sepals 5, united, petals 5, white or pink, united into a funnelform or salverform tube, stamens 5, ovary 4-celled, stigmas 1-2, fruit of 4 nutlets; flowers in dense lateral and terminal clusters; leaves alternate, entire; annual.

Stems prostrate; leaves ovate or rounded, 4-10 mm.
long   *C. Nuttállii*

ERITRÍCHIUM Schrader 1820 DWARF FORGET-ME-NOT

(Gr. *eri*, very, *trichios*, hairy)

Pl. 21, fig. 8.

Sepals 5, united, petals 5, white or blue, united into a salverform corolla, stamens 5, included, ovary 4-divided, style short, fruit of 4 nutlets; flowers in terminal spikes or racemes; leaves linear, entire, the lowest often opposite; annual.

PLATE 21.

1. Stems 1-3 in. high; leaves ovate to lanceolate,
   3-6 mm. long   *E. argénteum*
2. Stems 3-4 in. high; leaves linear, 10-15 mm. long *E. Howárdii*

HELIOTRÓPIUM Linné 1753 HELIOTROPE

(Gr. *helios*, sun, *tropos*, turn)

Sepals 5, united, petals 5, blue or white, united into a salver- or funnelform corolla, stamens 5, included, ovary entire or 2-4-grooved, style
terminal, short or slender, fruit 2-4-lobed, separating into 4 1-seeded
nutlets or 2 2-seeded carpels; flowers small, in one sided spikes or scattered; leaves alternate, mostly entire and stalked; annual.

1. Flowers solitary, white, 1.5-2 cm. long; leaves
   ovate to lanceolate, hairy   *H. convolvuláceum*
2. Flowers in 1-sided spikes, white with yellow eye,
   3-5 mm. long; leaves linear to spatulate   *H. curassávicum*

KRYNÍTZKIA Fischer & Meyer 1841

(Named for Krynitzki, a Russian botanist)

(Allocarya, Cryptanthe, Oreocarya)

Pl. 20, fig. 11-14; Pl. 21, fig. 2.

Sepals 5, united, petals 5, white, united into a salverform corolla,
stamens 5, included, ovary 4-divided, style short, fruit of 4 nutlets; flowers in terminal spikes or racemes; leaves linear, entire, the lowest often
opposite; annual or perennial.

1. Leaves alternate
   a. Calyx open in fruit; calyx and pedicel persist-
      ent
      (1) Fruit globose to ovoid   *K. Jámesii*
      (2) Fruit oblong-pyramidal
          (a) Corolla tube longer than calyx, and
              twice longer than corolla lobes; calyx
              with yellowish hairs and bristles
              x. Corolla white   *K. fulvocanéscens*
              y. Corolla yellow or yellowish   *K. leucopháea*
          (b) Corolla tube not longer than calyx, and
              hardly longer than corolla lobes
              x. Leaves of the flower cluster several
                 times longer than the short flower
                 branches; stems strict; flower cluster
                 oblong   *K. virgáta*

y. Leaves of the cluster equalling or much
    shorter than the flower branches
    (x) Stems tufted, spreading, 2-8 in.
        high; lower leaves gray, often
        silky, upper yellowish, bristly   *K. sericea*
    (y) Stems rarely tufted, erect, 8-15 in.
        high; leaves grayish green, usu-
        ally very bristly   *K. glomeráta*
b. Calyx mostly closed in fruit; fruit, calyx and
    pedicel falling off together
    (1) Nutlets of the fruit margined by a wing   *K. pterocárya*
    (2) Nutlets not winged
        (a) Nutlets or some of them, roughened or
            warted   *K. crassisépala*
        (b) Nutlets smooth   *K. Pattersóni*
c. Calyx splitting circularly in fruit, the lobed
    top falling away; stems 1-5 in. high, white-
    hairy; leaves linear   *K. circumscissa*
2. Leaves opposite, at least the lower; stems pros-
    trate, branched from the base, with single
    flowers for most of their length, 1-6 in. long   *K. califórnica*

LÁPPULA Moench 1794 STICKSEED
(Lat. *lappa*, bur, *-ula*, little)
Pl. 20, fig. 9-10; Pl. 21, fig. 9.

Sepals 5, united, petals 5, blue or white, united into a salver- or funnelform corolla, the tube very short, the throat closed by 5 scales, stamens 5, included, ovary 4-lobed, style short, fruit of 4 nutlets, the margins or backs armed with stout, often flattened, barbed prickles, the sides usually with small papillae; flowers in terminal racemes; leaves alternate, narrow, entire; annual or perennial.

1. Racemes with leafy bracts; fruits not deflexed
    a. Prickles in 1 row, distinct to variously fused *L. texána*
    b. Prickles in 2 rows   *L. láppula*
2. Racemes without leafy bracts; fruits deflexed
    a. Flowers 2-5 mm. wide; fruits 4-5 mm. wide *L. americána*
    b. Flowers 6-10 mm. wide; fruits 6-8 mm. wide *L. floribúnda*

LITHOSPÉRMUM Linné 1753 GROMWELL, PUCCOON
(Gr. *lithos*, stone, *sperma*, seed)
Pl. 21, fig. 3.

Sepals 5, united, petals 5, white, yellow, or blue, united into a funnel-

or salverform corolla, stamens 5, included, inserted on the throat of the corolla, ovary 4-divided, style slender or thread-like, stigma globose or 2-lobed, nutlets 4, or fewer, attached by their bases to the flat receptacles; flowers in leafy-bracted spikes or racemes; leaves alternate, entire, hairy or rough; annual or perennial.

1. Corolla lobes not toothed or fringed
  a. Corolla greenish-yellow, 6-10 mm. long; throat
    nearly naked   *L. pilósum*
  b. Corolla bright yellow to orange, 1-2 cm. long;
    throat crested
    (1) Corolla 6-8 mm. wide, bright yellow; at
      6-10000 ft.   *L. multiflórum*
    (2) Corolla 8-20 mm. wide, orange-yellow;
      at 3-5000 ft.
      (a) Stem and leaves soft gray-hairy; corolla
         tube naked at base within   *L. canéscens*
      (b) Stem and leaves rough hairy; corolla
         tube bearded at base within   *L. Gmelíni*
2. Corolla lobes toothed or fringed
  a. Corolla 2.5-4 cm. long; lobes fringed   *L. linearifólium*
  b. Corolla 8-20 mm. long; lobes toothed
    (1) Corolla 8-10 mm. long   *L. breviflórum*
    (2) Corolla 15-20 mm. long   *L. mandanénse*

MERTÉNSIA Roth 1797 MERTENSIA, FORGET-ME-NOT

(Named for Mertens, a German botanist)

Pl. 21, fig. 1, 5.

Sepals 5, united, petals 5, blue, purple or white, united into a tube-, funnel- or trumpet-shaped corolla, stamens 5, inserted on the tube of the corolla, included or scarcely exserted, ovary 4-divided, style thread-like, fruit of 4 nutlets, wrinkled when mature and attached above their bases; flowers in panicles, cymes or racemes; leaves alternate; perennial.

1. Filaments as long or longer than the anthers,
    and as broad; stems 6 in. to 5 ft. high, at 5-
    10000 ft.
  a. Calyx lobes oblong, obtuse, about ¼-⅕ the
    length of the corolla tube; stems 2-5 ft. high;
    leaves ovate   *M. sibírica*
  b. Calyx lobes lanceolate, acute, about ½-⅓ the
    length of the corolla tube; stems .5-2 ft.

high; stem leaves lance-ovate or spatulate
to linear
(1) Leaves lance-ovate to oblong, thin and
smooth; mostly in woodland   *M. praténsis*
(2) Leaves lanceolate, or oblanceolate to
linear, thickish, usually rough hairy;
mostly in open places   *M. lanceoláta*
2. Filaments much shorter and narrower than the
anthers; stems 2 to 12 in. high; at 10-14000 ft. *M. álpina*

MYOSÓTIS Linné 1753 FORGET-ME-NOT
(Gr. *mys*, mouse, *otis* ear, from the hairy leaves)
Pl. 21, fig. 4.

Sepals 5, united, petals 5, blue, pink or white, united into a salverform corolla, stamens 5, inserted on the corolla tube, included, ovary 4-
divided, style thread-like, fruit of 4 nutlets attached by their bases; flowers
in many-flowered elongated bractless more or less 1-sided racemes, or
sometimes leafy at the base; leaves alternate entire; annual, biennial or
perennial.

Stems 4-10 in. high; leaves soft-hairy, linear-oblong
to lanceolate   *M. alpéstris*

ONOSMÓDIUM   Michaux 1803   FALSE GROMWELL
(Of doubtful application)

Sepals 5, united, petals 5, yellowish or greenish white, united into
a tube- or funnel-shaped corolla, the lobes erect, the tube with a glandular 10-lobed band within at the base, stamens 5, inserted on the throat of
the corolla, included, ovary 4-parted, style thread-like, exserted, fruit
4 nutlets (commonly only 1 or 2 ripening), ovoid, shining, smooth, white,
attached by the bases; flowers in terminal leafy-bracted 1-sided spikes or
racemes; leaves alternate, entire, strongly veined; perennial.

Plants pale to green, hairy or shaggy, 1-3 ft. high;
leaves lance-ovate to oblong   *O. caroliniánum*

SÝMPHYTUM   Linné 1753   COMFREY
(Gr. *syn*, together, *phyo*, grow, from supposed healing properties)
Pl. 21, fig. 7.

Sepals 5, united, petals 5, yellow, blue or purple, united into a tubular
corolla, slightly dilated above, the throat with 5 crests below the lobes,

stamens 5, inserted on the corolla-tube, included, ovary 4-divided, style thread-like, fruit of 4 nutlets, slightly incurved, wrinkled, inserted by their bases; flowers in terminal simple or forked 1-sided racemes; leaves alternate, entire, those of the stem mostly clasping, the uppermost tending to be opposite, the lower long-petioled; perennial.

Stem 2-3 ft. high; leaves lanceolate to ovate, 3-8 in.
long; flowers 1-2 cm. long   *S. officinále*

SCROPHULARIALES SNAPDRAGON ORDER

SCROPHULARIÁCEAE SNAPDRAGON FAMILY

Sepals 4-5, united, petals 4-5, united into a 2-lipped or nearly regular corolla, stamens 2, 4 or 5, inserted on the corolla and alternate with its lobes, ovary with 2 cavities (or rarely 1), style slender, simple, stigma entire, 2-lobed or cleft, fruit usually a capsule; flowers mostly complete and irregular; herbs, shrubs or trees with opposite or alternate leaves.

1. Stamens 5, 1 usually without an anther
   a. Stamens with anthers 5   VERBASCUM
   b. Stamens with anthers 4, the fifth a filament
      only
      (1) Calyx deeply cleft; sterile filament con-
           spicuous; flowers usually blue or purple,
           2-4 cm. long   PENTSTEMON
      (2) Calyx lobed; sterile filament short; flow-
           ers white, 1-1.5 cm. long   CHIONOPHILA
2. Stamens with anthers 4, the fifth sometimes an
   inconspicuous scale or gland
   a. Sterile stamen a small scale or gland in the
      corolla tube
      (1) Flowers greenish-yellow or purplish in
           long terminal clusters   SCROPHULARIA
      (2) Flowers blue or blue and white, axillary COLLINSIA
   b. Sterile stamen wholly lacking
      (1) Corolla regular; stemless mud or water
           plants   LIMOSELLA
      (2) Corolla irregular, usually 2-lipped
         (a) Corolla with a spur at base   LINARIA
         (b) Corolla not spurred
           x. Corolla hardly 2-lipped; stamens not
              beneath an upper lip   GERARDIA

PLATE 22

SNAPDRAGON ORDER

SNAPDRAGON FAMILY

1. Veronica americana: Speedwell
2. Orthocarpus luteus
3. Veronica Buxbaumii: Speedwell
4. Mimulus Langsdorfii: Monkey Flower
7. Castilleia miniata: Painted Cup
8. Collinsia parviflora
9. Pedicularis canadensis
10. Linaria vulgaris: Butter and Eggs
11. Elephantella groenlandica: Little Elephant

BLADDERWORT FAMILY

5. Utricularia vulgaris: Bladderwort

BROOM-RAPE FAMILY

6. Thalesia uniflora

PLATE 22.

y. Corolla strongly 2-lipped; stamens beneath the upper lip
  (x) Bracts and often the calyx conspicuous and bright-colored
    m. Calyx 4-toothed; corolla lips somewhat equal   ORTHOCARPUS
    n. Calyx deeply cleft before and behind; upper corolla lip much longer than lower   CASTILLEIA
  (y) Bracts not conspicuous and bright-colored
    m. Calyx divided to the base, hence of 1 or 2 parts   CORDYLANTHUS
    n. Calyx usually toothed, sometimes 1-2-cleft also
      (m) Leaves entire or toothed
        r. Calyx 5-toothed, not inflated in fruit   MIMULUS
        s. Calyx 4-toothed, inflated in fruit   RHINANTHUS
      (n) Leaves pinnatifid; calyx not inflated
        r. Upper lip a long and trunk-like beak   ELEPHANTELLA
        s. Upper lip not long and trunk-like   PEDICULARIS
3. Stamens with anthers 2
  a. Corolla 4-lobed, almost regular; flowers blue or bluish   VERONICA
  b. Corolla 2-lipped or lacking
    (1) Calyx 5-divided, the parts almost separate   GRATIOLA
    (2) Calyx 4-parted   BESSEYA

BÉSSEYA Rydberg 1903 BESSEYA

(Named for the American botanist, Bessey)

(Synthyris Bentham)

Pl. 20, fig. 17.

Sepals 4, united, petals 4, purple, blue or pink, united into an oblong or bell-shaped corolla, more or less irregular, rarely wanting, stamens 2, inserted on the corolla, exserted, ovary with 2 cavities (rarely 3), style thread-like, stigma globose, fruit a capsule, compressed, obtuse or notched at the summit; flowers in terminal spikes or racemes; leaves alternate, sessile or clasping, the stem-leaves small and bract-like, the basal ones large and stalked; perennial.

1. Corolla present
    a. Leaves cleft to pinnatifid   *B. pinnatifida*
    b. Leaves merely toothed
        (1) Flowers reflexed; calyx lobes 2   *B. refléxa*
        (2) Flowers not reflexed; calyx lobes 3-4
            (a) Upper lip twice as long as calyx; corol-
                la purple; stems 2-6 in. high; at 11-
                14000 ft.   *B. alpina*
            (b) Upper lip but little longer that calyx;
                corolla white to yellowish or purple;
                stems 6-15 in. high; at 5-12000 ft.   *B. plantaginea*
2. Corolla lacking   *B. rúbra*

Castilléia   Mutis 1781   Painted Cup
(Name for Castillejo, a Spanish botanist)
Pl. 22, fig. 7.

Sepals united into a 2-cleft tubular calyx, usually colored like the corolla, petals red, yellow, purple or white, united into a very irregular 2-lipped corolla, its upper lip (hood or galea) arched, elongated, concave or keeled, compressed, entire, enclosing the 4 stamens, lower lip short, 3-lobed, stamens attached to the tube of the corolla, ovary with 2 cavities, style thread-like, stigma entire or 2-lobed, capsule ovoid or oblong; flowers in dense terminal leafy-bracted spikes, the bracts often brightly colored and larger than the flowers; leaves alternate; annual or perennial.

1. Annuals; leaves and bracts lance-linear, entire;
    hood much longer than the lip   *C. minor*
2. Perennials; upper leaves and bracts usually
    broadened and toothed or parted
    a. Calyx cleft much more deeply in front than
        behind
        (1) Corolla hood or galea about as long as the
            tube, and 6-10 times longer than the ob-
            scure lip; leaves linear, the uppermost
            and bracts 3-parted, red, rarely pale   *C. linarifólia*
        (2) Galea ⅓-½ as long as the tube; bracts
            yellowish or whitish

(a) Galea twice as long as the distinct, 3-cleft lip

  x. Corolla long exserted, about 2 in. long; leaves usually 3-5 cleft   *C. sessiliflóra*

  y. Corolla little exserted, about 1 in. long; leaves mostly entire   *C. breviflóra*

(b) Galea 4-5 times as long as the obscure lip; bracts yellowish; leaves linear, entire or 3-cleft   *C. fláva*

b. Calyx about equally cleft before and behind

(1) Stems with a close gray felt of hairs; bracts broad, entire or 3-toothed to deeply 3-cleft; corolla hood or galea usually shorter than tube   *C. intégra*

(2) Stems smooth or hairy but not gray-felted; bracts variable

(a) Galea nearly equal to or longer than the corolla tube, 4-8 times as long as the lip; bracts red to whitish

  x. Corolla 3-5 cm. long, much exserted   *C. miniáta*

  y. Corolla 2-3 cm. long, little exserted   *C. parviflóra*

(b) Galea much shorter than the corolla tube, 2-3 times as long as the lip; bracts most variable, yellowish to purple or red

  x. Plants 8-24 in. high; bracts mostly yellowish; at 7-10000 ft.   *C. pállida*

  y. Plant 1-8 in. high; bracts mostly brownish to purplish or red; at 11-14000 ft.   *C. p. occidentális*

CHIONóPHILA Bentham 1846 CHIONOPHILA

(Gr. *chion*, snow, *philos*, loving, from its habitat)

Pl. 20, fig. 17.

Sepals 5, united into a funnelform calyx, petals 5, cream-colored, united into a tubular corolla with slightly dilated throat, 2-lipped, upper lip erect, barely 2-lobed, lower with convex densely bearded base forming a palate, 3-lobed, stamens 4 inserted on the corolla tube, ovary with 2 cavities; flowers in a dense spike; leaves entire mostly in a basal tuft; high-alpine dwarf perennial.

Stems 1-6 in. high; flowers 10-15 cm. long   *C. Jámesii*

COLLÍNSIA   Nuttall 1817   COLLINSIA
(Named for Collins, a botanist)
Pl. 22, fig. 8.

Sepals 5, united into a bell-shaped calyx, petals 5, blue, pink, white or variegated, united into a 2-lipped corolla with short tube, upper lip 2-cleft, lobes erect or curved backwards, lower lip larger, 3-lobed, the lateral lobes spreading or drooping, flat, the middle one folded, keel-like, enclosing the 4 stamens and thread-like style, stamens in pairs, united to the corolla tube, which bears a gland on the upper side near the base, ovary with 2 cavities, stigma small, head-like, or 2-lobed, capsule ovoid or globose, 2-valved, the valves 2-cleft; flowers in whorls or solitary in the axils; leaves opposite or whorled; winter-annual.

Stems spreading, 2-6 in. high; flowers 5-7 mm. long *C. parviflóra*

CORDYLÁNTHUS   Nuttall 1846
(Gr. *kordyle*, club, *anthos*, flower)

Sepals united into a spathe, green, as are also the bracts, petals 5, dull yellow or purplish, united into a tubular, 2-lipped corolla, stamens 4, ovary with 2 cavities, style hooked at tip; flowers in small terminal clusters or sometimes scattered; leaves alternate, narrow, entire or parted; annual.

1. Calyx of 2 parts
    a. Corolla yellow or yellowish, 10-12 mm. long   *C. ramósus*
    b. Corolla purplish, 20-25 mm. long   *C. Wrightii*
2. Calyx of 1 part; corolla purplish, 2 cm. long   *C. Kingii*

ELEPHANTÉLLA   Rydberg 1900   LITTLE ELEPHANT
(Gr. *elephas*, elephant, from the shape of the upper lip)
Pl. 22, fig. 11.

Sepals 5, united into a tubular calyx, petals 5, purplish, united into a 2-lipped corolla, upper lip hooded with a curved beak, lower lip, 3-lobed, lobes spreading, the middle one smallest, stamens 4 in pairs, within the hood of the corolla, ovary with 2 cavities, capsule compressed, oblique or curved, beaked; flowers in terminal spikes; leaves pinnately cut; perennial.

Stems 4 in.-2 ft. high; leaves lanceolate, 2-6 in. long,
    often red-brown   *E. groenlándica*

GERÁRDIA   Linné 1753   GERARDIA
(Named for the English herbalist, Gerard)

Sepals 5, united into a bell-shaped calyx, petals 5, purple, violet,

yellow, red or rarely white, united into a slightly irregular, bell- or funnel-shaped corolla, slightly 2-lipped, stamens 4 in pairs, inserted on the corolla, included, ovary with 2 cavities, style thread-like, capsule globose or ovoid; flowers in racemes or panicles, or solitary and axillary; leaves mainly opposite and sessile; annual or perennial.
Stems erect, 1-2 ft. high; leaves linear, 1-2 in. long;

 corolla 10-15 cm. long   *G. besseyána*

GRATÍOLA Linné 1753 HEDGE HYSSOP
(Lat. *gratia,* favor, *-ola,* small, from its reputed healing qualities)

 Sepals 5, united, into a slightly unequal calyx, petals 5, yellow or whitish, united into an irregular somewhat 2-lipped corolla, its tube cylindric, upper lip entire or 2-cleft, lower lip 3-lobed, stamens 2 perfect, 2 sterile (or these lacking), ovary with 2 cavities, style thread-like, stigma slightly 2-lobed, capsule ovoid or globose, 4-valved; flowers stalked, solitary in the axils; leaves opposite, entire or toothed; annual or perennial.
Stems 4-12 in. high; leaves oblong, 1-2 in. long; corol-

 la 8-12 mm. long   *G. virginiána*

LIMOSÉLLA Linné 1753 MUDWEED
(Lat. *limus,* mud, *sella,* seat, from its habitat)

 Sepals 5, united into a bell-shaped calyx, petals 5, white, pink or purple, united into an open bell-shaped nearly regular corolla with short tube, stamens 4, inserted on the corolla tube, scarcely exserted, ovary with 2 cavities at the base, 1 above, style short, stigma head-shaped, capsule globose or oblong, becoming 1-celled; flowers solitary at the ends of leafless stems arising from the ground; leaves basal, entire; floating or creeping tufted annuals.
Plants 1-4 in. high; leaves spatulate, 1-5 in. long, flow-

 ers 2-3 mm. wide   *L. aquática*

LINÁRIA Jussieu 1789 BUTTER-AND-EGGS, TOAD-FLAX
(Lat. *linaria,* flax-like, from the resemblance)
Pl. 22, fig. 10.

 Sepals 5, united, petals 5, yellow, white, blue, purple or variegated, united into an irregular, 2-lipped corolla, spurred at the base, the upper lip erect, 2-lobed, the lower spreading 3-lobed, its base produced into a palate often nearly closing the throat, stamens 4 in pairs, ascending, inserted on the corolla, included, ovary with 2 cavities, style thread-like, capsule ovoid or globose, opening by 1 or mostly 3-toothed pores or slits below the summit; flowers in terminal racemes or spikes; leaves alternate, entire, dentate or lobed, or the lower opposite or whorled; annual, biennial or perennial.

1. Flowers yellow and orange, 2-3 cm. long   *L. vulgáris*
2. Flowers blue and white, 8-12 mm. long   *L. canadénsis*

MÍMULUS Linné 1753 MONKEY FLOWER
(Gr. *mimos*, comic actor, from the grinning corolla)
Pl. 22, fig. 4.

Sepals 5, united into a 5-angled, 5-toothed calyx, the upper tooth usually the largest, petals 5, pink, violet or yellow, united into an irregular 2-lipped corolla, tube cylindric, upper lip erect or turned backwards, lower lip spreading, 3-lobed, the lobes rounded, stamens 4 in pairs, inserted on the corolla tube, ovary with 2 cavities, style thread-like, stigma 2-lobed, capsule oblong or linear, enclosed by the calyx; flowers axillary, solitary, stalked; leaves opposite mostly toothed; perennial.

1. Flowers yellow
   a. Upper calyx tooth largest; fruiting calyx in-
      flated
      (1) Stems spreading, rooting at the joints   *M. Géyeri*
      (2) Stems erect, not rooting at the joints
         (a) Corolla 2-3 cm. long; perennial   *M. Langsdórfi*
         (b) Corolla 6-10 mm. long; annual   *M.·Hállii*
   b. Calyx teeth equal or nearly so; fruiting calyx
      not inflated; leaves sticky, musk-scented
      (1) Corolla 2-4 cm. long; perennial   *M. moschátus*
      (2) Corolla 10-12 mm. long; annual   *M. floribúndus*
2. Flowers red to purple
   a. Corolla 1.5-5 cm. long
      (1) Corolla 1.5-2 cm. long; stigma funnelform   *M. nánus*
      (2) Corolla 3-5 cm. long; stigma 2-lobed   *M. Lewísii*
   b. Corolla 6-8 mm. long; stigma 2-lobed   *M. rubéllus*

ORTHOCÁRPUS Nuttall 1818 ORTHOCARPUS
(Gr. *orthos*, straight, *karpos*, fruit)
Pl. 22, fig. 2.

Sepals united into a tubular or bell-shaped calyx, 4-cleft or sometimes split down both sides, petals 5, yellow, white or purplish, united into a very irregular, 2-lipped corolla with slender tube, upper lip little if any longer than the 3-lobed 1-3-pouched lower one, stamens 4 in pairs, inserted in the corolla and ascending under the upper lip, ovary with 2 cavities, style thread-like, stigma entire, capsule oblong; flowers in bracted usually dense spikes, the bracts sometimes brightly colored; leaves mostly alternate; annual, rarely perennial.

1. Flowers yellow   *O. lúteus*
2. Flowers white to rose-purple   *O. purpureo-álbus*

PEDICULÁRIS Linné 1753 PEDICULARIS

(Lat. *pedicula*, louse)

Pl. 22, fig. 9.

Sepals 5, united into a tubular calyx, cleft on the lower side or sometimes also on the upper or 2-5-toothed, petals 5, yellow, red, purple or white, united into a strongly 2-lipped corolla, the tube cylindric, the upper lip (galea) compressed, concave or folded, sometimes beaked, the lower lip erect or ascending, 3-lobed, the lobes spreading or turned backwards, the middle one the smallest, stamens 4 in pairs, inserted on the corolla and ascending within the upper lip, ovary with 2 cavities, capsule compressed, oblique or curved, beaked; flowers in terminal spikes or spike-like racemes; leaves alternate opposite or rarely whorled, usually pinnately cut or lobed; annual, biennial or perennial.

1. Leaves pinnatifid or apparently pinnate
  a. Flowers yellowish, or yellow, rarely reddish
    (1) Upper lip or galea with a distinct curved
        beak; alpine plants   *P. Párryi*
    (2) Galea without a distinct beak
      (a) Leaves divided to the midrib, appearing
          pinnate; calyx 5-lobed
        x. Galea with 2 lateral teeth; flowers
          greenish; stems 2-6 ft. high   *P. procéra*
        y. Galea without lateral teeth; flowers yel-
          low; stems .5-1.5 ft. high   *P. bracteósa*
      (b) Leaves with rounded lobes about half-
         way to the midrib; calyx cleft on the
         lower side; stems low and spreading *P. canadénsis*
  b. Flowers purple or purplish
    (1) Galea with a long curved beak; calyx cleft
        below   *P. ctenóphora*
    (2) Beak none, or short and straight
      (a) Calyx teeth much shorter than tube;
         corolla 8-20 mm. long   *P. scopulórum*

(b) Calyx teeth and tube about equal; corolla 20-25 mm. long   *P. cystoptérides*
2. Leaves merely round-toothed
  a. Flowers white; beak of galea long and coiled   *P. racemósa*
  b. Flowers purple, rarely whitish; beak none   *P. crenuláta*

PENTSTÉMON   Solander 1789   PENTSTEMON, BEARD-TONGUE

(Gr. *pente*, five, *stemon*, stamen, from the sterile stamen)

Pl. 23, fig. 1-6.

Sepals 5, united, petals 5, blue, purple, red or white, united into an irregular 2-lipped corolla, tube elongated, more or less enlarged above, upper lip 2-lobed, lower lip 3-lobed, stamens 5 inserted on the corolla, included, 4 of them fertile and in pairs, the fifth sterile, ovary with 2 cavities, style thread-like, stigma globose, capsule ovoid, oblong or globose; flowers in terminal racemes or panicles; leaves opposite or rarely whorled, or the upper occasionally alternate; perennial.

1. Corolla red
  a. Corolla strongly 2-lipped
    (1) Pedicel and calyx sticky-hairy; anther cells split to middle only   *P. Brídgesii*
    (2) Pedicel and calyx smooth; anther cells split to base; leaves lance-linear   *P. barbátus*
  b. Corolla slightly 2-lipped, the lobes nearly equal; leaves lance-ovate   *P. Eátoni*
2. Corolla blue, purple, rose or white
  a. Stems shrubby and woody at base
    (1) Corolla 2-4 cm. long; leaves obovate to oblanceolate, usually toothed   *P. fruticósus*
    (2) Corolla 1-2 cm. long
      (a) Leaves lanceolate to lance-ovate, sharply toothed   *P. deústus*
      (b) Leaves linear to spatulate, entire
        x. Leaves obovate to oblanceolate   *P. caespitósus*
        y. Leaves linear
          (x) Flowers alternate, single on very short stalks   *P. linarioídes*
          (y) Flowers opposite, in twos on long stalks   *P. ambíguus*
  b. Stems herbaceous, often hard but not shrubby and twig-like at base ·

(1) Leaves linear thread-like, densely tufted
at base; flowers purple or white   *P. laricifólius*

(2) Leaves lance-linear to ovate or rounded

  (a) Stems single or few, erect, 6-24 in. high

    x. Corolla narrow, 1-2 cm. long

      (x) Flower verticillate in 1 to several
head-like clusters, making an interrupted spike, yellowish to
blue; sepals usually white-margined and toothed   *P. confértus*

      (y) Flowers not in a head-like cluster;
sepals mostly entire and not
white-margined; blue   *P. grácilis*

    y. Corolla widened into a throat, 2-4 cm.
long   *P. Hárbouri*

  (b) Stems many, clustered, spreading, mostly
2-6 ft. high, from a spreading rootstock

    x. Anthers long-hairy

      (x) Corolla swollen above, 2.5-4 cm.
long; stems glaucous   *P. stríctus*

      (y) Corolla scarcely enlarged, 1.5-2 cm.
long; stems finely hairy   *P. Fremóntii*

    y. Anthers smooth or sparsely short-hairy

      (x) Sterile stamen smooth; corolla 2.5-
4 cm. long   *P. glában*

      (y) Sterile stamen bearded

        m. Stems sticky-hairy above, at least
the pedicels and calyx

          (m) Stems smooth; pedicel and
calyx sticky-hairy; flowers
wine-colored to nearly black,
sometimes pale   *P. glaúcus*

          (n) Stems hairy or glandular

           r. Sterile filament densely beard-
ed; corolla rose to purple, 2-
3 cm. long   *P. cristátus*

           s. Sterile filament sparsely short-
bearded; corolla white 1.5-2
cm. long   *P. álbidus*

        n. Stems not sticky-hairy

          (m) Upper leaves and flower

PLATE 23.

bracts clasping, rounded or
broadly ovate, the base
heart-shaped

r. Stems 2-6 ft. high, glaucous;
leaves oval to round; flowers
4-5 cm. long   *P. grandiflórus*

s. Stems 1-2 ft.; leaves linear to
lance-ovate; flowers 1.5-3
cm. long

  (r) Flower cluster short, dense,
the ovoid bracts nearly
concealing the blue flow-
ers beneath; a plains
species   *P. Háydeni*

  (s) Flower cluster often 6-10
in. long, interrupted, the
bracts round, pointed,
small; flowers rose-pur-
ple; at 7-9000 ft.   *P. cyathóphorus*

(n) Upper leaves and flower bracts
not clasping and cordate,
lance-ovate to linear

r. Corolla 1.5-2 cm. long; stems
1-10 in. high, usually tufted;
leaves lance-linear to long-
linear

  (r) Flowers purple, sterile stamen densely bearded;
at 10-13000 ft.   *P. Hállii*

  (s) Flowers deep blue, sterile
stamen short-bearded;
at 3-6000 ft.   *P. angustifólius*

s. Corolla 2-4 cm. long; stems
mostly 1-5 ft. high

  (r) Leaves narrow, lanceolate
or oblanceolate to linear;
stems strict, tall, 2-5 ft.
high   *P. unilaterális*

  (s) Leaves broader, lance-ovate to ovate or oblong;
stems usually clustered,

         ascending or spreading,
         1-2 ft. high

h. Flowers rose-purple, or
     pink; sepals entire;
     leaves ovate, pointed,
     glaucous   *P. secundiflórus*

i. Flowers blue; s e p a l s
     toothed; leaves lance-
     ovate to oblong, usually
     green   *P. gláber*

RHINÁNTHUS Linné 1753 RATTLE-BOX
(Gr. *rhinos,* nose, *anthos,* flower, from the beaked form)

Sepals 4, united into a compressed calyx, much inflated, papery and veiny in fruit, petals 5, yellow, blue, violet or variegated, united into a 2-lipped corolla, the upper lip (galea) compressed, arched, minutely 2-toothed below the entire apex, the lower lip 3-lobed and spreading, stamens 4 in pairs, inserted on the corolla, ovary with 2 cavities, capsule round in outline, flat; flowers in terminal 1-sided, leafy-bracted spikes or solitary in the upper axils; leaves opposite; annual.

Stems .5-2 ft. high; leaves lance-oblong, 1-2 in. long;
     flowers 10-15 mm. long   *R. crus-gálli*

SCROPHULÁRIA Linné 1753 FIGWORT
(Named for its reputed value in scrofula)

Sepals 5, united, petals 5, purple, greenish or yellow, united into an irregular corolla, tube globose to oblong, the 2 upper lobes longer, erect, the lateral ones ascending, the lower spreading or turned backwards, stamens 5, inserted on the corolla, 4 of them fertile and in pairs, mostly included, the fifth sterile, reduced to a scale on the roof of the corolla tube, ovary 2-celled, style thread-like, stigma head-like or straight, capsule ovoid; flowers in terminal open or close clusters; leaves mostly opposite, large; perennial.

Stems 2-6 ft. high; leaves 2-6 in. long; flowers 6-8
     mm. long   *S. nodósa*

VERBÁSCUM Linné 1753 MULLEIN
(The Latin name)

Sepals 5, united, petals 5, yellow, purple, red or white, united into a flat or slightly saucer-shaped corolla, the lobes a little unequal, stamens 5, inserted on the base of the corolla, filaments of the 3 upper or of all 5 hairy, ovary with 2 cavities, style flattened at the summit, capsule globose to oblong, 2-valved, the valves usually 2-cleft at the apex; flowers in terminal spikes, racemes or panicles; leaves alternate, toothed, pinnately cut or entire; biennial or rarely perennial.

1. Plants densely woolly; flowers in long dense
       spikes   *V. tháarpsus*
2. Plants smooth or sparsely hairy; flowers in
       racemes   *V. blattária*

VERÓNICA   Linné 1753   VERONICA
(Named for St. Veronica)
Pl. 22, fig. 1, 3.

Sepals mostly 4, sometimes 5, united, petals 4, (rarely 5), blue, purple, pink or white, united into a saucer-shaped corolla, with very short tube and unequal lobes, the lower lobe commonly the narrowest, stamens 2, spreading, inserted on either side of the upper corolla lobe, ovary with 2 cavities, style slender, stigma globose, capsule compressed, sometimes very flat, notched, heart-shaped or 2-lobed; flowers terminal or axillary, solitary or in racemes or spikes; leaves opposite and alternate, rarely whorled; annual or perennial.

1. Flowers in terminal clusters
   a. Capsule oblong, notched; leaves sessile   *V. alpína*
   b. Capsule nearly round, broadly heart-shaped
       above; lower leaves petioled   *V. serpyllifólia*
2. Flowers solitary or clustered in the axils of the
   leaves
   a. Flowers solitary
       (1) Flowers white or whitish; leaves linear to
           oblong   *V. peregrína*
       (2) Flowers blue; leaves ovoid   *V. Buxbáumii*
   b. Flowers in racemes
       (1) Leaves ovate to lance-ovate
           (a) Stem leaves petioled   *V. americána*
           (b) Stem leaves sessile and often clasping *V. anagállis*
       (2) Leaves linear to lance-linear   *V. scutelláta*

PINGUICULÁCEAE   BLADDERWORT FAMILY

Sepals 2-5, united, petals 5, united into a 2-lipped corolla, the upper lip usually erect, concave or the sides plaited, entire or 2-lobed, lower lip larger, spreading or turned back, 3-lobed with nectar-bearing spur beneath, stamens 2, on the corolla, ovary with 1 cavity, ovoid or globose, style short or none, stigma 2-lobed, fruit a capsule; flowers solitary or in racemes on naked stems, flower stalks with small bracts; leaves basal and tufted, or borne on floating branching stems, or reduced to minute scales; aquatic or on moist ground.

UTRICULÁRIA Linné 1753 BLADDERWORT
(Lat. *utriculus,* bladder, from the leaf bladders)
Pl. 22, fig. 5.

Sepals 2, united, petals 5, purple or yellow, united into a 2-lipped corolla, upper lip erect and entire, lower lip larger, 3-lobed, spurred at the base, stamens 2 on the corolla, ovary 1-celled, fruit a capsule; flowers in racemes or solitary at the summits of slender leafless stems, the flower-stalks with 2 little bracts; leaves finely divided; herbs floating in the water or rooting in the mud, the floating species with stems bearing finely divided leaves and covered with minute bladders.

1. Corolla 12-15 mm. wide; leaf-bladders 4-5 mm. *U. vulgáris*
2. Corolla 4-6 mm. wide; leaf-bladders 1-2 mm.   *U. minor*

OROBANCHÁCEAE   BROOM-RAPE FAMILY

Sepals 4-5, united, petals 5, united into a more or less 2-lipped corolla, the tube cylindric or expanded above, stamens 4 in pairs, on the tube of the corolla and alternate with its lobes, a fifth rudimentary one occasionally present, ovary 1-celled, style slender, stigma disk-like, 2-lobed or sometimes 4-lobed, capsule 1-celled, 2-valved; flowers in terminal spikes, or solitary in the axils of the scales; erect brown, yellowish, purplish or nearly white root-parasites with leaves reduced to alternate appressed scales.

1. Flower-stalk or calyx with 1 or more bracts;
   flowers nearly sessile in spikes   OROBANCHE
2. Flower-stalk and calyx without bracts; flowers
   solitary on long stalks   THALESIA

OROBÁNCHE Linné 1753 BROOM-RAPE
(Gr. *orobos,* vetch, *anchone,* strangler, from its parasitic habit)

Sepals 2-5, united into a calyx split both above and below nearly or quite to the base, the divisions 2-cleft or rarely entire, or 2-5-toothed, petals 5, reddish, yellowish, violet or nearly white, united into a 2-lipped corolla, upper lip erect, notched or 2-lobed, lower lip spreading, 3-lobed, stamens 4 in pairs on the tube of the corolla, included, ovary with 1 cavity, style slender, commonly persistent until after the splitting of the capsule, stigma shield- or funnel-shaped, entire or 2-lobed; flowers in spikes or racemes; leaves reduced to scattered scales the color of the flowers; root parasites.

1. Corolla 1.5-2 cm. long; anthers smooth   *O. ludoviciána*
2. Corolla 2-2.5 cm. long; anthers woolly   *O. multiflóra*

THALÉSIA   Rafinesque 1818   BROOM-RAPE
(Named for the Greek philosopher, Thales)
Plate 22, fig. 6.

Sepals 5, united into a bell-shaped calyx, petals 5, yellowish, white or violet, united into a 2-lipped corolla, the tube elongated, curved, upper lip erect-spreading, 2-lobed, the lower spreading, 3-lobed, lobes all nearly equal, stamens 4 in pairs on the tube of the corolla, included, ovary with 1 cavity, ovoid, style slender, deciduous, stigma shield-shaped or transversely 2-lobed; flowers on long bractless stalks; leaves reduced to scattered scales the color of the flowers; root-parasites.

1. Stem nearly absent; flowers 1-4; calyx-lobes
   lanceolate   *T. uniflóra*
2. Stem 2-5 in. high; flowers 3-15; calyx-lobes triangular   *T. fasciculáta*

MARTYNIÁCEAE   MARTYNIA FAMILY

Sepals 4-5, united into a 4-5-cleft calyx, petals 5, united into a 2-lipped corolla, lobes nearly equal, the 2 upper ones exterior in the bud, stamens 4 in pairs on the tube of the corolla, fertile or the posterior pair sterile, ovary with 1 cavity, with 2 broad ovule-bearing surfaces, or with 2-4 cavities by false partitions, style slender, stigma 2-lobed, fruit various in the different genera; flowers in racemes; herbs with opposite leaves, or the upper sometimes alternate.

MARTÝNIA   Linné 1753   UNICORN PLANT
(Named for the English botanist Martyn)

Sepals 5, united into a bell-shaped, inflated calyx, petals 5, violet, purple, whitish or mottled, united into a funnel- or bell-shaped corolla, the lobes nearly equal, spreading, stamens 4 on the tube of the corolla, ovary with 1 cavity, the ovules in 1 or 2 rows on 2 broad places of attachment in the center of the cavity, fruit an incurved, beaked 2-valved capsule, somewhat fleshy without, fibrous and woody within, ridged below or also above, 4-celled; flowers in short terminal racemes; leaves opposite or alternate, long-stalked; strong-scented annual.

Stems creeping, 1-5 ft. long; leaves 4-12 in. wide;
   flowers 4-5 cm. long   *M. louisiána*

LAMIALES   MINT ORDER
VERBENACEAE   VERBENA FAMILY

Sepals 4-5, united, petals 4-5, united into a regular or 2-lipped corolla, the tube usually cylindric, stamens 4 in pairs on the tube of the corolla, rarely only 2 or as many as the corolla lobes and alternate with them, ovary with 2-4 cavities (rarely 8-10) with 1-2 ovules in each cavity, style terminal, simple, stigmas 1 or 2, fruit dry, separating at maturity into 2-4 nutlets; flowers in terminal or axillary clusters; herbs or shrubs with opposite, whorled or rarely alternate leaves.

1. Corolla 4-lobed; nutlets 2   LIPPIA
2. Corolla 5-lobed; nutlets 4   VERBENA

LÍPPIA   Linné 1753   LIPPIA
(Named for Lippi, a French naturalist)

Sepals 2-4, united into a small calyx, petals 4, pale blue, purple or white, united into a 2-lipped corolla, tube cylindric, lobes broad, spreading, often notched, stamens 4 in pairs, on the tube of the corolla, ovary with 2 cavities, 1 ovule in each, style short, stigma oblique or curved backward, fruit dry, separating into two nutlets; flowers in axillary or terminal spikes or heads; leaves opposite, sometimes whorled or rarely alternate; perennial.

1. Leaves linear-wedge-shaped, 2-8-toothed above   *L. cuneifólia*
2. Leaves lanceolate to oblong, many toothed   *L. lanceoláta*

VERBÉNA   Linné 1753   VERBENA, VERVAIN
(Lat. *verbena,* a sacred branch)
Pl. 24, fig. 7.

Sepals 5, united into a tubular, 5-angled, more or less unequally 5-toothed calyx, petals 5, variously colored, united into a salver- or funnel-form corolla, 2-lipped or regular, stamens 4 in pairs on the corolla-tube, (rarely 2) included, ovary 4-celled, 1 ovule in each cavity, style usually short, 2-lobed at the summit, one of the lobes stigmatic, fruit dry, mostly enclosed by the calyx, at length separating into 4 nutlets; flowers in terminal solitary or clustered spikes; leaves mostly opposite; annual or perennial.

1. Flowers 8-25 mm. long, 4-20 mm. wide, in flat-
     topped clusters
   a. Corolla 4-8 mm. wide; leaves .5-1 in. long   *V. ciliáta*
   b. Corolla 8-20 mm. wide; leaves 1-4 in. long
      (1) Corolla 8-10 mm. wide; leaves twice pin-
           natifid   *V. bipinnatífida*

(2) Corolla 12-20 mm. wide; leaves once pin-
nnatifid   *V. canadénsis*
2. Flowers 4-10 mm. long, 2-8 mm. wide, in spikes
  a. Bracts of spike longer than the flowers; stems
    spreading   *V. bracteósa*
  b. Bracts of spike small and inconspicuous; stems
    erect
    (1) Corolla 3-4 mm. wide; plants smooth or
      sparsely hairy   *V. hastáta*
    (2) Corolla 6-8 mm. wide; plants densely soft-
      hairy   *V. stricta*

LAMIACEAE   MINT FAMILY

Sepals 5 (rarely 4), united into a regular or 2-lipped calyx, petals 4-5, united into a mostly 2-lipped but sometimes regular corolla, upper lip 2-lobed or entire, lower lip 3-lobed, stamens 4 in pairs on the corolla-tube, sometimes 2, ovary 4-lobed or parted, each lobe or division with 1 ovule, style 2-cleft at the summit, fruit of 4 1-seeded nutlets; flowers variously clustered; aromatic herbs or shrubs; mostly with 4-sided stems and simple opposite leaves without stipules.

1. Stamens 2
  a. Corolla nearly regular, 4-5 lobed, white; leaves
    sharply toothed or cut   LYCOPUS
  b. Corolla 2-lipped, mostly blue to rose or purple
    (1) Flowers blue, in terminal racemes or
      spikes; calyx 2-lipped or 3-lobed   SALVIA
    (2) Flowers rose to purple, rarely white, in
      head-like or axillary clusters
      (a) Flowers 2-4 cm. long, in dense mostly
        terminal heads   MONARDA
      (b) Flowers 5-12 mm. long, axillary, soli-
        tary or few in a cluster   HEDEOMA
2. Stamens 4
  a. Calyx 2-lipped
    (1) Calyx cap-shaped, lips entire   SCUTELLARIA
    (2) Calyx lips toothed
      (a) Flower bracts large, round, purplish PRUNELLA
      (b) Flower bracts neither round nor purple
        x. Corolla apparently with one long lip TEUCRIUM
        y. Corolla clearly 2-lipped   CLINOPODIUM

b. Calyx more or less equally 4-5-toothed, rarely
  10-toothed
  (1) Corolla regular or nearly so, 4-cleft　　MENTHA
  (2) Corolla 2-lipped
    (a) Calyx 10-toothed; leaves white-woolly MARRUBIUM
    (b) Calyx 4-5-toothed
      x. Upper tooth much larger than the other
        4; flowers light blue in a dense termi-
        nal spike　　　　　　　　　　　　DRACOCEPHALUM
      y. Teeth equal in size or nearly so
        (x) Calyx swollen in fruit; flowers pur-
          ple, 10-12 mm. long　　　　　PHYSOSTEGIA
        (y) Calyx not swollen in fruit
          m. Calyx teeth rigid, spiny; corolla
            hairy　　　　　　　　　　LEONURUS
          n. Calyx teeth not rigid and spiny
            (m) Flowers in heads　　　MONARDELLA
            (n) Flowers not in heads
              r. Lower or outer stamens short-
                er than the inner
                (r) Anther halves parallel and
                  touching　　　　AGASTACHE
                (s) Anther halves spreading NEPETA
              s. Lower or outer stamens longer
                than the inner　　　STACHYS

AGÁSTACHE　Clayton 1762　GIANT HYSSOP
(Gr. *agan*, much, many, *stachys*, spike)

Sepals 5, united into a narrow bell-shaped, somewhat oblique, slightly
2-lipped calyx, petals 5, yellowish, purplish or blue, united into a strongly
2-lipped corolla, upper lip erect, 2-lobed, lower lip spreading, 3-lobed,
stamens 4 in pairs on the corolla-tube, the upper or inner pair longer, ovary
deeply 4-parted, style 2-cleft, nutlets ovoid, smooth; flowers in dense
terminal spikes; leaves toothed, mainly ovate, stalked; perennial.

1. Flowers blue; calyx-teeth acute; leaves gray beneath　　　　　　　　　　　　　　　　　　*A. anethiodóra*
2. Flowers pale violet or purplish; calyx-teeth long-
  pointed; leaves green beneath　　　　　　*A. urticifólia*

CLINOPÓDIUM　　Linné 1753　　WILD BASIL
(Gr. *klinos*, bed, *podion*, little foot)

Sepals 5, united into a 2-lipped, tubular or oblong calyx, upper lip

3-toothed, lower 2-cleft, petals 5, purple, pink or white, united into a 2-lipped corolla, upper lip erect, entire or notched, lower spreading, 3-cleft, stamens 4 in pairs on the corolla-tube, ovary deeply 4-parted, style 2-cleft, nutlets ovoid, smooth; flowers variously clustered; leaves entire or sparingly toothed; annual or perennial.

Flowers purple, pink or white, 5-7 mm. wide; leaves
    ovate   *C. vulgáre*

DRACOCÉPHALUM Linné 1753 DRAGON HEAD
(Gr. *drakon,* dragon, *kephale,* head, from the corolla)

Sepals 5, united into a tubular calyx, with the upper tooth much larger than the others, or 2-lipped, the upper 3 teeth more or less united, petals 5, blue or purple, united into a 2-lipped corolla, upper lip erect, notched, lower lip spreading, 3-lobed, stamens 4 in pairs on the corolla-tube, the upper or inner pair longer, ovary deeply 4-parted, style 2-cleft, nutlets smooth, ovoid; flowers in axillary or terminal bracted clusters; leaves toothed, entire or cut; perennial.

Flowers pale blue, 5-7 mm. wide; leaves lanceolate to
    oblong, sharply toothed   *D. parviflórum*

HEDEÓMA Persoon 1807 PENNYROYAL
(Corrupted from Gr. *hedysma,* sweetness)
Pl. 24, fig. 8.

Sepals 5, united into a tubular calyx, hairy in the throat, 2-lipped or nearly equally 5-toothed, petals 5, blue or purple, united into a 2-lipped corolla, the upper lip erect, entire, notched or 2-lobed, the lower spreading 3-cleft, perfect stamens 2, sterile stamens 2, minute or none, ovary deeply 4-parted, style 2-cleft, nutlets ovoid, smooth; flowers in axillary clusters crowded into terminal spikes or racemes; leaves entire or scalloped; annual or perennial, strongly aromatic and pungent.

1. Soft gray-hairy perennial; flowers 8-12 mm. long;
    2 lower calyx-teeth nearly twice as long as
    upper   *H. Drummóndii*
2. Rough-hairy annual; flowers 5-6 mm. long;
    calyx-teeth about equal   *H. híspida*

LEONÚRUS Linné 1753 MOTHERWORT
(Gr. *leon,* lion, *oura,* tail)

Sepals 5, united into a tube- or bell-shaped calyx with 5 rigid, awl-shaped or bristle-like teeth, petals 5, white or pink, united into a 2-lipped

PLATE 24

MINTS—VERBENAS

MINT FAMILY

1. Scutellaria resinosa: Skull-cap
2. Prunella vulgaris: Heal-all
3. Mentha canadensis: Brook Mint
4. Monarda fistulosa: Horse Mint
5. Salvia Pitcheri: Blue Sage
6. Stachys palustris: Woundwort
8. Hedeoma Drummondii

VERBENA FAMILY

7. Verbena bracteosa

PLATE 24.

PRUNÉLLA Linné 1753 SELF-HEAL, HEAL-ALL
(Of uncertain origin)
Pl. 24, fig. 2.

Sepals 5, united into a deeply 2-lipped calyx, closed in fruit, petals 5, purple or white, united into a 2-lipped corolla, upper lip entire, arched, lower lip spreading, 3-lobed, stamens 4, the lower or outer pair longer, ovary deeply 4-lobed, style 2-cleft; flowers in terminal spikes or heads with large, often colored bracts; leaves opposite, entire or toothed; perennial.

Leaves oblong to ovate, entire or toothed; flowers
blue, 8-12 mm. long   *P. vulgáris*

SÁLVIA Linné 1753 SAGE
(Lat. *salvus*, well, from its medical properties)
Pl. 24, fig. 5.

Sepals 5, united into a 2-lipped calyx, petals 5, blue or bluish, united into a 2-lipped corolla, the upper lip concave or arched, entire to 2-lobed, lower lip spreading, 3-lobed, stamens with anthers 2, ovary 4-lobed, style 2-cleft; flowers in racemes, or spikes; leaves opposite, entire to toothed; annual or perennial.

1. Flowers 2-3 cm. long; stems 2-6 ft. high; peren-
   nial   *S. Pítcheri*
2. Flowers 8-12 mm. long; .5-2 ft. high; annual   *S. lanceoláta*

SCUTELLÁRIA Linné 1753 SKULL-CAP
(Lat. *scutella*, flat dish, from the calyx)
Pl. 24, fig. 1.

Sepals 5, united into a swollen, 2-lipped calyx, lips entire, upper crested and usually falling in fruit, petals 5, blue to purple, united into a 2-lipped corolla, upper lip arched, the lower spreading, stamens 4, the lower or outer pair slightly longer, ovary deeply 4-lobed, style 2-cleft; flowers 1-3 in the axils or in spike-like racemes; leaves opposite, entire to toothed; annual or perennial.

1. Flowers 2-3 cm. long, solitary
   a. Stems 4-15 in. high; leaves usually sticky-hairy
      and entire; corolla much enlarged in the
      throat; in dry habitats   *S. resinósa*
   b. Stems 1-3 ft. high; leaves not sticky, toothed;
      corolla little enlarged; in wet habitats   *S. galericuláta*
2. Flowers 6-10 mm. long, in racemes; leaves ovate
   to lance-ovate, toothed   *S. lateriflóra*

STÁCHYS   Linné 1753   WOUNDWORT
(Gr. *stachys,* spike, from the flower-cluster)
Pl. 24, fig. 6.

Sepals 5, united into a 5-toothed calyx, petals 5, purple to bluish, united into a 2-lipped corolla, upper lip erect, concave, lower lip spreading, 3-lobed, stamens 4, lower or outer pair longer, ovary 4-lobed, style 2-cleft; flowers in terminal spikes; leaves opposite, toothed; perennial.

Leaves lance-oblong, toothed; flowers purplish to reddish, 10-15 mm. long   *S. palústris*

TEÚCRIUM   Linné 1753   GERMANDER, WOODSAGE
(Gr. *teukrion,* germander)

Sepals 5, united into an unequally 5-toothed calyx, petals 5, pink, purplish or white, united into an irregular 5-lobed corolla, the terminal lobe much the larger, the other lobes appearing lateral, giving the flower a one-lipped appearance, stamens 4, the lower or outer pair the longer, ovary 4-lobed, style 2-cleft; flowers in terminal spikes; leaves opposite, entire, toothed or cut; perennial.

1. Leaves pinnately cleft; flowers solitary, axillary *T. laciniátum*
2. Leaves toothed; flowers in terminal spikes   *T. canadénse*

ROSALES   ROSE ORDER

ROSÁCEAE   ROSE FAMILY

Sepals 5, rarely 4-9, united, and often grown together with the ovary, petals usually 5, separate from each other, more or less united with the calyx, or lacking, stamens usually many, separate, pistils 1-many, separate or sometimes united with the calyx, ovary 1-celled with 1-several ovules, fruit follicles or achenes; flowers regular, usually perfect, solitary or clustered; herbs or shrubs with alternate simple or compound leaves.

1. Herbs
   a. Pistils 2-3
      (1) Flowers yellow, perfect; calyx bristly   AGRIMONIA
      (2) Flowers white, dioecious; calyx not bristly ARUNCUS
   b. Pistils 5-many
      (1) Flowers white, rarely cream-colored or
          yellowish
         (a) Leaves simple, basal; fruits long-hairy DRYAS
         (b) Leaves compound
           x. Leaves of 3-5 leaflets
             (x) Leaflets always 3; stems leafless,
                usually with runners   FRAGARIA

   (y) Leaflets 3-5; stems trailing, leafy RUBUS
  y. Leaves pinnate of many leaflets; stems
    leafless HORKELIA
 (2) Flowers yellow, pink or purple, occasionally cream-colored or white
  (a) Stamens 5; pistils 5-10
   x. Petals white; leaves many-cleft into
     linear segments CHAMAERHODUS
   y. Petals yellow, small; leaves of 3 leaflets SIBBALDIA
  (b) Stamens 10-many; pistils many
   x. Styles long, persistent and usually
     hooked or plumy in fruit
    (x) Styles naked or plumy, bent or
      jointed; flowers yellow or purplish GEUM
    (y) Styles naked or plumy, straight, not
      jointed; flowers yellow or pink-
      purple SIEVERSIA
   y. Style short, falling away from the ripe
     achenes
    (x) Styles attached at the base of the
      achenes; leaflets not silvery-silky DRYMOCALLIS
    (y) Styles lateral, attached near the
      middle of the achene; leaflets sil-
      very-silky ARGENTINA
    (z) Styles terminal, attached near the
      tip of the achenes
     m. Flowers yellow POTENTILLA
     n. Flowers red-purple COMARUM
2. Shrubs
 a. Leaves simple
  (1) Flowers solitary, or 2-3 in a cluster
   (a) Petals white;
    x. Stamens and pistils many; leaves round-
     ish, 3-5-lobed RUBUS
    y. Stamens 10; pistils 5; leaves entire KELSEYA
   (b) Petals yellow
    x. Leaves 3-7-pinnatifid; style becoming
     long and plumy COWANIA
    y. Leaves 3-lobed at tip; style not long
     and plumy PURSHIA
   (c) Petals none

    x. Leaves opposite; stems spiny; style not
       plumy   COLEOGYNE
    y. Leaves alternate; stems not spiny; style
       long and plumy   CERCOCARPUS
  b. Flowers several-many in a cluster
    (1) Leaves 3-7-cleft; style becoming long and
       plumy   FALLUGIA
    (2) Leaves lobed, toothed or entire; style not
       plumy
      (a) Flowers in panicles
        x. Ovary and fruit 1-seeded   HOLODISCUS
        y. Ovary and fruit several-seeded   SPIRAEA
      (b) Flowers in corymbs or spikes
        x. Flowers in corymbs; leaves mostly 3-5-
          lobed; stems 1-6 ft. high   OPULASTER
        y. Flowers in spikes; leaves entire; stems
          dwarf, in mats   PETROPHYTUM
  b. Leaves compound
    (1) Flowers yellow; leaflets 5-7, entire   DASYPHORA
    (2) Flowers white
      (a) Flowers in a panicle; leaves twice-pin-
        nately dissected   CHAMAEBATIARIA
      (b) Flowers 1-few in a cluster; leaves pin-
        nate of 3-5 leaflets   RUBUS
    (3) Flowers rose to red, rarely white; leaves
       pinnate of 3-11 (usually 5-9) leaflets   ROSA

AGRIMÓNIA   Linné 1753   AGRIMONY
(Of uncertain origin)

    Sepals 5, forming a hemispheric to top-shaped tube with hooked
bristles above, petals 5, yellow, stamens 5-15, carpels 2, stigma 2-lobed,
fruit 1-2 achenes; flowers in spiked racemes; leaves alternate, odd-pinnate,
with smaller lobes between the larger leaflets; perennial.

Stems 1-5 ft. high; leaves hairy to smooth; flowers
6-12 mm. wide   *A. eupatória*

ARGENTÍNA   Lamarck 1778   SILVERWEED
(Lat. *argentinus*, silvery, from the leaves)

    Sepals 5, united into a concave tube with 5 alternating bracts, petals
5, yellow, stamens 20-25, pistils many, style thread-like, attached near the

middle of the ovary; flowers solitary, axillary; leaves odd-pinnate, leaflets 7-25; perennial by runners.

Stems spreading, with runners; leaves silky-silvery
below, smooth, hairy or silvery above *A. anserína*

ARÚNCUS Adanson 1763 GOATSBEARD
(Gr. *aryngos,* goatsbeard)

Sepals 5, united, petals 5, white, stamens many, inserted on the calyx, pistils usually 3, becoming smooth few-seeded follicles; flowers dioecious in panicled spikes; leaves 2-3-pinnate; perennial.

Stems 2-6 ft. high; leaves about 1 ft. long; flowers 2-4
mm. wide *A. silvéster*

CERCOCÁRPUS H. B. K. 1823 MOUNTAIN MAHOGANY
(Gr. *kerkos,* tail, *karpos,* fruit)
Pl. 26, fig. 7, 8.

Sepals 5, united into a narrow tube, contracted above, petals none, stamens 15-25 in 2-3 rows on the calyx, pistil 1, forming a hairy achene, style hairy, persistent, becoming long and plumy in fruit, seed 1; flowers perfect, axillary or terminal, solitary or clustered; leaves alternate, simple, leathery; shrubs.

1. Leaves toothed, hairy, oval to obovate or roundish *C. parvifólius*
2. Leaves entire, revolute, smooth, leathery, lance-
oblong to linear *C. ledifólius*

CHAMAEBATIÁRIA Maximowicz 1879
(Resembling Chamaebatia, a low bramble)

Sepals 5, united into a calyx, petals 5, white, stamens many, pistils 5, hairy, follicles leathery, 1-valved, united at the base; flowers in terminal leafy panicles; leaves leathery, twice-pinnately dissected; shrub.

Stems diffusely branched; leaves narrowly lanceolate *C. millefólium*

CHAMAERHÓDUS Bunge 1829 GROUND ROSE
(Gr. *chamae,* on the ground, *rhodon,* rose)

Sepals 5, united into a bell-shaped calyx, petals 5, white, stamens 5, opposite the petals, pistils 5-10, style inserted near the base of the ovary; flowers in a two-forking cyme-like cluster; leaves once or twice ternately many-cleft; perennial.

Stems 4-12 in. high; basal leaves forming a rosette;
petals obovate *C. erécta*

PLATE 25

ROSE FAMILY

1. Rosa acicularis: Rose
2. Potentilla gracilis
3. Sieversia turbinata
4. Sieversia ciliata
5. Dasyphora fruticosa
6. Drymocallis arguta

PLATE 25.

COLEÓGYNE Torrey 1853
(Gr. *koleos*, sheath, *gyne*, pistil)

Sepals 5, petals 5, yellow, stamens many, style lateral, hairy at base, achene somewhat flattened, smooth; flowers terminal; leaves simple, leathery; somewhat spiny shrub.

Stems much branched; leaves linear-oblanceolate;
flowers showy   *C. ramosíssima*

CÓMARUM Linné 1753
(The Greek name of the arbutus)

Sepals 5, united, with 5 bracts between them, petals 5, purple, stamens many on a hairy disk, pistils many, style lateral, achenes smooth, 1-seeded; flowers in cymes or solitary, terminal or axillary; leaves alternate, pinnate; perennial.

Stems prostrate; leaflets oblong to oval, 1-3 cm. long;
flowers 2-3 cm. wide   *C. palústre*

COWÁNIA Don 1825 CLIFF ROSE
(Named for Cowan, an English explorer)
Pl. 26, fig. 9.

Sepals 5, united into a top-shaped calyx, petals 5, yellow, stamens many, inserted in 2 rows with the petals on the calyx-tube, pistils about 5, hairy, partly enclosed in the calyx-tube, styles becoming long plumy tails; flowers solitary or few in a cluster, terminal; leaves simple, leathery; shrub.

Stems .5-3 ft. high; leaves wedge-shaped, whitish below, .5-1 cm. long; flowers about 1 cm. wide   *C. mexicána*

DASÝPHORA Rafinesque 1838
(Gr. *dasys*, hairy, *phora*, bearing, perhaps from the shaggy achenes)
Pl. 25, fig. 5.

Sepals 5, united into a salverform calyx with 5 alternating bractlets, petals 5, yellow, stamens about 20, style club-shaped, glandular above, inserted near the base of the ovary, stigma 4-lobed, achenes densely woolly as also the receptacle; flowers terminal, solitary or in few-flowered cymes; leaves pinnate of 5-7 leaflets; shrub.

Stems erect, .5-6 ft. high, rarely prostrate; leaflets oblong to oblanceolate, 1-3 cm. long; flowers 1.5-3.5
cm. wide   *D. fruticósa*

Drýas   Linné 1753   Dryas
(Gr. *dryas*, wood-nymph)
Pl. 26, fig. 1.

Sepals 8-9, united, petals 8-9, white or yellow, stamens many on the calyx, pistils many, style terminal, persistent, becoming long and plumy in fruit; flowers solitary on leafless stalks; leaves simple, white beneath; low, tufted, herbaceous shrub.

Stems in a dense carpet; flowers-stalks 1-8 in. high;
leaves oblong to obovate, 1-3 cm. long; flowers 2-3
cm. wide   *D. octopétala*

Drymocállis   Fournier 1868
(Gr. *drymos*, oak-wood, *kallis*, beauty)
Pl. 25, fig. 6.

Sepals 5, united into a saucer-shaped calyx with 5 alternating bractlets, petals 5, creamy-white to yellow, stamens 20-30, in 5 groups, style inserted near the base of the ovary, thickened and glandular a little below the middle and tapering at both ends, stigma tiny; flowers in cymes; leaves pinnate, usually sticky-hairy; perennial.

Stems .5-4 ft. high; leaves usually sticky-glandular,
more rarely smooth; flowers white, yellowish, or
yellow; petals shorter, equalling or longer than the
sepals   *D. argúta*

Fallúgia   Endlicher 1840
(Named for Fallugio, an Italian botanist)
Pl. 26, fig. 2.

Sepals 5, united into a top-shaped calyx, with alternate narrow bractlets, petals 5, white, stamens many, inserted in 3 rows with the petals upon the calyx, pistils several, enclosed in the calyx, style lateral, persistent, hairy at the base; flowers clustered; leaves pinnately-lobed; low shrub.

Stems .5-2 ft. high; leaves hairy, lobes linear, 3-10 mm.
long; flowers 1.5-3 cm. wide   *F. paradóxa*

Fragária   Linné 1753   Strawberry
(Lat. *fragum*, strawberry)

Sepals 5, forming a top-shaped tube with 5 alternating bracts, petals 5, white, stamens many, pistils many on a convex or globoid receptacle which becomes pulpy in fruit, styles lateral, achenes many, seed-like; flowers in corymbs or racemes on leafless stalks, perfect or dioecious; leaves alternate, basal, of 3-leaflets; perennial by runners.

1. Nutlets in distinct pits in the fleshy fruit   *F. virginiána*
2. Nutlets on the surface of the fleshy fruit   *F. vésca*

GÉUM Linné 1753 AVENS
(Lat. name of the avens)

Sepals 5, united into a hemispheric or obconic tube, usually with 5 alternating bracts, petals 5, yellow or rose-purple, stamens many, pistils many, style thread-like, straight or jointed, persistent, somewhat hairy or plumose below; flowers solitary or in cyme-like clusters; leaves deeply pinnatifid to odd-pinnate; perennial.

1. Flowers yellow, erect; style bristle-like in fruit; terminal leaflet wedge-shaped, obovate or heart-shaped   *G. strictum*
2. Flowers purple or purplish, nodding; style plumy in fruit   *G. rivále*

HOLODÍSCUS Maximowicz 1879 HOLODISCUS
(Gr. *holos*, complete, *diskos*, disk)

Pl. 26, fig. 5.

Sepals 5, united into a saucer-shaped calyx, petals 5, white, stamens 20 on a circular disk about the ovary, pistils 5, becoming 1-seeded hairy fruits; flowers in terminal panicles; leaves alternate, simple, toothed or lobed; shrub.

Stems 1-10 ft. high; leaves spatulate or wedge-shaped to obovoid or ovate, toothed or lobed, silky beneath, .5-4 cm. long   *H. dumósus*

HORKÉLIA Chamisso and Schlechtendal 1827
(Named for Horkel, a German botanist)

Sepals 5, united into a calyx with 5 alternating bracts, petals 5, white or yellow, stamens 5-20 inserted on the calyx-tube, style thread-like, inserted near the base, pistils few; flowers in cymes or panicles; leaves pinnate with 10-20 pairs of leaflets; perennial.

Stems 4-8 in. high; petals spatulate, shorter than the sepals   *H. Górdonii*

KÉLSEYA　Rydberg 1900

(Named for Kelsey, an American botanist)

Sepals 5, united into a hairy calyx, petals 5, white, stamens 10, inserted on the margin of the disk, pistils 5; flowers solitary and hidden at the ends of the branches; leaves simple, imbricated; tufted perennial.

Stems 3-4 in. high; leaves oblong-spatulate, 2-4 cm.
long　　　　　　　　　　　　　　　　　　　　　*K. uniflóra*

OPULÁSTER　Medicus 1799　NINEBARK

(Lat. name of the wild cranberry tree)

Pl. 26, fig. 4.

Sepals 5, united into a bell-shaped calyx, petals 5, white, on the throat of the calyx, stamens 20-40, inserted with the petals, pistils 1-5, stigma terminal, globose, pods 1-5, more or less inflated, 2-4-seeded, splitting when ripe; flowers in terminal corymbs; leaves simple, palmately lobed; shrub. Bushy, 1-6 ft. high; carpels mostly 2-3, somewhat inflated or compressed, as long or longer than the
calyx　　　　　　　　　　　　　　　　　　　*O. opulifólius*

PETRÓPHYTUM　Nuttall 1840

(Gr. *petra*, rock, *phyton*, plant)

Sepals 5, united into a silky-hairy calyx, petals 5, white, stamens many, pistils 3-5, styles hairy below, follicles 1-2-seeded; flowers in a short spike, leaves entire, crowded into a rosette; stems woody, tufted or matted.

Stems in a dense mat; leaves oblong-spatulate, 8-10
mm. long　　　　　　　　　　　　　　　　　*P. caespitósum*

POTENTÍLLA　Linné 1753　POTENTILLA, CINQUEFOIL

(Lat. *potens*, powerful, from reputed medical properties)

Pl. 25, fig. 2.

Sepals 5, united into a concave or hemispheric tube with 5 alternating bracts, petals 5, rarely 4, yellow, rarely white or purple, stamens many, seldom fewer, pistils many, style terminal, deciduous; flowers solitary or in cymes; leaves compound, digitate or pinnate; annual or perennial.

1. Flowers many in leafy cymes; leaves mostly of
　　3-5-leaflets, digitate; style swollen toward the
　　base; mostly annuals
　　a. Achenes with a large wart or swelling on the
　　　　side　　　　　　　　　　　　　　　*P. paradóxa*

b. Achenes without a swelling
    (1) Flowers mostly 8-12 mm. wide; stamens
        15-20   *P. monspeliénsis*
    (2) Flowers mostly 4-6 mm. wide; stamens
        5-10   *P. rivális*

2. Flowers fewer and cymes less leafy; leaves mostly of 5-many leaflets; style not swollen at the base, except in perennials with well-developed rootstock
  a. Leaflets digitate
    (1) Leaflets 3, white-woolly beneath; style
        swollen toward the base   *P. nívea*
    (2) Leaflets 5-many
      (a) Stems tufted, spreading, 1-4 in. high;
          leaflets 5, white-woolly beneath   *P. concínna*
      (b) Stems mostly erect, .5-3 ft. high; leaflets
          5-9
        x. Leaflets toothed or cleft to the base or
           nearly, smooth to white-woolly   *P. grácilis*
        y. Leaflets toothed or cleft little below the
           middle   *P. dissécta*
  b. Leaves pinnate, of 5-many leaflets
    (1) Leaflets 5-7, small, usually less than .5 in. *P. rubricáulis*
        long
    (2) Leaflets mostly 7-many, .5-3 in. long
      (a) Style not longer than the mature achene,
          swollen below; leaflets mostly cleft or
          divided, green to white-woolly   *P. pennsilvánica*
      (b) Style usually longer than the mature
          achene, hardly or not at all swollen
          below; leaves silky-white to felted or
          nearly green; leaflets toothed to divided
        x. Leaves mostly gray-woolly on one or
           both sides, more rarely green and
           smoothish; leaflets mostly 1-3 in. long *P. hippiána*
        y. Leaves mostly green and smooth, more
           rarely white-hairy; leaflets mostly .5-
           1 in. long
          (x) Leaflets toothed   *P. criníta*
          (y) Leaflets cleft or divided   *P. platténsis*

PÚRSHIA   DeCandolle 1816
(Named for Pursh, an early American botanist)
Pl. 26, fig. 6.

Sepals 5, united into a funnel-shaped calyx, petals 5, yellowish, stamens about 25 in 1 row, inserted with the petals on the calyx, pistils 1 or sometimes 2, fruit soft-hairy, tapering at both ends, exserted; flowers solitary or clustered, terminal; leaves clustered, simple, lobed; low shrub.
Stems prostrate or erect, 1-5 ft. high; leaves spatulate
   or wedge-shaped, 3-lobed, white-hairy beneath, 5-15
   mm. long   *P. tridentáta*

RÓSA   Linné 1753   ROSE
(Lat. *rosa*, rose)
Pl. 25, fig. 1.

Sepals 5, united into a cup- or urn-shaped calyx, petals 5, white, pink or red, stamens many, inserted on a hollow disk, pistils many, hairy, becoming achenes enclosed in the berry-like calyx-tube or hip; flowers solitary or in corymbs; leaves alternate, odd-pinnate; erect or climbing usually prickly shrub.

   1. Flowers usually several in a corymb; leaflets
       mostly 9-11   *R. arkansána*
   2. Flowers usually solitary; leaflets mostly 5-7
     a. Stems with 2-3 larger conspicuous spines at
       base of the leaf stalk
       (1) Flowers 3-5 cm. wide; fruits 7-10 mm.
         wide   *R. Woódsii*
       (2) Flowers 5-8 cm. wide; fruits 12-20 mm.
         wide, often prickly   *R. nutkána*
     b. Stems very spiny, but without larger conspicuous spines at the base of the leaf stalk; fruit
       globose to pear-shaped   *R. aciculáris*

RÚBUS   Linné 1753   RASPBERRY, BLACKBERRY
(Lat. name of the bramble, from *ruber*, red)
Pl. 26, fig. 3.

Sepals 5, united into a short broad tube, petals 5, mostly white, stamens many, inserted on the calyx, pistils many, rarely few, inserted on a convex or elongated receptacle, ripening into little drupes and forming an aggregate fruit, style nearly terminal; flowers terminal or axillary, solitary or in racemes or panicles; leaves alternate, simple and lobed, or of 3-7 leaflets; low shrub or vine, rarely herbaceous, usually prickly.

1. Leaves 3-5-lobed; fruit scarcely edible
    a. Flowers single   *R. deliciósus*
    b. Flowers several in a cluster   *R. parviflórus*
2. Leaves of 3-7 leaflets; fruit edible
    a. Stems woody and prickly ·   *R. strigósus*
    b. Stems herbaceous, not prickly   *R. americánus*

SIBBÁLDIA Linné 1753
(Named for Sibbald, a Scotch botanist)

Sepals 5, united into a slightly concave calyx with 5 alternating bracts, petals 5, yellow, small, stamens 5, on the margin of the hairy disk, pistils 5-10 on short hairy stalks, style lateral, achenes 5-10, smooth; flowers in cymes on nearly leafless stalks; leaves alternate, of 3 leaflets; tufted perennials from a woody base.

Stems tufted, mat-like, 2-8 in. long; flowers 3-6 mm.
    wide   *S. procúmbens*

SIEVÉRSIA Willdenow 1811 SIEVERSIA
(Named for Sievers, a Russian botanist)
Pl. 25, fig. 3, 4.

Sepals 5, united into a saucer- or urn-shaped calyx, petals 5, yellow or rose-purple, stamens many, pistils many, style thread-like, not jointed, often plumy throughout in fruit; flowers usually 3-8; leaves interrupted-pinnate with many small intermediate leaflets; perennial.

1. Flowers rose to purple, 3-8, style plumy in fruit *S. ciliáta*
2. Flowers yellow, erect, single; style not plumy   *S. turbináta*

SPIRAÉA Linné 1753 MEADOWSWEET
(Gr. *spiraia*, meadowsweet)

Sepals 4-5, united into a bell-shaped tube, petals 4-5, white to pink or purple, stamens 20-60, inserted with the petals on the calyx-tube; pistils 5 as a rule, follicles usually 5, 2-several-seeded; flowers in terminal or axillary clusters; leaves alternate, simple, pinnatifid or pinnate; shrub.

Stems 1-3 ft. high; leaves oval to elliptic, 1-3 in. long;
    flowers white or rose   *S. lúcida*

MALÁCEAE APPLE FAMILY

Sepals 5, united into a tube grown to the ovary, petals usually 5, on the calyx-tube, stamens many, rarely few, ovary 1-5-celled with 1-2 ovules in each cell, styles 1-5, fruit a pome, i. e. the fleshy calyx-tube enclosing the bony, papery or leathery pistils or carpels; flowers regular, perfect, solitary or in racemes or cymes; trees or shrubs with alternate, simple or pinnate leaves.

1. Leaves simple
   a. Flowers solitary, or in racemes or in 2-3-flow-
      ered umbels
      (1) Leaves oblong-ovate or round; flowers
         white   AMELANCHIER
      (2) Leaves linear-oblanceolate; flowers pink PERAPHYLLUM
   b. Flowers in corymbs; leaves double-toothed or
      3-5-lobed   CRATAEGUS
2. Leaves pinnate; flowers in compound cymes   SORBUS

AMELÁNCHIER Linné 1753 JUNEBERRY
(The Savoy name)
Pl. 26, fig. 10.

Sepals 5, united into a bell-shaped tube, somewhat fused with the ovary, petals 5, white, stamens many, inserted on the throat of the calyx, styles 2-5, united, ovary wholly or partly inferior, 4-10-celled, fruit a small 4-10-celled berry-like pome; flowers in racemes or rarely solitary; leaves alternate, simple, serrate or entire; shrub or tree.

Stems 1-12 ft. high; leaves entire or serrate, smooth
  or hairy   *A. alnifólia*

CRATAÉGUS Linné 1753 HAWTHORN
(Gr. *krataigos*, hawthorn, from *krataios*, tough, strong)
Pl. 26, fig. 11.

Sepals 5, united into a cup- or bell-shaped tube, fused with the ovary, petals 5, white or pink, inserted on the calyx, stamens many, ovary inferior or nearly so, 1-5-celled, styles 1-5, fruit a small, drupe-like pome, containing 1-5 bony carpels, each usually 1-seeded; flowers in terminal corymbs; leaves alternate, doubly toothed, lobed or pinnatifid; trees or shrubs.

Shrubs or trees, 5-30 ft. high; leaves broadly spatulate to obovoid, usually with sharp or round shallow
  lobes, finely toothed, 1-3 in. long, .5-2 in. wide   *C. rivuláris*

PERAPHÝLLUM Nuttall 1838
(Gr. *pera*, leather pouch, *phyllon*, leaf)
Pl. 26, fig. 12.

Sepals 5, united, petals 5, pink, stamens many, inserted with the petals on the calyx, ovary 2-celled, styles 2, fruit globose; flowers solitary or in sessile 2-3-flowered umbels; leaves clustered at the ends of the branches; low shrub.

Stems 2-6 ft. high; leaves linear-oblanceolate, toothed
   or entire; flowers pink   *P. ramosíssimum*

SÓRBUS Linné 1753 MOUNTAIN ASH
(Lat. name of the pear)

Sepals 5, united into an urn-shaped calyx, petals 5, white, stamens many, inserted with the petals on the calyx-tube, ovary inferior, styles usually 3, fruit a small red berry-like pome; flowers in terminal branched cymes; leaves alternate, pinnate, the leaflets toothed; trees or shrubs.

Trunks 10-30 ft. high; leaflets 7-15, serrate, oblong, 2-
5 cm. long; flowers 7-10 mm. wide   *P. sambucifólia*

PRUNÁCEAE PLUM FAMILY

Sepals 5, united into a bell-shaped tube, free from the ovary, petals 5, white or pink, stamens many, inserted with the petals on the calyx, pistil 1, 1-celled, becoming a fleshy 1-seeded fruit with a stone; flowers regular, usually perfect, solitary or in racemes, umbels or corymbs; trees or shrubs with alternate, simple, toothed leaves.

PRÚNUS Linné 1753 PLUM, CHERRY
(The Latin name)
Pl. 26, fig. 13-15.

Characters of the family.
1. Flowers in umbels, appearing with or before the
    leaves; fruit 12-30 mm. in diam.
    a. Low shrubs, 1-4 ft. high; leaves elliptic to
       spatulate, toothed; flowers 8-12 mm. wide   *P. púmila*
    b. Tall shrubs, 6-20 ft. high; flowers 12-25 mm.
       wide
       (1) Leaves ovate, long-pointed; fruit 20-30
         · mm. wide   *P. americána*
       (2) Leaves lanceolate, acute; fruit 12-20 mm.
         wide   *P. angustifólia*
2. Flowers in corymbs or racemes, appearing after
    the leaves
    a. Flowers in corymbs, 12-15 mm. wide; fruit
       red   *P. pennsilvánica*

PLATE 27

PEA FAMILY

1. Thermopsis montana
2. Lupinus argenteus: Lupine
3. Petalostemon purpureus: Prairie Clover
4. Lathyrus ornatus: Sweet Pea
5. Vicia americana: Vetch

PLATE 27.

EDITH S. CLEMENTS. PINXT

b. Flowers in racemes, 8-12 mm. wide; fruit dark
purple to black *P. demissa*

MIMOSACEAE   SENSITIVE PLANT FAMILY

Sepals 3-6, united, petals 3-6, alike, separate or united, stamens 3-12 or many, separate or united, ovary 1-celled, ovules several to many, fruit a legume; flowers regular in heads, spikes or racemes; herbs with alternate, twice-pinnate leaves; perennial.

1. Leaflets closing when touched; petals united
   about halfway; pod spiny   SCHRANKIA
2. Leaflets hardly sensitive to touch; petals separate; pod smooth   DESMANTHUS

DESMÁNTHUS   Willdenow 1806   SENSITIVE PLANT
(Gr. *desmos,* band, *anthos,* flower)
(Acuan Medicus)

Sepals 5, united, petals 5, greenish or whitish, separate or nearly so, stamens 5 or 10, pod linear, flat, several-seeded, opening by 2 valves; flowers in axillary stalked heads; leaves twice pinnate, with many leaflets; perennial.

Stems 1-4 ft. high; pods many in a head, oblong-
curved, 1-2 cm. long   *D. illinoénsis*

SCHRÁNKIA   Willdenow 1896   SENSITIVE BRIER
(Named for Schrank, a German botanist)

Sepals 4-5, united, petals 4-5, pink to purple, united about halfway, stamens 8-12, separate or united at the base, pod linear, spiny, several-seeded, opening by 4 valves; flowers perfect or polygamous in axillary stalked heads or spikes; leaves twice pinnate, sensitive, of many leaflets; perennial.

Stems spreading, prickly, 2-4 ft. long; flower heads
10-25 mm. wide; pods densely spiny, 4-5 cm. long *S. uncináta*

CASSIACEAE   SENNA FAMILY

Sepals 5, separate or united, petals 5, separate, stamens 10 or less, separate or united, ovary 1-celled, fruit a legume, usually opening by 2 valves; flowers somewhat irregular in ours; annual or perennial herbs with solitary or clustered, alternate, simple or pinnate leaves.

1. Leaves once pinnate, not dotted with glands   CASSIA
2. Leaves twice pinnate, usually black-dotted   HOFFMANSEGGIA

CÁSSIA Linné 1753 PARTRIDGE PEA
(Gr. *cassia*, spice, from the Semitic)
(Chamaecrista Moench)
Pl. 29, fig. 2.

Sepals 5, united, petals 5, yellow, somewhat irregular, clawed, stamens 10, sometimes 5, often some imperfect, pod linear-oblong, flat with several-many seeds; flowers solitary; leaves alternate, even-pinnate; annual.

Stem 1-3 ft. high; leaflets oblong, 1-2 cm. long; flowers 2-4 cm. wide   *C. chamaecrista*

HOFFMANSÉGGIA Cavanilles 1797
(Named for Hoffmansegge)
Pl. 29, fig. 1.

Sepals 5, united, petals 5, yellow, regular or nearly so, stamens 10, separate, pod flat, linear to ovate, curved or straight, several-seeded; flowers in terminal or lateral racemes; leaves alternate, twice pinnate; annual or perennial.

1. Leaves, flowers and fruits dotted with black
      glands; pods 2-2.5 cm. long, 1 cm. wide, 2-3-
      seeded   *H. Jámesii*
2. Plants without black dots; pods 3-4 cm. long, 5-8
      cm. wide, 9-10-seeded   *H. drepanocárpa*

FABÁCEAE PEA FAMILY

Sepals 4-5, united into a calyx, rarely 2-lipped, petals usually 5, rarely 1, of 3 kinds, the large upper one or standard, 2 lateral wings and 2 inter-mediate ones forming a keel, stamens 10, rarely 9 or 5, separate, all united or nine united, pistil 1, simple, usually 1-celled but becoming 2-many-celled in fruit by cross partitions, ovules 1-many, fruit a legume, splitting by 2 valves, or indehiscent, occasionally a loment; flowers usually perfect, ir-regular, solitary or clustered; herbs, vines or shrubs with alternate usually compound leaves.

1. Herbs
   a. Leaves simple or apparently so   ASTRAGALUS
   b. Leaves of 3 leaflets
      (1) Leaflets entire
         (a) Stamens all separate from each other;
               flowers large, yellow   THERMOPSIS
         (b) Stamens with 9 united into a tube

   x. Pod several-seeded, splitting; leaves
      not dotted
      (x) Flowers 1-2 in a cluster   Lotus
      (y) Flowers several-many in a cluster   Astragalus
   y. Pod 1-seeded, not splitting; leaves dot-
      ted with glands   Psoralea
  (2) Leaflets toothed
   (a) Flowers in long tapering racemes   Melilotus
   (b) Flowers in loose spikes or dense heads,
      the latter rarely 2-few-flowered
   x. Flowers in loose spikes; pods coiled or
      curved, often spiny   Medicago
   y. Flowers in dense heads, rarely 2-few-
      flowered; pods straight   Trifolium
c. Leaves of 5-many leaflets
  (1) Leaflets dotted with glands
   (a) Leaves digitate, of 5 leaflets   Psoralea
   (b) Leaves pinnate, of 5-many leaflets
   x. Pod with hooked prickles   Glycyrrhiza
   y. Pod not prickly
      (x) Stamens 10; flowers pea-like   Dalea
      (y) Stamens 5; flowers not pea-like Petalostemon
  (2) Leaves not dotted with glands
   (a) Leaves odd-pinnate, not tendril-tipped
   x. Pod much narrowed between the seeds,
      flat, necklace-like   Hedysarum
   y. Pod not narrowed between the seeds
      (x) Leaflets digitate, usually 5-11; sta-
         mens 10, all united   Lupinus
      (y) Leaflets pinnate
      m. Stamens 10, all separate from each
        other   Sophora
      n. Stamens 10, 9 united into a tube
        (m) Tip of the keel with a point or
          hook   Aragalus
        (n) Tip blunt or rounded, not
          pointed or hooked   Astragalus
   (b) Leaves even-pinnate, usually tendril-
      tipped
   x. Style thread-like, hairy-tufted at or near
      the apex   Vicia

   y. Style flattened, hairs down the inner
    face   LATHYRUS
  2. Shrubs or trees
   a. Leaflets dotted with glands, 8-25 pairs; flowers
    purple, small; petal 1   AMORPHA
   b. Leaflets not dotted, 4-7 pairs; flowers rose-
    pink, pea-like   ROBINIA

AMÓRPHA Linné 1753 AMORPHA, FALSE INDIGO

(Gr. *a-*, without, *morphe*, form, from the absence of 4 petals)

Pl. 29, fig. 4-5.

Sepals 5, united into a bell-shaped calyx, petal 1, violet, blue or white, standard erect, folded about the stamens and the style, wings and keel lacking, stamens 10, united below, ovary 2-celled, pod hardly opening, 1-2-seeded; flowers in terminal spike-like racemes; leaves odd-pinnate, the leaflets dotted with tiny glands; shrub.

  1. Stems 3-15 ft. high; leaflets 2-5 cm. long; pods
   usually 2-seeded   *A. fruticósa*
  2. Stems 1-3 ft. high; leaflets .5-1.5 cm. long; pods
   usually 1-seeded
   a. Leaflets densely gray-hairy, 21-49; flower-
    spikes usually several   *A. canéscens*
   b. Leaflets smooth, or nearly so, 13-19; flower-
    spikes solitary   *A. nána*

ARÁGALUS Necker 1790

(Possibly modeled after Astragalus, from Gr. *ara*, curse)

(Oxytropis DeCandolle; Spiesia Necker.)

Pl. 28, fig. 1; Pl. 29, fig. 11, 12.

Sepals 5, united into a nearly equally toothed calyx, petals 5, red, blue, yellowish or white, standard erect, wings oblong, keel with a distinct beak, stamens 10, 9 united, pod 1-2 celled, 2-valved; flowers mostly in racemes, spikes or heads; leaves odd-pinnate, typically hairy; mostly stemless perennials.

  1. Flowers 6-7 mm. long; pods hanging, 5-6 times
   as long as the calyx   *A. defléxus*
  2. Flowers 1-2 cm. long; pods not hanging, enclosed
   in the calyx, or 1-3 times longer

a. Leaflets of the leaf opposite
  (1) Pod enclosed in the calyx, or the tip projecting somewhat
    (a) Flowers 1-3, rarely 5, in a cluster, purple; pod in the inflated calyx   *A. múlticeps*
    (b) Flowers several in a dense head or spike; pod filling the calyx and often breaking it
      x. Mature calyx split down one side; flowers violet with oblong wings   *A. lágopus*
      y. Mature calyx not split; flowers purple to white, with dilated wings   *A. nánus*
  (2) Pod much longer than the calyx
    (a) Pod bladdery-inflated, ovate; flowers violet, 2 in a cluster   *A. podocárpus*
    (b) Pod not bladdery-inflated
      x. Flowers 1-3 in a cluster; pods oblong; leaflet pairs 7-9   *A. Párryi*
      y. Flowers several to many in a head or spike
        (x) Flower stalk and cluster somewhat sticky-hairy; leaflet pairs 10-25   *A. víscidus*
        (y) Flower stalk and cluster not sticky-hairy
          m. Flowers 15-30 mm. long, red-purple to blue or white; leaflets silky or silvery to nearly smooth, lance-oblong to linear   *A. Lambérti*
          n. Flowers 10-15 mm. long
            (m) Flowers purple or violet   *A. montícola*
            (n) Flowers yellow or yellowish
              r. Leaflets 8-13; flowers 3-8 in a cluster; calyx black-hairy   *A. alpícola*
              s. Leaflets 25-31; flowers many in a dense cluster; calyx white-silky   *A. villósus*
b. Leaflets irregularly crowded, in whorls; plants silvery-silky, 6-18 in. high; flowers blue, 10-15 mm. long, in a long densely silky spike *A. spléndens*

PLATE 28

PEA FAMILY

1. Aragalus Lamberti: Loco Weed
2. Medicago sativa: Alfalfa
3. Trifolium dasyphyllum: Clover
4. Psoralea tenuiflora
5. Trifolium nanum: Dwarf Clover
6. Astragalus hypoglottis
7. Robinia neo-mexicana: Locust

PLATE 28.

EDITH S. CLEMENTS. PINXT

ROCKY MOUNTAIN FLOWERS

COCKAYNE, BOSTON

ASTRÁGALUS Linné 1753 ASTRAGALUS

(Greek name of a related plant)

Pl. 28, fig. 6; Pl. 29, fig. 13-28.

Sepals 5, united into a 5-toothed tube, petals 5, white, pink, red, blue or yellow, standard erect, wings oblong, keel blunt, stamens 10, 9 united, ovary 1-2-celled, many-seeded, pod 1-2-celled, fleshy to papery or woody, splitting or remaining closed; flowers in racemes or spikes, rarely solitary; leaves alternate, odd-pinnate, digitate or rarely simple; perennial or annual.

I. Leaves simple or of 3 leaflets
  1. Leaves simple or apparently so, rarely of 3-5 leaflets or at first pinnate
    a. Leaves simple, or rarely of 3-5 leaflets
      (1) Flowers purple; racemes several-flowered; stems tufted or mat-like; leaves silky   *A. caespitósus*
      (2) Flowers yellowish; stems 1-2 ft. high; leaves smooth   *A. asclepiadoídes*
    b. Leaves apparently simple, due to the falling of the pinnate leaflets   *A. júnceus*
  2. Leaves of 3 leaflets, silky-silvery; stems tufted
    a. Flowers purple
      (1) Flower cluster longer than the leaves; calyx partly enclosing the pod   *A. seríceus*
      (2) Flower cluster shorter than the leaves; calyx falling away   *A. tridactýlicus*
    b. Flowers yellowish to white; calyx enclosing pod   *A. triphýllus*
II. Leaves of 4-many leaflets, pinnate
  1. Pods 1-celled, cross wall wanting or imperfect
    a. Leaflets 4-6, spiny-pointed; flowers 1-3, yellowish to purple   *A. centrophýta*
    b. Leaflets not spiny-pointed, usually 6-many
      (1) Leaflets not jointed to the axis, but seeming continuous with it, rigid, linear and persistent; flowers white or yellowish; pods usually hanging, often horizontal or ascending   *A. pectinátus*
      (2) Leaflets distinctly jointed by a petiole to the axis, not persistent

(a) Pods 2-grooved above, the midrib and
    edges making 3 ridges, stalked·in the
    calyx, hanging

  x. Flowers violet, 10-15 mm. long; pods
    about 15 mm. long   *A. bisulcátus*

  y. Flowers white, purple-tipped, 7-10 mm.
    long; pods about 10 mm. long   *A. haydeniánus*

(b) Pods deeply grooved below, the midrib .
    much intruded

  x. Flowers white to yellowish; pods 2-3
    cm. long, stalk usually longer than
    the calyx

    (x) Stems and leaves long gray-hairy *A. Drummóndii*

    (y) Stems and leaves fine-hairy or
        smooth

      m. Calyx black-hairy; pod curved *A. scopulórum*

      n. Calyx white-hairy; pod mostly
        straight   *A. racemósus*

  y. Flowers purple; pods about 1 cm. long,
    stalk equal to or shorter than the calyx

    (x) Pod densely black-hairy; stalk
        equalling calyx   *A. alpínus*

    (y) Pod not black-hairy; stalk shorter
        than calyx or none

      m. Leaves ovate to rounded; pods
        mottled, little hairy   *A. sparsiflórus*

      n. Leaves oblong to linear; pods not
        mottled, often shaggy   *A. humistrátus*

(c) Pods not grooved above or below, the
    lower midrib intruded little if at all

  x. Pods distinctly to greatly inflated,
    papery; in one species less inflated
    and rather leathery, the upper midrib
    prominent

    (x) Stems very short or lacking

      m. Pods 6-15 mm. long, sessile, the
        upper midrib not acute and
        prominent

        (m) Pods mottled, globose, smooth,
           8-10 mm. wide; leaves linear
           to oblong   *A. jejúnus*

(n) Pods not mottled, hairy, ovoid,
6-15 mm. wide, leaflets lance-
oblong

   r. Leaflets 7-11; corolla whitish;
stalks 1-3-flowered; pods
ovate, 12-15 mm. long   *A. humíllimus*

   s. Leaflets 9-13; corolla violet to
white; stalks 5-12-flowered;
pods ovoid, 6-7 mm. long   *A. microcýstis*

n. Pods 2-3 cm. long, sessile, the upper midrib acute, prominent;
stalk of flower cluster none or
short to exceeding the leaves, the
latter lanceolate to ovoid, gray-
hairy; corolla yellow or yellowish   *A. lotiflórus*

o. Pods 5-7 cm. long, stalk short, oblong-ovate; flowers yellow to
white   *A. megacárpus*

(y) Stems 5-20 in. high

  m. Pods mottled with purple spots

    (m) Leaflets linear or thread-like,
some lacking, 1-5 cm. long;
pods ovoid, stalk equal to
calyx; flowers pale rose   *A. píctus*

    (n) Leaflets oval to roundish,
about 1 cm. long; pods
ovoid, stalk longer than
calyx, jointed; flowers whitish   *A. ártipes*

  n. Pods not mottled, though sometimes purplish

    (m) Pods smooth or nearly so

     r. Flowers white

      (r) Stalk of pod as long or
longer than the calyx;
clusters many-flowered *A. leptáleus*

      (s) Stalk of pod none; clusters
2-4-flowered   *A. americánus*

     s. Flowers purple; stalk of pod
short or none   *A. Eastwoódiae*

(n) Pods more or less hairy; flowers 3-15, yellowish or purp-
lish; leaves linear to ovate *A. triflórus*

y. Pods not inflated

(x) Pods with an incomplete cross wall,
caused by the intrusion of the
lower mid rib

m. Pods long-stalked

(m) Pods smooth; leaves linear to
lance-oblong; flowers white,
or tinged with violet

r. Pods papery; leaflets 7-13,
linear to lance-oblong; flow-
ers white, tinged with violet *A. aboríginum*

s. Pods leathery; leaflets 13-25,
obovoid; flowers yellowish   *A. Beckwithii*

(n) Pods black-hairy; leaves oblong to oval; flowers yel-
lowish, tinged with purple   *A. Macoúnii*

n. Pods not at all or scarcely stalked

(m) Wall of pod thin, soft and papery

r. Clusters many-flowered; flowers purple; leaves oval to
oblong   *A. élegans*

s. Clusters few-flowered; flowers
white or yellowish, purple-
tinged; leaves linear   *A. Brandégei*

(n) Wall of pod thick, stiff and
leathery or woody

r. Stems tall, 1-4 ft., smooth;
leaflets oblong to ovate; flowers white; pods tapering to
a short stalk-like base   *A. Pattersónii*

s. Stems low, tufted, 1-8 in. high;
leaves gray-hairy or silky

(r) Pods with long shaggy
wool

h. Flowers purple; leaves
nearly round, woolly   *A. utahénsis*

i. Flowers yellowish

        (h) Leaflets 3-7, obovate *A. Newbérryi*

        (i) Leaflets 9-17, lanceo-
            late to oblong   *A. Púrshii*

  (s) Pods short-hairy or smooth,
     not shaggy

    h. Stems and leaves long-
      hairy; leaflets obovoid;
      flowers various   *A. Párryi*

    i. Stems and leaves closely
      silky-hairy to nearly
      smooth

      (h) Leaflets smooth above
         or nearly so   *A. cibárius*

      (i) Leaflets silvery-silky;
         flowers violet to
         purple

        k. Pods tapering at the
          base   *A. amphióxys*

        l. Pods blunt at the base

        (k) Pods 1.5-2.5 cm.
           long, mostly
           straight   *A. missouriénsis*

        (l) Pods 3-5 cm. long,
          mostly curved *A. shortiánus*

(y) Pods without a trace of an intrud-
  ing partition

  m. Pods hard and woody

    (m) Flowers yellow; pods about 1
      cm. long   *A. flávus*

    (n) Flowers purple to whitish;
      pods 4-8 mm. long, more or
      less concave below   *A. grácilis*

  n. Pods papery to leathery

    (m) Stalk of pod usually twice as
      long as calyx; flowers white,
      12-15 mm. long; pods 2-4
      cm. long   *A. macrocárpus*

    (n) Stalk of pod usually shorter
      than calyx

    r. Pods flattened

(r) Stalk of pod distinct, 1-3
mm. long; pods 8-12 mm.
long; flowers white to
yellowish, purple-tinged,
keel rounded; leaflets 11-
21   *A. tenéllus*

(s) Stalk none or minute
  h. Pods oval to elliptic; pod
    8-12 mm. long; flowers
    purplish; leaflets 9-13   *A. wingaténsis*
  i. Pod oblong-linear to linear,
    15-30 mm. long; flow-
    ers yellowish to purple,
    keel beaked
    (h) Leaflets mostly thin
      and persistent, linear
      to elliptic   *A. campéstris*
    (i) Leaflets thickish, lin-
      ear, usually falling
      away, leaving the
      linear leaf-like axis *A. júnceus*
s. Pods nearly round, little if at
all flattened
  (r) Pods linear, 2-3 mm. wide;
    flowers white to purplish,
    8-10 mm. long   *A. flexuósus*
  (s) Pods oblong, 5-6 mm.
    wide; flowers purple
  h. Flowers 14-16 mm. long in
    a head; pods smooth   *A. Hállii*
  i. Flowers 8-10 mm. long in
    a loose raceme; pods
    finely hairy   *A. Féndleri*

2. Pods completely 2-celled
  a. Pods fleshy, plum-like, not splitting when ripe,
    2-4 cm. long; flowers deep red to purple or
    white; leaflets linear to oblong or obovoid   *A. crassicárpus*
  b. Pods papery and inflated, ovate, usually mot-
    tled, splitting when ripe, 1.5-3 cm. long;
    flowers purple to white or yellowish; leaflets
    obovate to elliptic or oblong   *A. diphýsus*

c. Pods neither fleshy nor inflated and papery
  (1) Pods linear-oblong, flattened, 12-25 mm.
    long, 2-3 mm. wide
    (a) Plants stemless or nearly so, silvery-silky *A. scapósus*
    (b) Plants stemmed, 3-15 in. high, finely
      hairy   *A. nuttalliánus*
  (2) Pods ovate to broadly oblong
    (a) Stems and leaves densely woolly or
      felted; leaflets 15-29; corolla purple
      x. Pods smooth   *A. mollíssimus*
      y. Pods densely woolly   *A. Bigelóvii*
    (b) Stem and leaves not densely woolly, but
      smooth or finely hairy
      x. Flowers yellowish to greenish; stems 1-
        5 ft. high; flowers spreading or re-
        flexed in a long cluster; pods smooth *A. caroliniáñus*
      y. Flowers blue to purple, more rarely
        whitish or yellowish, ascending, in a
        head-like cluster
        (x) Flower cluster ovoid; calyx black-
          hairy; leaflets mostly less than 1
          cm. long; pods with long spread-
          ing hairs   *A. hypoglóttis*
        (y) Flower cluster usually oblong; calyx
          white-hairy; leaflets 1-2 cm. long;
          pods with close gray or black hairs *A. adsúrgens*

DÁLEA Jussieu 1789 DALEA
(Named for Dale, an English botanist)
(Parosela Cavanilles 1802)
Pl. 29, fig. 6.

Sepals 5, united into an equally-toothed tube, petals 5, purple, red, yellow, or white, often long-clawed, wings and keel united below to the stamen-
tube, stamens 10 or 9, united, pod enclosed in the calyx, usually 1-seeded
and remaining closed; flowers in racemes or spikes; leaves odd-pinnate of
3-41 leaflets, dotted with tiny glands; herbs or shrubs.

  1. Flowers white, rose or purple, not yellow; plants
    mostly smooth
    a. Leaflets 5-13; flowers in a loose cluster
      (1) Stems shrubby; flowers rose-purple   *D. formósa*
      (2) Stems herbaceous

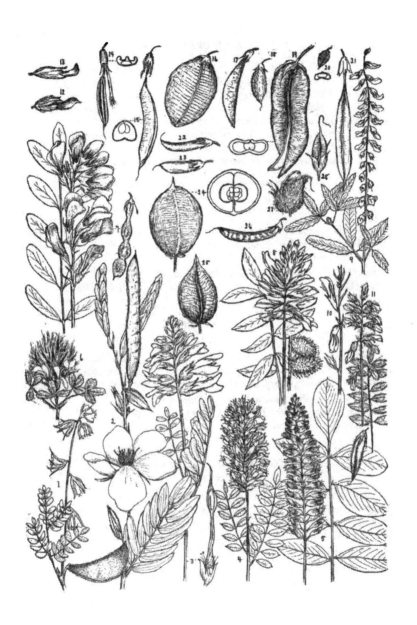

    (a) Flowers white   *D. enneándra*
    (b) Flowers red to purple   *D. lanáta*
  b. Leaflets 13-41; flowers in a dense spike, white
     or pink   *D. alopecuroídes*
2. Flowers yellow, or fading to purple
  a. Leaflets 3, palmate; flowers becoming purple   *D. Jámesii*
  b. Leaflets 5-7, sometimes 3, pinnate; flowers per-
     manently yellow or becoming purple   *D. aúrea*

GLYCYRRHÍZA   Linné 1753   WILD LIQUORICE
(Gr. *glykys,* sweet, *rhiza,* root)
Pl. 29, fig. 8.

Sepals 5, united into a tube, petals 5, white, stamens 10, 9 united, pod covered with prickles, remaining closed or nearly so; flowers in spikes; leaves odd-pinnate, of 11-19 leaflets; perennial.
Stems 1-4 ft. high; leaflets lanceolate to ovate, 2-4
  cm. long   *G. lepidóta*

HEDÝSARUM   Linné 1753
(Gr. *hedysaron,* the name of a vetch)
Pl. 29, fig. 7.

Sepals 5, united into a tube, petals 5, violet, purple, yellow or white, keel longer than the wings, stamens 10, 9 united, pod flat, constricted into joints; flowers in axillary racemes; leaves odd-pinnate of 11-23 leaflets.
Plants .5-3 ft. high, smooth or hairy; flowers blue to
  purple, yellow or white, 10-15 mm. long; calyx-teeth
  shorter to longer than the tube   *H. americánum*

LÁTHYRUS   Linné 1753   LATHYRUS, SWEET PEA
(Gr. *lathyros,* a kind of pulse)
Pl. 27, fig. 4.

Sepals 5, united into a tube, sometimes with slightly unequal teeth, petals 5, purple, blue, violet, yellowish or white, standard notched, wings and keel somewhat united, stamens 10, all united or 1 free, style hairy down the inner side, pod flat or somewhat rounded, splitting; flowers in racemes or sometimes solitary; leaves pinnate, of 6-12 leaflets, usually tendril-bearing at the tip; perennial.
1. Flowers purple, 2-3 cm. long; leaves with or with-
    out tendrils; leaflets linear to lanceolate or ob-
    long, mostly smooth, sometimes gray-hairy   *L. ornátus*

2. Flowers white, or yellowish, 12-20 mm. long
   a. Leaflets linear to oblong, 3-20 times longer
      than wide; stems erect, 4-12 in. high   *L. arizónicus*
   b. Leaflets ovate, mostly less than twice as long
      as wide, or rounded; stems climbing or trail-
      ing, 1-3 ft. high   *L. ochroleúcus*

Lótus Linné 1753 Trefoil
(The Greek for various plants)
Pl. 29, fig. 10.

Sepals 5, united into a tube, petals 5, reddish to yellow or white, stamens 10, 9 united, pod linear to oblong, somewhat flattened, splitting when mature; flowers solitary or clustered; leaves of 3 leaflets, rarely of a single leaflet; annual or perennial.
   1. Leaflets 3-5, oblong to linear; calyx teeth and
      tube about equal; keel not attenuate-curved;
      perennial   *L. Wríghtii*
   2. Leaflets 3, rarely 1 or 4, lance-ovate; calyx teeth
      much longer than the tube; keel attenuate-
      curved; annual   *L. purshiánus*

Lupínus Linné 1753 Lupine
(The Latin name)
Pl. 27, fig. 2.

Sepals 5, united into a 2-lipped calyx, petals 5, purple, blue, pink, white or yellow, standard with reflexed margins, wings oblong to obovate, keel incurved, stamens 10, united, ovary 1-celled, pod flattened, leathery; flowers in terminal spikes or racemes; leaves alternate, digitate, of 3-15 leaflets; perennial or annual.
   1. Low annuals, 2-8 in. high, with long hairs; pods
      mostly 1-2-seeded
     a. Racemes oblong to elongate; lower calyx lip
        entire or nearly so   *L. pusíllus*
     b. Racemes head-like; lower calyx lip 2-3-toothed *L. Kíngii*
   2. Perennials, usually 1-4 ft. high; pods mostly 3-8-
      seeded
     a. Plants low, tufted, often nearly stemless, 1-6
        in. high; flowers 5-7 mm. long   *L. caespitósus*
     b. Plants not tufted, 1-3 ft. high; flowers 6-18
        mm. long
       (1) Flowers 6-12 mm. long; calyx rounded to
           spurred; leaves smooth to hairy or silky *L. argénteus*

(2) Flowers 12-18 mm. long
   (a) Banner hairy   *L. seríceus*
   (b) Banner smooth or nearly so
     x. Leaflets 2-5 in. long, smooth or finely
       hairy   *L. Búrkei*
     y. Leaflets 1-2 in. long, more or less silky *L. ornátus*

Medicágo Linné 1753 Alfalfa, Nonesuch
(Gr. *medike*, alfalfa, Lat. *ago* like)
Pl. 28, fig. 2.

Sepals 5, united, petals 5, yellow or purple, stamens 10, 9 united, ovary 1-several-seeded, pod curved or spirally twisted, netted or spiny, remaining closed, 1-few-seeded; flowers in axillary heads or racemes; leaves alternate, of 3 toothed leaflets; annual or perennial.

  1. Flowers blue-purple, 5-7 mm. long; pods with 2-
     3 spirals   *M. satíva*
  2. Flowers yellow, 2-3 mm. long; pods with a partial
     spiral   *M. lupulína*

Melilótus Linné 1753 Sweet Clover
(Gr. *mel*, honey, *lotus*, a plant, from its fragrance)
Pl. 29, fig. 9.

Sepals 5, united, petals 5, white or yellow, stamens 10, 9 united, ovary with few ovules, pod usually remaining closed, with 1-few seeds; flowers in racemes; leaves of 3 toothed leaflets; annual or biennial.

  1. Flowers white, standard larger than wings   *M. álba*
  2. Flowers yellow, standard and wings equal   *M. officinális*

Petalostémon Michaux 1803 Prairie Clover
(Gr. *petalon*, petal, *stemon*, stamen, the two grown together)
(Kuhnistera Lamarck)
Pl. 27, fig. 3.

Sepals 5, united into a bell-shaped calyx with nearly equal teeth, petals 5, white to pink or purple, on long slender claws, standard large, wings and keel petals similar, their claws grown to the stamen-tube, stamens 5, ovary sessile, 2-ovuled; pod enclosed in the calyx, 1-2-seeded; flowers curiously irregular, not pea-like, in dense spikes or heads; leaves alternate, odd-pinnate, dotted with glands; perennial.

1. Flowers white
   a. Spike of flowers densely silky-hairy   *P. compáctus*
   b. Spike of flowers smooth; leaflets linear-oblong
       to spatulate or obovate   *P. cándidus*
2. Flowers rose-pink, rarely white
   a. Leaflets 3-5, linear; plants smooth or sparsely
       hairy   *P. purpúreus*
   b. Leaflets 7-17, linear-oblong to oblanceolate;
       plants densely hairy   *P. villósus*

PSORÁLEA   Linné 1753   PSORALEA

(Gr. *psoraleos*, scabby, from the dotted leaves)

Pl. 28, fig. 4.

Sepals 5, equal or the lower longest, united into a bell-shaped calyx, petals 5, white to blue, stamens 10, 9 or all united, pod ovoid, not splitting, 1-seeded; flowers in spikes or racemes; leaves digitate, of 1-5 leaflets; annual or perennial.

1. Flowers 4-8 mm. long, in racemes or open spikes;
      root not tuberous; stems 1-4 ft. high
   a. Plants densely silvery-silky; flowers in open
       spikes
      (1) Leaflets oblong to obovate; one calyx lobe
          much the longest   *P. argophýlla*
      (2) Leaflets linear to oblanceolate; calyx lobes
          nearly equal   *P. digitáta*
   b. Plants green or greenish, smooth or hairy;
       flowers in racemes or dense spikes
      (1) Plants smooth or nearly so; spikes short
          and dense; pods nearly round   *P. lanceoláta*
      (2) Plants finely gray-hairy; flowers in race-
          mes; pods ovoid to lance-ovate
         (a) Leaflets oblong to ovate or obovate   *P. tenuiflóra*
         (b) Leaflets narrowly linear   *P. linearifólia*
2. Flowers 10-16 mm. long, in dense spikes; root
      tuberous; stems mostly a foot or less high
   a. Plants with long spreading hairs
      (1) Stemless or nearly so; leaflets linear to
          oblong   *P. hypogaéa*
      (2) Stems 4-15 in. high; leaflets spatulate to
          obovate   *P. esculénta*

b. Plants with fine, closely appressed hairs
  (1) Plants low, nearly stemless   *P. mephítica*
  (2) Plants 1-2 ft. high   *P. cuspidáta*

Robínia Linné 1753 Locust
(Named for the brothers Robin)
Pl. 28, fig. 7.

Sepals 5, united into a tube, the 2 upper teeth also somewhat united, petals 5, white to rose, standard large, reflexed, stamens 10, 9 united, ovary stalked, ovules many, pod linear, flat, opening by 2 valves; flowers in axillary or terminal racemes; trees or shrubs with odd-pinnate leaves.
Shrubs 3-15 ft. high; leaflets oblong to elliptic; clusters large; flowers 15-25 mm. long   *R. neo-mexicána*

Sophóra Linné 1753 Sophora
(From the Arabic word for yellow)
Pl. 29, fig. 3.

Sepals 5, united into a bell-shaped tube, petals 5, white, stamens 10, distinct from each other or nearly so, ovary short-stalked, ovules many, pod stalked, terete, constricted between the seeds, usually remaining closed; flowers in terminal racemes or panicles; leaves odd-pinnate; perennial.
Stems 4-12 in. high; leaflets oblong to obovate, 5-15 mm. long; flowers 15-16 mm. long   *S. serícea*

Thermópsis R. Brown 1811 Thermopsis
(Gr. *thermos*, lupine, *opsis*, likeness)
Pl. 27, fig. 1.

Sepals 5, united, the 2 upper ones also sometimes united with each other, petals 5, yellow, stamens 10, separate, ovary sometimes short-stalked, ovules many, pod linear to oblong, flat, straight or curved; flowers in terminal or axillary racemes; leaves alternate of 3 leaflets; perennial.
1. Pods erect or ascending, straight or slightly curved *T. montána*
2. Pods horizontal, reflexed, strongly curved   *T. rhombifólia*

Trifólium Linné 1753 Clover, Alsike
(Lat. *tri-*, three, *folium*, leaf)
Pl. 28, fig. 3, 5.

Sepals 5, united into a bell-shaped calyx, petals 5, white, pink, red or yellow, usually persistent, stamens 10, 9 united, pod usually not splitting, 1-6-seeded; flowers in dense heads or spikes, often with an involucre; leaves of 3 leaflets, the latter toothed; annual or perennial.

1. Heads with a row of bracts at base, i. e., an involucre
   a. Plants tufted, mat-like, nearly stemless; bracts
   separate or nearly so
      (1) Leaflets entire, usually silky-hairy
         (a) Heads on a distinct, often long, stalk;
         bracts awl-shaped, often tiny   *T. dasyphýllum*
         (b) Heads nearly sessile; bracts 2, of 3 leaf-
         lets each   *T. andínum*
      (2) Leaflets toothed, smooth or nearly so;
         bracts oblong to obovate, blunt, en-
         tire   *T. Párryi*
   b. Plants with leafy stems, 4-20 in. high; bracts
   united, the lobes long-pointed and usually
   toothed; leaflets toothed, narrowly oblanceolate to obovate   *T. involucrátum*
2. Heads without an involucre
   a. Stems low, tufted; leaves basal
      (1) Flowers 1.2-3 cm. long; leaves smooth or
         nearly so
         (a) Flowers 1-3, 1.5-3 cm. long; leaflets
         mostly oblanceolate, toothed   *T. nánum*
         (b) Flowers mostly 10 or more, 12-15 mm.
            long
            x. Leaflets toothed, ovate to nearly round,
            1-1.5 cm. long   *T. Háydeni*
            y. Leaflets entire, elliptic to oblong, 1.5-2
            cm. long   *T. Brandégei*
      (2) Flowers 7-9 mm. long, several in a head;
         leaves hairy, ovate to oblong, toothed   *T. gymnocárpum*
   b. Stems leafy, scarcely tufted
      (1) Heads sessile; flowers red; leaves hairy   *T. praténse; red
         clover*
      (2) Heads on a distinct, often long, stalk
         (a) Stems creeping; heads white, on stalks
         3-6 in. high; leaves ovate to roundish,
         toothed   *T. répens; white
         clover*
         (b) Stems erect, .5-3 ft. high
            x. Cultivated or escaped from cultivation
            into roadsides and fields

    (x) Heads globose, pink to white; calyx
        and leaves smooth   *T. hýbridum; alsike*
    (y) Heads usually oblong to elongate,
        red; calyx and leaves hairy   *T. incarnátum; crim-*
                                          son clover

  y. Native; heads globose to oblong, yellow-
      ish, white or purplish; calyx usually
      long-hairy; leaflets lanceolate or ov-
      ate, hairy to smooth   *T. lóngipes*

Vícia Linné 1753 Vetch
(The Latin name)
Pl. 27, fig. 5.

    Sepals 5, united, the 2 upper somewhat longer, petals 5, blue, violet or yellow, rarely white, wings somewhat adherent to the keel, stamens 10, 9 or sometimes all united, style with a tuft of hairs at the tip, pod flat, splitting by 2 valves; flowers usually in axillary racemes; leaves alternate, pinnate, tendril-bearing; annual or perennial vines.

  1. Flowers 10-25 mm. long, 3-40 in a cluster, vari-
      ously blue-purple; leaflets linear to oblong or
      ovoid, smooth or hairy, round or truncate at
      tips; stipules various   *V. americána*
  2. Flowers 5-6 mm. long, 1-2 in a cluster, yellowish,
      with purple tip; leaflets linear to oblong   *V. prodúcta*

CRASSULÁCEAE STONECROP FAMILY

    Sepals 4-5, separate or united, free from the ovary, petals 4-5, distinct or slightly united at the base, rarely wanting, stamens 4-10, pistils 4-5, distinct or united below, ovules numerous in 2 rows, follicles 1-celled, splitting; flowers regular, usually in cymes, clusters often head-like; herbs with simple fleshy leaves.

  1. Stamens 8-10; flowers clustered; leaves fleshy
    a. Flowers pink to purple or dark red
      (1) Flowers pink, rarely white, axillary in
           racemes   Clementsia
      (2) Flowers purple to red-brown, terminal   Rhodiola
    b. Flowers yellow, in spreading 1-sided racemes Sedum
  2. Stamens 3-5; leaves hardly fleshy   Tillaeastrum

CLEMÉNTSIA Rose 1903
(Sedum Linné)
Pl. 30, fig. 1.

Sepals 4-5, united, petals 4-5, rose to nearly white, separate, stamens 8-10, pistils 4-5, separate or united at the base; flowers perfect, axillary in dense racemes, forming a head or spike-like cluster; leaves more or less crowded, fleshy, usually toothed; perennial.

Stems 4-18 in. high; leaves oblong to oblanceolate,
entire or toothed, 1-4 cm. long; petals lanceolate, 8-
15 mm. long   *C. rhodántha*

RHODÍOLA Linné 1753 KING'S CROWN
(Gr. *rhodon*, rose, perhaps from the rose-like odor of the root)
(Sedum Linné)
Pl. 30, fig. 3.

Sepals 4-5, united, petals 4-5, red-purple, separate, stamens 8-10, pistils 4-5, separate or united at the base; flowers polygamous or dioecious in a compound cyme, the latter dense and head-like; leaves crowded, fleshy, flat, entire or toothed; perennial.

Stems 1-25 cm. high; leaves obovate to oblong, entire
or dentate, .5-2.5 cm. long; flowers 4-8 mm. wide   *R. rósea*

SÉDUM Linné 1753 STONECROP
(Lat. *sedeo*, sit, from growing on walls and rocks)
Pl. 30, fig. 8.

Sepals 4-5, united, petals 4-5, yellow, separate, stamens 8-10, alternate ones usually attached to the petals, pistils 4-5, distinct or united at the base; flowers perfect as a rule, in terminal, usually 1-sided cymes; leaves alternate, often crowded, fleshy, entire or toothed; annual or perennial.

1. Leaves linear-cylindric; petals distinct
   a. Leaves flat above; stems branched at base, 5-12
      in. high   *S. Douglásii*
   b. Leaves round above; stems simple, tufted, 1-
      8 in. high   *S. stenopétalum*
2. Leaves elliptic to obovate; petals united at base *S. débilis*

TILLEÁSTRUM Britton 1903
(Named from its resemblance to Tillaea)

Sepals 3-5, united, petals 3-5, greenish, separate or united, stamens

PLATE 30.

3-5, pistils 3-5, separate, follicles few-several-seeded; flowers solitary or cymose, axillary or terminal; leaves fleshy, opposite, entire; aquatic or marsh herb.

Stems 1-6 cm. long; leaves linear-oblong, 4-6 mm.
  long; flowers 1 mm. wide   *T. aquáticum*

SAXIFRAGÁCEAE SAXIFRAGE FAMILY

Sepals mostly 5, united, free or grown to the ovary, petals 4-5, rarely none, stamens 4-10, pistils 1-several, often 2, separate or united, styles separate or united into one, fruit a capsule, follicle or berry; flowers perfect to dioecious, solitary or variously clustered; herbs or shrubs with alternate or opposite leaves.

1. Herbs
  a. Stamens with anthers 5, rarely 4
    (1) Leaves entire; flowers flat, saucer-shaped PARNASSIA
    (2) Leaves toothed or lobed; flowers bell-
        shaped
        (a) Petals cut or fringed   MITELLA
        (b) Petals entire
          x. Ovary 1-celled, 2-beaked; common   HEUCHERA
          y. Ovary 2-celled, 2-beaked; very rare SULLIVANTIA
  b. Stamens 8-10
    (1) Petals present; stamens 10
        (a) Petals entire   SAXIFRAGA
        (b) Petals 3-7-parted   LITHOPHRAGMA
    (2) Petals absent, sepals yellowish; stamens
        usually 8   CHRYSOSPLENIUM
2. Shrubs
  a. Stamens 8-10
    (1) Leaves alternate, lobed; ovary inferior;
        fruit a berry   RIBES
    (2) Leaves opposite, not lobed; ovary partly
        inferior; fruit a capsule
        (a) Leaves entire; flower solitary or 2-3;
          stamens 8   FENDLERA
        (b) Leaves toothed; flowers several in a
          cluster; stamens 10   JAMESIA
  b. Stamens many; ovary inferior; flowers large,
    white, solitary   PHILADELPHUS

CHRYSOSPLÉNIUM Linné 1753 GOLDEN SAXIFRAGE
(Gr. *chrysos*, gold, *splen*, spleen)

Sepals 4-5, united into an urn-shaped calyx, grown to the ovary, petals none, stamens 4-10, ovary 1-celled, 2-lobed, styles 2, capsule 2-lobed, 2-valved above; flowers tiny, greenish, solitary or clustered, axillary or terminal; leaves opposite or alternate, toothed; perennial.

Stems 2-6 in. high; leaves alternate, round, 1-3 cm.
wide; flowers 2 mm. wide   *C. tetrándrum*

FÉNDLERA Engelmann and Gray 1852
(Named for Fendler, an American botanical collector)
Pl. 31, fig. 11.

Sepals 5, united, grown together with the ovary, petals 4, separate, white, stamens 8, ovary 3-4-celled, capsule hard, splitting; flowers terminal, solitary or in 3-flowered cymes; leaves opposite, entire; shrub.

Stems 4-15 ft. high; leaves oblong, 1-3 cm. long;
flowers 1.5-2.5 cm. wide   *F. rupícola*

HEÚCHERA Linné 1753 HEUCHERA
(Named for Heucher, a German botanist)
Pl. 31, fig. 6.

Sepals 5, united into a saucer- or bell-shaped calyx, grown to the base of the ovary, petals 5, white, green or purplish, often tiny, inserted on the throat of the calyx, stamens 5, inserted with the petals, ovary 1-celled, styles 2, capsule 2-beaked, 2-valved; flowers in panicles or racemes; leaves mostly basal, simple, lobed; perennial.

1. Stamens projecting more or less
   a. Flowers in a dense cylindric spike; stems 4-10
      in. high   *H. bracteáta*
   b. Flowers in a panicle or a loose interrupted
      spike
      (1) Flowers in an open panicle; flower stalks
         smooth; leaves 1-2.5 cm. long   *H. rubéscens*
      (2) Flowers in a spike-like panicle; flower
         stalks bristly hairy; leaves 3-8 cn. long *H. híspida*
2. Stamens included in the calyx tube
   a. Calyx bell-shaped, whitish to pinkish
      (1) Petals none or minute; leaves and flower
         stalks densely hairy; leaf lobes with
         round teeth   *H. ovalifólia*

(2) Petals distinct, spatulate and clawed;
   leaves and flower stalks sparsely hairy;
     leaf lobes with spiny teeth   *H. Hállii*
b. Calyx saucer-shaped, greenish; petals tiny   *H. parvifólia*

JÁMESIA Torrey and Gray 1840
(Named for James, an American botanist)
Pl. 31, fig. 9.

Sepals 5, united into a calyx, grown together with the ovary, petals 5, white, stamens 10, the alternate shorter, ovary 1-celled, styles 3-5; flowers in terminal clusters; leaves opposite, simple, toothed; shrub.

Stems 2-6 ft. high; leaves gray-hairy below, 2-5 cm.
  long; flowers 1-2 cm. wide   *J. americána*

LITHOPHRÁGMA Nuttall 1840
(Gr. *lithos,* stone, *phragma,* hedge)
Pl. 31, fig. 4.

Sepals 5, united into a bell- or top-shaped calyx, somewhat grown to the ovary at the base, petals 5, white or pink, 3-7-parted, stamens 10, styles 2-3; flowers in terminal racemes; leaves mostly basal, palmately divided or parted; perennial.

1. Calyx bell-shaped, free from the ovary   *L. tenélla*
2. Calyx top-shaped, united to the lower half of the
   ovary   *L. parviflóra*

MITÉLLA Linné 1753 MITREWORT
(Gr. *mitra,* turban, from the form of the pod)
Pl. 31, fig. 5.

Sepals 5, united into a bell-shaped calyx, grown to the base of the ovary, petals 5, white to greenish-yellow, cleft or pinnatifid, stamens 10 or 5, ovary 1-celled, styles 2, capsule 2-valved at the tip; flowers in spike-like racemes; leaves mostly basal, simple; perennial.

1. Petals yellowish, 7-9-pinnatifid; stigma 2-lobed;
   stamens opposite the petals   *M. pentándra*
2. Petals white, trifid to entire; stigma entire; stamens alternate with the petals   *M. trífida*

PARNÁSSIA Linné 1753 PARNASSIA
(Named from Mount Parnassus)
Pl. 31, fig. 8.

Sepals 5, united into a short tube, free from or grown to the ovary, petals 5, white or cream-colored, stamens with anthers 5, imperfect stamens or staminodia usually many in clusters at the base of each petal, ovary 1-celled, ovules many, stigmas usually 4, capsule 1-celled, opening by 4 valves; flowers solitary, terminal; leaves mostly basal entire; perennial.

1. Petals fringed on the edges, with a short claw or
   stalk   *P. fimbriáta*
2. Petals not fringed and without a claw
   a. Leaves all basal; sterile stamens 3-5 in a clus-
      ter   *P. Kotzebúei*
   b. Stem bearing a leaf near the middle; sterile
      stamens 5-15 in a cluster
      (1) Petals 5-8 mm. long; leaves tapering at
          base   *P. parviflóra*
      (2) Petals 10-12 mm. long; leaves heart-shaped
          at base   *P. palústris*

PHILADÉLPHUS Linné 1753 MOCK ORANGE
(Gr. *philadelphon,* a sweet-flowering shrub)
Pl. 31, fig. 10.

Sepals 4-5, united into a top-shaped calyx, grown to the ovary, petals 4-5, white, separate, stamens 20-40, ovary 3-5-celled, styles 3-5, separate or united at base, capsule top-shaped, splitting by 3-5 valves; flowers solitary or clustered, terminal or axillary; leaves opposite, simple; shrub.

Leaves smooth or hairy, 1-3 cm. long; flowers 2-3.5
   cm. wide   *P. microphýllus*

RÍBES Linné 1753 CURRANT, GOOSEBERRY
(From the German *riebs,* gooseberry)
Pl. 30, fig. 4, 6; pl. 31, fig. 12, 13.

Sepals 4-5, united into a cylindric-, saucer-, or bell-shaped calyx, green, white, pink or yellow, petals 4-5, stamens 4-5, inserted with the petals on the throat of the calyx, ovary 1-celled, styles 2, separate or united, fruit a berry; flowers in racemes or 1-few in axillary clusters; leaves alternate, often clustered, usually lobed; shrubs.

1. Stems prickly, and often bristly
   a. Flower saucer-shaped; berry usually bristly,
      red or black   *R. lacústre*
   b. Flower bell-shaped to tubular; berry usually
      smooth
      (1) Calyx hairy   *R. leptánthum*

(2) Calyx smooth
   (a) Calyx lobes longer than tube; fruit
      smooth   *R. oxyacanthoídes*
   · (b) Calyx lobes shorter than tube; fruit us-
      ually bristly   *R. setósum*
2. Stems smooth
  a. Flowers yellow, 10-25 mm. long; fruit smooth,
    black, rarely yellow   *R. aúreum*
  b. Flowers greenish to white or red
    (1) Berries bristly
      (a) Leaves smooth; fruit globose
        x. Flower saucer-shaped; floral bracts tiny,
          1-2 mm. long   *R. prostrátum*
        y. Flower bell-shaped; bracts 4-6 mm.
          long   *R. Wólfii*
      (b) Leaves hairy, usually sticky; fruit ovoid;
        flower bell-shaped   *R. viscosíssimum*
    (2) Berries smooth or nearly so
      (a) Flower clusters hanging; calyx tubular
        x. Calyx hairy; fruit red   *R. céreum*
        y. Calyx smooth; fruit black   *R. flóridum*
      (b) Flower clusters erect or ascending; calyx
        bell-shaped   *R. hudsoniánum*

Saxífraga Linné 1753 Saxifrage
(Lat. *saxum*, rock, *frango*, break, from the habitat)
Pl. 30, fig. 2, 5, 7, 9, 10; Pl. 31, fig. 1-3.

Sepals 5, united, free from or grown to the base of the ovary, petals 5, white, to yellow or red, usually alike, stamens 10, ovary superior or partly inferior, 2-celled, 2-lobed above, capsule 2-beaked, many-seeded; flowers solitary or in corymbs or panicles; leaves alternate or opposite, entire to pinnatifid; perennial.

1. Flowers white or whitish to purple
  a. Flowers purple
    (1) Leaves opposite, sessile, fleshy, ovate, en-
      tire; stems prostrate; flowers solitary   *S. oppositifólia*
    (2) Leaves alternate, stalked, mostly basal, re-
      niform, lobed; stems erect; flowers large,
      in an oblong cluster   *S. Jámesii*
  b. Flowers white to whitish, pinkish or yellowish
    (1) Stems leafy

PLATE 31

SAXIFRAGES—MENTZELIAS

SAXIFRAGE FAMILY

1. Saxifraga nivalis: Saxifrage
2. Saxifraga debilis
3. Saxifraga caespitosa
4. Lithophragma parviflora
5. Mitella pentandra: Mitrewort
6. Heuchera Hallii
7. Heuchera parvifolia
8. Parnassia parviflora
9. Jamesia americana
10. Philadelphus microphyllus: Mock Orange
11. Fendlera rupicola
12. Ribes cereum: Currant
13. Ribes aureum

MENTZELIA FAMILY

14. Mentzelia nuda

EVENING PRIMROSE FAMILY

15. Anogra coronopifolia

(a) Leaves usually wider than long, 3-7-lobed
    x. Flower usually solitary, terminal, nodding; upper leaves with bulbils   *S. cérnua*
    y. Flowers 2-5, erect; bulbils absent   *S. débilis*
(b) Leaves usually longer than wide, lobed to entire
    x. Leaves entire, linear to oblong, ciliate, spiny-tipped, petals with orange or purple dots   *S. bronchiális*
    y. Leaves usually 3-5-toothed or cleft, mostly spatulate, not spiny-tipped; petals white, pinkish or yellowish, 2-7 mm. long   *S. caespitósa*
(2) Stems leafless
    (a) Stems 1-3 ft. high; leaves round, heart-shaped at base; flowers in a large open panicle   *S. punctáta*
    (b) Stems 1-15 in. high; leaves lanceolate to broadly ovate, tapering or rounded at base, entire to coarsely toothed; flowers 4-10 mm. wide, mostly in a head or a raceme of head-like clusters   *S. niválís*
2. Flowers yellow
    a. Flowers 8-15 mm. wide; basal leaves forming a dense rosette
        (1) Stems 1-8 in. high, with runners at base; leaves ciliate, 10-15 cm. long   *S. flagelláris*
        (2) Stems 1-3 in. high, without runners; leaves smooth, 4-6 mm. long   *S. chrysántha*
    b. Flowers 1.5-2.5 cm. wide; stems without basal rosette, 6-12 in. high   *S. hírculus*

SULLIVÁNTIA   Torrey and Gray 1842
(Named for Sullivant, an American botanist)

Sepals 5, united into a bell-shaped calyx grown to the base of the ovary, petals 5, white, stamens 5, ovary 2-celled, 2-beaked, styles 2; flowers in panicled cymes; leaves mostly basal, wavy-toothed or lobed; perennial.
Stems 4-12 in. high, sticky-hairy; leaves rounded, lobed and toothed, 2-5 cm. wide   *S. Hapemánnii*

LYTHRALES   LOOSESTRIFE ORDER

LYTHRÁCEAE   LOOSESTRIFE FAMILY

Sepals 4-6, united into a cylindric, 8-12-ribbed calyx, petals 4-6, rarely none, pink to purple, stamens 8-12, inserted on the calyx-tube, ovary 2-celled, stigma globose, capsule enclosed in the calyx, opening by 2 valves or irregularly; flowers perfect, solitary to clustered; herbs or shrubs with opposite, alternate or whorled, entire leaves.

LÝTHRUM Linné 1753 LOOSESTRIFE
(Gr. *lythron*, blood, from the color)

Characters of the family.

Stems 1-4 ft. high; leaves lance-oblong, 1-3 cm. long;
  flowers 6-10 mm. wide   *L. alátum*

ONAGRÁCEAE   EVENING PRIMROSE FAMILY

Sepals usually 4, rarely 2-6, united into a calyx grown to the ovary and often prolonged into a tube beyond it, petals usually 4, rarely 2-9 or none, separate, stamens usually 2, 4 or 8, ovary usually 4-celled, rarely 1-6-celled, stigma globose, disk-like or 4-lobed, ovules many, fruit a capsule or nut; flowers solitary or clustered, usually axillary; annual or perennial herbs, rarely shrubs, with alternate or opposite leaves.

1. Petals 4
   a. Stigma 4-lobed
      (1) Flowers white, pink or red
         (a) Fruit 4-celled, many-seeded, splitting
             when ripe
            x. Flowers red or rose-purple; seeds hairy
               (x) Calyx-tube extending above the
                   ovary; style straight   ZAUSCHNERIA
               (y) Calyx-tube not extending above the
                   ovary; style recurved at first CHAMAENERIUM
            y. Flowers white to pink
               (x) Stamens equal in length   ANOGRA
               (y) Stamens of two lengths
                  m. Leafy-stemmed; leaves 1-2 cm.
                     long; flowers 2-2.5 cm. wide GAURELLA
                  n. Stemless or nearly so; leaves 3-10
                     in. long; flowers 2-6 in. wide PACHYLOPHUS
         (b) Fruit small, closed, 1-4-seeded; flowers
             1-sided   GAURA

(2) Flowers yellow, at least at first
  (a) Plant stemmed; leaves entire or toothed
    x. Petals less than 1 cm. long; seeds hairy EPILOBIUM
    y. Petals 1-4 cm. long; seeds not hairy ONAGRA
  (b) Plants stemless; leaves pinnatifid LAVAUXIA
b. Stigma entire or merely 4-toothed
  (1) Stigma disk-like; flowers yellow
    (a) Calyx-tube several times longer than the
        ovary GALPINSIA
    (b) Calyx-tube not longer than the ovary MERIOLIX
  (2) Stigma globose or club-shaped
    (a) Calyx-tube not extending above the
        ovary; flowers white to rose GAYOPHYTUM
    (b) Calyx-tube extending above the ovary
    x. Seeds hairy; flowers white to rose EPILOBIUM
    y. Seeds not hairy; flowers mostly yellow
      (x) Calyx-tube longer than the ovary;
          capsule 4-winged; flowers yellow TARAXIA
      (y) Calyx-tube shorter than the ovary;
          capsule not winged
        m. Capsule linear, sessile; flowers
           yellow, white or pink SPHAEROSTIGMA
        n. Capsule club-shaped, stalked; flow-
           ers yellow CHYLISMA
2. Petals 2, white; fruit bristly-hairy CIRCAEA

ANÓGRA Spach 1835 ANOGRA
(An anagram of Onagra)
Pl. 31, fig. 15.

Sepals 4, united into a long tube extending beyond the ovary, petals 4, white or pink, separate, stamens 8, equal, ovary 4-celled, linear, stigma 4-cleft, capsule oblong to linear, 4-angled, splitting; flowers solitary, axillary, opening in the daytime, buds drooping; leaves alternate, pinnatifid; annual or perennial.

1. Corolla 3.5-8 cm. wide; tips of the sepals united
   with each other in the bud; annual *A. albicaulis*
2. Corolla 2-3.5 cm. wide; the fine tips of the sepals
   free from each other in the bud; perennial
  a. Leaves deeply pinnatifid; stems little woody,
     and bark not shredding; calyx tube hairy in-
     side *A. coronopifólia*

b. Leaves wavy-toothed or entire, rarely pinnatifid; stems woody, bark shredding; calyx
tube smooth inside *A. pállida*

CHAMAENÉRIUM Adanson 1763 FIREWEED
(Gr. *chamae*, on the ground, *nerion*, rose-bay)
Pl. 32, fig. 1.

Sepals 4, united into a tube, not extending beyond the ovary, the 4
lobes falling off, petals 4, red-purple, somewhat irregular in form or position, stamens 8, ovary 4-celled, stigma 4-cleft, capsule 4-celled, 4-angled,
elongated; flowers in terminal racemes; leaves alternate, entire or wavy;
perennial.

1. Stems 1-5 ft. high; leaves lanceolate, short-petioled, 2-8 in. long; bracts small; style hairy at
   base *C. angustifólium*
2. Stems .5-1.5 ft. high; leaves mostly sessile, lance-
   ovate, 1-2 in. long; bracts leaf-like; style
   smooth *C. latifólium*

CHYLÍSMA Nuttall 1840
(Gr. *chylisma*, the juice of plants)

Sepals 4, united into a funnelform or obconic calyx, petals 4, yellow,
stamens 8, unequal, stigma globose, capsule linear to club-shaped; flowers
in terminal racemes; leaves simple or pinnate; annual.

Flower stem 2-4 in. high; leaves ovoid, entire; flow-
·ers 4-5 mm. long *C. scapoídea*

CIRCAÉA Linné 1753 ENCHANTER'S NIGHTSHADE
(Named for the enchantress Circe)

Sepals 2, united into a hairy tube extending but slightly beyond the
ovary, petals 2, white, stamens 2, alternating with the petals, ovary 1-2-
celled, ovules 1 in each cavity, stigma globoid, fruit obovoid, not splitting,
covered with hooked bristly hairs; flowers in terminal and lateral racemes;
leaves opposite, simple, toothed; perennial.

1. Stems 4-8 in. high; leaves coarsely toothed and
   heart-shaped at base *C. alpína*
2. Stems 1-2 ft. high; leaves finely wavy-toothed,
   round or truncate at base *C. pacífica*

EPILÓBIUM Linné 1753 WILLOW HERB
(Gr. *epi*, upon, *lobion*, little pod, from the corolla)

Sepals 4, united into a calyx tube extending beyond the ovary, petals
4, white to pink or rose-purple, separate, stamens 8, ovary 4-celled, ovules

numerous, stigma 4-lobed or club-shaped, capsule cylindric, opening by 4 valves; flowers axillary or terminal, solitary or clustered; leaves alternate or opposite, entire to toothed; annual or perennial.

1. Flowers yellowish or cream-colored; stigma 4-lobed; stems woody at base　　　　　　　　　　*E. suffruticósum*
2. Flowers white, pink, red or purplish; stigma entire or nearly so
    a. Annual, usually much branched; leaves linear to lance-linear; petals 6-10 mm. long, rose to lilac; pods club-shaped, 2-3 cm. long　*E. paniculátum*
    b. Perennial by rosettes, stolons or underground stems
        (1) Leaves linear to lance-linear, closely gray-hairy; flowers pink or white, 4-8 mm. wide　　　　　　　　　　*E. lineáre*
        (2) Leaves lanceolate to ovate, not gray-hairy
            (a) Plants with rosettes or scaly shoots; seeds warted under the microscope　*E. adenocaúlum*
            (b) Plants with stolons or underground stems; seeds smooth under the microscope　　　　　　　　　*E. alpínum*

GALPÍNSIA　Britton 1894

(An anagram of Salpingia)

Sepals 4, united into a long funnelform tube extending beyond the ovary, petals 4, yellow, stamens 8, equal, ovary 4-celled, elongated, stigma disk-like, capsule elongated; flowers solitary, axillary; leaves alternate, simple, entire or toothed; perennial.

Stems spreading, 4-6 in. high; leaves linear-oblong to lanceolate, entire or toothed, 1-5 cm. long; flowers 2-5 cm. wide　　　　　　　　　　　　　　*G. Hartwégi*

GAÚRA　Linné 1753　GAURA

(Gr. *gauros,* proud)

Pl. 32, fig. 2.

Sepals 4, united into a narrow tube extending beyond the ovary, the lobes reflexed, petals 4, white to pink or red, clawed, unequal, stamens 8, ovary 1-celled, stigma 4-lobed, fruit nut-like, not splitting, 1-4-seeded; flowers irregular, in terminal racemes or spikes; leaves alternate, simple, sessile; annual, biennial or perennial.

1. Flowers 3-4 mm. wide; fruit 8-ribbed; stems 3-10 ft. high　　　　　　　　　　　　　　　*G. parviflóra*

2. Flowers 1-2 cm. wide; fruit 4-angled
    a. Stems .5-2 ft. high; flowers more or less red   *G. coccínea*
    b. Stems 2-5 ft. high; flowers white to pink   *G. biénnis*

GAURÉLLA Small 1896
(Diminutive of Gaura)

Sepals 4, united into a cylindric tube, purplish, petals 4, white or pink, stamens 8, the alternate ones longer, ovary 4-angled, stigmas linear, capsule ovoid-pyramidal, beaked, 4-angled; flowers solitary, axillary; leaves alternate, simple; perennial.

Stems spreading, 4-8 in. high, grayish; leaves lance-
    linear, entire or toothed, 1-2 cm. long; flowers 2-2.5
    cm. wide   *G. canéscens*

GAYÓPHYTUM Jussieu 1832
(From Gay, a botanical traveller, and Gr. *phytʒn*, plant)

Sepals 4, united into a tube, not prolonged beyond the ovary, lobes reflexed, petals 4, white or rose, stamens 8, alike or sometimes in 2 sets, stigma globose to club-shaped, capsule linear to club-shaped; flowers solitary, axillary; leaves alternate, entire, linear; annual.

1. Pods on stalks 1-2 mm. long   *G. caésium*
2. Pods on stalks usually 5-15 mm. long
    a. Flowers 5-10 mm. wide; stigma club-shaped   *G. diffúsum*
    b. Flowers 2-4 mm. wide; stigma globose   *G. ramosíssimum*

LAVÁUXIA Spach 1835
(Named for Delavaux, a French botanist)

Sepals 4, united into a tube several times longer than the ovary, petals 4, white, pink or yellow, separate, stamens 8, the alternate longer, ovary 4-celled, 4-winged, stigma 4-cleft; flowers solitary; leaves basal, pinnatifid; stemless perennial or annual.

1. Flowers 1-2 in. wide, yellow then pink; fruits
    beaked   *L. trilóba*
2. Flowers 3-4 in. wide, yellow; fruits not beaked   *L. brachycárpa*

MERÍOLIX Rafinesque 1818
(Of doubtful origin and meaning)
Pl. 32, fig. 3.

Sepals 4, united into a tube shorter than the ovary, petals 4, separate, yellow, stamens 8, ovary 4-celled, 4-angled, stigma disk-like, 4-toothed, pods linear, 4-angled; flowers axillary, solitary, regular; leaves alternate, entire or toothed; biennial or perennial.

Plate 32

EVENING PRIMROSES—CACTI

EVENING PRIMROSE FAMILY

1. Chamaenerium angustifolium: Fireweed
2. Gaura coccinea
3. Meriolix serrulata
4. Onagra biennis: Evening Primrose

MENTZELIA FAMILY

5. Mentzelia multiflora

CACTUS FAMILY

6. Opuntia humifusa: Prickly Pear
7. Cactus viviparus

PLATE 32.

EDITH S. CLEMENTS. PINXT

Stems 6-15 in. high; leaves linear-oblong or lanceolate,
toothed, 1-3 in. long; flowers 1-2.5 cm. wide   *M. serruláta*

ONÁGRA   Adanson 1763   EVENING PRIMROSE
(Gr. *onagra*, wild ass, from a fancied resemblance of its leaves to an
ass's ears)
Pl. 32, fig. 4.

Sepals 4, united into a tube longer than the ovary, petals 4, yellow,
white or pink, separate, stamens 8, ovary 4-celled, stigma 4-cleft, capsule
4-angled; flowers in terminal spikes, opening in the evening; leaves alternate, entire to toothed; annual or biennial.

  1. Calyx tube 1-2 in. long
    a. Petals yellow, 1-2 cm. long   *O. biénnis*
    b. Petals yellow or pinkish, 2-4 cm. long   *O. Hoókeri*
  2. Calyx tube 2-4 in. long   *O. Jámesii*

PACHÝLOPHUS   Spach 1835   EVENING PRIMROSE
(Gr. *pachys*, thick, *lophos*, crest, from the pod)

Sepals 4, united into a tube several times longer than the ovary, petals
4, white or pink, separate, stamens 8, the alternate longer, stigma 4-cleft,
ovary short, capsule pyramidal; flowers solitary; leaves basal, entire to
pinnatifid; mostly stemless perennials.

Plants stemless or rarely with a short stem; leaves
smooth to densely hairy, entire to pinnatifid; flowers
2-6 in. wide; calyx tube 2-8 in. long   *P. caespitósus*

SPHAEROSTÍGMA   Seringe 1828
(Gr. *sphaira*, ball, *stigma*, spot)

Sepals 4, united into a short tube, petals 4, yellow, white or rose,
separate, stamens 8, ovary 4-celled, stigma globose, capsule 4-angled; flowers axillary and solitary or in terminal spikes; leaves alternate, entire or
toothed; annual or perennial.

  1. Flowers yellow, often turning red   *S. contórtum*
  2. Flowers white or rose   *S. minutiflórum*

TARÁXIA   Nuttall 1840
(From its resemblance to Taraxacum)

Sepals 4, united into a tube longer than the ovary, petals 4, yellow or
white, separate, stamens 8, ovary 4-celled, stigma globose, pod 4-grooved
or angled; flowers axillary; leaves basal, pinnatifid or entire; stemless
perennial.

1. Leaves entire or wavy, smooth   *T. subacaúlis*
2. Leaves pinnatifid, finely hairy   *T. breviflóra*

ZAUSCHNÉRIA Presl 1831
(Named for Zauschner, a German botanist)

Sepals 4, united into a tube extending beyond the ovary, bearing 8 small scales inside at the upper end, petals 4, red, stamens 8, 4 longer, ovary 4-celled, stigma 4-lobed, capsule linear, 4-angled; flowers large, in racemes; leaves mostly opposite, simple, toothed; perennial, or woody at base.

Stems .5-1 ft. high; leaves ovate, 1 in. long; calyx-
tube 12-15 mm. long   *Z. califórnica*

GUNNERÀCEAE   WATER MILFOIL FAMILY

Sepals 2-4, united into a calyx grown to the ovary, petals 2-4 or none, stamens 1-8, ovary 1-4-celled, styles 1-4, fruit a nutlet or drupe of 2-4 1-seeded carpels; flowers perfect, monoecious or dioecious, solitary or clustered; perennial or annual aquatic herbs with alternate or whorled leaves, the submerged ones usually dissected.

1. Leaves entire, 6-12 in a circle   HIPPURIS
2. Leaves finely cut, 3-5 in a circle   MYRIOPHYLLUM

HIPPÚRIS Linné 1753 BOTTLE BRUSH
(Gr. *hippos,* horse, *oura,* tail)

Sepals united into an entire calyx, petals 0, stamen 1 on the margin of the calyx, ovary 1-celled, style 1, fruit a 1-celled, 1-seeded drupe; flowers axillary, perfect or imperfect; leaves simple, entire, whorled; aquatic perennial.

Stems .5-2 ft. high; leaves linear or lanceolate, 1-3
cm. long   *H. vulgáris*

MYRIOPHÝLLUM Linné 1753 WATER MILFOIL
(Gr. *myrios,* countless, *phyllon,* leaf)

Sepals usually 2-4, united into a short tube, petals 2-4, greenish, stamens 4-8, ovary 2-4-celled with 1 ovule in each cell, styles 4, fruit maturing into 4 1-seeded closed carpels; flowers monoecious or perfect, axillary or becoming spiked; leaves whorled or alternate, the aerial ones entire to cleft, submerged ones finely dissected; aquatic perennial.

1. Flowers in a spike, the bracts small, ovate   *M. spicátum*
2. Flowers in the axils of pinnatifid leaves   *M. verticillátum*

CACTALES CACTUS ORDER

CACTÁCEAE CACTUS FAMILY

Sepals many, united or separate; grown to the ovary, petals many, in several rows, mostly separate, stamens many, inserted on the throat of the calyx, ovary 1-celled, fruit a berry, mostly fleshy but sometimes nearly dry; flowers usually solitary, sessile, terminal or lateral; fleshy plants with continuous or jointed stems, the latter often ridged or tubercled; leafless or nearly so, with spines arising from cushions of minute bristles.

1. Stems jointed, the joints flat or cylindric   OPUNTIA
2. Stems not jointed, but with ridges or nipples
    a. Stems with ribs or ridges
       (1) Flowers greenish to red or purple   ECHINOCEREUS
       (2) Flowers yellow   ECHINOCACTUS
    b. Stems with nipple-like projections
       (1) Flowers and fruits arising between the nipples   CACTUS
       (2) Flowers arising from the nipples   ECHINOCACTUS

CÁCTUS Linné 1753 NIPPLE CACTUS
(Gr. name of a prickly plant)
Pl. 32, fig. 7.

Sepals many, united into a bell-shaped or funnelform calyx, grown to the ovary, petals in several rows, yellowish-green to purple, ovary smooth, berry ovoid or club-shaped; flowers borne at the bases of the tubercles; leaves none; stems solitary or clustered, globose or ovoid, with tubercles or nipples; tubercles conic or cylindric, woolly and with clusters of spines at the apex.

1. Central spine one or none in each cluster; flowers yellowish-green; plants single or clustered *C. missouriénsis*
2. Central spine 3-12 in each cluster; flowers purple *C. vivíparus*

ECHINOCÁCTUS Link and Otto 1827
(Gr. *echinos*, hedgehog, *kaktos*, cactus)

Sepals many, united into a tube grown to the ovary, petals numerous, rose, purple to yellow, berry usually covered with scales and tufts of bristles; flowers borne on tubercles at or near points from which the spines are developed; stems globose, oblong or cylindric, leafless, tubercled; tubercles arranged in straight or spiral rows, often forming ridges.

1. Stems with nipples
   a. Central spines 8-10; radial spines 20-30; flow-
      ers greenish-yellow to purple   *E. Simpsoni*
   b. Central spines 1-3; radial spines 8-9; flowers
      rose   *E. glaúcus*
2. Stems with ribs or ridges; central spines 4; radial
    spines 9-11; flowers yellow   *E. Whípplei*

ECHINOCÉREUS ENGELMANN 1848
(Gr. *echinos,* hedge hog, *Cereus,* a genus of cacti)

Sepals many, united into a tube grown to the ovary, petals many,
purple, red to yellowish-green, fruit spiny; flowers borne on the ribs or
tubercles, close to fully developed clusters of spines; stems ovoid, cylindric
or oval, ribbed, the ribs somewhat tubercled.

1. Ribs usually 13; flowers greenish-yellow   *E. viridiflórus*
2. Ribs 5-12; flowers red to purple
   a. Ribs 5-7; flowers red
     (1) Radial spines 3-5, nearly round; central
        spine absent   *E. paucispínus*
     (2) Radial spines 6-8, angled; central spine 3-
        8 cm. long .   *E. gonacánthus*
   b. Ribs 8-12
     (1) Central spine 1, black; radial spines usual-
        ly 7; flowers violet-purple   *E. Féndleri*
     (2) Central spines 1-3, white or yellowish;
        radial spines 8-12; flowers red   *E. aggregátus*

OPÚNTIA Miller 1759 PRICKLY PEAR
(Gr. name of a plant)
Pl. 32, fig. 6.

Sepals many, united into a tube grown to the ovary, petals many, yellow, red or purple, slightly united at base, stamens very numerous in several
rows, berry pear-shaped, smooth or spiny; flowers usually somewhat lateral;
stems jointed, branching, the joints flat or cylindric with small, awl-shaped,
deciduous leaves, the areoles axillary, usually spine-bearing.

1. Joints of the stem flat, oval to round
   a. Fruits fleshy, smooth or nearly so; flowers yel-
     low
     (1) Spines none or a single large reflexed one
        and 1-2 small ones   *O. humifúsa*

(2) Spines 1-8, not greatly unlike in length
  (a) Spines twisted, 3-5   *O. tortispína*
  (b) Spines not twisted, 1-8
    x. Spines 1-3, brownish; joints round to
       obovate   *O. camánchica*
    y. Spines 5-7; joints oblong   *O. schweriniána*
 b. Fruit dry, usually spiny; flowers yellow or red
  (1) Flowers yellow, spines 8-15   *O. polyacántha*
  (2) Flowers red; spines 2-4   *O. rhodántha*
2. Joints of the stem flattish to somewhat terete,
  separating easily
 . a. Flowers yellowish; joints 1-2 in. long; spines
    usually 4   *O. frágilis*
  b. Flowers pink or reddish; joints 2-4 in. long;
    spines 3-5   *O. rútila*
3. Joints long, cylindric or angled; stems 2-15 ft.
  high
  a. Plants spreading, about 2 ft. high; edges of
    stem not comb-like   *O. Dávisii*
  b. Plants erect, 4-15 ft. high; edges of the stem
    comb-like   *O. arboréscens*

LOASALES MENTZELIA ORDER

LOASÁCEAE MENTZELIA FAMILY

Sepals 4-5, united into a long tube, grown to the ovary, petals 4-10 on the throat of the calyx, stamens many, inserted with the petals, ovary 1-celled, style entire or 2-3-lobed; flowers solitary or in racemes or cymes, regular, perfect; herbs with opposite or alternate leaves, usually armed with hooked hairs.

MENTZÉLIA Linné 1753 MENTZELIA
(Named for Mentzel, a German botanist)
(Touterea E. & W.; Acrolasia Rydberg)
Pl. 31, fig. 14; pl. 32, fig. 5.

Sepals 5, united into a cylindric or club-shaped calyx, grown to the ovary, petals 5-10, cream-colored to yellow, stamens 20-many, ovary 1-celled, styles 3, somewhat united, capsule opening at the top, seeds often winged; flowers terminal, solitary or in cymes; leaves alternate, entire to pinnatifid; annual or perennial.

1. Flowers 1-2 cm. wide; petals 5, yellow
    a. Leaves sessile, ovate to lance-linear, entire to
       sometimes pinnatifid   *M. albicaúlis*
    b. Leaves with a distinct short petiole, ovate to
       oblong, toothed or angled   *M. oligospérma*
2. Flowers 1-5 in. wide; petals usually 10, cream-
    colored or yellow
    a. Flowers cream-colored, opening at evening and
       closing in the morning
       (1) Flowers 1.5-2.5 in. wide   *M. núda*
       (2) Flowers 3-5 in. wide   *M. ornáta*
    b. Flowers yellow or golden
       (1) Flowers 1-2 in. wide, usually opening in
          the evening   *M. multiflóra*
       (2) Flowers 2.5-5 in. wide, day-blooming   *M. levicaúlis*

CUCURBITÁCEAE GOURD FAMILY

Sepals usually 5, united and grown to the ovary, petals usually 5, separate or united, stamens usually 3, ovary 1-3-celled, style simple or lobed, fruit a pepo, splitting or non-splitting; flowers solitary or in racemes, monoecious or dioecious; climbing or trailing herbaceous vines with alternate lobed leaves.

1. Flowers solitary, yellow; trailing vine   Cucurbita
2. Flowers in a raceme, greenish-white; climbing or
    clambering   Micrampelis

CUCÚRBITA Linné 1753 WILD PUMPKIN
(The Latin name of the gourd)

Sepals 5, united into a bell-shaped calyx, petals 5, yellow, united, stamen flower with 3 stamens, pistil flower with a 1-celled ovary, stigmas 3-5, sterile stamens 3, fruit a pepo with a thick rind; flowers single, axillary, monoecious; leaves lobed, toothed; stems prostrate, tendril-bearing.

Stems 5-20 ft. long; leaves 4-12 in. long; flowers 2-4
in. long   *C. foetidíssima*

MICRÁMPELIS Rafinesque 1808 WILD CUCUMBER
(Gr. *mikros*, small, *ampelis*, vine)

Sepals 5-6, united into a bell-shaped calyx, petals 5-6, white, united, stamen flower with 3 stamens, pistil flower with a 2-celled ovary, fruit more or less bladdery, 1-2-celled, densely spiny; flowers in racemes, monoecious; leaves digitately 3-7-lobed; annual climber with tendrils.

Stems 10-25 ft. high; leaves 2-5 in. long; fruit flat elliptic, 1.5-2 in. long   *M. lobáta*

CELASTRALES BITTERSWEET ORDER

CELASTRACEAE BITTERSWEET FAMILY

Sepals 4-5, united, petals 4-5, separate, stamens 4-5, inserted on the disk, alternate with the petals, ovary 3-4-celled, stigma entire or 3-5-lobed, fruit a fleshy or dry 2-5-celled pod, splitting when ripe; flowers regular, usually purplish, solitary or in terminal or axillary clusters; trees or shrubs, sometimes climbing, with alternate or opposite simple leaves.

1. Flowers 5-parted; erect shrubs, often with spiny
   branches   FORSELLESIA
2. Flowers 4-parted; spreading or trailing evergreen
   shrubs without spines   PACHYSTIGMA

FORSELLÉSIA Greene 1893
(Named for Forselles, a Swedish botanist)
Pl. 33, fig. 2.

Sepals 5, united, petals 5, white, separate, long-linear, stamens 5-10, ovary 1-celled, with 2 ovules, fruit dry, ovoid, pointed; flowers solitary, axillary; leaves alternate, simple; low shrub, often spiny.

Stems 1-2 ft. high; leaves oblong to spatulate, 1-2 cm.
long; petals about 1 cm. long   *F. spinéscens*

PACHYSTÍGMA Rafinesque 1818
(Gr. *pachys,* thick, *stigma,* stigma; incorrectly Pachystima)
Pl. 33, fig. 1.

Sepals 4, united, petals 4, brownish, separate, stamens 4, ovary 2-celled, immersed in the disk, stigma 2-lobed, capsule 2-celled, 1-2-seeded, splitting; flowers axillary, solitary or clustered; leaves opposite, simple, leathery, evergreen; low shrub.

Stems .5-3 ft. high; leaves oblong to oblanceolate 1-3
in. long   *P. myrsinítes*

VITÁCEAE GRAPE FAMILY

Sepals 4-5, united into an entire or toothed calyx, petals 4-5, separate or cohering, falling early, stamens 4-5, ovary 1, usually immersed in the disk, 2-6-celled, fruit mostly a 2-celled berry; flowers greenish, perfect, polygamous or dioecious, in racemes, cymes or panicles; climbing shrubs with tendrils and alternate, lobed or compound leaves.

1. Leaves simple, lobed   VITIS
2. Leaves usually of 5 leaflets   PARTHENOCISSUS

Vítis Linné 1753 Grape
(The Latin name)

Sepals 4-5, united into a calyx, petals greenish, coherent and falling without expanding, stamens 4-5, ovary mostly 2-celled, berry globose, or ovoid, few-seeded; flowers mostly dioecious or polygamous, in racemes or panicles; leaves simple, usually digitately lobed; climbing or trailing woody vines with tendrils.

Leaves 3-7-lobed, 4-6 in. long; berry 8-12 mm. wide *V. vulpína*

Parthenocíssus Planchon 1887 Virginia Creeper, American Ivy
(Gr. *parthenos,* maiden, *kissos,* ivy)
Pl. 33, fig. 7.

Sepals 5, united into a calyx, petals 5, greenish, stamens 5, ovary 2-celled, berry 1-4-seeded, not edible; flowers perfect or polygamous-monoecious, in compound cymes or panicles; leaves digitate, leaflets 5-7; climbing or trailing woody vines, the tendrils coiling, or with adhering disks.

Leaflets lance-oblong to ovate, 2-6 in. long; berry 10-
12 mm. wide   *P. quinquefólia*

RHAMNÁCEAE   BUCKTHORN FAMILY

Sepals 4-5, united into a tube, petals 4-5, or none, stamens 4-5, inserted with the petals on the calyx, ovary 2-5-celled, free or immersed in the disk, fruit a drupe or capsule, often 3-celled; flowers in axillary or terminal cymes or panicles, perfect or polygamous; trees or shrubs, often thorny, with alternate simple leaves.

1. Fruit fleshy, berry-like; petals with a short claw
     or wanting   Rhamnus
2. Fruit dry, 3-lobed, becoming 3 nutlets; petals
     with a long claw   Ceanothus

Ceanóthus Linné 1753 Redroot
(Greek name of a plant)
Pl. 33, fig. 4-6.

Sepals 5, united into a hemispheric or top-shaped calyx, petals 5, white to pink, hood-like, clawed, stamens 5, ovary immersed in the disk and grown to it at the base, 3-lobed, style 3-cleft, fruit dry, 3-lobed, separating into 3 nutlets when ripe; flowers in terminal or axillary cyme-like panicles; leaves alternate, simple; shrubs.

1. Leaves large, 1-4 in. long; stems not spiny
   a. Leaves leathery, shining, roundish to ovate, 2-
      4 in. long   *C. velutínus*
   b. Leaves thin, soft-hairy, ellipsoid, 1-2 in. long *C. ovátus*
2. Leaves small, 1-2.5 cm. long; stems usually spiny *C. Féndleri*

RHÁMNUS Linné 1753 BUCKTHORN

(The Greek name)

Pl. 33, fig. 3.

Sepals 4-5, united into a bell-shaped calyx, petals 4-5, or none, green-ish, ovary free from the disk, styles 3-4-cleft, drupe berry-like; flowers axillary, in cymes, racemes or panicles, perfect or polygamous; leaves alter-nate, simple; shrubs or small trees.

1. Leaves ovate to elliptic, 5-10 cm. long; stamens
   5; petals absent   *R. alnifólia*
2. Leaves lanceolate, 3-5 cm. long; stamens 4; petals
   present   *R. Smíthii*

ELAEAGNÁCEAE   SILVERBERRY FAMILY

Sepals 4, united into a saucer-shaped to tubular calyx, petals none, stamens 4 or 8, ovary 1-celled, 1-seeded, fruit drupe-like, the base of the perianth enclosing the achene or nut; flowers polygamous or dioecious, clustered in the axils, rarely solitary; shrubs or trees with silvery-scaly or stellate-hairy entire, alternate or opposite leaves.

1. Leaves alternate; flowers perfect; stamens 4   ELAEAGNUS
2. Leaves opposite; flowers dioecious; stamens 8   LEPARGYRAEA

ELAEÁGNUS Linné 1753 SILVERBERRY

(Gr. *elaia*, olive-tree, *agnos*, sacred)

Pl. 33, fig. 10.

Sepals 4, united into a tubular calyx, constricted above the ovary, petals none, stamens 4 on the throat of the perianth, style long, thread-like, fruit drupe-like, the fleshy or mealy base of the perianth enclosing the nut; flowers solitary or 2-4 together in the axils, silvery outside, yellowish with-in; leaves alternate, entire, silvery-scaly; shrubs.

Stems 3-12 ft. high; leaves oblong to lance-ovate, 1-4
   in. long   *E. argéntea*

Plate 33.

BITTERSWEET FAMILY

1. Pachystigma myrsinites
2. Forsellesia spinescens

BUCKTHORN FAMILY

3. Rhamnus Smithii: Buckthorn
4. Ceanothus velutinus: Redroot
5. Ceanothus ovatus
6. Ceanothus Fendleri

GRAPE FAMILY

7. Parthenocissus quinquefolia: Virginia Creeper

SILVERBERRY FAMILY

8. Lepargyraea argentea: Buffalo Berry
9. Lepargyraea canadensis
10. Elaeagnus argentea: Silverberry

SANDALWOOD FAMILY

11. Comandra pallida: Toad Flax

MISTLETOE FAMILY

12. Phoradendrum juniperinum: Mistletoe
13. Razumovskya cyrtopoda

LEPARGYRAÉA   Rafinesque 1817   BUFFALO BERRY

(Gr. *lepos,* scale, *argyraios,* silvery)

(Shepherdia Nuttall)

Pl. 33, fig. 8-9.

Sepals 4, united into an urn-shaped calyx, petals none, the pistillate flower with an 8-lobed disk nearly closing the mouth, style somewhat exserted, stamens 8, fruit drupe-like, the fleshy perianth base enclosing the nut; flowers axillary, clustered, dioecious or polygamous; pistillate flowers solitary to few; leaves opposite, entire, brown or silvery-scurfy; shrubs.

1. Stems usually thorny, 6-20 ft. high; leaves oblong, silvery above and below, 1-2 in. long   *L. argéntea*
2. Stems not thorny, 3-8 ft. high; leaves ovoid, silvery below only, 1-1.5 in. long   *L. canadénsis*

SANTALÁCEAE SANDALWOOD FAMILY

Sepals 4-5, grown to the ovary, petals none, stamens 5, anthers connected by a tuft of hairs to the sepals, ovary 1-celled, ovules 2-4, style 1, fruit drupe-like or nut-like, 1-seeded, crowned by the persistent calyx-lobes; flowers greenish-white, perfect, in terminal, umbel-like clusters; perennial herbs, sometimes parasitic, with alternate, sessile leaves.

COMÁNDRA   Nuttall 1818   TOAD FLAX

(Gr. *kome,* hair, *aner, andros,* man)

Pl. 33, fig. 11.

Characters of the family.

Stems 4-10 in. high; leaves linear to lance-oblong; flowers small, white   *C. pállida*

LORANTHÁCEAE MISTLETOE FAMILY

Sepals 2-4, petals none, stamens 2-4, ovary inferior, 1-celled, fruit a 1-seeded berry; flowers dioecious, in spikes or panicles; evergreen parasites on trees or shrubs, yellowish-green to brownish, branches 2-forking with swollen joints; leaves reduced to opposite leathery scales.

1. Parasitic on juniper and cedar; berry globose, translucent   PHORADENDRUM
2. Parasitic on pines and spruces; berry compressed, opaque.   RAZUMOVSKYA

PHORADÉNDRUM Nuttall 1849 MISTLETOE
(Gr. *phora,* borne, *dendron,* wood, from its habit)
Pl. 33, fig. 12.

Sepals usually 3, united into a globular calyx, grown to the ovary, petals none, stamens 3, berry 1-seeded; flowers greenish, dioecious, in axillary spikes; leaves reduced to triangular scales; parasites.

Stems round or square, 4-12 in. high; berry whitish
or reddish   *P. juniperínum*

RAZUMÓVSKYA Hoffmann 1808
(Named for Count Razumovski)
Pl. 33, fig. 13.

Sepals 3 in the stamen flower, 2 in the pistil flower, petals none, stamens usually 3, berry 1-seeded; flowers greenish, dioecious, solitary, in apparent spikes or panicles; leaves reduced to united scales; parasites.

1. Parasitic on pines
    a. On lodgepole pine   *P. americána*
    b. On limber pine   *P. cyanocárpa*
    c. On pinyon   *P. divaricáta*
    d. On yellow pine   .   *P. cryptópoda*
2. Parasitic on Douglas fir   *P. Doúglasi*

SAPINDALES MAPLE ORDER

ACERÁCEAE MAPLE FAMILY

Sepals 5, united, petals 5, or none, stamens 4-12, ovary 2-lobed, 2-celled, styles 2, fruit of 2 winged, 1-seeded samaras; flowers polygamous or dioecious, in axillary or terminal racemes or cymes; trees or shrubs with opposite simple and lobed or odd-pinnate leaves.

ÁCER Linné 1753 MAPLE, BOXELDER
(Lat. *acer,* maple-tree)
Pl. 34, fig. 1, 2.

Characters of the family.

1. Leaves of 3-5 ovate toothed or lobed leaflets;
    flowers dioecious   *A. negúndo*
2. Leaves simple, 3-lobed or parted, or some cut in-
        to 3 leaflets; flowers polygamous
    a. Wings of fruit broad; flower cluster stalked   *A. glábrum*

Plate 34

MAPLES—OAKS.

MAPLE FAMILY

1. Acer glabrum: Mountain Maple
2. Acer negundo: Boxelder

SUMAC FAMILY

3. Rhus Rydbergii: Poison Ivy
4. Rhus glabra: Sumac
5. Rhus trilobata

BIRCH FAMILY

6. Betula glandulosa: Alpine Birch
7. Betula fontinalis: Birch
8. Alnus tenuifolia: Alder
9. Corylus rostrata: Hazelnut

BEECH FAMILY

10. Quercus Gunnisoni: Oak
11. Quercus Gambelii
12. Quercus undulata

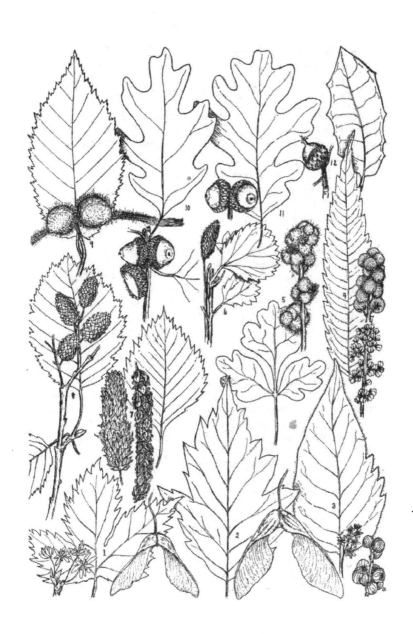

b. Wings of fruit narrow; flower cluster nearly
    sessile   *A. grandidentátum*

ANACARDIÁCEAE· SUMAC FAMILY

Sepals 4-6, united, petals 4-6, rarely none, stamens 5, ovary usually 1-celled, styles 3, fruit usually a drupe; flowers polygamous, in axillary or terminal panicles; trees or shrubs with alternate, 3-foliate, odd-pinnate leaves.

Rhús Linné 1753 Sumac, Poison Ivy
(Gr. *rhous,* sumac, perhaps from the Celtic for red)
Pl. 34, fig. 3-5.

Characters of the family.
1. Leaflets 3
  a. Leaflets 1-4 in. long, broadly ovate, toothed;
    stems little branched, 3 in.-2 ft. high; poison-
    ous to the touch   *R. Rydbérgii*
  b. Leaflets .5-1 in. long, wedge-shaped to obo-
    vate, usually lobed; stems bushy, 1-8 ft. high *R. trilobáta*
2. Leaflets 11-31, lanceolate, 2-6 in. long; stems 3-
    12 ft. high   · *R. glábra*

BETULÁCEAE BIRCH FAMILY

Sepals 2-4, united, or none, petals 0, stamens 2-10, ovary 1-2-celled, fruit a 1-seeded nut, sometimes with an involucre; flowers monoecious in catkins; trees or shrubs with alternate, simple often lobed, toothed leaves.
1. Fruits in spikes or catkins
  a. Bracts of the fruiting catkin papery, 3-lobed,
    falling with the small nut   Betula
  b. Bracts of the fruiting catkin thick, not 3-lobed,
    persistent   Alnus
2. Fruit a large nut in a tubular involucre, paired Corylus

Álnus Linné 1753 Alder
(Lat. *alnus,* alder)
Pl. 34, fig. 8.

Sepals of the stamen flower 3-5, united, of the pistil flower none, petals 0, stamens 2-5, stamen catkins with 4-5 bractlets and 3 or 6 flowers upon each stalked, shield-shaped scale, pistil catkins with 2 flowers in the axil of each bract, with 2-4 bractlets, woody in fruit; leaves alternate doubly toothed; trees or shrubs.

Trunks 10-30 ft. high; leaves ovate-oblong, 2-4 in.
   long; catkins 8-12 mm. long   *A. tenuifólia*

BÉTULA   Linné 1753   BIRCH
(Lat. *betula*, birch-tree)
Pl. 34, fig. 6-7.

Sepals of the stamen flowers 4, united, of the pistil flowers none, stamens 2; stamen-flowers usually 3 in the axil of each bract, with 2 bractlets, pistil flowers usually 2-3 in the axil of 3-lobed or entire bracts; fruit a winged nut; leaves alternate, toothed or lobed; shrubs or trees.

   1. Bark white or gray; trees   *B. papyrífera*
   2. Bark dark brown or greenish brown; shrubs
      a. Stems 5-20 ft. high; leaves ovate, 3-6 cm. long;
         catkins 2-3 cm. long   *B. fontinális*
      b. Stems 1-8 ft. high; leaves cuneate to obovate,
         1-2.5 cm. long; catkins 1-2 cm. long   *B. glandulósa*

CÓRYLUS   Linné 1753   HAZEL-NUT
(Gr. *korys*, helmet, probably from the involucre)
Pl. 34, fig. 9.

Sepals of the stamen flowers none, of the pistil flowers 4-5, petals none, stamens 4; stamen flowers solitary in the axil of each bract, with 2 bractlets, pistil flowers solitary in the axil of a bract, with 2 bractlets enlarging in fruit and forming a leaf-like involucre about the nut; leaves alternate, toothed; shrubs.

Stems 1-6 ft. high; leaves ovate, 2.5-4 in. long; nut
   ovoid, 1-1.5 mm. high   *C. rostráta*

FAGÁCEAE   BEECH FAMILY

Sepals 4-8, united, petals none, stamens 4-20, ovary 3-7-celled, fruit a 1-seeded nut; flowers monoecious, staminate in catkins, pistillate solitary or clustered; leaves alternate, simple, entire to lobed; trees or shrubs.

QUÉRCUS   Linné 1753   OAK
(Lat. *quercus*, oak)
Pl. 34, fig. 10-12.

Sepals of the stamen flowers usually 6, united, of the pistil flowers completely united into a tube, petals none, stamens 6-12, ovary 3-celled,

fruit an involucre with many bracts, a cup at the base or nearly enclosing
the 1-seeded nut or acorn; flowers greenish, staminate many in drooping
catkins, pistillate solitary; leaves entire to pinnatifid, sometimes evergreen;
trees or shrubs.

1. Scales of the acorn cup with long spreading
   tips; usually trees   *Q. macrocárpa*
2. Scales not long and spreading; usually shrubs
   a. Leaves deciduous, deeply round-lobed, smooth
      to hairy
      (1) Acorns keg-shaped, about ⅓ covered by
          the cup   *Q. Gunnisóni*
      (2) Acorns ovoid, about ½ covered by the cup *Q. Gambélii*
   b. Leaves evergreen or somewhat so, sinuately
      toothed, the teeth sharp-pointed or spiny   *Q. unduláta*

APIALES PARSLEY ORDER

ARALIÁCEAE GINSENG FAMILY

Sepals usually 5, united into a tube grown to the ovary, petals usually
5, white or greenish, separate, stamens 5, alternate with the petals, ovary
5-celled, styles 5, fruit a berry; flowers mostly perfect, in umbels; perennial
herbs with alternate leaves divided into three 3-5-pinnate parts.

ARÁLIA Linné 1753 ARALIA, WILD SARSAPARILLA
(Of uncertain origin and meaning)
Pl. 35, fig. 1.

Characters of the family.

Stems short or none; leaflets 3-5, 2-5 in. long; umbels
usually 3   *A. nudicaúlis*

CORNÁCEAE DOGWOOD FAMILY

Sepals 4, united into a calyx grown to the ovary, petals 4, white, greenish or purple, rarely wanting, stamens usually 4, ovary 2-celled, stigma 1,
fruit a drupe, 2-celled and 2-seeded; flowers in cymes or heads, the latter
margined with large petal-like bracts; shrubs or trees with whorled, opposite or alternate, simple usually entire leaves.

CÓRNUS Linné 1753 CORNEL, DOGWOOD
(Lat. *cornus,* dogwood)
Pl. 35, fig. 2-3.

Characters of the family.

1. Plant herb-like, 2-10 in. high ; upper leaves ovoid,
    in a whorl; flower cluster resembling a flower,
    with 4-6 petal-like bracts, 1-2.5 cm. wide   *C. canadénsis*
2. Shrubs with opposite leaves, 3-10 ft. high
    a. Leaves woolly beneath   *C. Baileyi*
    b. Leaves smooth or sparsely hairy beneath   *C. stolonifera*

APIÁCEAE PARSLEY FAMILY

Sepals 5, united and grown to the ovary, the lobes or teeth often inconspicuous, petals 5, on the margin of the calyx, often 2-lobed and sometimes irregular, stamens 5, ovary 2-celled, styles 2, often borne on a flattened or conic base, the stylopodium, ovule 1 in each cell, fruit dry, of 2 carpels, usually separating, when ripe, along their faces, i. e. commissure, often flattened parallel to the commissure, i. e., dorsally, or at right angles to the commissure, i. e., laterally, or nearly round; each carpel with 5 main ribs and sometimes with 4 secondary ones, all or some of them often winged, the wall of the carpel usually with oil-tubes in the intervals between the ribs and on the side toward the commissure; flowers perfect, sometimes polygamous, in simple or compound umbels, rarely in head-like clusters; leaves alternate, simple to variously compound; herbs.

1. Fruit with hooked bristles; leaves digitately divided   Sanicula
2. Fruit without hooked bristles; leaves various
    a. Leaves simple, perfoliate   Bupleurum
    b. Leaves, or at least some of them, not simple
        (1) Fruit linear-club-shaped, usually bristly on the margins   Washingtonia
        (2) Fruit not linear-club-shaped and not bristly
           (a) Fruit strongly flattened parallel to the commissure, i. e. dorsally
             x. Oil-tubes solitary in the intervals
               (x) Stylopodium conic
                 m. Stems 1-2 ft. high; leaves pinnate, of 5-9 leaflets   Oxypolis
                 n. Stems 2-8 ft. high; leaves ternate with 3 large leaflets   Heracleum
               (y) Stylopodium flat or none
                 m. Plants stemmed, 1-4 ft. high
                    (m) Flowers white, greenish or purplish   Angelica
                    (n) Flowers yellow   Pastinaca

    n. Plants stemless or nearly so
      (m) Calyx-teeth and stylopodium
          evident   CYNOMARATHRUM
      (n) Calyx-teeth and stylopodium
          none   LOMATIUM
y. Oil-tubes more than 1 in the intervals
  (x) Plants stemmed, 1-3 ft. high
    m. Flowers white, greenish or purp-
        lish
      (m) Leaves 2-3-ternate, then 1-2-
          pinnate   CONIOSELINUM
      (n) Leaves 1-2-pinnate or 1-ter-
          nate and then 1-2-pinnate   ANGELICA
    n. Flowers yellow or purple   PSEUDOCYMOPTERUS
  (y) Plants stemless or nearly so
    m. Lateral wings of the carpel thin
      (m) Calyx-teeth and stylopodium
          evident   CYNOMARATHRUM
      (n) Calyx-teeth and stylopodium
          none   LOMATIUM
    n. Lateral wings of the carpel thick
      (m) Dorsal ribs very prominent or
          slightly winged   PSEUDOCYMOPTERUS
      (n) Dorsal ribs thread-like or
          prominently winged
        r. Leaves 1-2-pinnate   CYMOPTERUS
        s. Leaves 3-5-pinnate   LEPTOTAENIA
(b) Fruit flattened little or not at all dorsal-
    ly, sometimes flattened at right-angles
    to the commissure, i. e. laterally
x. Oil-tubes solitary in the intervals
  (x) Flowers white; stylopodium conic
    m. Involucre present; leaflets usually
        linear to thread-like   CARUM
    n. Involucre none; leaflets lance-
        linear to lanceolate   CICUTA
  (y) Flowers yellow; stylopodium flat or
      none
    m. Carpel with equal broad ribs
      (m) Fruit globose, scarcely flat-
          tened; stems tufted 1-4 in.
          high   OREOXIS

    (n) Fruit ovate, flattened; stems
        1-3 ft. high   HARBOURIA
  n. Carpels with winged or thread-like
     ribs
    (m) Ribs or some of them with
        wings   THASPIUM
    (n) Ribs not winged
      r. Fruit cylindric; plant stemless;
        leaves pinnate   ALETES
      s. Fruit ovoid, flattened; stems 2-
        3 ft. high; leaves simple or
        ternate   ZIZIA
y. Oil-tubes more than 1 in the intervals
  (x) Stylopodium conic
    m. Fruit round; leaves once-pinnate;
      aquatic   BERULA
    n. Fruit ovate to oblong
      (m) Plants stemmed; leaves ter-
        nate then pinnate   LIGUSTICUM
      (n) Plants stemless; leaves once-
        pinnate   LIGUSTICELLA
  (y) Stylopodium flat or none
    m. Carpels with winged ribs
      (m) Seed with a narrow deep
        groove on the face   AULOSPERMUM
    (n) Seed-face plane or with a broad
        shallow concavity
      r. Leaves 1-3-pinnate; flowers
        white, pink purple   PHELLOPTERUS
      s. Leaves ternate; flowers yellow PTERYXIA
    n. Carpels with the ribs not winged
      (m) Ribs thread-like   MUSINEUM
      (n) Some of the ribs thick and
        corky
      r. Dorsal ribs filiform; lateral ribs
        thick and corky   OROGENIA
      s. All the ribs equally prominent
        and corky
        (r) Leaves entire, clasping or
          perfoliate   BUPLEURUM
        (s) Leaves pinnate; aquatic   SIUM

ALÉTES Coulter and Rose 1900
(Gr. *aletes,* wanderer)
Pl. 35, fig. 15, 25.

Sepals 5, united and grown to the ovary, the teeth prominent, petals 5, white, stamens 5, ovary 2-celled, styles 2 without a base or stylopodium, fruit oblong or short cylindric, the ridges equal and distinct, oil-tubes solitary in the intervals, 2 next the commissure and 1 in each ridge; leaves pinnate with toothed leaflets; stemless perennial.

Flower-stalks shorter than the leaves; leaflets variously lobed or cleft; fruit 4–6 mm. long *A. acaúlis*

ANGÉLICA Linné 1753
(Named for supposed medicinal properties)
Pl. 35, fig. 21.

Sepals 5, united and grown to the ovary, teeth none or small, petals 5, usually white, more rarely greenish-yellow or purplish, stamens 5, ovary 2-celled, stylopodium flattened, fruit ovoid, compressed dorsally, dorsal and intermediate ribs prominent, lateral ribs broadly winged, oil-tubes 1-several in the intervals, 2–10 on the commissure side; leaves once or twice pinnate or ternate-pinnate; leafy stemmed perennial.

1. Leaves ternately divided, then once or twice pinnate
    a. Oil-tubes solitary in the intervals
        (1) Fruit smooth *A. Lyállii*
        (2) Fruit rough or hairy *A. roseána*
    b. Oil-tubes many *A. ámpla*
2. Leaves once or twice pinnate
    a. Leaves once pinnate; involucel absent *A. pinnáta*
    b. Leaves twice pinnate; involucel of conspicuous bracts *A. Gráyi*

AULOSPÉRMUM Coulter and Rose 1900
(Gr. *aulos,* groove, *sperma,* seed)

Sepals 5, united and grown to the ovary, the teeth evident, petals 5, white, yellow or purple, stamens 5, ovary 2-celled, stylopodium none, fruit oblong to round with 3-5 rather broad wings on each half, oil-tubes several in the intervals, 2 or more on the commissure side; leaves usually 1-3-pinnate, often much dissected; stemless or stemmed perennial.

1. Stem more or less evident; fruit 4–8 mm. long
    a. Flowers yellow *A. lóngipes*

b. Flowers white to purplish   *A. ibapénse*

2. Stem lacking; flowers yellowish-purple; fruit 8-
    10 mm. long   *A. purpúreum*

BÉRULA   Hoffmann 1821
(The Latin name of the water-cress)
Pl. 35, fig. 16.

Sepals 5, united and grown to the ovary, teeth inconspicuous, petals 5, white, stamens 5, ovary 2-celled, stylopodium conic, fruit nearly globose, the ribs thin, oil-tubes many and close together on the commissure side; flowers in compound umbels with both involucre and involucels; leaves pinnate; stemmed aquatic or marsh perennial.

Stems .5-3 ft. high; leaflets 7-19, ovate to linear-oblong; fruits about 1.5 mm. long   *B. erécta*

BUPLEÚRUM   Linné 1753
(Gr. *bous*, ox, *pleuron*, side, rib, from the ribbed leaves)
Pl. 35, fig. 14.

Sepals 5, united and grown to the ovary, teeth none, petals 5, yellow or greenish-yellow, stamens 5, ovary 2-celled, stylopodium conic, fruit oblong or oval, slightly compressed, carpels angled with thin equal ribs, oil-tubes none; flowers in compound umbels with conspicuous involucels; leaves simple, entire, clasping or perfoliate; stemmed annual or perennial.

Leaves oblong to lanceolate or linear, more or less
clasping   *B. americánum*

CÁRUM   Linné 1753   CARAWAY
(The Greek name of the caraway)

Sepals 5, united and grown to the ovary, teeth tiny, petals 5, white, stamens 5, ovary 2-celled, stylopodium conic, fruit ovate or oblong, somewhat flattened, carpels somewhat 5-sided, the ribs thin or none, oil-tubes solitary in the intervals, 2 on the commissure side; flowers in compound umbels; leaves pinnate or ternate; stemmed biennial or perennial.

1. Leaves once-pinnatifid; native   *C. Gaírdneri*

2. Leaves twice-pinnatifid; cultivated or escaped as
    a weed   *C. cárui*

CICÚTA   Linné 1753
(The Latin name)
Pl. 35, fig. 12.

Sepals 5, united and grown to the ovary, teeth small, petals 5, white, stamens 5, ovary 2-celled, stylopodium low conic, fruit ovate to oblong,

slightly flattened with low corky ribs, oil-tubes solitary in the intervals, 2
on the commissure side; flowers in compound umbels; leaves 2-3-pinnate;
stem perennial.

Stems 3-8 ft. high; leaves 2-3-pinnate; leaflets lanceolate; fruits 2-3 mm. long   *C. maculáta*

CONIOSELÍNUM   Hoffmann 1814
(From the names of two similar genera)

Sepals 5, united and grown to the ovary, teeth none, petals 5, white,
stamens 5, ovary 2-celled, stylopodium low conic, fruit oval to oblong,
flattened dorsally, carpels with prominent ribs, the lateral ribs broadly
winged, oil-tubes usually 2-3 in the intervals and 4-8 on the commissure
side; flowers in compound umbels; leaves pinnate; stemmed perennial.

Stems 2-5 ft. high; leaves twice pinnate; leaflets pinnatifid; fruit 4 mm. long   *C. scopulórum*

CYMÓPTERUS   Rafinesque 1819
(Gr. *kyme,* wave, *pteron,* wing, from the fruit)
Pl. 35, fig. 27.

Sepals 5, united and grown to the ovary, teeth usually distinct, petals
5, white or yellow, stamens 5, ovary 2-celled, stylopodium none, fruit ovoid,
flattened dorsally, carpels with 3-5 equal wings, oil-tubes 1-several in the
intervals; flowers in terminal umbels; leaves once to twice pinnate; stemless dry land perennial.

1. Flowers white
   a. Each carpel of the fruit broadly 3-5-winged   *C. acaúlis*
   b. Each carpel with but 2 lateral wings   *C. lapidósus*
2. Flowers yellow
   a. Leaves 2-3-pinnate   *C. Féndleri*
   b. Leaves once pinnate or merely lobed   *C. Newbérryi*

CYNOMARÁTHRUM   Coulter and Rose 1900
(Gr. *kyon, kynos,* dog, *marathron,* fennel)

Sepals 5, united and grown to the ovary, teeth evident, petals 5, yellow,
stamens 5, ovary 2-celled, stylopodium flat; fruit oblong, flattened dorsally,
each carpel with distinct or winged ribs, broadly winged laterally, oil-tubes
usually 3-5 in the intervals, 6-10 on the commissure side; flowers in terminal
umbels; leaves 1-2-pinnate; mostly stemless perennial.

1. Pedicels 2-6 mm. long, shorter than the fruit;
   leaves smooth   *C. Nuttállii*

2. Pedicels 12-18 mm. long, longer than the fruit;
   leaves rough *C. Eastwoódae*

HARBOÚRIA Coulter and Rose 1888
(Named for Harbour, an early collector in the Rocky Mountains)
Pl. 35, fig. 13.

Sepals 5, united and grown to the ovary, the teeth evident, petals 5, yellow, stamens 5, ovary 2-celled, stylopodium low or none, fruit ovate, flattened laterally, each carpel with broad, prominent ribs, oil-tubes solitary in the intervals, 2 on the commissure side; flowers mostly in paired umbels; leaves ternately compound with thread-like divisions; stemmed perennial.

Stems 1-2.5 ft. high; fruit 4 mm. long *H. trachypleúra*

HERÁCLEUM Linné 1753
(Gr. *Herakleios,* of Hercules, from its great size)
Pl. 35, fig. 29.

Sepals 5, united and grown to the ovary, petals 5, white, stamens 5, ovary 2-celled, stylopodium conic, fruit obovoid, strongly flattened dorsally, the carpels with thin dorsal and intermediate ribs, and broad lateral wings, oil-tubes solitary in the intervals, 2-4 on the commissure side; leaves large, ternately-compound; flowers in compound umbels; tall stemmed perennial.

Stems 3-8 ft. high; leaves of 3 leaflets, often a foot or
   more long; fruits 8-12 mm. long *H. lanátum*

LEPTOTAÉNIA Nuttall 1840
(Gr. *leptos,* thin, *taenia,* band)
Pl. 35, fig. 20.

Sepals 5, united and grown to the ovary, teeth usually none, petals 5, yellow or purple, stamens 5, ovary 2-celled, stylopodium none, fruit oblong, flattened dorsally, each carpel with thin dorsal and intermediate ribs, the lateral ribs with thick corky wings, oil-tubes 3-6 in the intervals, 4-6 on the commissure side, sometimes wanting; flowers in compound umbels; leaves pinnate, much dissected; tall perennial.

1. Leaves cut into very fine divisions; oil-tubes usually none *L. multífida*
2. Leaves less dissected; oil-tubes present *L. Eátoni*

LIGUSTICÉLLA Coulter and Rose 1909
(Diminutive of Ligusticum)

Sepals 5, united and grown to the ovary, teeth evident, petals 5, yellowish-green, stamens 5, ovary 2-celled, stylopodium conic, fruit ovate, flattened laterally, each carpel with all the ribs thin, oil-tubes 2-3 in the intervals, 4 on the commissure side; flowers in terminal umbels; leaves once pinnate; stemless perennial.

Plants 4-12 in. high; leaflets 7-13, oval; fruit 3 mm.
long *L. Eastwoódae*

LIGÚSTICUM Linné 1753
(Named from the country Liguria)
Pl. 35, fig. 19.

Sepals 5, united and grown to the ovary, teeth tiny or none, petals 5, white or pinkish, stamens 5, ovary 2-celled, stylopodium conic, fruit oblong or ovate, little or not at all flattened, each carpel with prominent equal ribs, oil-tubes 2-5 in the intervals, 6-10 on the commissure side; leaves ternately or pinnately compound; stemmed perennial.

1. Stems leafy; ribs of the fruit somewhat winged
   a. Fruit 4-5 mm. long   *L. símulans*
   b. Fruit 6-7 mm. long
      (1) Leaf segments narrowly linear   *L. filicínum*
      (2) Leaf segments lanceolate to lance-ovate   *L. Pórteri*
2. Stems naked or nearly so; leaf segments linear or
   .   thread-like   *L. tenuifólium*

LOMÁTIUM Rafinesque 1819 WILD PARSLEY
(Gr. *lomation*, little fringe, perhaps from the leaves)
(Cogswellia Rafinesque)
Pl. 35, fig. 22.

Sepals 5, united and grown to the ovary, teeth inconspicuous, petals 5, yellow, white, or purple, stamens 5, ovary 2-celled, stylopodium none, fruit oblong to round, strongly flattened dorsally, each carpel with thread-like dorsal and intermediate ribs, the lateral ribs winged, oil-tubes 1-several in the intervals, rarely none, 2-10 on the commissure side; leaves ternate, pinnate or dissected; stemmed or stemless.

1. Flowers yellow or purple
   a. Stems from tubers
      (1) Umbels open; fruit 6-8 mm. long on pedi-
         cels 4-8 mm. long   *L. ambíguum*
      (2) Umbels dense; fruit 9-10 mm. long, nearly
         sessile   *L. leptocárpum*
   b. Stems from a thick root or rootstock
      (1) Plant smooth or nearly so; fruit smooth
        (a) Fruits 5-6 mm. long; leaves 2-pinnate *L. montánum*

(b) Fruits 8-16 mm. long; leaves ternate,
    then pinnate
    x. Fruit 10-12 mm. long; wings narrow,
      ribs inconspicuous   *L. bicolor*
    y. Fruit 8-16 mm. long; wings more than
      half as broad as carpel; ribs thread-
      like   *L. Gráyi*
  (2) Plant hairy, at least when young; fruits
    usually hairy also
    (a) Leaves finely dissected, ternate then pin-
      nate   *L. foeniculáceum*
    (b) Leaves 1-2-ternate   *L. platycárpum*
2. Flowers white
  a. Fruit oblong, 6-20 mm. long; bracts of the in-
    volucel not papery-margined   *L. macrocárpum*
  b. Fruit oval to round, 4-6 mm. long; bracts of
    the involucel papery-margined   *L. nudicaúle*

MUSÍNEUM   Rafinesque 1820
(A Greek name for fennel)
Pl. 35, fig. 17.

Sepals 5, united and grown to the ovary, teeth prominent, petals 5,
yellow, stamens 5, ovary 2-celled, stylopodium low, fruit ovate to oblong,
somewhat flattened laterally, each carpel flattened dorsally with thin narrow ribs, oil-tubes usually 3 in the intervals, 2-4 on the commissure side;
leaves ternate or pinnate, usually much dissected; low or stemless perennial.

1. Stems 6-10 in. high; leaf segments mostly oblong
  to ovate   *M. divaricátum*
2. Plant stemless; leaf segments narrowly linear   *M. tenuifólium*

OREÓXIS   Rafinesque 1830
(Gr. *oros, oreos,* mountain, perhaps from the habitat)
Pl. 35, fig. 11.

Sepals 5, united and grown to the ovary, teeth prominent, petals 5,
yellow, stamens 5, ovary 2-celled, stylopodium none, fruit globose, each
carpel with thick equal corky ribs, oil-tubes 1-3 in the intervals, 2 on the
commissure side; leaves pinnate; the leaflets cleft into narrow segments;
tufted alpine perennial.

1. Plants smooth or nearly so; oil-tubes more than 1
  in the intervals   *O. húmilis*
2. Plants finely hairy; oil-tubes 1 in the intervals   *O. alpína*

Plate 35

PARSLEYS—HONEYSUCKLES

GINSENG FAMILY

1. Arália nudicaulis: Wild Sarsaparilla

DOGWOOD FAMILY

2. Cornus canadensis: Cornel
3. Cornus Baileyi: Dogwood

MOSCHATEL FAMILY

4. Adoxa moschatellina

HONEYSUCKLE FAMILY

5. Lonicera involucrata: Honeysuckle
6. Viburnum pauciflorum: Bush Cranberry
7. Sambucus racemosa: Elderberry

MADDER FAMILY

8. Galium boreale: Bedstraw

PARSLEY FAMILY

9-30. Fruit clusters and fruits, the latter natural size except where indicated

9. Sanicula marilandica: x2
10. Washingtonia obtusa
11. Oreoxis alpina, x2
12. Cicuta maculata, x2
13. Harbouria trachypleura, x2
14. Bupleurum americanum, x2
15. Aletes acaulis
16. Berula erecta, x2
17. Musineum divaricatum, x3
18. Sium cicutifolium, x2
19. Ligusticum Porteri
20. Leptotaenia multifida
21. Angelica Grayii
22. Lomatium nudicaule
23. Pseudocymopterus montanus
24. Pseudocymopterus anisatus
25. Aletes acaulis
26. Oxypolis Fendleri, x2
27. Cymopterus acaulis
28. Phellopterus purpurascens
29. Heracleum lanatum
30. Orogenia linearifolia, x2

OROGÉNIA   Watson 1871
(Gr. *oros,* mountain, *genos,* born)
Pl. 35, fig. 30.

Sepals 5, united and grown to the ovary, teeth tiny, petals 5, white, stamens 5, ovary 2-celled, fruit oblong, each carpel strongly flattened dorsally, dorsal and intermediate ribs thin, lateral ribs greatly corky-thickened; leaves 1-2-ternate, leaflets entire; stemless perennial.

Stalks 1-5 in. high from a tuber; leaves 2-3; fruit 3-4
  mm. long   *O. linearifólia*

OXÝPOLIS   Rafinesque 1830
(Of uncertain origin and meaning)
Pl. 35, fig. 26.   ·

Sepals 5, united and grown to the ovary, teeth evident, petals 5, white, · stamens 5, ovary 2-celled, stylopodium low conic, fruit ovoid, somewhat flattened laterally, each carpel with thin dorsal and intermediate ribs, the lateral ribs winged, oil-tubes solitary in the intervals, 2-6 on the commissure side; leaves once pinnate or ternate, or sometimes reduced to the · petiole alone; stemmed perennial.

Stems 1-2.5 ft. high from a group of tubers; leaflets
  5-9, ovate to lance-ovate; fruit 3-4 mm. long   *O. Féndleri*

PASTINÁCA   Linné 1753
(Lat. name of the parsnip, from *pastus,* food)

Sepals 5, united and grown to the ovary, teeth none, petals 5, yellow stamens 5, ovary 2-celled, stylopodium low, fruit oval, much flattened dorsally, each carpel with thread-like dorsal and intermediate ribs, the lateral ribs winged, oil-tubes solitary in the intervals and 2-4 on the commissure side; leaves pinnate; stemmed biennials.

Stems 2-5 ft. high; leaflets ovate, 1-3 in. long; fruit
  5-8 mm. long   *P. satíva*

PHELLÓPTERUS   Nuttall 1840
(Gr. *phellos,* cork, *pteron,* wing)
Pl. 35, fig. 28.

Sepals 5, united and grown to the ovary, teeth evident, petals 5, white to pink or purple, stamens 5, ovary 2-celled, stylopodium none, fruit oblong to round, each carpel with 3-5 broad wings, oil-tubes 1-3 in the intervals, 4-8 on the commissure side; leaves 13-pinnate; stemless or short-stemmed perennial.

1. Flowers white; fruit 6-8 mm. long   *P. montánus*
2. Flowers pinkish to purple
    a. Bracts of the involucel 1-3-nerved
        (1) Fruits oblong, 8 mm. long   *P. bulbósus*
        (2) Fruits round, 10-12 mm. long   · *P. purpuráscens*
    b. Bracts of the involucel many-nerved; fruit 12-
        15 mm. long   *P. multinervátus*

PSEUDOCYMÓPTERUS   Coulter and Rose 1888
(Gr. *pseudes,* false, from its relationship to Cymopterus)
· Pl. 35, fig. 23-24; Pl. 36, fig. 7.

Sepals 5, united and grown to the ovary, teeth evident, petals 5, usually yellow to purple, stamens 5, ovary 2-celled, stylopodium none, fruit oblong to rounded, each carpel with prominent and intermediate ribs, the lateral ribs rather broadly and thickly winged, oil-tubes 1-4 in the intervals, 2-8 on the commissure side; leaves twice pinnate; stemless or stemmed perennial.

1. Stems leafy, .5-3 ft. high; flowers yellow to purple *P. montánus*
2. Stemless, leaves basal; flowers white or yellow   *P. anisátus*

PTERÝXIA   Nuttall 1840
(Gr. *pteryx,* wing, from the wings of the fruit)

Sepals 5, united and grown to the ovary, teeth evident, petals 5, yellow, stamens 5, ovary 2-celled, stylopodium none, fruit oblong to round, each carpel strongly flattened dorsally, dorsal and intermediate ribs prominent or broadly winged, lateral ribs broadly winged, oil-tubes several in the intervals; leaves ternate, then pinnately dissected; stemless perennial.

1. Flowers yellow; fruit oblong, 6-7 mm. long   *P. calcárea*
2. Flowers white; fruit roundish, 4 mm. long   *P. albiflóra*

SANÍCULA   Linné 1753
(From the Latin *sano,* to heal)
Pl. 35, fig. 9.

Sepals 5, united and grown to the ovary, teeth conspicuous, petals 5, greenish-white, stamens 5, ovary 2-celled, fruit slightly flattened, more or less globose, covered with hooked bristles, carpels ribless, the oil-tubes usually 5; flowers in small globose umbels, the clusters with leaf-like involucres; leaves digitately 3-7-divided; stemmed perennial.

Stems 1-4 ft. high; leaflets oblanceolate to obovate;
    fruit 5-6 mm. long   *S. marilándica*

Síum   Linné 1753
(The Greek name of a marsh plant)
Pl. 35, fig. 18.

Sepals 5, united and grown to the ovary, teeth tiny, petals 5, white, stamens 5, ovary 2-celled, stylopodium low, fruit flattened laterally, ovate to oblong, each carpel with prominent nearly equal ribs, oil-tubes 1-3 in the intervals, 2-6 on the commissure side; leaves pinnate; stemmed aquatic or marsh perennial.

Stems 2-6 ft. high; leaflets 3-8 pairs, linear to lanceolate, toothed; fruit 3 mm. long   *S. cicutifólium*

Tháspium   Nuttall 1818
(Gr. *thapsia*, plant with a yellow dye)

Sepals 5, united and grown to the ovary, teeth evident, petals 5, yellow, stamens 5, ovary 2-celled, stylopodium none, fruit ovoid, each carpel with all the ribs strongly winged, oil-tubes solitary in the intervals, 2 on the commissure side; leaves ternate; tall stemmed perennial.

Stems 2-5 ft. high; basal leaves mostly heart-shaped,
stem-leaves once-ternate; fruits globose-ovoid, 4-5
mm. long   *T. trifoliátum*

Washingtónia   Rafinesque 1818
(Named for George Washington)
Pl. 35, fig. 10.

Sepals 5, united and grown to the ovary, teeth none, petals 5, white or purple, stamens 5, ovary 2-celled, stylopodium conic, fruit more or less club-shaped, usually tapering to the base, and hairy; leaves 2-3-ternate; stemmed perennial.

  1. Fruits bristly-hairy
    a. Involucel present; style and base 2 mm. long;
      fruits 12 mm. long   *W. longístylis*
    b. Involucel wanting as a rule; style and base
      less than 1 mm. long; fruits 15-20 mm. long *W. obtúsa*
  2. Fruits smooth; style and base 1-2 mm. long;
    fruits 12-16 mm. long   *W. occidentális*

Zízia   Koch 1825
(Named for Ziz, a German botanist)

Sepals 5, united and grown to the ovary, teeth prominent, petals 5, yellow, stamens 5, ovary 2-celled, stylopodium none, fruit ovoid to oblong,

somewhat flattened, the ribs thread-like, oil-tubes solitary in the intervals with a small one beneath each rib; flowers in compound umbels; lower leaves sessile, deeply heart-shaped, stem-leaves mostly ternate; perennial. Stems 2-3 ft. high; lower leaves 4-6 in. long; fruit
ovate, 3 mm. long   *Z. cordáta*

RUBIALES MADDER ORDER
RUBIÁCEAE MADDER FAMILY

Sepals 4, united into a tube grown to the ovary, petals 4, white, greenish or yellow, united into a saucer-shaped corolla, stamens usually 4, ovary 2-celled, ovule 1 in each cell, styles 2, fruit separating into 2 closed carpels; flowers in axillary or terminal cymes or panicles, usually perfect; annual or perennial herbs with whorled, simple, mostly entire leaves.

GÁLIUM Linné 1753 BEDSTRAW
(Gr. *gala*, milk, which some species curdle)
Pl. 35, fig. 8.

Characters of the family.

1. Flowers with stamens and pistils
  a. Annual
      (1) Leaves usually 4 in a whorl; stems smooth *G. bifólium*
      (2) Leaves 6-8 in a whorl; stems rough-angled *G. aparíne*
  b. Perennial
      (1) Stems erect; leaves 3-nerved; fruit white-
          hairy, often smooth   *G. boreále*
      (2) Stems weak; leaves 1-nerved
        (a) Leaves sharp-pointed at tip, oval   *G. triflórum*
        (b) Leaves not sharp-pointed
          x. Fruit with hooked hairs   *G. trífidum*
          y. Fruit without hooked hairs
            (x) Leaves obovate, 8-10 mm. long;
               fruit smooth   *G. Brandégei*
            (y) Leaves lanceolate, 1-2 cm. long;
               fruit rough   *G. aspérrimum*
2. Flowers with only stamens or pistils; leaves
  linear   *G. coloradénse*

CAPRIFOLIÁCEAE HONEYSUCKLE FAMILY

Sepals 3-5, united and grown to the ovary, petals 5, united into a saucer-shaped tubular corolla, often 2-lipped, stamens usually 5 on the tube of the corolla, ovary 1-6-celled, stigma globose or 2-5-lobed, fruit a 1-6-celled berry, drupe or capsule; flowers mostly clustered, sometimes in pairs; shrubs, herbs, or vines with opposite simple or pinnate leaves.

1. Corolla shallow, mostly saucer-shaped; stigma on
     a very short style; fruit drupe-like
     a. Leaves simple   VIBURNUM
     b. Leaves pinnate   SAMBUCUS
2. Corolla long, bell-shaped to tubular; stigma on a
     long style; fruit a berry or dry
     a. Stems trailing; flowers terminal, paired   LINNAEA
     b. Stems erect or climbing, a foot or more high;
         flowers clustered, or axillary when paired
         (1) Corolla regular, bell-shaped   SYMPHORICARPUS
         (2) Corolla irregular, usually tubular   LONICERA

LINNAÉA   Gronovius 1753   TWIN FLOWER
(Named for Linnaeus, the great Swedish botanist)
Pl. 36, fig. 4.

Sepals 5, united, petals 5, pink or purplish, united into a bell-shaped regular corolla, stamens 4 on the corolla tube, in 2 pairs, ovary 3-celled with a single perfect ovule, fruit 3-celled, 1-seeded; flowers terminal, in pairs on long stalks; leaves opposite, evergreen, simple; somewhat woody, creeping herb.

Stems 3-8 in. high; leaves 1-2 cm. long; flowers 10-15
    mm. long   *L. boreális*

LONÍCERA   Linné 1753   HONEYSUCKLE
(Named for Lonitzer, a German botanist)
(Distegia Rafinesque)
Pl. 35, fig. 5.

Sepals 5, united, the teeth small, petals 5, white to pink, red or yellow, united into a mostly tubular 2-lipped corolla, stamens 5 on the corolla tube, ovary 2-3-celled, ovules many, stigma globose, berry fleshy, 2-3-celled, few-seeded; flowers in clusters or twos; leaves opposite simple entire; shrubs or woody climbers.

1. Flowers in pairs; erect shrubs
     a. Bracts of the cluster large and leaf-like, en-
         closing the fruit   *L. involucráta*
     b. Bracts small or none
         (1) Berry bluish-black   *L. caerúlea*
         (2) Berry red   *L. utahénsis*

2. Flowers 4-several in a cluster; stems climbing
   or clambering   *L. glaucéscens*

SAMBÚCUS Linné 1753 ELDERBERRY
(The Latin name for the elder)
Pl. 35, fig. 7.

Sepals 3-5, united, petals 3-5, white, united into a saucer-shaped corolla, stamens 5, at the base of the corolla, ovary 3-5-celled, styles 3-parted, fruit a berry-like drupe with 3-5 nutlets; flowers in large compound cymes; leaves opposite, pinnate; shrubs.

   1. Flower cluster flat-topped; fruit purplish-black,
      5-6 mm. wide   *S. canadénsis*
   2. Flower cluster panicle-like, not flat-topped
     a. Cluster convex; fruit black   *S. melanocárpa*
     b. Cluster conic or somewhat so; fruit bright red *S. racemósa*

SYMPHORICÁRPUS Jussieu 1789 SNOWBERRY, WOLFBERRY
(Gr. *symphoros*, borne together, *karpos*, fruit, from the clustered berries)
Pl. 36, fig. 5.

Sepals 4-5, united, petals 4-5, white or pink, united into a bell-shaped corolla, stamens 4-5 on the corolla tube, ovary 4-celled, stigma globose or 2-lobed, berry 4-celled, 2-seeded; flowers in axillary or terminal clusters; leaves opposite, simple, entire or nearly so; shrubs.

   1. Corolla 3-5 mm. long
     a. Stamens and style projecting from the corolla;
       clusters many-flowered   *S. occidentális*
     b. Stamens and style not projecting; clusters few-
       flowered   *S. racemósus*
   2. Corolla 6-12 mm. long
     a. Corolla 6-8 mm. long, the tube 2-3 times the
       length of the lobes   *S. rotundifólius*
     b. Corolla 8-12 mm. long, the tube 4-5 times the
       length of the lobes   *S. oreóphilus*

VIBÚRNUM Linné 1753 BUSH CRANBERRY, CRANBERRY TREE
(The Latin name)
Pl. 35, fig. 6.

Sepals 5, united into a tube, petals 5, white or pink, united into a shallow corolla, stamens 5 on the corolla tube, ovary 1-3-celled, style 3-lobed, drupe 1-seeded; flowers in compound cymes, the outer sometimes without stamens or pistils; leaves opposite, entire to lobed; shrub.

Plate 36

PARSLEYS—HONEYSUCKLES—BLUEBELLS

PARSLEY FAMILY

7. Pseudocymopterus montanus

HONEYSUCKLE FAMILY

4. Linnaea borealis: Twin Flower
5. Symphoricarpus occidentalis: Snowberry

BLUEBELL FAMILY

1. Campanula Parryi: Bluebell
2. Campanula rotundifolia
6. Campanula uniflora

VALERIAN FAMILY

3. Valeriana silvatica: Valerian

PLATE 36.

EDITH S. CLEMENTS, PINXT

1. Leaves not lobed, with a single midrib, the veins
   pinnate; fruit bluish-black   *V. lentágo*
2. Leaves mostly 3-lobed, with 3 prominent veins;
   fruit red
   a. Outer flowers of the cluster large, without sta-
      mens and pistils; clusters 3-4 in. wide; rare *V. ópulus*
   b. Outer flowers not large and sterile; clusters
      less than 1 in. wide; common   *V. pauciflórum*

ADOXÁCEAE MOSCHATEL FAMILY

Sepals 2-3, united and grown to the ovary, petals 4-6, gréen, united into a regular saucer-shaped corolla, stamens twice as many, in pairs on the corolla tube, ovary 3-5-celled, style 3-5-parted, fruit a drupe with 3-5 nutlets; flowers in terminal globose clusters; low perennial herbs with basal and opposite, ternate leaves.

ADÓXA Linné 1753 MOSCHATEL, MUSKROOT
(Gr. *a*, without, *doxa*, glory, from its small green flowers)
Pl. 35, fig. 4.

Characters of the family.
Stems 2-6 in. high; leaf-segment 3-cleft or 3-parted;
flowers 3-6 in a head   *A. moschatéllina*

CAMPANULES BLUEBELL ORDER

CAMPANULÁCEAE BLUEBELL FAMILY

Sepals mostly 5, united and grown to the ovary, petals 5, united into a regular or irregular corolla, the latter bell-shaped, saucer-shaped or 2-lipped, stamens 5 on the corolla tube, ovary 2-5-celled, rarely 1-celled, stigma 2-5-lobed, fruit a capsule or berry; flowers solitary or clustered, mostly terminal; annual or perennial herbs with alternate, entire, toothed or lobed leaves.

1. Corolla regular; anthers separate from each other
   a. Corolla bell-shaped; flowers all alike   CAMPANULA
   b. Corolla saucer-shaped; earlier flowers small
      and green, without corolla   SPECULARIA
2. Corolla irregular; anthers united around the
   style
   a. Corolla split to the base on one side   LOBELIA
   b. Corolla not split   LAURENTIA

CAMPÁNULA   Linné 1753   BLUEBELL
(Diminutive of It. *campana*, bell)
Pl. 36, fig. 1, 2, 6.

Sepals 5, united, petals 5, usually blue or purple, rarely white, united
into a bell-shaped corolla, stamens 5, free from the corolla, ovary 3-5-
celled, stigma 3-5-lobed, capsule crowned by the long calyx-lobes, opening
by 3-5 small holes; flowers solitary or clustered; leaves alternate, entire
or toothed, rarely lobed; annual or perennial.

1. Flowers nodding; corolla deeply bell-shaped, 1.5-
    3 cm. long; fruit nodding   *C. rotundifólia*
2. Flowers erect, spreading or horizontal, not nod-
    ding
    a. Corolla tubular bell-shaped, 8-12 mm. long;
       flowers solitary; at 12-14,000 ft.   *C. uniflóra*
    b. Corolla broadly open; flowers often 2 or more;
       at 5-12,000 ft.
       (1) Flowers about 1 cm. wide, several-many
            in an open cluster   *C. aparinoídes*
       (2) Flowers 2-3 cm. wide, 1-few in a cluster   *C. Párryi*

LAURÉNTIA   Micheli 1729
(From Laurent, a French botanist)

Sepals 5, united, petals 5, blue, united into a closed tube, 2-lipped,
stamens 5, united by the anthers, ovary 2-celled, fruit a capsule, opening at
the top; flowers few, axillary; leaves alternate, simple; perennial.
Stems 4-5 in. high; leaves linear, 1.5-3 cm. long   *L. exímia*

LOBÉLIA   Linné 1753   LOBELIA, CARDINAL FLOWER
(Named for de L'Obel, a Flemish botanist)

Sepals 5, united, petals 5, red, blue or white, united into a 2-lipped
corolla, split to the base on one side, stamens 5, united by the anthers,
ovary 2-celled, capsule 2-valved from the top; flowers in long racemes;
leaves alternate, simple; perennial.

1. Flowers red, 2-2.5 cm. long   *L. cardinális*
2. Flowers blue, rarely white, 1-1.5 cm. long   *L. syphilítica*

SPECULÁRIA   Heister 1830   VENUS' LOOKING GLASS
(Latin *speculum*, looking-glass)

Sepals 3-5, united, petals 5, blue, united into a saucer-shaped corolla,
the earlier flowers without petals, stamens 5, ovary 3-celled, stigma 3-lobed,
capsule opening by lateral valves; flowers axillary, the earlier small, green,

closed, the later with a blue corolla; leaves alternate, simple, entire or toothed; annual.

1. Leaves linear to lance-oblong, sessile
2. Leaves rounded or broadly ovate, clasping by a *S. leptocárpa*
   heart-shaped base *S. perfoliáta*

ASTERALES ASTER ORDER
VALERIANÁCEAE VALERIAN FAMILY

Sepals united and grown to the ovary, the lobes none in flower but becoming a feathery pappus in fruit, petals usually 5, united into a regular or irregular corolla, stamens 3 on the corolla tube, ovary 1-3-celled, fruit an achene with feathery pappus; flowers perfect or dioecious in clustered. cymes; herbs with opposite simple to pinnate leaves.

VALERIÁNA Linné 1753 VALERIAN
(Lat. *valeo*, to be strong, from the strong odor)
Pl. 36, fig. 3.

Characters of the family.

1. Flowers in a flat-topped cluster; leaves thin, netted-veined, the segments usually toothed *V. silvática*
2. Flowers in a long panicle-like cluster; leaves
   thick, parallel-veined, the segments entire *V. edúlis*

ASTERÁCEAE ASTER OR COMPOSITE FAMILY

Sepals usually 5, united and grown to the ovary, usually developing in fruit into a pappus of awns, bristles, hairs, scales or teeth, sometimes lacking, petals usually 5, united into a regular tubular corolla in the disk flowers and into an irregular ribbon-like corolla in the marginal or ray flowers, stamens usually 5, united by their anthers, on the corolla tube, style 2-cleft at the apex, the ray flowers often without stamens or style, ovary 1-celled, becoming a 1-seeded achene usually crowned by the pappus; flowers grouped in dense clusters called heads, each one popularly regarded as a flower, enclosed in an involucre made up of one or more rows of bracts, often with chaffy scales between the single flowers; heads solitary or clustered on the stems; herbs or shrubs, very variable as to leaves.

1. Heads rayless, with tube- or disk-flowers only
   a. Heads white, yellow, red, etc., not green and
      inconspicuous

(1) Heads large, rose-purple to cream-colored,
    usually with spiny bracts; leaves spiny;
    pappus hairy   CARDUUS
(2) Heads not large or spiny; leaves rarely
    spiny
  (a) Flowers red or purple
    x. Leaves in whorls of 3-5   EUPATORIUM
    y. Leaves alternate .
      (x) Heads in spikes or racemes   LACINIARIA
      (y) Heads in flat-topped panicles   VERNONIA
  (b) Flowers yellow, cream-colored or white
    x. Pappus hairy
      (x) Receptacle with chaffy scales among
          the flowers   FILAGO
      (y) Receptacle without chaff
        m. Shrubs
          (m) Heads dioecious   BACCHARIS
          (n) Heads perfect   TETRADYMIA
        n. Herbs
          (m) Heads white
            r. Leaves large and arrow-shaped PETASITES
            s. Leaves not large and arrow-
               shaped
              (r) Leaves opposite; involucre
                  and leaves not woolly   EUPATORIUM
              (s) Leaves alternate or basal;
                  involucre   and   leaves
                  more or less woolly
                h. Heads dioecious
                  (h) Stems mostly low, with
                      basal leaves   ANTENNARIA
                  (i) Stems tall and leafy   ANAPHALIS
                i. Heads monoecious   GNAPHALIUM
          (n) Heads cream-colored, yellow or
              . yellowish
            r. Flowers cream-colored
              (r) Leaves more or less oppo-
                  site;   involucre   bell-
                  shaped   COLEANTHUS
              (s) Leaves alternate; involucre
                  oblong   KUHNIA

s. Flowers yellow
  (r) Heads narrow, cylindric,
      few-flowered
    h. Bracts of involucre in dis-
       tinct vertical rows   CHRYSOTHAMNUS
    i. Bracts of involucre not in
       vertical rows   ISOCOMA
  (s) Heads broad, many-flow-
      ered
    h. Bracts of involucre in 2-
       3 rows   HAPLOPAPPUS
    i. Bracts in 1 row
      (h) Leaves opposite   ARNICA
      (i) Leaves alternate   SENECIO
·y. Pappus not hairy, but of scales, awns or
   lacking
  (x) Receptacle with chaffy scales among
      the flowers; pappus usually of 2-
      6 awns
    m. Bracts of involucre separate   BIDENS
    n. Inner bracts of involucre united in-
       to a cup   THELESPERMA
  (y) Receptacle not chaffy
    m. Pappus a crown, or none
      (m) Pappus a fringed crown;
          leaves ·opposite, long-tailed PERICOME
      (n) Pappus a low, entire crown or
          none; leaves dissected
        r. Pappus usually a crown   TANACETUM
        s. Pappus usually none   MATRICARIA
    n. Pappus of scales or awns
      (m) Leaves entire or toothed
        r. Leaves entire, mostly basal;
           involucre not sticky, the
           bracts in 2-3 rows   ACTINELLA
        s. Leaves toothed, on the stem;
           involucre sticky, the bracts
           in several rows   GRINDELIA
      (n) Leaves parted or dissected
        r. Flowers yellow   BAHIA
        s. Flowers yellowish or whitish

(r) Scales of the pappus 10-20 HYMENOPAPPUS
(s) Scales of the pappus 4-14 CHAENACTIS
b. Heads green or greenish-yellow, inconspicuous
  (1) Leaves not lobed or divided
    (a) Leaves opposite   IVA
    (b) Leaves alternate
      x. Fruit a spiny bur with 2 achenes   XANTHIUM
      y. Achenes not in a bur
        (x) Receptacle chaffy
          m. Pappus of several scales   DICORIA
          n. Pappus none   PARTHENICE
        (y) Receptacle without chaff; pappus
            none   ARTEMISIA
  (2) Leaves lobed to pinnatifid
    (a) Some of the leaves opposite; spines of
        fruit in 1 row   AMBROSIA
    (b) Leaves regularly alternate
      x. Spines of fruit in several rows   FRANSERIA
      y. Achenes not in a spiny fruit
        (x) Bracts imbricated, not sharp-pointed ARTEMISIA
        (y) Bracts in one row, sharp-pointed OXYTENIA
2. Heads with rays
  a. Receptacle with chaffy scales among the disk-
    flowers
    (1) Rays not yellow
      (a) Rays white
        x. Leaves finely dissected
          (x) Rays 2-6   ACHILLEA
          (y) Rays 10-18   ANTHEMIS
        y. Leaves entire to pinnatifid
          (x) Rays 4-9; pappus none   MELAMPODIUM
          (y) Rays 8-13; pappus hairy   LAYIA
        z. Leaves 2-3-pinnatifid into linear seg-
           ments; involucre white-bordered   LEUCAMPYX
      (b) Rays pink to purple; chaff spiny   BRAUNERIA
    (2) Rays yellow
      (a) Rays pistillate, i. e., with a style
        x. Achene broadly winged; pappus of 2
          awns   XIMENESIA
        y. Achene scarcely or not at all winged
          (x) Rays 2-5

      m. Rays large and broad, 4-5; pappus
          of a few awns   CRASSINA
      n. Rays small, 2-5; pappus none   MADIA
    (y) Rays 10 or more
      m. Pappus none; leaves 6-12 in. long BALSAMORRHIZA
      n. Pappus present
         (m) Inner involucral scales united
               into a cup; pappus of 2 awns
               or scales   THELESPERMA
         (n) Inner scales not united into a cup
           r. Pappus of 2-6 barbed awns   BIDENS
           s. Pappus awns not barbed
              (r) Rays less than 1 in. long;
                 involucral scales in 2 dif-
                 ferent rows   COREOPSIS
              (s) Rays an inch or more long
                h. Leaves opposite; pappus a
                   crown or 1-3 teeth   HELIOPSIS
                i. Leaves alternate; pappus
                   a crown of 5-10 teeth WYETHIA
  (b) Rays neutral, i. e., without a style
    x. Disk globoid, conic or cylindric
      (x) Pappus a 4-toothed crown, or if
          none, the disk purple-black
      m. Achenes flattened   RATIBIDA
      n. Achenes 4-angled   RUDBECKIA
      (y) Pappus inconspicuous or none; disk
          yellow   GYMNOLOMIA
    y. Disk convex to flat
      (x) Pappus of 2 awns only   HELIANTHUS
      (y) Pappus of scales and 2 awns, or of
          scales alone   HELIANTHELLA
b. Receptacle not chaffy
  (1) Pappus hairy
    (a) Rays yellow
    x. Leaves opposite
      (x) Rays 1-4 cm. long   ARNICA
      (y) Rays 2-4 mm. long   HAPLOESTHES
    y. Leaves alternate
      (x) Involucral bracts equal, in 1 row,
         often with small ones at base SENECIO

   (y) Involucral bracts in 2-several rows
    m. Heads broad, many-flowered; rays
     many
     (m) Pappus bristles in 2 rows, the
      outer much shorter   CHRYSOPSIS
     (n) Pappus bristles equal, in 1 row HAPLOPAPPUS
    n. Heads narrow, few-flowered; rays
     3-20   SOLIDAGO
  (b) Rays not yellow
   x. Pappus of many hair-like bristles
    (x) Involucral scales usually in 1-2
     rows; rays usually many, narrow
    m. Rays longer than the width of the
     disk   ERIGERON
    n. Rays tiny, not longer than the
     width of the disk   LEPTILUM
    (y) Involucral scales usually in several
     rows; rays broad
    m. Bracts in 2-5 rows, not spreading
     or reflexed as a rule   ASTER
    n. Bracts in many rows, mostly
     spreading or reflexed MACHAERANTHERA
   y. Pappus of a few hair-like bristles or
    scales or both   TOWNSENDIA
 (2) Pappus not hairy, but of scales, awns, etc.,
  or none
  (a) Rays yellow
   x. Ray 1; leaves opposite; pappus none FLAVERIA
   y. Rays more than 1
    (x) Achenes 4-angled
    m. Plants permanently densely woolly ERIOPHYLLUM
    n. Plants not densely woolly, or only
     when young
     (m) Plants sticky-hairy   HULSEA
     (n) Plants not sticky-hairy
     r. Leaves entire   PLATYSCHKUHRIA
     s. Leaves parted or divided BAHIA
    (y) Achenes 5-10 ribbed
    m. Receptacle with bristles among the
     disk-flowers; pappus of 5-10
     pointed scales   GAILLARDIA

n. Receptacle without bristles
  (m) Leaves alternate or basal, usually without glands
    r. Involucral scales spreading or reflexed; stems 2-6 ft. high HELENIUM
    s. Involucral scales not spreading or reflexed; stems less than 2 ft. high as a rule
      (r) Involucre densely woolly; leaves parted or divided; alpine RYDBERGIA
      (s) Involucre not densely woolly; leaves entire or if divided, not alpine ACTINELLA
  (n) Leaves usually opposite, with distinct oil-glands
    r. Leaves entire, narrow PECTIS
    s. Leaves divided DYSODIA
  (z) Achenes flattened, roundish or swollen, sometimes striate
    m. Heads small, disk-flowers 1-12; rays 1-10
      (m) Rays 2-3-lobed, 4-15 mm. long PSILOSTROPHE
      (n) Rays not lobed, 1-2 mm. long GUTIERRETZIA
    n. Heads large, disk- and ray-flowers many; involucres gummy GRINDELIA
  (b) Rays white to purple
    x. Marginal flowers not true rays, merely ray-like CHAENACTIS
    y. Marginal flowers true rays
      (x) Rays rose-purple POLYPTERIS
      (y) Rays white CHRYSANTHEMUM
3. Heads with all the flowers ray-like or strap-shaped, the central sometimes imperfect and closed; typically with milky juice
a. Pappus of blunt scales; flowers blue CICHORIUM
b. Pappus of plumy, hair-like bristles or bristle-like scales
  (1) Achenes with a beak, bristles interwoven TRAGOPOGON
  (2) Achenes not beaked
    (a) Flowers pink; pappus plumy PTILONIA

(b) Flowers yellow; pappus of narrow scales
    x. Bracts of involucre in 1 row   ADOPOGON
    y. Bracts in 2 or more rows
      (x) Pappus scales tipped with a plumy
          bristle   PTILOCALAIS
      (y) Pappus scales bristle-like   NOTHOCALAIS
c. Pappus of hair-like bristles which are not
  plumose
  (1) Pappus in 2 rows, the inner deciduous
     and falling together, the outer 1-8 and
     persistent   MALACOTHRIX
  (2) Pappus persistent or the bristles falling
     separately
    (a) Flowers rose to purple
      x. Stems annual, 4-8 in. high   PRENANTHELLA
      y. Stems perennial usually a foot or more
        high
        (x) Leaves few or none   LYGODESMIA
        (y) Leaves many   PRENANTHES
    (b) Flowers yellow, blue or white
      x. Stems leafless; heads solitary
        (x) Achenes spiny-warted about the top TARAXACUM
        (y) Achenes not spiny-warted   AGOSERIS
      y. Stems leafy; heads usually several-many
        (x) Achenes flattened
          m. Achenes broad at top, not beaked SONCHUS
          n. Achenes narrowed at top or beaked LACTUCA
        (y) Achenes not flattened
          m. Pappus white   CREPIS
          n. Pappus not white, dark or brown-
            ish   HIERACIUM

ADOPÓGON   Necker 1790 GOATSBEARD
(Gr. *hados,* pleasing, *pogon,* heard)
(Krigia Schreber)

Heads with yellow or orange perfect strap-flowers, achenes oblong, ribbed, pappus of an outer row of 10-15 scales and an inner row of hair-like bristles; receptacle flat, without chaff, involucre bell-shaped, bracts in 1-2 rows; heads solitary; leaves alternate or basal, entire to pinnatifid; annual or perennial.

Stems 1-2 ft. high, 1-leaved; heads about 1.5 in. wide *A. virginicus*

ACHILLÉA Linné 1753 MILFOIL, YARROW
(Named for Achilles)

Heads with white or pink pistillate ray flowers, disk flowers yellow, perfect, achenes oblong or obovate, slightly flattened, pappus none; receptacle flat or convex, with chaff, involucre bell-shaped, the bracts imbricated in several rows; heads in flat-topped corymbs; leaves alternate, finely dissected; perennial.

Stems 1 in. to 3 ft. high; leaves finely dissected, 1-10
  in. long; rays 4-6, white to rose   *A. millefólium*

ACTINÉLLA Nuttall 1818
(Gr. *aktís, aktinos,* ray)
(Hymenoxys Cassini)
Pl. 40, fig. 6; Pl. 41, fig. 2.

Heads with yellow ray flowers, rarely rayless, ray-flowers pistillate, 3-toothed, disk flowers perfect, yellow to brownish, achenes top-shaped, 5-10-ribbed or angled, usually hairy, pappus of 5-12 usually pointed scales; receptacle convex to conic, without chaff, involucre bell-shaped or hemispheric, bracts imbricated in 2-3 rows; heads single or clustered; leaves alternate or basal, often dotted with glands; stemmed or stemless, annual or perennial.

1. Leaves entire
  a. Stems with 1-4 leaves in addition to those at
    the base   *A. leptóclada*
  b. Stems leafless, the leaves all basal, smooth to
    variously hairy   *A. acaúlis*
2. Leaves ternately cut into linear lobes
  a. Perennial from a branched caudex; heads solitary to many   *A. Richardsónii*
  b. Annual from a tap root   *A. multiflóra*

AGÓSERIS Rafinesque 1817
(Gr. *aix, agos,* goat, *seris,* chicory)
(Troximon Nuttall)
Pl. 37, fig. 4.

Heads with yellow, orange or purple strap-shaped perfect flowers, the tip 5-toothed, achenes oblong to linear or obovate, 10-ribbed with a short or long beak, pappus of white, hair-like bristles; receptacle flat, involucre bell-shaped or oblong, the bracts imbricated in several rows; heads solitary on leafless stalks; leaves simple to pinnatifid; annual or perennial.

1. Heads yellow, the rays occasionally purplish
  outside or when old

Plate 37

ASTER FAMILY

1. Laciniaria punctata: Blazing Star
2. Lactuca pulchella: Blue Lettuce
3. Coleanthus grandiflorus
4. Agoseris glauca
5. Tragopogon porrifolius: Salsify
6. Carduus undulatus: Thistle
7. Crepis runcinata

PLATE 37.

a. Achene 3-4 mm. long, with a thread-like beak
   10-15 mm. long   *A. grandiflóra*
b. Achene 7-12 mm. long, with a short stout beak
   1-4 mm. long   *A. glaúca*
2. Heads orange to purple; achene 6-8 mm. long,
   with a thread-like beak, 5-10 mm. long   *A. aurantíaca*

AMBRÓSIA Linné 1753 RAGWEED, KINGHEAD
(The Latin name)

Heads without rays, monoecious, achenes ovoid or obovoid, pappus none, involucre closed, usually with 4-8 tubercles or spines, staminate heads open, many-flowered, corolla present, involucre 5-12-lobed, heads spiked or racemed, pistillate heads 1-flowered, without corolla, solitary or clustered; leaves alternate or opposite, lobed or divided; annual or perennial.

1. Leaves digitately 3-5-lobed; stems 3-15 ft. high   *A. trífida*
2. Leaves 1-3-pinnatifid; stems 1-5 ft. high
   a. Fruiting involucre with 4-6 spines about the
      summit; annual   *A. artemisifólia*
   b. Fruiting involucre spineless or with 3-4 tuber-
      cles; perennial by rootstocks   *A. psilostáchya*

ANÁPHALIS DeCandólle 1837 PEARLY EVERLASTING
(Greek name of some plant)

Heads without rays, dioecious, staminate and pistillate flowers with corolla and hair-like pappus, achenes oblong; receptacle convex without chaff, involucre oblong to bell-shaped, the bracts papery, pearly white, imbricated in several rows; heads in corymbs; leaves alternate, entire, white-woolly; perennial.

Stems 1-2 ft. high; leaves 2-5 in. long, lance-linear,
  · green above, woolly below; heads 6 mm. high   *A. margaritácea*

ANTENNÁRIA Gaertner 1791 CATSFOOT
(Latin *antenna*, feeler)
Pl. 38, fig. 2.

Heads without rays, usually dioecious, staminate and pistillate flowers with hair-like pappus, achenes oblong, round or somewhat flattened; receptacle convex or flat without chaff, involucre oblong to bell-shaped, usually woolly, the bracts papery, imbricated in several rows; heads in dense clusters, corymbs or racemes; leaves alternate, basal, mostly entire, woolly; perennial.

1. Plants with stolons, forming mats
  a. Heads in a dense head-like cluster
    (1) Involucres brown, greenish-brown or
       brownish   *A. alpína*
    (2) Involucres white or pink, greenish at base
      (a) Involucres 4-6 mm. high
         x. Basal leaves obovate to spatulate, dense-
           ly silvery-white, 1-1.5 cm. long   *A. dioéca*
         y. Basal leaves narrowly lanceolate or ob-
           lanceolate, greenish-silvery, 2-3 cm.
           long   *A. corymbósa*
      (b) Involucres 7-10 mm. high; leaves spatu-
         late to obovate   *A. apríca*
  b. Heads in an open raceme-like cluster   *A. racemósa*
2. Plants in tufts, or single, without stolons
  a. Heads solitary; stems tufted, 1-2 in. high;
     leaves spatulate, 1-3 cm. long   *A. dimórpha*
  b. Heads in a corymb-like or head-like cluster;
     stems .5-2 ft. high; leaves linear to lanceo-
     late or oblanceolate, 2-10 cm. long   *A. carpáthica*

ÁNTHEMIS Linné 1753 MAYWEED
(Gr. *anthemis*, flower)

Heads with white, neutral or pistillate ray-flowers, disk-flowers yellow, perfect, achenes oblong, 10-angled, 10-ribbed, roughened, pappus none or a short border; receptacle convex to oblong, with chaff, involucre hemispheric, bracts with papery margins, imbricated in several series; heads at the ends of the branches; leaves alternate, pinnatifid or dissected, strong-scented; annual. or perennial.
Stems .5-2 ft. high; leaves finely dissected   *A. cótula*

ÁRNICA Linné 1753 ARNICA
(Origin and meaning uncertain)
Pl. 40, fig. 2.

Heads with yellow ray-flowers, the latter sometimes wanting, ray-flowers pistillate entire, or 2-3-toothed, disk-flowers yellow, perfect, achenes linear, 5-10-ribbed, pappus a single row of barbed, hair-like bristles; receptacle flat without chaff, involucre bell-shaped or top-shaped, bracts nearly equal in 1-2 series; heads solitary or few in a corymb; leaves mostly opposite, simple, entire or toothed; perennial.

1. Basal leaves, and often some stem leaves, deeply
     heart-shaped, densely hairy to smooth or near-
     ly so   *A. cordifólia*
2. Leaves not cordate
     a. Stem leaves usually 4–8 pairs
          (1) Leaves lance-ovate to lanceolate or ob-
                long, acute or blunt at tip, 2–3 in. long   *A. Chamissónis*
          (2) Leaves long lanceolate, 3–6 in. long, taper-
                ing into a point 1–2 in. long   *A. longifólia*
     b. Stem leaves 1–3 pairs, upper pair usually bract-
          like
          (1) Heads without rays, usually 3–13; leaves
                lance-ovate to lanceolate   *A. Párryi*
          (2) Heads with rays, single or 2–3; leaves
                ovate to lanceolate   *A. alpína*

ARTEMÍSIA   Linné 1753   WORMWOOD, SAGEBRUSH
(Named for Artemisia, wife of Mausolus)

Heads without ray-flowers, the disk-flowers all perfect and fertile, or
the central ones sometimes sterile, the marginal ones pistillate and fertile,
achenes obovate to oblong, pappus none; receptacle flat to hemispheric,
without chaff, involucre oblong to hemispheric, the bracts imbricated in a
few rows; heads variously clustered, the flowers greenish or yellow; leaves
alternate, entire to divided, often woolly; herbs or shrubs.

1. Stems spiny; achenes cobwebby with long hairs;
     leaves digitately 3–5-parted   *A. spinéscens*
2. Stems not spiny; achenes not cobwebby
     a. Stems shrubby, 5 in. to 10 ft. high
          (1) Leaves entire, linear to lance-linear, dense-
                ly white-hairy; stems 1–2.5 ft. high   *A. cána*
          (2) Leaves 3-toothed or 3-cleft
               (a) Leaves wedge-shaped, 3-toothed or 3-
                     lobed at the tip, uppermost entire
                     x. Stems usually 1–10 ft. high; flower
                          cluster much branched; heads 2 mm.
                          wide   *A. tridentáta*
                     y. Stems 4–10 in. high; flower cluster nar-
                          row, spike-like; heads 3 mm. wide   *A. arbúscula*
               (b) Leaves 3-cleft into thread-like lobes, the
                     upper entire and thread-like
                     x. Leaves 1–2 cm. long, lobes 3–10 mm.
                          long; heads oblong, 2 mm. wide   *A. trífida*

y. Leaves 1-2 in. long, lobes 1 in. or more
   long; heads round, 1 mm. wide   *A. filifólia*

b. Stems herbaceous, occasionally woody at the
   base

  (1) Leaves entire or coarsely 3-5-lobed

    (a) Leaves entire, linear, green; involucres
   green, 2-3 mm. wide; heads many in
   a long panicle   *A. dracunculoides*

    (b) Leaves entire to coarsely and irregular-
   ly 3-5-lobed, felted on both faces, or
   green above; involucres white or gray,
   felted, woolly or hairy   *A. ludoviciána*

  (2) Leaves, at least the lower, regularly 5-7-
   lobed or pinnatifid to finely dissected

    (a) Long woolly hairs between the flowers;
   leaves usually gray-hairy

      x. Heads many, 3-5 mm. wide; leaves
   short, finely dissected; stems 6-18 in.
   high, usually mat-like; at 3-9000 ft. *A. frígida*

      y. Heads 1 to about 10, 5-12 mm. wide,
   often nodding; leaves longer, pinnatifid; stems 1-10 in. high, clustered or
   single; at 10-13000 ft.   *A. scopulórum*

    (b). No long woolly hairs between the flow-
   ers of the head

      x. Leaves smooth, green at least above

        (x) Stems from a caudex or woody base

          m. Leaf segments linear to thread-
   like   *A. canadénsis*

          n. Leaf segments broad, lanceolate to
   oblong

            (m) Leaves mostly 1-pinnatifid;
   heads 20-30-flowered   *A. díscolor*

            (n) Leaves mostly 2-pinnatifid;
   heads 30-40 flowered   *A. franserioídes*

        (y) Stems merely from a tap root, bien-
   nial; leaf segments toothed as a
   rule   *A. biénnis*

      y. Leaves more or less gray-hairy

        (x) Heads many in a large panicle   *A. canadénsis*

(y) Heads fewer in a narrow spike-like
cluster
m. Stems and involucres white-felted *A. Wrightii*
n. Stems and involucres hairy to
smooth   *A. boreális*

Áster Linné 1753 Aster

(Gr. *aster*, star)

Pl. 38, fig. 5.

Heads with white, pink, blue, violet or purple pistillate ray-flowers, disk-flowers yellow, becoming brown, purple or red, perfect, achenes usually flattened and nerved, pappus of hair-like bristles; receptacle flat to convex, without chaff, involucre hemispheric to top-shaped, the bracts usually unequal and imbricated in several rows, sometimes about equal and in 2-3 rows; heads solitary or in corymbs or panicles; leaves alternate, simple; perennial or rarely annual.

1. Annuals
    a. Bracts linear or linear-lanceolate, pointed   *A. angústus*
    b. Bracts oblong to oblanceolate, blunt or rounded *A. frondósus*
2. Perennials
    a. Bracts spiny-pointed; stems tufted, 1-headed
       (1) Leaves not spiny-toothed, spatulate or
          oblanceolate; heads 10-15 mm. wide;
          rays white   *A. villósus*
       (2) Leaves spiny-toothed, spatulate; heads 10-
          12 mm. high; rays purple   *A. coloradénsis*
    b. Bracts not spiny-pointed
       (1) Bracts broad with keel-like midrib, papery,
          usually fringed and purple-tipped
          (a) Involucres 12-20 mm. wide; leaves
             mostly 1.5-2.5 cm. wide   *A. Engelmánnii*
          (b) Involucres 6-10 mm. wide; leaves usu-
             ally less than 1 cm. wide
            x. Stems usually simple; bracts purple,
               acute   *A. élegans*
            y. Stems usually much branched; bracts
               scarcely purple, outer rounded or
               blunt   *A. glaúcus*
       (2) Bracts mostly narrow, without keel-like
          midrib

(a) Stems 1-headed, 2-4 in. high; leaves
linear to spatulate; rays white to violet; at 10-14000 ft.

  x. Stems erect; basal leaves usually none;
stem leaves many, crowded, gray-
hairy, spiny-tipped, less than 1 cm.
long; heads 6-12 mm. wide; rays 10-
12 mm. long, violet   *A. alpinus*

  y. Stems spreading; basal leaves many,
green, 3-9 cm. long; stem leaves few
or none; heads 12-18 mm. wide; rays
12-16 mm. long, purple   *A. pulchéllus*

(b) Stems usually few-many-headed, .5-6
ft. high; at 3-9000 ft.

  x. Involucres and peduncles glandular-
hairy

    (x) Stem leaves linear, or lance-linear,
1-5 mm. wide

    m. Involucre 4-5 mm. high; rays 4-5
mm. long, violet   *A. pauciflórus*

    n. Involucre 5-8 mm. high; rays 8-15
mm. long

      (m) Rays violet, 8 mm. long   *A. Féndleri*

      (n) Rays deep blue, 12-15 mm.
long   *A. campéstris .*

    (y) Stem leaves lanceolate or oblong to
ovate; .5-6 cm. wide

    m. Leaves ovate to lance-ovate, coarse-
ly sharp-toothed, 2-6 cm. wide,
involucre 10-12 mm. high; rays
violet   *A. conspícuus*

    n. Leaves oblong to spatulate, entire

      (m) Stems 1-2 ft. high; rays 15-30

      r. Rays 15-25, blue-purple; in-
volucre 8-12 mm. high;
heads few; leaves spatulate *A. integrifólius*

      s. Rays 25-30, violet; involucre
4-6 mm. high; heads many;
leaves lance-oblong   *A. oblongifólius*

      (n) Stems 2-6 ft. high; rays 50-70,
purple; involucre 8-12 mm.
high; leaves lance-oblong   *A. novae-ángliae*

y. Involucres and peduncles not glandular-
hairy
  (x) Outer bracts as long or longer than
the inner, often leaf-like   *A. foliáceus*
  (y) Outer bracts shorter than the inner,
not leaf-like
    m. Bracts more or less hairy on the
back
      (m) Stems 2-6 in. high; leaves
bristly ciliate, less than 1
cm. long; heads single at the
end of each branch, 1-1.5
cm. wide; rays white, 12-15 *A. ericoídes*
      (n) Stems 1-4 ft. high, leaves
somewhat ciliate, 1-5 cm.
long; heads not single on the
branches
        r. Bracts pointed with a short
white bristle; heads usually
many in a panicle; invol-
ucre 4-8 mm. high; rays
mostly white, sometimes
bluish   *A. multiflórus*
        s. Bracts n o t bristle-pointed;
heads few in a cyme-like
cluster; rays violet   *A. gríseus*
    n. Bracts smooth on the back
      (m) Stems and peduncles smooth
        r. Rays white; leaves linear or
lance-linear; stems 1-2 ft.
high
          (r) Heads few-several in a
flat-topped cluster; stems
simple   *A. ptarmicoídes*
          (s) Heads many in a panicle;
stems much branched *A. Pórteri*
        s. Rays lilac to blue-purple;
leaves lance-oblong to spatulate or ovate, upper with
clasping base; stems 1-5 ft.
high   *A. lévis*

Plate 38

ASTER FAMILY

1. Solidago missouriensis: Goldenrod
2. Antennaria dioeca: Catsfoot
3. Erigeron macranthus: Daisy
4. Machaeranthera Bigelovii; Purple Aster
5. Aster foliaceus
6. Gutierrezia sarothrae
7. Chrysopsis villosa: Golden Eye
8. Grindelia squarrosa: Gum Weed

PLATE 38.

(n) Stems and peduncles hairy, or
 at least with hairy lines
 r. Lower leaves ovate and heart-
  shaped, long-petioled; rays
  blue to violet   *A. lindleyánus*
 s. Leaves lanceolate, spatulate to
  linear
  (r) Lower leaves spatulate or
   oblong-spatulate; heads
   mostly few-several, in
   flat-topped clusters *A. adscéndens*
  (s) Leaves lanceolate to linear
  h. Bracts of 1-2 different
   lengths; rays violet to
   purple   *A. longifólius*
  i. Bracts of 3-5 different
   lengths; rays often white *A. salicifólius*

BÁCCHARIS Linné 1753
(Named for Bacchus)

Heads without rays, dioecious, achenes ribbed, somewhat flattened,
pappus of hair-like bristles, shorter in the staminate flowers; receptacle
flat without chaff, involucre bell-shaped, the bracts imbricated in several
rows; heads in panicles or corymbs; leaves alternate, simple; herbs or
shrubs.

1. Stems herbaceous, except for a woody base
 a. Leaves linear, entire; pappus elongating in
  fruit, 4 times as long as the 8-10-ribbed
  achene   *B. Wrightii*
 b. Leaves long-lanceolate, somewhat toothed;
  pappus little elongated in fruit; achene 5-
  ribbed   *B. glutinósa*
2. Shrubs, 3-10 ft. high
 a. Pistillate heads 5-10 mm. broad; involucral
  bracts all acute   *B. salicína*
 b. Pistillate heads 3-5 mm. broad; outer bracts
  obtuse   *B. Emóryi*

BÁHIA Lagasca 1816 BAHIA
(Named for Bahi, a Spanish botanist)
Pl. 41, fig. 1.

Heads with yellow pistillate ray-flowers or none, disk-flowers perfect,
yellow, achenes linear to oblong, 4-angled, pappus of several papery scales;

receptacle flat, without chaff, involucre bell-shaped or hemispheric, the bracts nearly equal, in 1-2 rows; heads solitary or in corymbs; leaves opposite or alternate, parted or divided; annual or perennial.

1. Perennial ·from a woody root; rays 5-6, short;
   leaves 3-5 parted *B. oppositifólia*
2. Annual
   a. Rays present; leaves mostly alternate *B. dissécta*
   b. Rays none; leaves mostly opposite *B. neo-mexicána*

BALSAMORRHÍZA Hooker 1833 BALSAM ROOT
(Gr. *balsamon,* balsam, *rhiza,* root)

Heads with yellow ray-flowers, disk-flowers yellow, perfect, achenes of the ray-flowers 3-angled or flattened, of the disk-flowers 4-angled; receptacle flat or convex with lance-linear chaff, involucre broad, the bracts imbricated or nearly equal and the outer enlarged; heads mostly solitary on few-leaved or naked stalks; leaves large, mostly basal, simple to pinnatifid; perennial.

1. Leaves entire or toothed *B. sagittáta*
2. Leaves, or some of them, pinnatifid
   a. Stems and leaves smooth or slightly hairy *B. macrophýlla*
   b. Stems and leaves white-hairy to woolly *B. incána*

BÍDENS Linné 1753 BEGGAR'S TICKS, BUR-MARIGOLD
(Latin *bi-,* two, *dens,* tooth, from the pappus)
Pl. 40, fig. 1.

Heads with white or yellow neutral rays or none, disk-flowers perfect, yellow to brown, achenes flat, angled or rounded, wedge-shaped to linear, pappus of barbed awns; receptacle flat, with chaff, involucre bell-shaped to hemispheric, bracts in 2 rows, separate or somewhat united at the base, the outer often larger and leaf-like; heads solitary or in corymbs or panicles; leaves opposite, or alternate above, toothed, lobed or dissected; annual or perennial.

1. Leaves simple, toothed
   a. Rays present *B. lévis*
   b. Rays none *B. comósa*
2. Leaves, or some of them, divided or dissected
   a. Rays none; achenes oval to obovate, flat, 2-
      awned *B. frondósa*
   b. Rays present; achenes long-linear, angled, 2-4-
      awned

(1) Leaf-segments linear; achenes 2-awned   *B. tenuisécta*

(2) Leaf-segments triangular to oblong;
     achenes 3-4-awned   *B. bipinnáta*

BRAUNÉRIA Necker 1790

(Named for Brauner, a German botanist)

Heads with pink to rose-purple neutral rays, disk-flowers perfect, brown, achenes 4-sided, pappus a crown of teeth; receptacle conic, with stiff pointed chaff, involucre hemispheric, the bracts imbricated in 2-4 rows; heads solitary on long stalks; leaves alternate or opposite, entire or toothed; perennial.

Stems bristly, 1-3 ft. high; leaves lanceolate, 3-8 in.
    long; rays 10-20, 1-2.5 in. long   *B. pállida*

CÁRDUUS Linné 1753 THISTLE

(The Latin name of the thistle) .

Pl. 37, fig. 6.

Heads without rays, rarely dioecious, disk-flowers with long, deeply-cleft corolla tube, perfect as a rule, achenes oblong to obovate, flattened or 4-angled, pappus of several rows of hair-like bristles; receptacle flat or convex, bristly, involucre ovoid to globose, the bracts usually imbricated in many rows and spiny-tipped; heads large, solitary or clustered; leaves alternate or basal, toothed to pinnatifid, usually spiny; biennial or perennial.

1. Heads 1.5-3 in. high, perfect
   a. All the bracts, or at least the inner ones, with
       broadened fringed tips; flowers yellow or
       yellowish
     (1) All the bracts with broadened fringed tips,
         not cobwebby, the spines short or none;
         leaves green above, white-felted below   *C. americánus*
     (2) Inner bracts with broadened fringed tips,
         outer with spines .5-10 mm. long
       (a) Leaves green and smooth when mature,
           oblong-ovate; bracts cobwebby   *C. Párryi*
       (b) Leaves green and hairy or white below,
           long and narrow; bracts not cobwebby *C. Drummóndii*
   b. None of the bracts with broadened fringed
       tips; white, yellow or purple
     (1) Bracts without a sticky ridge or line on the
         back

(a) Bracts more or less densely cobwebby,
    not imbricated in rows; heads yellow-
    ish; leaves white woolly to nearly
    smooth   *C. hookeriánus*

(b) Bracts not cobwebby

   x. All bracts tipped with spines, cóttony;
       heads dark purple; weeds   *C. lanceolátus*

   y. Inner bracts, and sometimes the outer
       also, pointed but not spiny; heads
       white to rose-purple

      (x) Bracts spreading or reflexed, dense-
          ly white-woolly; leaves densely
          white-woolly   *C. neo-mexicánus*

      (y) Bracts not spreading or reflexed, or
          at the tips only; bracts not dense-
          ly white-woolly; stem simple,
          branched or none   *C. Drummóndii*

(2) Bracts with a sticky ridge, line or spot on
     the back, closely imbricated in several
     rows

   (a) Heads yellowish or yellow   *C. platténsis*
   (b) Heads rose to purple, rarely white   *C. undulátus*

2. Heads less than 1 in. high, dioecious; weed   *C. arvénsis*

CHAÉNACTIS   DeCandolle 1836

(Gr. *chaino*, to gape, *actis*, ray, from the enlarged throat of the corolla)

Heads without rays, but the marginal flowers somewhat enlarged,
often simulating rays, disk-flowers yellow, white or purplish, achenes linear,
4-angled or flattened, pappus of scales; receptacle flat, without chaff, involucre bell-shaped to hemispheric; heads solitary or in cymes; leaves
alternate, usually pinnately-dissected; annual or perennial.

1. Marginal flowers manifestly enlarged, becoming
    unequally 5-lobed or ray-like; pappus of 4
    scales   *C. stevioídes*

2. Marginal corollas not enlarged and irregular;
    pappus of 8-14 scales   *C. Douglásii*

CHRYSÁNTHEMUM   Linné 1753   OX-EYE DAISY, WHITE WEED
(The Greek name, meaning Golden Flower)

Heads with white pistillate rays, disk-flowers yellow, perfect, achenes
roundish or angled, 5-10-ribbed, pappus none or a cup of scales; receptacle

flat to hemispheric without chaff, involucre hemispheric, bracts imbricated in several rows; heads usually solitary on long stalks; leaves alternate, coarsely toothed or cut; annual or perennial.

Stems 1-3 ft. high; stem-leaves linear-spatulate, 1-3 in.
long; rays 20-30   *C. leucánthemum*

CHRYSÓPSIS Nuttall 1818 GOLDEN EYE, GOLDEN ASTER
(Gr. *chrysos*, golden, *opsis*, look, from the color)
Pl. 38, fig. 7.

Heads with yellow pistillate ray-flowers, disk-flowers yellow, usually perfect, achenes flattened, linear-oblong to obovate, pappus double, inner row of hair-like bristles and the outer of smaller scales or bristles; receptacle flat, without chaff, involucre hemispheric to bell-shaped, the bracts imbricated in several rows; heads solitary or corymbose on the branches; leaves alternate, sessile, entire or toothed; perennial.

Stems 4 in. to 2 ft. high; leaves lance-linear to spatulate or nearly ovate, 1-8 cm. long, bristly, shaggy,
hairy or sticky; heads 1-2 cm. wide, sessile or variously stalked   *C. villósa*

CHRYSOTHÁMNUS Nuttall 1840 GOLDEN BUSH, FALSE
GOLDEN ROD
(Gr. *chrysos*, golden, *thamnos*, bush)

Heads without rays, the disk-flowers yellow or cream-colored, perfect, achenes oblong to ovoid, pappus of hair-like bristles; receptacle without chaff, involucre oblong to cylindric, the bracts imbricated in several rows, often in distinct vertical ridges, usually stiff and papery; heads in racemes, panicles or cymes; leaves alternate, entire, spatulate to linear; shrubs, or becoming shrubby.

1. Bracts more or less long-pointed
  a. Achenes hairy; bracts not in ridges
    (1) Outer bracts long-tapering, some usually
        exceeding the flowers, and leaf-like;
        heads in a long leafy spike- or raceme-
        like cluster
      (a) Heads 10-15-flowered; bracts about 12;
          leaves lance-linear   *C. Párryi*
      (b) Heads 5-flowered; bracts 15-18; leaves
          narrowly linear   *C. Hówardii*

  (2) Outer bracts not exceeding the flowers or
    leaf-like; leaves thread-like, green
    and smooth   *C. Greénei*
 b. Achenes smooth; bracts keeled, in 5 distinct
  vertical ridges
  (1) Leaves spatulate or oblanceolate, gray-
    hairy   *C. depréssus*
  (2) Leaves narrowly linear to thread-like
    (a) Bracts thick, strongly keeled, smooth. *C. pulchéllus*
    (b) Bracts thin, not strongly keeled, cob-
      webby-ciliate   *C. Bigelóvii*
2. Bracts not long-pointed, obtuse to acute
 a. Achenes hairy
  (1) Branches, at least the young ones more or
    less white-woolly or felted; bracts
    smooth, ciliate or hairy; leaves linear to
    lance-oblong   *C. gravéolens*
  (2) Branches green, never woolly or felted;
    bracts smooth to ciliate; leaves linear to
    lance-oblong   *C. Douglásii*
 b. Achenes not hairy   *C. Váseyii*

CICHÓRIUM Linné 1753 CHICORY
(Latinized from the Arabic)

Heads with strap-shaped flowers alone, the latter perfect, blue, rarely white, achenes 5-angled or ribbed, not beaked, pappus of 2-3 rows of short scales; receptacle flat, without chaff, involucre of 2 rows of bracts, the outer spreading; heads usually 1-4 in sessile clusters; leaves alternate and basal, entire to pinnatifid; perennial with milky juice.

Stems 1-3 ft. high; basal leaves 3-6 in. long, spatulate,
 pinnatifid; heads 1-1.5 in. wide   *C. íntybus*

COLEÁNTHUS Cassini 1817 THOROUGHWORT
(Gr. *koleos*, sheath, *anthos*, flower)
Pl. 37, fig. 3.

Heads with tube-flowers alone, the latter white to yellowish, perfect, achenes 10-ribbed, oblong, pappus of hair-like bristles, receptacle flat or convex without chaff, involucre oblong to bell-shaped, the bracts imbricated in several rows; heads in panicles or cymes; leaves opposite or alternate, simple, toothed; perennial.

 1. Leaves ovate or oblong-ovate, often heart-shaped
   at base

a. Leaves sessile or nearly so, the teeth spiny-
  pointed   *C. atractyloídes*
b. Leaves petioled, the teeth not spiny-tipped
  (1) Heads 10-25-flowered
    (a) Leaves 2-4 cm. long; involucral bracts
      erect, not spreading   *C. Wríghtii*
    (b) Leaves 5-10 mm. long; involucral bracts
      spreading and reflexed   *C. microphýllus*
  (2) Heads 30-50-flowered
    (a) Heads drooping   *C. grandiflórus*
    (b) Heads erect   *C. ámbigens*
2. Leaves lance-oblong to linear, sessile; heads 40-
  50-flowered   *C. linifólius*

CORÉOPSIS Linné 1753 TICKSEED
(Gr. *koris*, tick, *opsis*, look, from the form of the achene)

Heads with yellow to brown neutral ray-flowers, disk-flowers yellow, perfect, achenes flat, oblong to rounded, often winged, pappus of 2 short teeth or none; receptacle flat, with chaff, involucre hemispheric, the bracts in 2 distinct rows, united at the base, the outer row usually narrower and shorter; heads solitary or in corymbs; leaves opposite or alternate, entire to pinnately-divided; annual or perennial.

1. Rays brown at the base or brown all over; leaves
  1-2-pinnately divided into linear segments   *C. tinctória*
2. Rays bright yellow; leaves spatulate or oblong,
  entire   *C. lanceoláta*

CRASSÍNA Scepin 1758 ZINNIA
(Named for Crassus, an Italian botanist)

Heads with yellow or yellowish pistillate rays, becoming papery and persistent, disk-flowers yellow, perfect, achenes flattened, usually wingless, pappus of 2-4 erect awns; receptacle conic, with chaff, involucre bell-shaped to cylindric, the bracts papery, imbricated in several rows; heads solitary on the branches; leaves opposite, entire, sessile; annual or perennial.

Stems 6-12 in. high; leaves linear or lance-linear, 1-3
cm. long; rays 4-5, 10-16 mm. long   *C. grandiflóra*

CRÉPIS Linné 1753 HAWKSBEARD
(Gr. *krepis*, sandal, perhaps from the basal leaves)
Pl. 37, fig. 7.

Heads of strap-shaped yellow or orange perfect flowers, achenes linear-oblong, 10-20-ribbed, not beaked, pappus of hair-like white bristles; receptacle flat, without chaff, involucre ovoid to cylindric, the main bracts in 1 row with shorter basal ones; heads in panicles or corymbs; leaves alternate or basal, entire to pinnatifid; annual or perennial.

1. Stems none or 4-10 in. high; heads very many,
the involucre 6-8 mm. long, 2-3 mm. wide;
achenes broadened at the tip into a disk
   a. Stemless or nearly so, the tufts from creeping
   rootstocks   *C. nána*
   b. Stems 4-10 in. high from a tap root   *C. élegans*
2. Stems 1-3 ft. high; heads few-many; achenes not
broadened into a disk
   a. Stems and leaves smooth or glaucous, occasionally with coarse hairs, not finely gray-hairy; leaves mostly entire or with coarse teeth, rarely deeply pinnatifid
      (1) Involucres and peduncles smooth   *C. glaúca*
      (2) Involucres and peduncles coarsely hairy,
      the latter often woolly   *C. runcináta*
   b. Stems and leaves gray-hairy to woolly; leaves
   usually deeply pinnatifid
      (1) Involucres narrow, 1 cm. or less long, 2-3
      mm. wide, smooth, except for the woolly-edged bracts at the base; inner bracts
      5-8; flowers 5-8   *C. acumináta*
      (2) Involucres 1-2 cm. long, 4-6 mm. wide,
      gray-hairy or woolly; inner bracts 9-
      24; flowers 10-30   *C. occidentális*

Dicória Torrey and Gray 1848
(Gr. *di-*, twice, *koris*, bug, from the two achenes)

Heads without rays, with 1-2 pistillate flowers without corolla and 6-12 staminate ones, achenes oblong, margined with teeth, pappus small of several little scales; receptacle flat, chaff of 2 narrow scales, involucre of 5 leafy bracts; heads in a sparse panicle, some all staminate; leaves alternate, at least above, usually entire; annual.

Leaves lance-oblong to spatulate, 2-3 cm. long; pistillate flowers solitary in the head   *D. Brandégei*

Dysódia Cavanilles 1801 Dysodia
(Gr. *dysodia*, ill-smelling)
(Hymenatherum Cassini; Lowellia Gray)
Pl. 41, fig. 6.

Heads with yellow pistillate ray-flowers, disk-flowers perfect, yellow, achenes 3-5-angled, pappus of 6-10 scales, toothed or fringed with hair-like bristles; receptacle flat, hairy or bristly, involucre hemispheric to cylindric, the bracts in 1 series, more or less united; heads solitary or somewhat panicled; leaves alternate or opposite, pinnately parted or dissected; annual.

1. Leaves mostly opposite, strong-scented; rays usually 2-5, 3-4 mm. long   *D. pappósa*
2. Leaves mostly alternate, not strong-scented; rays about 12, 6 mm. long   *D. aúrea*

ERÍGERON Linné 1753 DAISY
(Gr. *er,* spring, *geron,* old man, from the woolly heads and time of blooming)
(Wyomingia Nelson)
Pl. 38, fig. 3.

Heads with white, violet or purple pistillate ray-flowers, disk-flowers yellow, perfect, achenes flattened, usually 2-nerved, pappus of hair-like bristles in 1-2 rows; receptacle flat, without chaff, involucre hemispheric to bell-shaped, the bracts nearly equal in 1-2, rarely 3-4 rows; heads solitary or in corymbs or panicles; leaves alternate or basal, entire to pinnatifid; annual or perennial.

1. Rays inconspicuous, short or wanting, usually erect; leaves entire
   a. Heads in a flat-topped corymb or panicle   *E. ácris*
   b. Heads in a narrow raceme   *E. a. racemósus*
2. Rays conspicuous, spreading or flat; leaves various
   a. Bracts of the involucre in 1-2 nearly equal rows
      (1) Perennial, as shown by old stems, runners, rootstocks, caudexes, etc.
         (a) Stems spreading by runners, 2-10 in. high; leaves linear to spatulate; rays white, rose or purplish   *E. flagelláris*
         (b) Stems without runners
            x. Leaves basal, deeply divided or cleft, 1-3-ternate, 3-5-fid or pinnatifid; stems tufted, 2-8 in. high; heads 1-1.5 cm. wide; rays white to blue-purple   *E. compósitus*
            y. Leaves entire or toothed
               (x) Involucres copiously white or black cobwebby-woolly, especially at base

m. Stems 1-8 in. high, mostly single;
leaves mostly basal, stem leaves
small; rays white to blue   *E. uniflórus*

n. Stems 6-15 in. high, clustered, very
leafy; leaves entire to toothed;
rays white to rose-purple   *E. elátior*

(y) Involucres white-bristly to glandular or smooth, but not woolly

  m. Stems 2-8 in. high, 1-headed, tufted;
leaves mostly basal

    (m) Involucre dotted-glandular;
leaves smooth, spatulate to
obovate; rays violet   *E. leiómerus*

    (n) Involucre with at least some
white-bristly hairs, often
densely so, sometimes glandular also

      r. Leaves obovate, gray-hairy;
rays violet   *E. téner*

      s. Leaves linear to linear-oblance-
olate, hairy; rays white to
blue-purple

        (r) Leaves glandular as well
as hairy   *E. glandulósus*

        (s) Leaves not glandular, more
or less gray-hairy   *E. radicátus*

n. Stems 8 in.-3 ft. high, or if lower
with several heads, more or less
leafy; heads in most very large

  (m) Heads small, the disk usually 1
cm. or less; stems tufted

    r. Stems with long bristly white
hairs; leaves mostly linear,
rays white to blue   *E. púmilus*

    s. Stem with soft close hairs;
leaves lanceolate to spatulate;
rays white to blue   *E. caespitósus*

  (n) Heads large, the disk 1-2 cm.
wide; stems single or
clustered

r. Involucral bracts spreading and
reflexed   *E. salsuginósus*

s. Involucral bracts erect and appressed

   (r) Upper stem leaves greatly
reduced, mostly few and
bract-like, hairy to near-
ly smooth   *E. ásper*

   (s) Stem leaves not bract-like,
usually many and gradu-
ally reduced   .   *E. macránthus*

(2) Annual or biennial, without rootstocks,
runners, etc.

  (a) Stem leaves broad, clasping by a heart-
shaped base; rays usually pink   *E. philadélphicus*

  (b) Stem leaves not broad and clasping

    x. Stems much branched at the base, 4-12
in. high; rays usually rose or purplish *E. divérgens*

    y. Stems simple at base, branched above,
1-2 ft. high; rays white   *E. ramósus*

b. Bracts of the involucre in 3 or 4 rows, the
outer usually shorter; stems tufted from a
woody base with long woody roots; leaves
spatulate to linear, more or less silvery-hairy

(1) Heads 12-15 mm. high; involucres 2-2.5
cm. wide; rays 12-15 mm. long; achenes
hairy   *E. argentátus*

(2) Heads 6-10 mm. high; involucres 1-1.5 cm.
wide; rays 6-15 cm. long; achenes
smooth or hairy   *E. cánus*

ERIOPHÝLLUM Lagasca 1818

(Gr. *erion*, wool, *phyllon*, leaf, from the woolly plant)

Heads with yellow ray-flowers, the disk-flowers yellow, perfect, achenes
narrow club-shaped to wedge-oblong, usually 4-angled, pappus of scales;
receptacle flat to convex, involucre hemispheric, of separate or united bracts
in 1-2 series; heads solitary or scattered; leaves alternate or opposite; entire or lobed, annual or perennial.

1. Stems 1-4 in. high; heads sessile or nearly so   *E. Wallácei*
2. Stems 4-12 in. high; heads stalked   *E. integrifólium*

PLATE 39

ASTER FAMILY

1, 6. Ratibida columnaris: Cone Flower
   2. Rudbeckia laciniata: Golden Glow
   3. Thelesperma gracile
   4. Rudbeckia hirta: Blackeyed Susan
   5. Gymnolomia multiflora
   7. Helianthus petiolaris: Sunflower
   8. Thelesperma trifidum

PLATE 39.

EUPATÓRIUM Linné 1753 BONESET, JOE PYEWEED
(Named for Mithridates Eupator)

Heads with white, blue or purple perfect tube-flowers, achenes oblong, 5-angled, pappus of hair-like bristles; receptacle flat to conic, without chaff, involucre hemispheric to oblong, bracts imbricated in 2-several rows; heads in cymose panicles; leaves opposite or whorled, usually simple; perennial.

1. Leaves opposite, 1-2 in. long
 a. Bracts of the involucre nerved or ribbed   *E. Féndleri*
 b. Bracts of the involucre not nerved   *E. texénse*
2. Leaves usually in whorls of 3, 2-5 in. long   *E. maculátum*

FILÁGO Linné 1753
(Latin *filum*, thread, *ago*, like, from the cottony wool)

Heads without rays, outer pistillate flowers in several rows, central flowers few, perfect, mostly sterile, achenes flattened or rounded, pappus none; receptacle convex to conic with chaff, involucre of a few papery bracts; heads clustered, with leafy bracts; leaves alternate, entire; white, woolly annual.

Stems 2-6 in. high; leaves spatulate, 8-15 mm. long   *F. prolífera*

FLAVÉRIA Jussieu 1789
(Lat. *flavus*, yellow, from its use as a yellow dye) ·

Heads with a single yellow, pistillate ray, 2-5-flowered, disk-flowers perfect, yellow, achenes oblong or linear, 8-10-ribbed, pappus none; involucre of 2-5 equal bracts; heads in clusters; annual.

Stems 8-20 in. high; leaves linear to lanceolate, entire or toothed   *F. angustifólia*

FRANSÉRIA Cavanilles 1793
(Named for Franser, a Spanish botanist)

Heads without ray-flowers, monoecious, staminate heads in terminal spikes or racemes, pistillate heads solitary or clustered, achenes obovoid, pappus none; receptacle of the staminate heads chaffy, the involucre hemispheric, open, 5-12-lobed, involucre of the pistillate heads globose or ovoid, closed, 1-4-beaked, with several rows of spines, forming a bur in fruit; leaves entire to pinnatifid; annual or perennial.

1. Leaves simple or once-pinnatifid   *F. Gráyi*
2. Leaves 2-3-pinnatifid
 a. Fruiting involucre 1-flowered, its spines flat
  and thin; annual   *F. acanthicárpa*
 b. Fruiting involucre 2-flowered, its spines short
  and conic; perennial

(1) Spines of the involucre usually hooked;
racemes of staminate heads usually pan-
icled   *F. tenuifólia*

(2) Spines not hooked; raceme of staminate
heads usually solitary   *F. tomentósa*

GAILLÁRDIA Fougeroux 1786 GAILLARDIA

(Named for Gaillard de Marentonneau, a French botanist)

Pl. 40, fig. 3.

Heads with yellow, orange or purple neutral, rarely pistillate ray-flowers, disk-flowers orange to purplish, perfect, achenes top-shaped, 5-ribbed,
usually densely woolly, pappus of 5-12 awned scales; receptacle convex
to globose, usually bristly, involucre low hemispheric, bracts imbricated
in 2-3 rows with spreading or reflexed tips; heads solitary on long stalks;
leaves alternate or basal, entire to pinnatifid; annual or perennial.

1. Lobes of the disk-flowers pointed, often tipped
with a tooth, with long beaded hairs on the outside   *G. aristáta*

2. Lobes of the disk-flowers short, broad and obtuse, without beaded hairs   *G. pinnatifida*

GNAPHÁLIUM Linné 1753 EVERLASTING

(Gr. *gnaphalion,* name of a woolly plant)

Heads without ray-flowers, pistillate flowers in several rows, central
flowers perfect, achenes oblong to obovate, round or flattened, pappus of
hair-like bristles; receptacle flat to conic, without chaff, involucre oblong
to bell-shaped, the bracts imbricated in several rows, usually papery and
woolly; heads in racemes, corymbed spikes or dense clusters; leaves alternate, mostly entire; annual or perennial.

1. Heads with leafy bracts; involucres more or less
woolly all over; stems simple or branched;
leaves variously woolly   *G. palústre*

2. Heads without leafy bracts; involucre woolly only
at base
a. Leaves woolly on both surfaces
(1) Leaf-bases running down the stem   *G. chilénse*
(2) Leaf-bases not running down the stem   *G. Wrightii*
b. Leaves green above, sticky-hairy, running down
the stem   *G. decúrrens*

GRINDÉLIA Willdenow 1807 GUMWEED
(Named for Grindel, a Russian botanist)
Pl. 38, fig. 8.

Heads with yellow pistillate ray-flowers or none, disk-flowers yellow, perfect or staminate, achenes oblong-ovoid, 4-5-ribbed, pappus of 2-8 awns or bristles, soon falling; receptacle flat or convex, without chaff, involucre hemispheric, the bracts imbricated in several-many rows, often spreading and reflexed; heads solitary at the ends of branches; leaves alternate, usually spiny-toothed, often clasping; perennial, often woody at base.

1. Heads hemispheric; involucral bracts narrow,
   the reflexed tips awl-shaped; rays often absent *G. squarrósa*
2. Heads broad and flat; involucral scales broad, the
   reflexed tips flat   *G. texána*

GUTIERRÉZIA Lagasca 1816 GUTIERREZIA
(Named for Gutierrez, a Spanish noble)
Pl. 38, fig. 6.

Heads with 1-10 yellow, pistillate ray-flowers, disk flowers 1-10, yellow, perfect or some staminate, achenes ovoid, rounded, ribbed or 5-angled, pappus of several scales; receptacle flat to conic, without chaff, involucre ovoid to oblong, bracts somewhat papery, imbricated in a few rows; heads in corymbose panicles; leaves alternate, linear, entire; perennial, often woody at base.

Stems bushy-branched, 6-25 in. high; leaves linear,
1-4 cm. long; heads 3-4 mm. high; rays 1-10   *G. saróthrae*

GYMNOLÓMIA H. B. K. 1820 GYMNOLOMIA
(Gr. *gymnos*, naked, *loma*, fringe, from the absent pappus)
Pl. 39, fig. 5.

Heads with yellow pistillate ray-flowers, disk-flowers yellow or brown, perfect, achenes 4-angled, pappus a toothed crown or none, receptacle conic, with chaff, involucre hemispheric to bell-shaped, bracts in 2-3 rows; heads solitary on the branches; leaves alternate or opposite, simple, entire or toothed; perennial.

Stems 1-5 ft. high; leaves linear to lanceolate; rays
10-15   *G. multiflóra*

HAPLOÉSTHES Gray 1859
(Gr. *haploos*, simple, *esthes*, garment, from the few bracts of the involucre)

Heads with yellow pistillate ray-flowers, disk-flowers perfect, yellow, achenes linear, rounded, ribbed, pappus of bristles; receptacle flat, without chaff, involucre bell-shaped, of 4-5 nearly equal fleshy bracts, the outer overlapping the inner; heads in loose cymes; leaves opposite, entire; perennial.

Stems 1-2 ft. high; leaves linear or filiform; rays oval,
  2-4 mm. long   *H. Gréggii*

HAPLOPÁPPUS Cassini 1828 HAPLOPAPPUS

(Gr. *haploos*, simple, *pappos*, pappus)

Heads with yellow, pistillate rays or none, disk-flowers yellow, perfect, achenes linear to top-shaped, pappus of hair-like bristles; receptacle flat to convex, without chaff, involucre usually broad, the bracts more or less imbricated, often with leaf-like tips; heads solitary or in corymbs; leaves alternate, entire to pinnatifid, sometimes spiny-toothed; annual or perennial.

1. Involucre of firm or rigid well-imbricated bracts;
     pappus dark or reddish
   a. Heads rayless; achenes silky; leaves lanceolate
        to spatulate-oblong, toothed   *H. Nuttállii*
   b. Heads with rays .5-1 in. long; achenes smooth;
        leaves entire
      (1) Stems equally very leafy up to the sessile
            or sub-sessile head; leaves lanceolate;
            rays .5 in. long   *H. Fremóntii*
      (2) Stems with few sparse leaves above, the
            heads stalked
         (a) Bracts of the involucre ovate to oblong;
               rays nearly or quite an inch long   *H. cróceus*
         (b) Bracts oblong to lance-linear; rays .5 in.
               long   *H. integrifólius*
   c. Heads with rays 6-12 mm. long; achenes hairy
      (1) Rays 7-10; leaves narrowly linear, entire;
            stems 1-3 in. high   *H. multicaúlis*
      (2) Rays 15-50; leaves mostly toothed to pin-
            natifid
         (a) Stems usually simple with a tuft of basal
               leaves; leaves entire or spiny-toothed:
               rays 20-50
            x. Heads usually solitary   *H. uniflórus*
            y. Heads 3-15   *H. lanceolátus*
         (b) Stems branching and leafy; leaves
               toothed to pinnatifid, teeth spiny-tipped;
               rays 15-30

x. Plants sticky-hairy; leaves toothed to
pinnatifid *H. rubiginósus*

y. Plants gray-hairy to smooth; leaves 1-2-
pinnately parted *H. spinulósus*

2. Bracts of the involucre not well-imbricated or
rigid, more or less equal; pappus white or whitish; leaves entire

a. Heads solitary; rays conspicuous

(1) Rays 15-20; leaves soft, not persistent

(a) Plants green, not woolly

x. Plants soft-hairy or smooth; involucral
bracts oblong, the outer leaf-like and
very obtuse; achenes hairy *H. pygmaéus*

y. Plants sticky-hairy; involucral bracts
lanceolate, acute; achenes smooth or
nearly so *H. Lyállii*

(b) Plants woolly or felted, at least the involucre; leaves narrowly spatulate to
linear; bracts lanceolate, pointed;
achenes silky *H. lanuginósus*

(2) Rays 6-15; leaves stiff and persistent;
achenes hairy; stems nearly leafless, 1-
headed, 1-6 in. high *H. acáulis*

b. Heads in cymes or clusters; rays 12-20, small
and narrow; achenes smooth or nearly so;
stems 5-2 ft. high; leaves oblong-ovate to
spatulate *H. Párryi*

3. Bracts of the involucre more or less equal, with
conspicuous leafy tips or passing into leaves;
pappus soft; leaves linear, entire; rays 2-5 or
none

a. Plants densely white-felted; heads about 1 in.
high; rays none *H. macronéma*

b. Plants not felted; heads 15-18 mm. high; rays
2-5 or none *H. suffruticósus*

HELÉNIUM Linné 1753 SNEEZEWEED
(The Greek name of some plant)
Pl. 41, fig. 3.

Heads with yellow to orange pistillate or neutral ray-flowers, disk-
flowers yellow, perfect, achenes top-shaped, ribbed, pappus of 5-8 entire,
toothed or awned scales; receptacle convex to oblong, without chaff, in-

PLATE 40.

volucre low hemispheric, the bracts in 1-2 rows, spreading or reflexed; heads solitary on the branches; leaves alternate, simple, toothed, often decurrent; annual or perennial.

1. Rays orange to purplish; stems not winged by
    the leaf-bases
    a. Rays 2-4 cm. long; leaves spatulate to lance-
        oblong, mostly entire   *H. Hoópesii*
    b. Rays about 1 cm. long; leaves linear to linear-
        lanceolate, usually parted into 3-5 linear di-
        visions   *H. helenioídes*
2. Rays bright yellow, 3-cleft at tip; stem winged by
    the decurrent bases of the lanceolate to lance-
    ovate leaves   *H. autumnále*

HELIANTHÉLLA Torrey and Gray 1840 HELIANTHELLA
(Diminutive of Helianthus, which it resembles)
Pl. 40, fig. 7.

Heads with yellow neutral ray-flowers, disk-flowers yellow or purple, perfect, achenes flattened, somewhat winged, pappus of scales or awns or both; receptacle with chaff, involucre hemispheric, the bracts in 2-3 rows, more or less leaf-like; heads solitary; leaves alternate, simple, mostly entire; perennial.

1. Disk yellowish
    a. Disk 2-3 cm. wide; rays 2.5-4 cm. long; stems
        2-5 ft. high   *H. quinquenérvis*
    b. Disk 1-2 cm. wide; rays 1.5-3 cm. long; stems
        1-2 ft. high   *H. Párryi*
2. Disk dark purple
    a. Heads several; rays 5-6 mm. long   *H. microcéphala*
    b. Heads mostly solitary; rays 2-3 cm. long   *H. uniflóra*

HELIÁNTHUS Linné 1753 SUNFLOWER
(Gr. *helios*, sun, *anthos*, flower)
Pl. 39, fig. 7.

Heads with yellow neutral ray-flowers, disk-flowers yellow, brown or purple, perfect, achenes oblong or obovate, flattened or somewhat 4-angled, pappus of 2 scales or awns falling readily; receptacle flat, conic, with chaff, involucre hemispheric, the bracts imbricated in several rows; heads solitary or in corymbs; leaves opposite or alternate, simple; annual or perennial.

1. Disk brown or purplish
    a. Leaves all, or nearly all, opposite, thick,
        leathery, toothed, lanceolate to lance-oblong *H. rígidus*

   b. Leaves mostly alternate, only the lower oppo-
      site
      (1) Leaves linear or lance-linear; perennial   *H. orgyális*
      (2) Leaves ovate; annual
         (a) Leaves entire or nearly so; bracts of the
            involucre lanceolate, gray-hairy   *H. petioláris*
         (b) Leaves toothed; bracts oblong to ovate,
            long-pointed, hairy and ciliate   *H. ánnuus*
  2. Disk yellow
    a. Leaves opposite; stems rough and bristly, 1-3
      ft. high   *H. púmilus*
    b. Some of the upper leaves alternate
      (1) Stem leaves rough and somewhat hairy   *H. Maximiliáni*
      (2) Stem smooth, often glaucous
         (a) Leaves mostly sharply toothed, hairy
            beneath   *H. grosse-serrátus*
         (b) Leaves entire or finely toothed, not hairy
            beneath   *H. Nuttállii*

HELIÓPSIS Persoon 1807 OX-EYE
(Gr., *helios,* sun, *opsis,* likeness)

Heads with yellow pistillate ray-flowers, rays persisting, disk-flowers yellow, perfect, achenes 3-4-angled, pappus a short, toothed crown, or of 1-3 awns; receptacle convex to conic, with chaff, involucre hemispheric, the bracts imbricated in 2-3 rows; heads solitary, terminal and axillary; leaves opposite, simple, perennial.

Stems 2-5 ft. high; leaves ovate or lance-ovate, toothed,
  2-5 in. long; rays an inch long or more   *H. scábra*

HIERÁCIUM Linné 1753 HAWKWEED
(Gr. *hierax,* hawk)

Heads with yellow, orange or red perfect strap-flowers, achenes oblong to cylindric, not beaked, 10-15-ribbed, round or 4-5-angled, pappus of brown or brownish hair-like bristles; receptacle flat, without chaff, involucre bell-shaped to cylindric, the bracts in 1-3 rows, often with smaller basal ones; heads solitary or in corymbs or panicles; leaves alternate or basal, entire to toothed or lobed; perennial.

  1. Bracts of the involucre in 2-4 rows; stems leafy
    a. Leaves, at least the upper, clasping; involucre
      hairy   *H. canadénse*
    b. Leaves not clasping; involucre smooth   *H. umbellátum*

2. Bracts of the involucre in 1 row with some short
   basal ones; stems naked or with few leaves
   a. Flowers white or yellowish   *H. albiflórum*
   b. Flowers yellow
      (1) Achenes tapering gradually to a narrow tip *H. Féndleri*
      (2) Achenes cylindric, not tapering above
          x. Involucres black-hairy   *H. grácile*
          y. Involucres white-hairy   *H. Scoúleri*

Húlsea   Torrey and Gray
(Named for Hulse, an American physician)

Heads with yellow or purple ray-flowers, disk-flowers perfect, yellow, achenes linear-wedge-shaped, flattened or somewhat 4-angled, hairy, pappus of 4 scales; receptacle flat, without chaff, involucre hemispheric with bracts in 2-3 series; flowers solitary as a rule; leaves alternate, sessile, entire to pinnatifid; perennial.

Plants fleshy; leaves lobed, 2-4 in. long; rays 7-9 mm.

long   *H. carnósa*

Hymenopáppus   L'Héritier 1803   Hymenopappus
(Gr., *hymen,* membrane, *pappos,* pappus)
Pl. 41, fig. 4.

Heads without rays, disk-flowers white to yellow, perfect, achenes obovoid to long wedge-shaped, 4-5-angled, pappus of 10-20 scales, sometimes short or none; receptacle flat, naked, involucre hemispheric to bell-shaped, bracts 6-12 in 1-2 rows, usually colored, the margins papery; heads solitary or in corymbs; leaves alternate or basal, usually pinnatifid or dissected; perennial or biennial.

Stems 4 in. to 2 ft. high; leaves 1-3-pinnatifid, gray-
hairy or felted to green and nearly smooth; corolla-
throat 2-4 times the length of the lobes; pappus
scales of various lengths   *H. tenuifólius*

Isocóma   Nuttall 1841
(Gr., *isos,* equal, *kome,* tuft, perhaps from the pappus)

Heads without rays, disk-flowers yellow, perfect, achenes short, silky-hairy, pappus of darkish hair-like bristles; receptacle flat, without chaff, the bracts imbricated in several rows, often papery; heads in a corymb-like cyme; leaves simple, entire or somewhat deeply toothed, usually sticky; perennial, somewhat woody at base.

Stems 1-2 ft. high; leaves narrowly linear; heads 8-
10 mm. high, 7-15 flowered   *I. Wrightii*

Íva   Linné 1753   Marsh Elder
(Named from Ajuga iva, from its similar smell)

Heads without rays, the marginal flowers 1-6, pistillate, disk-flowers greenish, perfect but sterile, achenes obovoid, flattened, pappus none; receptacle flat, with chaff, involucre hemispheric or cup-shaped, bracts few; heads solitary or variously clustered; leaves opposite or alternate, simple; annual or perennial.

1. Heads 4-6 mm. wide, solitary in the leaf-axils;
   leaves sessile, oblong to spatulate   *I. axilláris*
2. Heads 1-2 mm. wide, crowded in panicled spikes;
   leaves ovate, petioled   *I. xanthifólia*

Kúhnia   Linné 1753   False Boneset
(Named for Kuhn, an American botanist)

Heads without rays, tube-flowers perfect, cream-colored, achenes oblong, striate, pappus of feathery, hair-like bristles; receptacle flat, without chaff, involucre oblong, the bracts striate, imbricated in several rows; heads in terminal corymbs; leaves alternate, simple; perennial.

Stems 1-2 ft. high; leaves linear to lance-ovate, entire
or toothed; heads 8-16 mm. high   *K. eupatorioídes*

Laciniária   Hill 1762   Blazing Star
(Lat. *lacinia*, fringe, from the appearance of the heads)
(Liatris Schreber)
Pl. 37, fig. 1.

Heads without rays, tube-flowers rose-purple, perfect, achenes oblong or club-shaped, ribbed, pappus of feathery hair-like bristles; receptacle flat, without chaff, involucre oblong to ovoid, the bracts imbricated in several rows; heads in spikes or racemes; leaves alternate, entire, long and narrow; perennial.

1. Heads 3-6-flowered, less than 1 cm. wide as a
   rule; bracts pointed   *L. punctáta*
2. Heads many-flowered, 1-2.5 cm. wide; bracts
   rounded   *L. scariósa*

Lactúca   Linné 1753   Lettuce
(The Latin name from *lac*, milk)
Pl. 37, fig. 2.

Heads with yellow, white or blue perfect strap-flowers, achenes linear to oval, flat, 6-10-ribbed, narrow above or contracted into a beak, pappus of white or brown hair-like bristles; receptacle flat, without chaff, involucre cylindric, the bracts in several rows; heads in panicles; leaves alternate, entire to pinnatifid; annual, biennial or perennial.

1. Pappus white; achenes with a distinct beak
   a. Flowers yellow or reddish-yellow
     (1) Leaves with spiny margins and often with spiny mid-ribs
       (a) Heads 6-12-flowered; involucre 8-12 mm. high   *L. scaríola*
       (b) Heads 12-many-flowered; involucre 15-20 mm. high   *L. ludoviciána*
     (2) Leaves without spiny margins or mid-rib; involucre 8-12 mm. high   *L. canadénsis*
   b. Flowers blue, purplish or white
     (1) Involucre 12-14 mm. high; achenes 1-3-nerved   *L. graminifólia*
     (2) Involucre 16-18 mm. high; achenes striate *L. pulchélla*
2. Pappus brown; achenes beakless; flowers blue to yellowish or whitish   *L. spicáta*

LÁYIA Hooker and Arnott 1833
(Named for Lay, a British naturalist)

Heads with white or rose-colored rays, disk-flowers yellow, perfect, achenes flattened, ray-achenes without pappus, disk-achenes with a pappus of 10-20 bristles; receptacle flat, with chaff, involucre with flattened bracts, enclosing the ray-achenes; heads mostly solitary on the ends of branches; leaves alternate, usually pinnatifid; annual.

Stems 8-15 in. high, much-branched; leaves lanceolate to linear, the lower pinnatifid; rays 8-13, 3-lobed   *L. glandulósa*

LÉPTILUM Rafinesque 1818 HORSEWEED
(Gr. *leptos,* narrow, from the small heads)

Heads with white or purplish pistillate ray-flowers, disk-flowers perfect, yellow or yellowish, achenes flattened, oblong; receptacle flat, without chaff, involucre bell-shaped, the bracts in 2-3 rows; heads in racemes or branched panicles; leaves alternate, simple; annual or biennial.

1. Stems 1-6 ft. high; involucre smooth; rays white *L. canadénse*
2. Stems 3-12 in. high; involucre hairy; rays purplish   *L. divaricátum*

LEUCÁMPYX Gray 1874
(Gr. *leukos*, white, *ampyx*, head-band, from the white-bordered bracts)

Heads with white or cream-colored pistillate rays, disk-flowers yellow, perfect, achenes wedge-shaped, incurved, flattened, pappus none; receptacle convex, with chaff, involucre hemispheric, the bracts imbricated in 2-3 rows, broadly white-papery at the top; heads more or less corymbose; leaves alternate, 2-3-pinnately parted; perennial.

Stems 1-2 ft. high; rays 10-12 mm. long; achenes
  black   *L. Newbérryi*

LYGODÉSMIA Don 1829 MILK PINK
(Gr. *lygos*, a pliant twig, *desme*, a bundle, referring to the rush-like stems)

Heads with pink or rose perfect strap-flowers, achenes terete, faintly striate or angled, linear to club-shaped, pappus of white or whitish hair-like bristles; receptacle flat, without chaff, involucre of one row of main bracts, with one or more shorter rows below; heads 3-12-flowered, usually terminal; leaves alternate, linear or scale-like; annual or perennial.

1. Stems .5-1.5 ft. high, perennial; leaves mostly
     less than 3 in. long
     a. Heads 5-flowered; involucre 10-12 mm. high *L. júncea*
     b. Heads 6-10-flowered; involucre 20-25 mm.
        high   *L. grandiflóra*
2. Stems 1-4 ft. high, annual; leaves 2-6 in. long;
     heads 8-9-flowered   *L. rostráta*

MACHAERÁNTHERA Nees 1832 PURPLE ASTER
(Gr. *machaera*, sickle, *ánthera*, anther)
Pl. 38, fig. 4.

Heads with pale violet to purple pistillate rays, disk-flowers yellow, becoming red or brown, perfect, achenes top-shaped, usually hairy, pappus of hair-like bristles; receptacle convex or flat, without chaff, involucre bell-shaped, the bracts imbricated in many rows, usually spreading or reflexed; heads in corymbs or panicles; leaves alternate, entire to pinnatifid, the lobes often bristle-tipped; annual, biennial or perennial.

1. Leaves entire to ciliate or spiny toothed
     a. Bracts of the involucre with reflexed often awl-
        shaped tips usually longer than the erect
        basal portion; flower clusters typically very
        sticky-hairy
        (1) Stems 1-4 ft. high bearing usually many
            heads; leaves mostly lance-oblong, broad-
            ened and clasping at the base; tips of
            bracts mostly awl-shaped   *M. Bigelóvii*

(2) Stems 2-8 in. high, tufted, usually 1-head-
ed; leaves usually spatulate, tapering to
the base, not clasping; tips of the bracts
broad and flat   *M. Pattersónii*

b. Bracts of the involucre erect or with flat reflexed tips shorter than the basal portion;
leaves mostly gray-hairy, oblanceolate to
linear; stems usually much branched, many-
headed, .5-2 ft. high   *M. canéscens*

2. Leaves 1-3-pinnatifid   *M. tanacetifólia*

MÁDIA Molina 1782 TARWEED
(From the Chilian name of the common species)

Heads with yellow pistillate rays, the rays rarely lacking, disk-flowers yellow, perfect, achenes flattened, enclosed in the folded bracts, pappus none; receptacle flat or convex, with a single row of bracts enclosing the disk-flowers, involucre ovoid or oblong, angled by the projecting backs of the bracts; heads axillary and terminal; leaves mostly alternate, entire or toothed, sticky; annual.

Stems 1-2 ft. high; leaves linear; rays 2-5, sometimes
none   *M. glomeráta*

MALACÓTHRIX DeCandolle 1838
(Gr. *malakos*, soft, *thrix*, hair)

Heads with yellow or white perfect strap-flowers, achenes oblong or linear, ribbed, 4-5-toothed, pappus of hair-like bristles in 2 rows; receptacle flat, without chaff, involucre bell-shaped, main bracts in 1-2 rows with several rows of shorter ones; heads solitary or panicled; leaves alternate or basal, mostly pinnatifid; annual or perennial.

1. Achene crowned by a 15-toothed white border   *M. sonchoídes*
2. Achene with an entire crown   *M. Féndleri*

MATRICÁRIA Linné 1753 CAMOMILE
(Lat, *matrix*, womb, from its medicinal virtues)

Heads without rays in our species, disk-flowers yellow, perfect, achenes oblong, 3-5-ribbed, pappus a crown, or none; receptacle conic or hemspheric, without chaff, involucre hemispheric, the bracts imbricated in a few rows; heads solitary on the branches; leaves alternate, dissected; annual or perennial.

Stems 6-8 in. high; leaves 2-3-pinnately dissected;
heads 6-8 mm. wide   *M. discoídea*

Melampódium   Linné 1753
(Gr. *melas*, black, *podion*, little foot)

Heads with white pistillate ray-flowers, disk-flowers yellow, perfect, achenes obovoid, somewhat curved, pappus none; receptacle convex or conic, with chaff, involucre hemispheric, bracts in 2 rows, 4-5 outer broad, the inner hooded, more or less embracing the ray-flowers; heads solitary; leaves opposite, mostly entire; perennial.

Stems 4-12 in. high; leaves linear to spatulate, 1-2 in.
long; rays 5-9, 2-3-lobed   *M. cinéreum*

Nothocálais   Greene 1886   False Dandelion
(Gr. *nothos*, false; Calais)

Heads with yellow perfect strap-flowers, achenes spindle-shaped, narrowed above, 10-ribbed, pappus of 10-30 scales, often with hair-like bristles as well; receptacle flat, without chaff, involucre bell-shaped, bracts in 2-4 rows; heads solitary; leaves basal, entire; perennial.

Leaves lance-linear, 4-8 in. long; heads 1-2 in. wide   *N. cuspidáta*

Oxyténia   Nuttall 1848
(Gr. *oxytenes*, pointed, from the rigid leaves)

Heads without rays, pistillate flowers about 5, without corolla, staminate flowers 10-20, achenes obovate, hairy, pappus none or a single scale; receptacle convex, with chaff, involucral bracts about 5, long-pointed; heads in dense panicles; leaves alternate, 3-5-parted into narrow divisions; shrubby perennial.

Stems 3-6 ft. high, sometimes leafless; leaves 4-6 in.
long; heads 4 mm. high   *O. acerósa*

Partiiénice   Gray 1853
(Gr. *parthenice*, virgin)

Heads without rays or the latter inconspicuous, pistillate flowers 6-8, staminate flowers 40-50, achenes oblong-obovate, falling away, enclosed by bracts, pappus none; receptacle convex, with chaff around the outer series of staminate flowers, involucre of 5 greenish outer bracts and 6-8 large roundish, papery inner ones; heads in panicles; leaves alternate, simple; annual.

Stems 3-6 ft. high; leaves ovate, 6-12 in. long; heads
greenish-white, 4 mm. wide   *P. móllis*

Péctis   Linné 1753
(Lat. *pecten*, comb, from the pappus)

Heads with yellow pistillate ray-flowers, disk-flowers yellow, perfect, achenes linear, striate, pappus of 4-6 somewhat united short scales, often with 2 awns; receptacle flat, without chaff, involucre oblong, the bracts in 1 row; heads in cymes; leaves opposite, narrow, entire, dotted with glands; annual.

Stems 4-12 in. high; leaves linear, .5-2 in. long; heads
5-6 mm. wide   *P. angustifólia*

PERICÓME   Gray 1853
(Gr. *peri*, around, *kome*, hair, from the hairy achenes)

Heads without rays, the disk-flowers yellow, perfect, achenes linear-oblong with margins long-hairy, pappus a crown of fringed scales; involucre bell-shaped, the bracts united by their edges; heads in cymes; leaves opposite, long-tapering; perennial.

Stems very bushy, 2-5 ft. high and wide; leaves
hastate, 2-4 cm. long; heads 9-12 mm. wide   *P. caudáta*

PETÁSITES   Gaertner 1791   COLTSFOOT
(Gr. *petasites*, a broad-rimmed hat, from the broad leaves)

Heads tubular, or some with white pistillate rays, disk-flowers white or purplish, perfect but sterile, achenes linear, pappus of hair-like bristles; receptacle flat, without chaff, involucre bell-shaped to cylindric, the bracts equal in 1 row; heads often dioecious, or somewhat so, in racemes or corymbs; leaves basal, broad; perennial.

Flower-stalks .5-2 ft. high; leaves triangular-ovate,
heart-shaped at base, white-woolly below, 4-10 in.
long   *P. sagittáta*

PLATYSCHKÚHRIA   Rydberg 1906
(Gr. *platys*, flat, Schkuhria)

Heads with yellow pistillate ray-flowers, disk-flowers yellow, perfect, achenes linear-wedge-shaped, pappus of about 10 lance-linear abruptly pointed scales; receptacle flat, without chaff, involucre bell-shaped or hemispheric, the bracts nearly equal in 1-2 rows; heads solitary or somewhat corymbose; leaves alternate, entire; perennial.

Stems 4-12 in. high; leaves oval to spatulate; heads
10-12 mm. high; rays 6-9   *P. integrifólia*

POLÝPTERIS   Nuttall 1818
(Gr. *polys*, many, *pteris*, wing)

Heads with rose-purple pistillate ray-flowers in ours, the rays 3-cleft, disk-flowers purplish, perfect, achenes linear to wedge-shaped, 4-angled, pappus of 8-12 pointed scales; receptacle flat, without chaff, involucre bell-shaped, the bracts in 1-2 rows, usually colored; heads in corymbs; leaves alternate or opposite, usually entire; annual.

Plate 41

PLATE 41.

Stems 1-3 ft. high, sticky; leaves lanceolate, 2-4 in.
long; rays 8-10   *P. hookeriána*

Prenanthélla Rydberg 1906
(Diminutive of Prenanthes)

Heads with rose or pink perfect strap-flowers, achenes wedge-shaped, 4-5-ribbed, pappus of white, hair-like bristles; receptacle flat, without chaff, involucre oblong, with 1 row of oblong bracts and 1-2 small basal ones; heads solitary at the ends of the branches; leaves alternate, entire to pinnatifid; annual.

Stems 4-10 in. high; leaves spatulate to oblong; involucre 4 mm. high, 4-5-flowered   *P. exígua*

Prenánthes Linné 1753 Rattlesnake Root
(Gr. *prenes*, drooping, *anthos*, flower)

Heads of white, yellowish or purplish perfect strap-flowers, achenes oblong or cylindric, round or 4-5-angled, ribbed, pappus of white to reddish-brown, hair-like bristles; receptacle flat, without chaff, involucre cylindric, the main bracts in 1-2 rows, a few small ones at the base; heads in panicles; leaves alternate, dentate to pinnatifid; perennial.

1. Basal leaves obovate; involucre somewhat hairy   *P. racemósa*
2. Basal leaves arrow-shaped; involucre smooth   *P. sagittáta*

Psilostróphe DeCandolle 1838
(Gr. *psilos*, naked, *strophe*, ridge)

Heads with 3-4 yellow pistillate ray-flowers, disk-flowers 5-12, yellow, perfect, achenes linear, striate, pappus of 4-6 scales; receptacle small, without chaff, involucre cylindric, bracts white-woolly, 4-10 in one row; heads in corymbs; leaves alternate, entire to pinnatifid; annual or perennial.

Stems 4-12 in. high; leaves entire to 3-lobed or pinnatifid; rays 3-5, broad and 2-3-lobed; pappus scales
acute to obtuse   *P. tagetína*

Ptilocálais Greene 1886
(Gr. *ptilon*, feather; Calais)

Heads with yellow perfect strap-flowers, achenes linear, pappus of white, hair-like bristles, scale-like at base; receptacle flat, without chaff, involucre cylindric, the main bracts in 1 row with a few short basal ones; heads solitary on the ends of branches; leaves entire to pinnately parted; perennial.

Stems 4-12 in. high; leaves spatulate-obovate or parted into linear lobes; heads 8-20-flowered   *P. nútans*

PTILÓRIA   Rafinesque 1832
(Gr. *ptilon*, feather)
(Stephanomeria Nuttall)

Heads with pink perfect strap-flowers, achenes oblong to linear, 5-ribbed, sometimes beaked, pappus of hair-like bristles; receptacle flat, without chaff, involucre cylindric to oblong, main bracts in 1 row with a few shorter ones; heads solitary or panicled; leaves alternate or basal, entire to pinnatifid, those of the stem often mere scales; annual, biennial or perennial.

  1. Perennial   *P. tenuifólia*
  2. Annual or biennial
    a. Bristles of the pappus plumy to the base; in-
      volucre 4–8-flowered   *P. virgáta*
    b. Bristles of the pappus not plumy below the
      middle; involucre 5-flowered   *P. exígua*

RATÍBIDA   Rafinesque 1818   CONE FLOWER
(Of unknown origin and meaning)
Pl. 39, fig. 1, 6.

Heads with yellow to purple-brown neutral ray-flowers, disk-flowers yellow, perfect, achenes oblong, flattened, margined or winged, pappus of 1-2 teeth, often with small intermediate scales; receptacle oblong to cylindric, with chaff, scales of the involucre in 2-3 rows; heads solitary on the ends of the branches; leaves alternate, pinnately divided; perennial.

  1. Rays 2-4 cm. long, yellow or more or less purple-
    brown; disk cylindric 1-2 in. long   *R. columnáris*
  2. Rays 5-9 mm. long, usually brown-purple; disk
    oblong, 1 cm. long   *R. tagétes*

RUDBÉCKIA   Linné 1753   BLACKEYED SUSAN, GOLDEN GLOW
(Named for Rudbeck, a Swedish botanist)
Pl. 39, fig. 2, 4.

Heads with yellow to orange-yellow neutral ray-flowers, or none, disk-flowers purple or yellow, perfect, achenes oblong, 4-angled, pappus crown-like or of 2-4 short teeth or none; receptacle convex to conic, with chaff, involucre hemispheric, the bracts imbricated in 2-4 rows; heads solitary; leaves alternate, entire to pinnatifid; perennial to biennial.

  1. Rays present
    a. Leaves entire or toothed; stems 1-3 ft. high,
      rough-hairy   *R. hírta*

b. Leaves 3-7-divided; stems 3-6 ft. high, usually
  smooth   *R. laciniáta*

2. Rays none
  a. Leaves entire or toothed; disk 3-5 cm. long   *R. occidentális*
  b. Leaves pinnately parted; disk 5-7 cm. long   *R. montána*

RYDBÉRGIA Greene 1898 RYDBERGIA
(Named for the American botanist Rydberg)
Pl. 41, fig. 7.

Heads with yellow pistillate ray-flowers, disk-flowers yellow, perfect, achenes top-shaped, ribbed or angled, hairy, pappus of 5-12 white scales, usually long-pointed; receptacle flat, without chaff, involucre hemispheric, the woolly bracts in several rows; heads solitary; leaves 2-5-parted or lobed into linear divisions, upper sometimes entire; alpine perennial.

1. Leaves and involucre woolly; rays 30 or more,
   12-16 mm. long   *R. grandiflóra*
2. Leaves smooth or nearly so; involucre merely
   hairy; rays 12-16, 6-8 mm. long   *R. Brandégei*

SENÉCIO Linné 1753 GROUNDSEL
(Lat. *senex*, old man, perhaps from the white pappus)
Pl. 40, fig. 4.

Heads with yellow pistillate ray-flowers or none, disk-flowers yellow, perfect, achenes oblong, rounded, ribbed, pappus of hair-like bristles; receptacle flat, without chaff, involucre bell-shaped to cylindric, the main bracts in 1 row, usually with some shorter ones; heads solitary or in corymbs or panicles; leaves alternate or basal, entire or pinnatifid; annual or perennial.

1. Heads large, 15-25 mm. high
  a. Heads with rays
    (1) Stem leaves clasping at base, usually sharp-
        ly toothed   *S. ampléctens*
    (2) Stem leaves distinctly petioled, not clasping
        (a) Leaves round or nearly so, smooth,
            mostly basal; heads erect   *S. soldanélla*
        (b) Leaves spatulate to obovate, tapering in-
            to the petiole; heads nodding
            x. Stems 1-6 in. high; leaves somewhat
               lobed, white woolly; heads single;
               rays 10-15 mm. long   *S. taraxacoídes*

y. Stems 6-12 in. high; leaves toothed,
smooth; heads 1-6; rays 20-30 mm.
long   .   *S. Hólmii*

b. Heads rayless, nodding; stems .5-4 ft. high;
leaves lanceolate to lance-ovate   *S. Bigelóvii*

2. Heads medium to small, 5-15 mm. long

  a. Heads distinctly nodding, many; stems
branched, 1-4 ft. high; leaves lanceolate, entire, toothed or lobed, 2-6 in. long   *S. cérnuus*

  b. Heads not nodding

    (1) None of the leaves pinnatifid or pinnate

      (a) Stems equally many-leaved to the top

        x. Leaves linear   *S. spartioídes*

        y. Leaves lanceolate to ovate or obovate

          (x) Heads rayless 5-6 mm. high; leaves
spatulate to obovate, coarsely
toothed

          (y) Heads with rays, 8-15 mm. high   *S. rapifólius*

            m. Stems 4-12 in. high; leaves blunt,
oblong to ovoid, coarsely sharp-
toothed or lobed, 1-2 in. long;
heads 10-12 mm. high   *S. Fremóntii*

            n. Stems 1-6 ft. high; leaves lanceo-
late to lance-ovate, 3-10 in. long,
many-toothed

              (m) Stems 8-15 in. high; leaves 3-
8 on a stem; heads 1-8, 12-
15 mm. high   *S. crássulus*

              (n) Stems 2-6 ft. high; leaves
many on a stem; heads 8-
10 mm. high

                r. Leaves long-lanceolate, taper-
ing to the base, 4-8 in. long,
1-3 cm. wide   *S. sérra*

                s. Leaves triangular-ovate, heart-
shaped or truncate at base,
2-6 in. long, 1-2 in. wide   *S. trianguláris*

      (b) Stems few-leaved or the upper much re-
duced in size

        x. Stems simple, 2-5 ft. high; leaves fleshy,
usually glaucous, entire or toothed,
lance-oblong, 4-8 in. long   *S. hydróphilus*

y. Plants clustered or tufted from rootstocks, .5-2.5 ft. high
  (x) Stems leafy
     m. Rays wanting   *S. rapifólius*
     n. Rays present
       (m) Heads 12-15 mm. high   *S. crássulus*
       (n) Heads 8-12 mm. high
          r. Leaves glaucous; basal leaves
            obovate to broadly spatulate *S. microdóntus*
          s. Leaves not glaucous, white-
            woolly at first   *S. lúgens*
          t. Leaves persistently white-hairy
            or woolly
             (r) Stems 1-2 ft. high; leaves
                2.5-5 in. long; heads 2-
                4 mm. wide   *S. atrátus*
             (s) Stems 4-15 in. high; leaves
                1-2 in. long, upper often
                lobed; heads 6-7 mm.
                wide   *S. cánus*
  (y) Stems with the leaves all or nearly
     all basal
     m. Leaves usually white-woolly, lin-
       ear-spatulate to oblong-spatulate,
       mostly entire   *S. wernerifólius*
     n. Leaves usually green, roundish,
       toothed or lobed above   *S. petraéus*
(2) Leaves, at least some of them, pinnatifid
   to pinnate
 (a) Stems equally many-leaved to the top
   x. Leaves or their segments linear or
     thread-like, white-woolly to smooth   *S. Douglásii*
   y. Leaves pinnatifid, the divisions not lin-
     ear but toothed or lobed   *S. eremóphilus*
 (b) Stems with the leaves much reduced up-
     wards, often to mere scales
   x. Stems and leaves persistently white-
     woolly, rarely becoming smooth
      (x) Basal leaves entire   *S. cánus*
      (y) Basal leaves toothed to pinnatifid   *S. Féndleri*

y. Stems and leaves white-woolly only
when young, typically green and
smooth at flowering; leaves variously
toothed to pinnatifid, more rarely
entire, round, oblong or lanceolate to
spatulate; heads sometimes without
rays, the latter yellow to orange-red *S. aúreus*

SOLIDÁGO Linné 1753 GOLDENROD
(Lat. *solidus*, whole, *-ago*, like, from its former use in medicine)
Pl. 38, fig. 1.

Heads with yellow pistillate ray-flowers, disk-flowers yellow, mostly
perfect, achenes round or angled, usually ribbed, pappus of hair-like
bristles; receptacle flat or convex, without chaff, involucre oblong to bell-
shaped, the bracts imbricated in several rows; heads in terminal axillary
panicles, corymbs, cymes, etc.; leaves alternate, simple; perennial.

1. Heads in a flat-topped spreading cluster
   a. Rays fewer than the disk flowers, 1-10
      (1) Heads 8-10 mm. high, 30-40-flowered;
          rays 7-10; leaves ovate to oblong, very
          rough   *S. rígida*
      (2) Heads 6-8 mm. high, 5-8-flowered; rays
          1-3; leaves linear or lance-linear   *S. púmila*
   b. Rays more numerous than the disk flowers, 12-
      20; heads 4-6 mm. high, disk flowers 8-14;
      leaves linear or lance-linear   *S. lanceoláta*
2. Heads in a terminal cone-like, or a raceme-, spike-
   or head-like cluster, which is not flat-topped
   a. Stems and leaves smooth or nearly so
      (1) Leaves distinctly 3-veined
          (a) Stems 4-15 in. high; stem leaves ob-
              lanceolate to linear; in dry soil   *S. missouriénsis*
          (b) Stems 1-5 ft. high; stem leaves lanceo-
              late; along streams   *S. serótina*
      (2) Leaves not 3-veined
          (a) Stems 2-4 ft. high; heads 3-4 mm. wide,
              very many in a much branched pan-
              icle-like cluster; at 4-7000 ft.   *S. speciósa*
          (b) Stems 1 in.-2 ft. high; heads 5-7 mm.
              wide, mostly few in a compact head-
              or raceme-like cluster; at 7-13000 ft.

x. Bracts of the involucre sharp-pointed to
tapering-pointed .... *S. multiradiáta*
y. Bracts of the involucre obtuse or
rounded .... *S. húmilis*
b. Stems and leaves hairy, at least the leaves
  (1) Leaves lanceolate, soft-hairy; stems 2-6
    ft. high; heads 3-4 mm. high; rays 9-15 *S. canadénsis*
  (2) Leaves oblanceolate, spatulate to elliptic
    or ovate, rough-hairy or gray-hairy;
    heads 4-6 mm. high; rays 5-9
    x. Leaves oblanceolate to spatulate, rough-
      hairy .... *S. nemorális*
    y. Leaves elliptic to ovate or obovate,
      densely gray-hairy .... *S. móllis*

SÓNCHUS Linné 1753 Sow Thistle
(The Greek name)

Heads with yellow perfect strap-flowers, achenes linear to oval, somewhat flattened, ribbed, not beaked, pappus of white hair-like bristles; receptacle flat, without chaff, involucre ovoid to bell-shaped, the bracts imbricated in 2 or more rows; heads in corymbs or panicles; leaves alternate,
usually clasping, entire to pinnatifid and prickly-margined; annual or
perennial.

1. Involucre 20-25 mm. high, sticky-hairy; heads
  1-2 in. wide .... *S. arvénsis*
2. Involucre 12-16 mm. high, smooth; heads an inch
  or less wide
  a. Basal ears of the clasping leaves acute;
    achenes striate, wrinkled crosswise ...... *S. oleráceus*
  b. Ears of the leaves rounded; achenes ribbed,
    not wrinkled crosswise .... *S. ásper*

TANACÉTUM Linné 1753 Tansy
(Latinized from Fr. *tanasie*, Gr. *athanasia*, immortality)

Heads usually rayless, marginal flowers yellow, pistillate, sometimes
forming short rays, disk-flowers yellow, perfect, achenes 5-angled or ribbed,
pappus none or a short crown; receptacle flat or convex, without chaff,
involucre hemispheric to bell-shaped, bracts imbricated in several rows;
heads in corymbs; leaves alternate, 1-3-pinnately divided or dissected;
perennial.

1. Leaves simple, oblong to linear and entire or 3-
    5-lobed at the tip   *T. Nuttállii*
2. Leaves 3-5-parted into linear lobes, as a rule   *T. capitátum*

TARÁXACUM Haller 1768 DANDELION

(Gr. *tarasso*, to disturb, in allusion to its medicinal properties)

Heads with yellow perfect strap-flowers, achenes oblong to linear-spindle-shaped, 4-5-angled, roughened or spiny, tapering into a long beak, pappus of hair-like bristles; receptacle flat, without chaff, involucre oblong to bell-shaped, main bracts nearly equal in 1 row with several rows of outer shorter spreading bracts; heads solitary; leaves basal, wavy-toothed to pinnatifid; perennial.

Leaves toothed to pinnatifid, sometimes nearly entire;
    flower-stalk 1-15 in. long; heads 1-2 in. wide   *T. officinále*

TETRADÝMIA DeCandolle 1837

(Gr. *tetradymos*, four together, the heads often but 4-flowered)

Heads without rays, the disk-flowers yellow or yellowish, perfect, achenes cylindric, rounded, often very woolly; receptacle flat, without chaff, involucre oblong to cylindric, of 4-6 concave overlapping bracts; heads cymose or clustered; leaves alternate, entire, sometimes clustered, occassionally modified into spines, usually densely felted; shrubs.

1. Heads 4-flowered; involucral bracts 4-5; achenes
    hairy to smooth; stems 1-2 ft. high
    a. Branches spiny   *T. Nuttállii*
    b. Branches not spiny; white wool permanent or
        disappearing   *T. canéscens*
2. Heads 5-9-flowered; involucral scales 5-6;
    achenes white-woolly; stems 2-4 ft. high;
    branches spiny   *T. spinósa*

THELESPÉRMA Lessing 1831 THELESPERMA

.   (Gr. *thele*, nipple, *sperma*, seed)

Pl. 39, fig. 3, 8.

Heads with yellow neutral ray-flowers or none, disk-flowers yellow to brownish, perfect, achenes linear to oblong, somewhat pappillose, pappus of 2 barbed awns, sometimes none; receptacle flat, with chaff, involucre hemispheric to bell-shaped, the inner bracts united to the middle or above into a cup, the outer short, narrow and spreading; heads solitary on the ends of the branches; leaves opposite, entire and linear or finely dissected; annual or perennial.

1. Rays none or 4-6 mm. long; awns of the pappus much longer than the width of the achene   *T. grácile*
2. Rays usually present, 12-15 mm. long; awns of the pappus shorter than the width of the achene, or none
    a. Awns or scales of the pappus 2; lobes of disk-corolla linear to lanceolate, longer than the throat   *T. trífidum*
    b. Pappus a tiny 4-5-toothed crown or none; lobes of disk corollas oblong to ovate, shorter than the throat   *T. subnúdum*

TOWNSÉNDIA Hooker 1834 TOWNSENDIA
(Named for Townsend, an American botanist)

Heads with pink, purple or white pistillate ray-flowers, disk-flowers mostly perfect, achenes of the disk compressed, those of the rays usually 3-angled, pappus of bristles or scales or both; receptacle flat, without chaff, involucre hemispheric to bell-shaped, bracts imbricated in several rows; heads solitary on the branches; leaves alternate or basal, entire; tufted perennials.

1. Bracts of the involucre tapering to a long point
    a. Stem with many spreading branches from the base; pappus of the ray flower a crown of short scales   *T. grandiflóra*
    b. Stem erect, not branched at base; pappus with 2 awns or wholly of bristles
        (1) Pappus wholly of bristles; stem 1-8 in. or lacking   *T. Párryi*
        (2) Pappus a crown of scales with 2 awl-shaped awns; stems 6-15 in. high   *T. exímia*
2. Bracts of the involucre short-pointed, acute or obtuse
    a. Stems 1-10 in. high, at least when mature; leaves and stems gray-hairy
        (1) Leaves spatulate; pappus of ray flower of both bristles and scales   *T. Wátsoni*
        (2) Leaves narrowly oblanceolate to linear; pappus almost wholly of bristles or scales
            (a) Pappus of the ray flower of many bristles; stems 1-5 in. high   *T. incána*

(b) Pappus of the ray flower of scales and
    1-2 bristles; stems finally 4-10 in. high   *T. strigósa*
b. Stems none, or less than an inch high at maturity
  (1) Plants gray or white-hairy
    (a) Leaves linear, closely and finely gray-
      hairy; heads 12-20 mm. high   *T. exscápa*
    (b) Leaves spatulate, densely woolly; heads
      7-10 mm. high   *T. spathuláta*
  (2) Plants green, hairy to smooth
    (a) Heads 2-3 cm. high, without the rays   *T. Rothróckii*
    (b) Heads 6-12 mm. high
      x. Leaf blades hairy; heads 10-12 mm.
        high   *T. scapígera*
      y. Leaf blades smooth; heads 5-8 mm.
        high   *T. glabélla*

TRAGOPÓGON Linné 1753 SALSIFY, GOATSBEARD

(Gr. *tragos*, goat, *pogon*, beard, from the pappus)

Pl. 37, fig. 5.

Heads with yellow or purple perfect strap-flowers, achenes linear, round or 5-angled, ribbed, with a long beak, pappus of brownish, plumy, interwoven bristles; receptacle flat, without chaff, involucre cylindric or bell-shaped, the equal bracts in 1 row; heads solitary; leaves alternate, entire; biennial or perennial.

1. Heads purple; bracts of the involucre much longer than the flowers   *T. porrifólius*
2. Heads yellow; bracts of the involucre equalling
  or shorter than the flowers   *T. praténsis*

VERNÓNIA Schreber 1791 IRONWEED

(Named for Vernon, an English botanist)

Heads without rays, the tube-flowers usually purple, perfect, achenes ovate to oblong, 8-10-ribbed, pappus mostly of hair-like bristles; receptacle flat, without chaff, involucre hemispheric to oblong, the bracts imbricated in several to many rows; heads in panicled cymes; leaves usually alternate, simple; perennial.

Leaves linear to lance-oblong, spiny-toothed to nearly
  entire; heads 6-10 mm. high   *V. fasciculáta*

WYÉTHIA Nuttall 1834
(Named for Wyeth, a botanical collector)

Heads with yellowish or white pistillate rays, the latter sometimes with sterile filaments, disk-flowers yellow, perfect, achenes oblong, 4-5-angled, pappus a fringed or 5-10-toothed crown, 1 or more of the teeth often awn-like; receptacle convex, with chaff, involucre bell-shaped, the bracts in 2-3 rows; heads solitary; leaves alternate, usually entire; perennial.

1. Rays white to straw-color   *W. helianthoídes*
2. Rays bright yellow
    a. Rays 2.5-4 cm. long
       (1) Plants smooth throughout   *W. amplexicaúlis*
       (2) Plants hairy   *W. arizónica*
    b. Rays 10-15 mm. long; plants rough   *W. scábra*

XÁNTHIUM Linné 1753 COCKLEBUR
(Gr. *xanthos*, yellow, from yielding a yellow dye)

Heads without rays, monoecious, staminate heads densely clustered at the ends of branches, the involucre of 1-3 rows of bracts, receptacle cylindric, chaffy, corolla present; pistillate heads axillary, forming a closed involucre, 1-2-beaked and covered with hooked spines, with 2 achenes, pappus none; leaves alternate, lobed or toothed; annual.

Stems 1-6 ft. high; leaves ovate to rounded; bur 2-2.5
    cm. long, with hooked or curved beak   *X. canadénse*

XIMENÉSIA Cavanilles 1793
(Named for Ximenes, a Spanish physician)
Pl. 40, fig. 5.

Heads with yellow pistillate ray-flowers, disk-flowers yellow, perfect, achenes flat, winged, pappus of 2 awns or in the ray of 1-3 awns; receptacle convex, with chaff, involucre hemispheric, the bracts more or less imbricated, equal and spreading; heads solitary or few; leaves alternate or sometimes opposite, simple, toothed; annual.

Stems 1-3 ft. high; leaves ovate and heart-shaped to
lance-ovate, 2-5 in. long; rays 12-15, about an inch
long   *X. encelioídes*

ALISMALES   ARROWHEAD ORDER
ALISMÁCEAE   ARROWHEAD FAMILY

Sepals 3, green, petals 3, colored, stamens 6-many, pistils many or rarely few, fruit an achene; flowers perfect, monoecious or dioecious, in racemes or panicles; aquatic or marsh herbs with leafless stems and basal simple leaves.

1. Flowers perfect; leaves not arrow-shaped   ALISMA
2. Flowers monoecious or dioecious; leaves arrow-
    shaped   SAGITTARIA

ALÍSMA Linné 1753 WATER PLANTAIN
(Name of uncertain origin and meaning)

Sepals 3, green, petals 3, white or rose-tinted, stamens 6-9, pistils usually 12-18, achenes flattened, curved and ribbed; flowers many in panicle-like clusters; leaves erect or floating, ovate to lance-linear; perennial.
Flower-stalks 1-4 ft. high; leaves ovate to elliptic;
flowers 5-7 mm. wide   *A. plantago-aquática*

SAGITTÁRIA Linné 1753 ARROWHEAD
(Lat. *sagitta,* arrow, from the shape of the leaf)
Pl. 44, fig. 2.

Sepals 3, green, petals 3, white, stamens usually numerous, pistils numerous, achenes flattened in rounded heads; flowers monoecious or dioecious, in whorls of 3's, staminate usually above; leaves basal, arrow-shaped, or the blade lost; aquatic or marsh perennial.

1. Basal lobes of the leaf lance-linear, forming ⅔ to
    ¾ the length of the whole leaf   *S. longilóba*
2. Basal lobes more or less triangular and broad,
    forming ¼ to ½ the length of the whole leaf
  a. Beak of the achene more than ¼ its length   *S. latifólia*
  b. Beak of the achene less than ¼ its length   *S. arifólia*

TYPHACEAE CAT-TAIL FAMILY

Sepals none, and petals reduced to bristles, stamens 2-7, filaments united, pistil 1, stalked, ovary 1-2-celled, styles 1-2, bristly hairs among the stamens and pistils; flowers monoecious in dense terminal spikes, staminate spike above the pistillate; marsh or aquatic plants with creeping root-stocks and erect cylindric stems and long-linear, flat, sword-like leaves, sheathing at the base.

TÝPHA Linné 1753 CAT-TAIL
(The Greek name)

Characters of the family.

1. Leaves 6-12 mm. wide; spikes dark brown to
    black, often 1 in. or more wide, the pistillate
    and staminate parts usually touching; stigmas
    spatulate or rhomboid   *T. latifólia*

2. Leaves 4-12 mm. wide; spikes light brown; staminate and pistillate parts usually separate, 4-15
   mm. wide; stigmas linear to linear-oblong *T. angustifólia*

SPARGANIÁCEAE BUR-REED FAMILY

Sepals and petals reduced to a few chaffy scales, stamens usually 5,
filaments distinct, ovary usually 1-celled, fruit nut-like; flowers monoecious,
densely crowded in round heads, staminate heads above, spathes linear, just
below or some distance below the heads; marsh or aquatic plants with
creeping rootstocks, erect or floating stems, and alternate, linear, sheathing
leaves.

SPARGÁNIUM Linné 1753 BUR-REED

(Gr. *sparganon*, band, from the ribbon-like leaves)

Pl. 44, fig. 4.

Characters of the family.
1. Nut-like fruits sessile, angled; fruiting heads 2-
   3 cm. wide   *S. eurycárpum*
2. Nutlets stalked, round or spindle-shaped; fruit-
   ing heads 4-20 mm. wide
   a. Flower cluster branched; fruiting heads 1-2
      cm. wide   *S. andrócladum*
   b. Flower cluster simple
      (1) Staminate heads 4-6, pistillate heads 2-6,
          the latter 10-15 mm. wide in fruit *S. símplex*
      (2) Staminate heads 1-2, pistillate heads 1-3,
          the latter 4-10 mm. wide in fruit   *S. mínimum*

NAIADÁCEAE PONDWEED FAMILY

Sepals and petals, or perianth, 4 or none, stamens usually 1-4, pistils
1-9, ovary 1-celled, carpels usually 1-seeded, rarely splitting; flowers perfect, monoecious or dioecious, axillary or in spikes; aquatic plants with
submerged leafy stems and alternate or opposite leaves.

1. Leaves alternate; flowers perfect; stamens 2 or 4
   a. Perianth of 4 parts   POTAMOGETON
   b. Perianth none   RUPPIA
2. Leaves mostly opposite or clustered; flowers
   monoecious or dioecious; stamen 1
   a. Leaves entire; flowers clustered   ZANNICHELLIA
   b. Leaves spiny-toothed; flowers solitary   NAIAS

NÁIAS Linné 1753 NAIAS
(Gr. *naias*, water-nymph, from the habitat)

Perianth of the staminate flower double, outer entire or 4-horned, the inner hyaline, adhering to the single anther, pistillate flower a single ovary with 2-4 stigmas, carpels solitary; flowers monoecious or dioecious, solitary, axillary; leaves usually opposite or whorled, sheathing at base; submerged aquatic.

1. Leaves tapering to a point, 12-25 mm. long, 1-2
mm. wide *N. fléxilis*
2. Leaves rather obtuse at tip, 1-2 cm. long, .5-1
mm. wide *N. guadaloupénsis*

POTAMOGÉTON Linné 1753 PONDWEED
(Gr. *potamos*, river, *geiton*, neighbor, from the habitat)
Pl. 44, fig. 1.

. Perianth of 4 parts, stamens 4, pistils 4, separate, fruit of 4 1-seeded drupelets; flowers perfect, green or red, in spikes; leaves alternate or the uppermost opposite, usually of 2 kinds, submerged and floating; submerged or floating aquatic.

1. Stems with both floating and submerged leaves
a. Submerged leaves with the flat blade present
(1) Submerged leaves of 2 forms, elliptic and
lanceolate *P. amplifólius*
(2) Submerged leaves alike
(a) Submerged leaves linear
x. Leaves thread-like with attached stipules *P. diversifólius*
y. Leaves lance-linear with free stipules *P. heterophýllus*
(b) Submerged leaves not linear
x. Some or all of the leaves petioled
(x) Upper leaves petioled, lower sessile; floating leaves spatulate to
oblanceolate *P. alpínus*
(y) All the leaves petioled; floating
leaves elliptic *P. lonchítes*
y. All the leaves sessile or short-petioled *P. Zízii*
b. Submerged leaves without the usual flat blade;
floating leaves ovate to elliptic *P. nátans*
2. Stems without floating leaves
a. Leaves lanceolate to ovate
(1) Leaves heart-shaped and perfoliate *P. perfoliátus*

(2) Leaves tapering to the base; sessile or
short-petioled   *P. lúcens*

b. Leaves linear
  (1) Leaves 1-3 in. long; stipules free
    (a) Leaves with 2 glands at the base, 1 mm.
wide   *P. pusíllus*
    (b) Leaves without glands at the base, 1-2
mm. wide   *P. foliósus*
  (2) Leaves 2-12 in. long; stipules attached
    (a) Stigma sessile or nearly so   *P. filifórmis*
    (b) Stigma on a distinct style   *P. pectinátus*

RÚPPIA Linné 1753 RUPPIA
(Named for Rupp, a German botanist)

Perianth none, flowers 2 or more, consisting of 2 stamens and 4 pistils, cluster enclosed at first in the sheath-like base of the leaf, fruit a drupe, each on a slender stalk which, like the stalk of the spadix, appears after flowering; leaves alternate, hair-like, sheathing at the base; submerged aquatic in salt or alkaline water.

Stems 2-3 ft. long; leaves 1-3 in. long, .5 mm. or less
wide; pedicels 4-6 in a cluster, the peduncle coiled *R. marítima*

ZANNICHÉLLIA Linné 1753 ZANNICHELLIA
(Named for Zannichelli, an Italian botanist)

Perianth none, flowers monoecious, 1 staminate and 2-5 pistillate flowers in the same axil, stamen 1, pistil 1, fruit a ribbed or toothed nutlet; flowers and leaf-buds at first enclosed in an envelope; leaves thread-like, whorled; submerged aquatic.

Leaves 1-3 in. long, .5 mm. or less wide; fruits 2-6
in a cluster, 2-4 mm. long   *Z. palústris*

JUNCAGINÁCEAE   ARROW GRASS FAMILY

Perianth usually of 6 parts, in 2 rows, greenish, stamens 3-6, pistils 3-6, united, separating into 3-6 carpels when ripe; flowers in terminal spikes or racemes on long leafless stalks; marsh herbs with basal, half-round leaves, sheathing below.

TRIGLÓCHIN Linné 1753 ARROW GRASS
(Gr. *tri-*, three, *glochin*, point, from the 3-pointed fruit)
Pl. 44, fig. 3.

Characters of the family.

1. Carpels 3; fruit linear or club-shaped, tapering
   to the base   *T. palústris*
2. Carpels 6; fruit oblong or ovoid, base broad   *T. marítima*

LILIALES LILY ORDER
COMMELINÁCEAE SPIDERWORT FAMILY

Sepals 3, green, petals 3, colored, stamens usually 6, ovary 2-3-celled, stigma entire or slightly 2-3-lobed, capsule 2-3-celled, splitting; flowers in cymes, usually with leafy bracts; perennial or annual herbs with regular or irregular, perfect flowers and alternate, entire, sheathing leaves.

1. Flowers regular; stamens with anthers usually
   6; bracts leaf-like   TRADESCANTIA
2. Flowers irregular; stamens with anthers usually
   3; bracts spathe-like   COMMELINA

COMMELÍNA Linné 1753 DAY FLOWER
(Named for Commelin, a Dutch botanist)

Sepals 3, somewhat unequal, petals 3, blue, one of them smaller, stamens with anthers 3, rarely 2, imperfect stamens usually 3, filaments smooth, capsule 3-celled, 3-6-seeded; flowers in cymes with spathe-like bracts; leaves alternate, entire, sheathing; perennial.

Stems 1-3 ft. high; leaves lanceolate or lance-linear,
   3-5 in. long; flowers about 1 in. wide   *C. virgínica*

TRADESCÁNTIA Linné 1753 SPIDERWORT
(Named for Tradescant, an English gardener)
Pl. 42, fig. 2.

Sepals 3, green, petals 3, blue, purple or pink, rarely white, alike, stamens 6, ovary 3-celled, capsule 3-celled, 3-12-seeded; flowers in terminal or axillary umbels, usually with leaf-like bracts; leaves alternate, narrow, long and entire; perennial.

Stems .5-4 ft. tall; leaves linear- to lance-linear,
   smooth and glaucous to hairy; flowers 1-2 in. wide *T. virginiána*

LILIÁCEAE LILY FAMILY

Sepals 3, usually colored like the petals, petals 3, usually separate, sometimes united, stamens 6, ovary 3-celled, styles separate or united, stigma 3-lobed or globose, fruit a capsule; flowers usually perfect, solitary or in racemes, umbels or panicles; stemless or leafy-stemmed perennials from bulbs or corms, or sometimes from root-stocks, often with long, grass-like leaves.

1. Styles distinct
    a. Leaves broad, ovate to oblanceolate; stems leafy; flowers greenish   VERATRUM
    b. Leaves linear or grass-like; flowers yellow or white
        (1) Flowers yellow; stems sticky-hairy   TOFIELDIA
        (2) Flowers white; stems not sticky-hairy
            (a) Leaves needle-shaped, 2 mm. wide or less; rare   XEROPHYLLUM
            (b) Leaves linear, 4-15 mm. wide; common ZYGADENUS
2. Styles united
    a. Flowers axillary, solitary or 1-few in a cluster
        (1) Parts of the perianth separate; leaves heart-shaped and clasping at base   STREPTOPUS
        (2) Parts of the perianth united into a cylindric tube; leaves not heart-shaped and clasping   POLYGONATUM
    b. Flowers terminal
        (1) Flowers on a leafy stem
            (a) Flowers white or whitish to lilac
                x. Flowers in a raceme or panicle   WAGNERA
                y. Flowers solitary or 2-3 in an umbel
                    (x) Flowers nodding; leaves ovate to lance-oblong   DISPORUM
                    (y) Flowers erect; leaves linear, grass-like
                        m. Flowers 1-3 in. wide; petals fringed at base   CALOCHORTUS
                        n. Flowers 1-2 cm. wide; petals not fringed   LLOYDIA
            (b) Flowers yellow to orange or purple
                x. Flowers erect, orange, 2-3 in. wide   LILIUM
                y. Flowers nodding, purple or yellow and purple-dotted, 1 in. wide or less   FRITILLARIA
        (2) Plants stemless
            (a) Leaves stiff, spiny-pointed, 1-3 ft. long; flowers white in a long raceme   YUCCA
            (b) Leaves not stiff and spiny-pointed
                x. Flowers yellow, nodding   ERYTHRONIUM

Plate 42

LILY FAMILY

1. Allium cernuum: Onion
3. Erythronium parviflorum: Spring Lily, Dogtooth Violet
4. Lilium philadelphicum: Lily
5. Zygadenus elegans
6. Calochortus Gunnisonii: Mariposa Lily

SPIDERWORT FAMILY

2. Tradescantia virginiana: Spiderwort

PLATE 42.

EDITH S. CLEMENTS. PINXT

ROCKY MOUNTAIN FLOWERS

COCKAYNE, BOSTON

y. Flowers white to pink or blue
  (x) Flowers in a raceme, blue or white QUAMASSIA
  (y) Flowers in an umbel
    m. Flowers blue   BRODIAEA
    n. Flowers white to pink
      (m) Flowers with a tube 1-2 in.
          long, few from an under-
          ground root-stalk   LEUCOCRINUM
      (n) Flowers without a tube, many
          on a long stalk   ALLIUM

ALLIUM Linné 1753 ONION
(Lat. name of the garlic)
Pl. 42, fig. 1.

Sepals and petals 3 each, similar, stamens 6, ovary 3-celled, stigmas small, ovules 1-6 in each cell; flowers white to rose, in a simple terminal umbel, with 2-3 papery bracts; leaves basal, narrowly linear, sheathing; bulbous perennial.

1. Leaves hollow, terete; flowers rose-color, longer
    than their pedicels; parts of the perianth 8-12
    mm. long   *A. sibíricum*
2. Leaves not hollow
  a. Flowers mostly replaced by little bulbs   *A. canadénse*
  b. Flowers rarely replaced by little bulbs
    (1) Flower-umbel nodding; each valve of the
      capsule with 2 short crests   *A. cérnuum*
    (2) Flower-umbel erect
      (a) Each valve of the capsule with 2 crests *A. reticulátum*
      (b) Valves of the capsule not crested
        x. Coats of the bulb very fibrous and net-
          like; perianth parts 6 mm. long   *A. Nuttállii*
        y. Coats of the bulb thin and papery, never
          fibrous; perianth parts 8-12 mm. long
          (x) Bulb oblong with a root-stock be-
             low   *A. brevístylum*
          (y) Bulb small and nearly round
            m. Leaves longer than the short flow-
              er-stem; perianth parts acute   *A. Brandégei*
            n. Leaves shorter than the flower-
              stem; perianth parts with point-
              ed, recurved tips   *A. acuminátum*

BRODIAÉA Smith 1811
(Named for Brodie, a Scotch botanist)

Sepals and petals each 3, similar, blue, stamens 6, ovary 3-celled, style 1; flowers in terminal umbels with several bracts; leaves basal, linear; perennial stemless herb from corm-like bulb.

Flower stem 1-2 ft. high; tube of the flower about
equalling the lobes   *B. Douglásii*

CALOCHÓRTUS Pursh 1814 MARIPOSA LILY
(Gr. *kalos*, beautiful, *chortus*, herb)
Pl. 42, fig. 6.

Sepals 3, narrow, green, petals 3, white to purple, glandular and hairy at base, stamens 6, ovary 3-celled, style short or none, stigmas 3, recurved; flowers solitary or 1-3; leaves alternate, long-linear; perennial with a corm.

1. Gland across the base of each petal oblong;
   anthers acute   *C. Gunnisónii*
2. Gland round or oval; anthers obtuse   *C. Nuttállii*

DISPÓRUM Salisbury 1812
(Gr. *di*, two, *spora*, seed, referring to the 2 ovules in each cell)

Sepals and petals 3 each, similar, whitish or greenish-yellow, stamens 6, ovary 3-celled, style 1, stigma entire or 3-cleft; flowers terminal, solitary or few in a simple umbel; leaves alternate, broad sessile or clasping; perennial from a root-stalk.

Stems 1-2 ft. high; leaves ovate to lance-oblong, 1.5-
3.5 in. long; flowers 8-15 mm. long   *D. trachycárpum*

ERYTHRÓNIUM Linné 1753 SPRING LILY, DOGTOOTH VIOLET
(Gr. *erythros*, red, from the color of the European species)
Pl. 42, fig. 3.

Sepals and petals 3 each, similar, yellow, stamens 6, ovary 3-celled, style 1, stigma 3-lobed; flowers nodding, solitary or 1-5; leaves in pairs below the middle and appearing basal, usually lance-oblong; perennial from a corm.

Flower stem 4-12 in. high; leaves oblong, more or less
tapering; flowers solitary or 2-5, 2-3 cm. long   *E. parviflórum*

FRITILLÁRIA Linné 1753 FRITILLARIA
(Lat. *fritillus*, dice-box)

Sepals and petals 3 each, yellow or purple, with a nectary at base, stamens 6, ovary 3-celled, style 1, stigma 3-lobed; flowers nodding, solitary or few in a raceme; leafy-stemmed perennial from a bulb.

1. Flowers purple and mottled   *F. atropurpúrea*
2. Flowers yellow or orange, tinged with purple   *F. pudíca*

LEUCOCRÍNUM   Nuttall 1837   SAND LILY
(Gr. *leukos*, white, *krinon*, lily)
Pl. 44, fig. 8.

Sepals and petals 3 each, white, similar, linear-oblong, forming a long tube, stamens 6 near the top of the tube, ovary 3-celled, style 1; flowers in an umbel, from the rootstock, leaves basal, linear, from a rootstock.
Leaves 2-10 in. long; flower-tube 1-2 in. long   *L. montánum*

LÍLIUM   Linné 1753   LILY
(The Latin name)
Pl. 42, fig. 4.

Sepals and petals 3 each, reddish-orange, similar, with a nectar-groove at base, stamens 6, ovary 3-celled, style 1, stigma 3-lobed; flowers solitary, or few, terminal; leaves whorled or alternate; leafy-stemmed perennial from a bulb.
Stems 1-3 ft. high; leaves lanceolate, 1-4 in. long;
     flowers 2-4 in. long   *L. philadélphicum*

LLÓYDIA   Salisbury 1812
(Named for Lloyd, an English botanist)
Pl. 44, fig. 9.

Sepals and petals 3 each, white, similar, stamens 6, ovary 3-celled, style 1; flower usually solitary, erect; leaves alternate, thread-like, the bases papery; stems from a bulb with a root-stalk.
Stems 2-8 in. high; flowers 1-2 cm. wide; at 10-14000
     ft.   *L. serótina*

POLYGONÁTUM   Adanson 1763   SOLOMON'S SEAL
(Gr. *polys*, many, *gonu*, knee, from the joints of the rootstock)

Sepals and petals united into a 6-lobed tube, greenish, stamens 6 on the tube, ovary 3-celled, style 1, fruit a berry; flowers axillary, 2-10 in an umbel; leaves ovate to lance-oblong, alternate, sessile; leafy-stemmed from a horizontal rootstock.
Stems 2-8 ft. high; leaves ovate to lanceolate, 2-6 in.
     long; flowers 1-2 cm. long   *P. commutátum*

QUAMÁSIA   Rafinesque 1818   WILD HYACINTH

(Latinized from Quamash, the Indian name)

Sepals and petals 3 each, blue or white, similar, stamens 6, ovary 3-celled, style 1, stigma 3-lobed; flowers in a terminal raceme; leaves basal, linear; stemless perennial from an edible bulb.

Flower-stems 1-2 ft. high; raceme 3-8 in. long; flowers 1-2 cm. long   *Q. hyacinthína*

STRÉPTOPUS   Michaux 1803   TWISTED STALK

(Gr. *streptos*, twisted, *pous*, foot, from the twisted flower-stalk)

Pl. 44, fig. 11.

Sepals and petals 3 each, greenish or purplish, similar, stamens 6, ovary 3-celled, style 1, fruit a berry; flowers solitary or 2 together, axillary, nodding; leaves alternate, broad, clasping; leafy-stemmed herb from a rootstalk.

Stems 1-5 ft. high with spreading branches; leaves
ovate to lance-oblong, 2-5 in. long; flowers 8-15 mm.
long   *S. amplexifólius*

TOFIÉLDIÁ   Hudson 1778   ASPHODEL

(Named for Tofield, an English botanist)

Petals and sepals 3 each, white or green, similar, stamens 6, ovary 3-celled, 3-lobed at tip, styles 3, capsule 3-lobed and 3-beaked, many-seeded; flowers in a terminal raceme, usually with bractlets; leaves basal, 2-ranked, linear; stemless perennial from a rootstock.

Stems .5-2 ft. high, 2-4-leaved near base; leaves 2-7
in. long; flowers 6-8 mm. wide   *T. glutinósa*

VERÁTRUM   Linné 1753   FALSE HELLEBORE

(Lat. name of the hellebore)

Pl. 44, fig. 7.

Sepals and petals 3 each, greenish-white, similar, stamens 6, ovary 3-celled, styles 3, capsule 3-lobed, seeds broadly winged; flowers monoecious or polygamous in large, terminal panicles; leaves alternate, broad, clasping; stem perennial from a poisonous rootstock.

Stems 2-8 ft. high; leaves lanceolate, 6-12 in. long;
panicle 1-3 ft. long; flowers 16-25 mm. wide   *V. víride*

WÁGNERA Adanson 1763 SPIKENARD, SOLOMON'S SEAL   ·
(Named for Wagner)
Pl. 44, fig. 10.

Sepals and petals 3 each, white or greenish-white, similar, stamens 6, ovary 3-celled, style 1, stigma 3-lobed, fruit a berry; flowers in a terminal raceme or panicle; leaves alternate, broad, usually sessile; leafy-stemmed perennial from a rootstock.

1. Flowers in a simple raceme
  a. Flower-stalk short, little if at all longer than the flowers and the fruit; leaves lanceolate, acute   *W. stelláta*
  b. Flower-stalk 2-3 times as long as the flowers and the fruit; leaves lance-linear, long-pointed   *W. sessilifólia*
2. Flowers in a panicle
  a. Leaves short-petioled   *W. racemósa*
  b. Leaves sessile, clasping   *W. amplexicaúlis*

XEROPHÝLLUM Michaux 1803 TURKEY BEARD
(Gr. *xeros*, dry, *phyllon*, leaf)

Sepals and petals 3 each, white, similar, persisting when dry, stamens 6, ovary 3-celled, styles 3; flowers many in a dense terminal raceme; leaves long and needle-like; leafy-stemmed perennial from a woody rootstock.

Stems 2-5 ft. high, densely leafy below; leaves 6-18 in. long, 1-2 mm. wide; flowers 5-6 mm. long   *X. asphodeloídes*

YÚCCA Linné 1753 SPANISH BAYONET
(The Haytian name)

Sepals and petals 3 each, white to cream-color, similar, stamens 6, ovary 3-celled, style 1, stigmas 3, fruit fleshy; flowers large, nearly globose, nodding in a terminal raceme or panicle; leaves basal, long, lance-linear, stiff and sharp-pointed, evergreen; stem woody, underground.

1. Leaves usually 1-5 cm. wide
  a. Fruit an erect, brown, splitting capsule   *Y. Harrimániae*
  b. Fruit a fleshy, edible, purple berry   *Y. baccáta*
2. Leaves .5-1 cm. wide; fruit an erect capsule   *Y. glaúca*

ZYGADÉNUS Michaux 1803 ZYGADENUS
(Gr. *zygon*, yoke, *aden*, gland)
Pl. 42, fig. 5.

Sepals and petals 3 each, white, yellowish or greenish, similar, with

1-2 glands at the base, stamens 6, ovary 3-celled, styles 3, capsule 3-lobed; flowers perfect or polygamous, in a terminal raceme or panicle; leaves alternate, linear; leafy-stemmed perennial from a bulb or root-stalk.

1. Perianth grown together with the base of the
   ovary; gland heart-shaped   *Z. élegans*
2. Perianth free from the ovary; gland ovate to
   rounded
   a. Parts of the perianth with a claw; stamen fila-
      ments attached to the base of the perianth
      (1) Flowers 4-6 mm. long; leaves 4-6 mm.
         wide   *Z. venenósus*
      (2) Flowers 5-8 mm. long; leaves 5-9 mm.
         wide   *Z. intermédius*
   b. Parts of the perianth without a claw, 6-10 mm.
      long; stamen filaments free from the perianth *Z. Nuttállii*

SMILACÁCEAE   SMILAX FAMILY

Sepals and petals 3 each, greenish, similar, stamens 6, ovary 3-celled, stigmas 1-3, fruit a berry; flowers dioecious in axillary umbels; leaves alternate, net-veined, several-ribbed; vines with woody or herbaceous, usually prickly stems.

SMÍLAX   Linné 1753   GREENBRIER
(Gr. name of the bindweed)

Characters of the family.
Stems 3-6 ft. high; leaves ovate or lance-ovate, 7-9-
   ribbed, 2-5 in. long; berries blue-black   *S. herbácea*

JUNCÁCEAE   RUSH FAMILY

Perianth of 6 parts, in 2 rows, stamens 3 or 6, pistil 1- or 3-celled, stigmas 3, fruit a capsule; flowers small, regular, greenish, mostly in compound umbels, panicles or corymbs, or densely crowded into spikes or heads; grass-like perennials, rarely annuals.

1. Sheaths of the leaves closed; capsule 3-seeded   JUNCODES
2. Sheaths of the leaves open; capsule many-seeded JUNCUS

JUNCÓDES   Adanson 1763   WOOD RUSH
(Lat. *juncus*, rush, Gr. *eidos*, like)

Perianth of 6 similar, greenish-brown parts, stamens 6, ovary 1-celled, seeds 3; flowers with bracts, in open or spike-like clusters; leaves grass-like; perennial.

1. Flowers in an open panicle; stems 1-4 ft. high   *J. parviflórum*
2. Flowers in a head or spike
   a. Spikes 1-2, nodding   *J. spicátum*
   b. Heads 2-several, erect   *J. intermédium*

JÚNCUS Linné 1753 RUSH

(Lat. *juncus,* rush, from *jungo,* bind, from their use)

Pl. 44, fig. 12, 13.

Perianth of 6 similar, greenish-brown parts, stamens 6 or 3, ovary 1-celled or 3-celled, stigmas 3, capsule usually many-seeded; flowers small, yellow, greenish, in panicles or corymbs or in dense heads or spikes; leaves terete, channelled or grass-like; perennial.

1. Leaves with internal cross-walls showing as bands or knots, especially when the leaf is pinched in the fingers
   a. Leaves roundish, or but slightly flattened
     (1) Stamens 3; seeds tailed   *J. Tweédyi*
     (2) Stamens 6; seeds merely pointed
       (a) Parts of the perianth and capsule pointed or acute
         x. Inner perianth parts longer than the outer   *J. nodósus*
         y. Inner perianth parts shorter than the outer
           (x) Capsule with beak a little longer than the perianth   *J. Tórreyi*
           (y) Capsule with beak shorter than the perianth   *J. nevadénsis*
       (b) Parts of the perianth and capsule obtuse *J. richardsoniánus*
   b. Leaves distinctly flattened and equitant
     (1) Stamens 3   *J. ensifólius*
     (2) Stamens 6
       (a) Heads solitary   *J. mertensiánus*
       (b) Heads 2 or more   *J. saximóntanus*
2. Leaves without knots or cross bands
   a. Flower-cluster terminal
     (1) Flowers solitary in panicles
       (a) Stems much branched and leafy   *J. bufónius*
       (b) Stems not branched, naked
         x. Leaves flat

    (x) Parts of the perianth greenish;
        capsule shorter than the perianth *J. ténuis*
    (y) Parts of the perianth brown; cap-
        sule equalling the perianth   *J. confúsus*
  y. Leaves terete   *J. Váseyi*
 (2) Flowers in heads
  (a) Leaves flat
    x. Stamens 3   *J. marginátus*
    y. Stamens 6   *J. longístylis*
  (b) Leaves hollow and tube-like
    x. Head usually single, 3-flowered; leaves
        flattened above   *J. triglúmis*
    y. Heads 1-3, 3-12-flowered; leaves terete
        above   *J. castáneus*
b. Flower-cluster lateral and sessile; stems leafless
 (1) Cluster usually of 1-3 flowers
  (a) Stems entirely without leaves   *J. subtriflórus*
  (b) Stems somewhat leafy
    x. Capsule blunt, equalling the perianth *J. Hállii*
    y. Capsule pointed, longer than the
        perianth   *J. Párryi*
 (2) Cluster of several to many flowers
  (a) Perianth and capsule brown; capsule
    long-pointed   *J. bálticus*
  (b) Perianth and capsule green; capsule
    barely pointed   *J. filifórmis*

•

PONTEDERIÁCEAE   PICKEREL WEED FAMILY

Perianth of 6 parts, corolla-like, nearly regular, stamens 3, ovary more or less 3-celled, stigma 3-lobed, fruit a many-seeded capsule enclosed in the withered perianth-tube; flowers 1-several, enclosed by a spathe; bog or aquatic perennials with petioled leaves with broad blades, or grass-like.

HETERÁNTHERA Roemer and Schultes 1794 MUD PLANTAIN

(Gr. *heteros*, different, *anthera*, anther)

Characters of the family.

Stems 6-15 in. long; leaves ovate, about 1 in. long;
  flowers white or blue   *H. limosa*

ARALES ARUM ORDER

LEMNÁCEAE DUCKWEED FAMILY

Flowers rarely seen, consisting of a single stamen or a single pistil, fruit a 1-6-seeded utricle; flowers monoecious, 1 or more on the edge or upper surface of the plant; plant a disk-shaped or irregular leaf-like body, usually with 1-several rootlets; tiny, floating, aquatic perennials without true leaves.

LÉMNA Linné 1753 DUCKWEED
(Possibly from Gr. *limne*, lake)
Pl. 44, fig. 5, 6.

Characters of the family.

1. Plant body or thallus lanceolate, often connected
   in a chain *L. trisúlca*
2. Plant body or thallus elliptic to ovoid or round
   a. Thallus 3-5-nerved
      (1) Thallus more or less strongly swollen be-
          neath *L. gíbba*
      (2) Thallus not swollen beneath
          (a) Thallus small, 2-3 mm. long, abruptly
              narrowed to a very short stalk *L. perpusílla*
          (b) Thallus 2-6 mm. long, not abruptly nar-
              rowed to a stalk *L. minor*
   b. Thallus not nerved
      (1) Thallus thin, without pappules; root-cap
          curved, tapering *L. cyclostása*
      (2) Thallus thick, with a row of pappules,
          root-cap scarcely curved, cylindric *L. mínima*

HYDRALES WATERWEED ORDER

HYDROCHARITÁCEAE WATERWEED FAMILY

Perianth of 6 parts, in 2 rows, at least the 3 inner petal-like, stamens 9, ovary 1-celled with 3 placenta, stigmas 3, fruit closed, few-seeded; flowers dioecious or polygamous from a 2-cleft spathe; submerged plants with opposite or whorled, crowded, entire or minutely toothed leaves.

PHILÓTRIA Rafinesque 1818 WATERWEED
(Gr. *philos*, loving, *tria*, three, the leaves often in 3's)

Characters of the family.

Stems .5-3 ft. long; leaves linear to elliptic, usually
3-4 in a whorl, .5-1.5 cm. long *P. canadénsis*

IRIDALES IRIS ORDER
IRIDÁCEAE IRIS FAMILY

Sepals and petals 3 each, similar in color, sometimes more or less united, and the tube grown to the ovary, stamens 3, inserted on the perianth, ovary usually 3-celled, style 3-cleft, the branches sometimes petal-like, capsule 3-celled, 3-angled or lobed; flowers regular or irregular, solitary or clustered, ·enclosed below by bracts; perennial herbs with grass-like, equitant, 2-ranked leaves.

1. Sepals and petals unlike in form; flowers 2-3 in.
    long; plants 1-3 ft. tall; style branches petal-
    like, concealing the stamens   IRIS
2. Sepals and petals alike in form; flowers 1-2 cm.
    long; style-branches not petal-like; stems 4-15
    in. high   SISYRINCHIUM

ÍRIS Linné 1753 IRIS
(Gr. *iris*, rainbow, referring to the color of the flower)
Pl. 43, fig. 5.

Sepals 3, spreading or reflexed, colored like the 3 erect petals but usually broader and larger, stamens 3, ovary 3-celled, style-branches petal-like, arched over the stamens, and bearing the stigmas under the 2-lobed tips, capsule oblong or oval; flowers terminal 1-few; leaves long and grass-like, equitant; perennial herb from a rootstock.
Stems .5-3 ft. tall; flowers 1-2, pale blue, to purple,
    rarely white, 2-3 in. long   *I. missouriénsis*

SISYRÍNCHIUM Linné 1753 BLUE-EYED GRASS
(Gr. *sisyrinchion*, a kind of iris)
Pl. 43, fig. 1.

Sepals and petals 3 each, blue, similar, usually abruptly pointed, stamens 3, ovary 3-celled, capsule mostly globose, flowers in a terminal umbel from a pair of green bracts; leaves grass-like; perennial.
Stems 4-15 in. high, 2-edged or 2-winged; leaves
    mostly basal, 1-3 mm. wide; flowers 1-2 cm. wide *S. angustifólium*

ORCHIDALES ORCHID ORDER
ORCHIDÁCEAE ORCHID FAMILY

Sepals 3, similar, petals 3, 2 alike, the third usually larger and different in form and color, forming a lip or sack, often spurred also, stamens 1-2, united with the style into a column, pollen in 2-8 pear-shaped masses, or pollinia, attached at the base of a sticky disk, style often forming a beak at the base of the anther, stigma a sticky surface beneath the beak of the style, or in a cavity between the anther sacks, ovary below the perianth, 1-celled, many-angled, capsule 3-valved, seeds very numerous; flowers irregular, solitary or in spikes or racemes; perennial herbs with entire sheathing leaves, sometimes scale-like, arising from corms, bulbs or tuberous roots.

1. Stems reddish-brown or purplish, the leaves represented by sheathing scales; rootless, the underground stems resembling branched coral   CORALLORRHIZA
2. Stems and leaves green
    a. Flowers mostly solitary and terminal, large, rose, purple or yellow
       (1) Flower solitary, rose; lip sack-like, with a tuft of yellow hairs   CALYPSO
       (2) Flowers 1-3, yellow or purple; lip a large sack, not tufted   CYPRIPEDIUM
    b. Flowers more than 1, usually in spikes or racemes, mostly white or greenish
       (1) Leaves all basal
         (a) Basal leaf 1; flowers greenish-yellow   LYSIELLA
         (b) Basal leaves several in a close rosette; flowers white or greenish-white   PERAMIUM
       (2) Stems leafy
         (a) Leaves 2, opposite, just below the raceme   LISTERA
         (b) Leaves more than 2 and alternate
           x. Capsules erect or ascending
             (x) Flowers spirally twisted on the spike
             m. Flowers white, fragrant   SPIRANTHES
             n. Flowers greenish, not fragrant   PIPERIA
             (y) Flowers not spirally twisted
             m. Petals lanceolate, lip entire   LIMNORCHIS
             n. Petals linear or thread-like; lip lobed   COELOGLOSSUM
           y. Capsules deflexed at maturity   EPIPACTIS

CALÝPSO Salisbury 1807 CALYPSO
(Named for the goddess, Calypso)
Pl. 43, fig. 6.

Sepals and lateral petals similar, rose, lip sack-like, 2-parted below,

Plate 43

IRIDS—ORCHIDS

IRIS FAMILY

1. Sisyrinchium angustifolium: Blue-eyed Grass
5. Iris missouriensis: Iris

ORCHID FAMILY

2. Corallorrhiza multiflora: Coral Root
3. Cypripedium pubescens: Ladies' Slipper
4. Peramium repens: Rattlesnake Plantain
6. Calypso borealis

PLATE 43.

with a patch of yellow hairs, column dilated, petal-like, the lid-like anther just below the summit, pollinia 2; flower solitary; terminal, bracted; leaf solitary, petioled, basal, the stem with 2-3 scales; perennial from a bulb. Stems 4-8 in. high; leaf ovate to rounded, 1-2 in. long;

flowers 1-2 cm. long *C. bulbósa*

COELOGLÓSSUM Hartman 1820
(Gr. *koilos*, hollow, *glossa*, tongue)

Sepals 3, ovate-lanceolate, the lateral petals narrow, linear or thread-like, greenish, lip oblong-spatulate, lobed at the summit, more than twice as long as the sack-like spur, pollinia with long stalks; flowers greenish in a leafy-bracted spike; leaves alternate, entire; leafy-stemmed biennial from a tuber.

Stem .5-2 ft. high; leaves lanceolate to ovate, 2-5 in.

long; flowers 6-8 mm. long *C. bracteátum*

CORALLORRHÍZA Robert Brown 1813 CORAL ROOT
(Gr. *corallion*, coral, *rhiza*, root)
Pl. 43, fig. 2.

Sepals 3, nearly equal, lateral petals about as long as the sepals, purple to brownish-red, lip whitish, 1-3-ridged, toothed or lobed, spotted or lined, sometimes with a sack or spur, column nearly free, slightly incurved, somewhat 2-winged, pollinia 4 in 2 pairs; flowers in terminal racemes; leaves all reduced to sheathing scales; saprophyte or root-parasite with coral-like underground stem.

1. Flowers a dull purple; lip not deeply 3-lobed
   a. Raceme 3-12-flowered; a small spur or sack
      attached to the summit of the ovary *C. innáta*
   b. Raceme 10-25-flowered; spur none *C. striáta*
2. Flowers brownish-red, 10-30 in a raceme; spur
   distinct, yellowish; lip deeply 3-lobed *C. multiflóra*

CYPRIPÉDIUM Linné 1753 LADIES' SLIPPER
(Gr. *kypris*, Venus, *pedion*, boot)
Pl. 43, fig. 3.

Sepals 3, separate or two of them united under the lip, lateral petals linear to lanceolate, greenish-brown, often twisted, lip a large swollen sack, purple, yellow or white, column declined, with an anther on either side and a dilated petal-like sterile stamen above covering the summit of the style; flowers solitary or several, drooping; leaves broad, many-veined; perennial from tufted roots.

1. Flowers yellow, usually solitary
   a. Lip 1.5-3 in. long   *C. pubéscens*
   b. Lip 1.5-3 cm. long   *C. parviflórum*
2. Flowers purple or yellow, 2-several in a cluster;
   leaves 2, opposite   *C. Knightae*

EPIPÁCTIS   Robert Brown 1813   HELLEBORINE
(Greek name of a plant)

Sepals and petals separate, similar, greenish, purple-veined, lip broad, concave below, constricted near the middle, the upper part broad and petal-like, column short, erect, pollinia 2-parted; flowers few in leafy-bracted, terminal racemes; leafy-stemmed perennial from a creeping root-stalk.

Stems 1-3 ft. high; leaves ovate to lanceolate; sack-
like base of the lip with wing-like margins   *E. gigantéa*

LIMNÓRCHIS   Rydberg 1900   GREEN ORCHID
(Gr. *limne*, lake, *orchis*, orchid)

Sepals and petals greenish, free, spreading, similar, lip linear or lance-olate, entire, the spur shorter to longer than the lip, column very short; flowers greenish to white, in terminal spikes or racemes; leaves alternate, lanceolate to ovate; perennial with fibrous or tuberous roots.

1. Flowers white; spur club-shaped, shorter than
   the lip   *L. boreális*
2. Flowers greenish or greenish-purple
   a. Lip 4-5 mm. long, not exceeded by the spur
      (1) Spur shorter than the lip   *L. stricta*
      (2) Spur equalling the lip   *L. viridiflóra*
   b. Lip 6-8 mm. long, exceeded by the spur   *L. sparsiflóra*

LÍSTERA   Robert Brown 1813   TWAYBLADE
(Named for Lister, an English botanist)

Sepals and petals nearly alike, spreading or reflexed, free, anther with-out a lid, joined with the column, pollinia 2; flowers greenish yellow to purplish, spurless, in terminal racemes; leaves 2, opposite, near the middle of the stem, 1-2 small scales at the base of the stem; small herb with fibrous roots.

1. Stems sticky-hairy; lip wedge-shaped, 2-lobed   *L. convallarioídes*
2. Stems smooth; lip linear, 2-cleft   *L. cordáta*

Lysiélla Rydberg 1900
(Dim. of Lysia)

Sepals and petals greenish-yellow, free, similar, spreading, lip linear-lanceolate, entire, spur shorter than the curved ovary, beak of stigma without appendages, stem with a single obovate leaf at base; low herbs from a rootstalk.

Stems 2-8 in. high; leaf 2-5 in. long; flowers 5-6 mm.
  long, the lip deflexed   *L. obtusáta*

Perámium Salisbury 1812 Rattlesnake Plantain
(Gr. *peras*, limit, line, from the barred leaves)
Pl. 43, fig. 4.

Sepals and petals white, the upper sepal united with the 2 petals into a hood, lip entire, concave or sack-like, the apex reflexed, anther attached to the column by a short stalk, pollinia 1 in each sack; flowers in bracted spikes; leaves basal, usually splotched with white; perennial from fleshy roots.

1. Stems 3-10 in. high; leaves 1-3 cm. long; spike
   1-sided; lip plainly sack-like   *P. répens*
2. Stems 8-20 in. high; leaves 3-6 cm. long; spike
   not 1-sided; lip hardly sack-like   *P. Menziésii*

Pipéria Rydberg 1901
(Named for Piper, an American botanist)

Sepals and petals greenish or white, lance-linear to ovate, truncate or hastate at base, lip oblong, obtuse, lobed near the base, stigma a small beak between the anthers, spur linear or club-shaped barely longer than the lip; flowers spirally arranged in a bracted spike; leaves mostly basal, those of the stem reduced, generally dead or withering at flowering time; herb with tuberous roots.

Stems 1-2 ft. high, leafy below; leaves oblanceolate;
  flowers greenish   *P. unalaschénsis*

Spiránthes Persoon 1807 Ladies' Tresses
(Gr. *speira*, spiral, *anthos*, flower) .

Sepals free or united with the petals into a hood, lip concave, erect, embracing the column and often adhering to it, spreading and wavy, or toothed at the apex, column arched below, stigma ovate, extending into a pointed beak, pollinia 2; flowers white, spurless, spirally twisted in a 1-3-

Plate 44

ARROWHEADS—SEDGES

PONDWEED FAMILY

1. Potamogeton pectinatus: Pondweed

ARROWHEAD FAMILY

2. Sagittaria arifolia: Arrowhead

ARROWGRASS FAMILY

3. Triglochin maritima: Arrow Grass

BUR-REED FAMILY

4. Sparganium simplex: Bur-reed

DUCKWEED.FAMILY

5. Lemma trisulca: Duckweed
6. Lemna minor

LILY FAMILY

7. Veratrum viride: False Hellebore
8. Leucocrinum montanum: Sand Lily
9. Lloydia serotina
10. Wagnera stellata: Spikenard, Solomon's Seal
11. Streptopus amplexifolius: Twisted Stalk

RUSH FAMILY

12. Juncus balticus: Rush
13. Juncus longistylis

SEDGE FAMILY

14. Eriophorum polystachyum: Cotton Grass
15. Cyperus inflexus: Galingale
16. Scirpus pauciflorus: Dwarf Rush
17. Scirpus lacustris: Bulrush
18. Heleocharis palustris: Spike Rush
19. Elyna Bellardi

rowed spike; leaves alternate, linear to lanceolate; perennial herb with fleshy or tuberous roots.

Stems 4-15 in. high; leaves linear or linear-oblanceolate, 2-8 in. long; flowers 6-8 mm. long, white or
greenish-white, fragrant   *S. stricta*

POALES   GRASS ORDER

CYPERACEAE   SEDGE FAMILY

Sepals and petals none or represented by bristles or scales, stamens 1-3, ovary 1-celled, style 2-3-cleft, fruit an achene; flowers perfect or staminate and pistillate, arranged in small dense clusters or spikelets, 1 or rarely 2 in the axil of each bract or glume; spikelets solitary or clustered, 1-many-flow-ered; leaves narrow with closed sheaths; grass-like or rush-like herbs, with usually solid, triangular, cylindric or flattened stems.

1. Flowers perfect, i. e., stamens and pistil in the
   axil of each scale
   a. Spikelets flattened, with the scales in 2 rows;
      perianth bristles wanting   CYPERUS
   b. Spikelets not flattened; scales roundish, im-
      bricated all around; perianth bristles usu-
      ally present
      (1) Perianth bristles 1-many; stamens usually 3
         (a) Bristles 1-12, usually less than 1 cm.
             long
             x. Leaves usually present; base of style
                enlarged or narrow, falling away from
                the achene   SCIRPUS
             y. Leaves reduced to a single sheath at
                base; base of style persisting on the
                achene as a tubercle   HELEOCHARIS
         (b) Bristles usually many, 1-3 cm. long,
             giving the spikelets a cottony ap-
             pearance   ERIOPHORUM
      (2) Perianth bristles wanting; stamen 1   HEMICARPHA
2. Flowers staminate or pistillate, in the same or
   in different spikelets
   a. Achene enclosed in a sack or perigynium   CAREX
   b. Achene without a perigynium   ELYNA

CÁREX Linné 1753 SEDGE

(Lat. *carex*, sedge, perhaps from Gr. *keirein*, to cut, from the sharp leaves)

Pl. 45, fig. 1-17.

Spikes (spikelets) pistillate, staminate or both pistillate and staminate, solitary or in racemes, panicles or dense clusters; perianth none, staminate flowers with 3 stamens, pistillate flowers a single pistil with style and 2-3 stigmas within a bract or perigynium, achene 3-angled or lens-shaped; flowers monoecious or dioecious, solitary in the axil of the scale; leaves 3-ranked; stems mostly 3-angled; grass-like perennials, usually from a rootstock.

1. Spike single, terminal, staminate above, pistillate below, except in dioecious plants
  a. Stigmas 3
    (1) Perigynia horizontal and spreading or reflexed when mature, mostly lanceolate
      (a) Leaves flat; rootstock creeping, the stems mostly in rows   *C. nigricans*
      (b) Leaves inrolled; stems tufted, the rootstocks matted   *C. pyrenaíca*
    (2) Perigynia erect or ascending, not horizontal
      (a) Perigynia rough or hairy
        x. Spike buff, staminate and pistillate; perigynia roughened; stems tufted   *C. filifólia*
        y. Spike purple-brown, staminate or pistillate; perigynia hairy; with creeping rootstocks   *C. scirpoídea*
      (b) Perigynia entirely smooth
        x. Scales 1-3 cm. long, leaf-like, hiding the large green perigynia   *C. durifólia*
        y. Scales not large and leaf-like, less than 1 cm. long
          (x) Stems 2-6 in. high; spikes or perigynia brown
            m. Perigynia erect when ripe, hidden by the scales; at 11-14000 ft.   *C. rupéstris*
            n. Perigynia spreading and visible when ripe; at 7-10000 ft.   *C. obtusáta*
          (y) Stems 8-16 in. high; perigynia, and spikes usually green

m. Perigynia 1-2, obovate, 4-5 mm.
    long   *C. Géyeri*
n. Perigynia 3-6, oblong, 2 mm. long *C. leptálea*
b. Stigmas 2; spike brown, about 1 cm. long;
    perigynia beaked, often spreading; leaves
    inrolled, thread-like; stems 3-10 in. high   *C. redowskyána*
2. Spikes two or more
  a. Spikes all essentially alike, both pistillate and
    staminate, but the latter flowers often few
    or inconspicuous; stigmas 2
    (1) Spikes crowded in a dense round or ovoid
        head, or if in an oblong spike, the latter
        usually less than 2 cm. long
      (a) Heads pale
        x. Spikes of the head many; heads 1.5-
           2.5x1-2 cm.; perigynia beaked, hid-
           den by the long pointed scale   *C. Douglásii*
        y. Spikes 3-12; heads 1-1.5x1 cm.; peri-
           gynia winged, beaked, longer and
           broader than the acute scale   *C. arthrostáchya*
      (b) Heads brown
        x. Spikes 2-6
          (x) Stems 2-8 in. high; leaves inrolled,
             thread-like
            m. Spikes in a roundish head 1 cm.
               wide   *C. incúrva*
            n. Spikes in an oblong head 1-1.5 cm.
               x5-8 mm.   *C. stenophýlla*
          (y) Stems 8-15 in. high; leaves flat;
             heads 1 cm.x5 cm.   *C. Bonplándii*
        y. Spikes several-many
          (x) Perigynia winged
            m. Heads ovoid 1.5-2 cm.x1-1.5 cm.;
               perigynium longer than the scale *C. festíva*
            n. Heads oblong 1-1.5 cm.x8-10 mm.;
               perigynium and scale about equal *C. Hoódii*
          (y) Perigynia not winged, abruptly
            short-beaked, hidden by the scale;
            heads 1.5-2.5 cm. long   *C. gayána*
    (2) Spikes more than 5 mm. long, densely
        crowded throughout or at least above,

rarely scattered, in an oblong to cylindric
cluster 2-5 cm. long

(a) Perigynia winged
  x. Beak nearly as long as body or longer
    (x) Perigynia broadly winged   *C. siccáta*
    (y) Perigynia narrowly winged   *C. leporína*
  y. Beak ⅓-½ as long as body; perigynia
    broadly winged   *C. fcstucácea*
(b) Perigynia not winged, sometimes with
  a ridge-like margin
  x. Beak 1-2 times longer than body   *C. stipáta*
  y. Beak equalling or shorter than body
    (x) Beak equalling the body   *C. teretiúscula*
    (y) Beak shorter than body
      m. Leaves 1-3 mm. wide; scales acute
        or pointed   *C. muricáta*
      n. Leaves 2-4 mm. wide; scales ob-
        tuse   *C. Sartwéllii*

(3) Spikes less than 5 mm. long, sometimes
  longer in C. deweyana, rarely crowded,
  mostly widely separated in a narrow
  cylindric cluster 2-7 cm.x4-8 mm.

(a) Flower cluster raceme-like, the spikes
  mostly 1-3-flowered, 1.5-5 mm. long;
  perigynia ovoid, minutely beaked,
  larger than the scale   *C. tenélla*
(b) Flower cluster of 3-9 distinct 3-15-flow-
  ered spikes
  x. Perigynia with a beak more than one-
    half as long to as long as the body
    (x) Perigynia spreading or reflexed
      when mature, 2-3 mm. long;
      spikes 8-15-flowered   *C. stérilis*
    (y) Perigynia erect, 4-5 mm. long;
      spikes 3-8-flowered   *C. deweyána*
  y. Perigynia 1-2 mm. long, not spreading,
    with a minute beak less than one-half
    as long as the body; spikes 10-20-
    flowered   *C. canéscens*
b. Terminal spike staminate or in the next often
  pistillate above and staminate below, the
  lateral spikes usually pistillate; stigmas 3

(1) Terminal staminate spike absent or inconspicuous, spikes often drooping, 2-5 in
a dense head, or contiguous; the scales
dark purple-brown to black; stigmas 3
(a) Spikes round or ovoid, 7-20 mm.x5-12
mm., 1-4, usually 3 in a dense head 1-2
cm.x1-1.5 cm., often drooping   *C. atráta*
(b) Spikes oblong to cylindric, 1-5, usually
separate, 7-30 mm.x3-6 mm. wide,
often long-stalked and drooping
x. Spikes drooping, 1-3 cm.x5-6 mm.   *C. bélla*
y. Spikes not drooping
(x) Spikes 2-3, often crowded, 7-12
mm.x3-4 mm.   *C. alpína*
(y) Spikes 3-5, mostly separate, 1-2 cm.
x5-6 mm.   *C. Raynóldsii*
(2) Terminal spike or spikes staminate, rarely
partly staminate
(a) Lateral pistillate spikelets 1-3, 1-few-
flowered, 3-10 mm. long, or raceme-
like and 1-2 cm. long
x. Lateral spikelets raceme-like, .5-2 cm.
long, the perigynia rarely crowded,
globoid or with a tiny abrupt point,
yellow to golden, smooth, ribbed   *C. aúrea*
y. Lateral spikelets 3-8 mm. long, mostly
with crowded perigynia, the latter
not yellow or golden, hairy or smooth,
not ribbed
(x) Spikes erect; perigynia hairy
m. Stems erect, with running rootstocks; perigynia 3-4 mm. long;
beak about one-fourth of the
body   *C. pennsilvánica*
n. Stems densely tufted, mat-like;
spikes often hidden by leaves;
perigynia 1-2.5 mm. long; beak
one-half to as long as body   *C. umbelláta*
(y) Spikes nodding, 4-10 mm. long, 2
mm. wide; perigynia smooth, pale
.green, 2 mm. long; beak about
one-third as long as body   *C. capilláris*

(b) Lateral pistillate spikelets many-flowered, cylindric, 2-8 cm. long
x. Beak conspicuously 2-toothed, the teeth
often 1-2 mm long; stigmas 3
(x) Perigynia hairy
m. Perigynia 5-8 mm. long, tapering
gradually into a beak about as
long as the body; teeth spreading, 1-2 mm. long   *C. aristáta*
n. Perigynia 2-4 mm. long, abruptly
beaked, the beak about one-third
as long as the body; teeth less
than 1 mm. long   *C. lanuginósa*
(y) Perigynia smooth
m. Staminate spike usually 1; scales
with a rough awn 2-4 times
longer than the ovoid base   *C. hystricína*
n. Staminate spikes usually 2; scales
acute or with an awn not longer
than the lance-ovate base
(m) Perigynia spreading hori-
zontally at maturity, usually
2 mm. or less wide at base   *C. utriculáta*
(n) Perigynia ascending, usually
2.5-3 mm. wide at base   *C. moníle*
y. Beak minutely or not at all toothed
(x) Beak as long or longer than the
body; stigmas 3
m. Spikes brown, 1-2 cm. long; perigynia densely crowded, lanceolate, tapering gradually into a
beak about as long as the body *C. abláta*
n. Spikes pale green, 2-5 cm. long;
perigynia often separate, roundish, abruptly narrowed into a
slender beak longer than the
body   *C. longiróstris*
(y) Beak none up to one-third as long
as body; stigmas 2 as a rule
m. Perigynia inflated; beak about as
long as body   *C. saxátilis*

Plate 45

SEDGES—GRASSES

SEDGE FAMILY

1. Carex tenella : Sedge
2. Carex muricata
3. Carex stenophylla
4. Carex festiva
5. Carex siccata
6-7. Carex atrata
8. Carex alpina
9. Carex festucacea
10. Carex aquatilis
11. Carex aurea
12. Carex rupestris
13. Carex pennsilvanica
14. Carex umbellata
15. Carex lanuginosa
16. Carex capillaris
17. Carex utriculata

GRASS FAMILY: BLUE GRASS TRIBE

18. Bromus ciliatus : Brome Grass
19. Festuca ovina : Fescue
20. Panicularia nervata : Manna Grass
21. Poa pratensis : Blue-grass
22. Melica Porteri : Melic Grass
23. Distichlis stricta : Salt-grass
24. Catabrosa aquatica : Whorl Grass
25. Munroa squarrosa
26. Eragrostis major
27. Triodia acuminata
28. Koeleria cristata
29. Redfieldia flexuosa
30. Eatonia obtusata

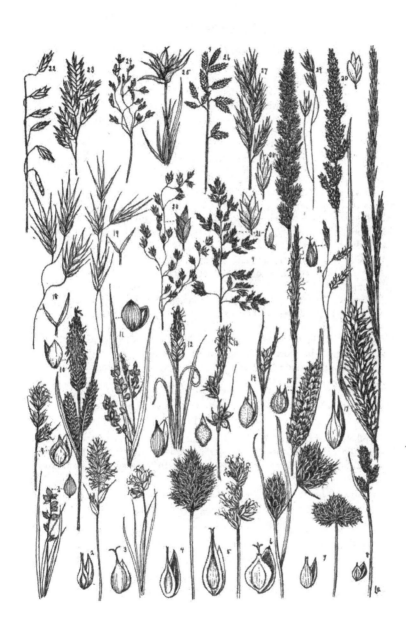

n. Perigynia somewhat flattened; beak
 short or none
 (m) Spikes dark brown-purple, 1-
  1.5 cm. long   *C. Tólmiei*
 (n) Spikes variously green and
  purple, 2-4 cm. long *C. aquátilis*

CYPÉRUS Linné 1753 GALINGALE
(The Greek name)
Pl. 44, fig. 15.

Spikelets flattened, scales falling away from the axis at maturity, in umbels or heads; flowers perfect, wth concave or keeled, 2-ranked scales, perianth none, stamens 1-3, style 2-3-cleft; leaves more or less basal, grass-like, 1 or more of the upper leaves forming an involucre; annual or perennial with triangular stems.

1. Stems 1-6 in. high; annual; spikelets 4-6 mm.
 long; scales with a long, recurved point; stamen 1   *C. infléxus*
2. Stems .5-2.5 ft. high; perennial; spikelets 6-16
 mm. long; scales without a recurved point;
 stamens 3
 a. Spikelets in 1-7 dense, globose heads *C. filicúlmis*
 b. Spikelets in loose clusters, several of which
  are sessile and some stalked *C. Schweinitzii*

ELÝNA Schröter 1806 ELYNA
(Gr. *elynos,* covering, perhaps from the overlapping scales)
Pl. 44, fig. 19.

Spikelets in a narrow, terminal, cylindric spike, scales of the spikelet 3-4, usually only 1 flower-bearing; perianth-bristles wanting, style 3-cleft, achene 3-angled; leaves narrowly linear, basal; tufted arctic and mountain sedges.
Stems 4-15 in. high; spike 1.5-3 cm. long; achenes 3-
4 mm. long, appressed   *E. Bellárdi*

ERIÓPHORUM Linné 1753 COTTON GRASS
(Gr. *erion,* wool, *phora,* bearing, from the cotton-like bristles)
Pl. 44, fig. 14.

Spikelets terminal, solitary or in heads or umbels, often with a 1-several-leaved involucre; flowers perfect, with spirally imbricated, usually fertile scales; perianth-bristles 6-many, white or brown, 1-3 cm. long, stamens 1-3, style 3-cleft achene 3-angled; leaves linear, stems triangular to round; bog-perennial from a rootstock.

1. Bristles 2.5-3 cm. long; achenes obovate; bracts
   ovate to lance-ovate; involucral leaves 2-4   *E. polystáchyum*
2. Bristles 1.5-2.5 cm. long; achenes linear-oblong;
   involucral leaf usually only 1   *E. grácile*

HELEÓCHARIS   Robert Brown 1810   SPIKE RUSH
(Gr. *helos*, marsh, *charis*, grace, from the habitat)
Pl. 44, fig. 18.

Spikelets solitary, terminal, without an involucre; flowers perfect, with concave, spirally imbricated scales; perianth-bristles usually 1-12, stamens 2-3, style 2-3-cleft, achenes lens-shaped or 3-angled, base of the style forming a swollen tip to the achene; leaves reduced to basal sheaths; stems simple, round, angular, flattened or grooved; annual or perennial.

1. Style 2-cleft; achenes lens-shaped or bi-convex
   a. Perennial from horizontal rootstocks
      (1) Stems 1-4 in. high; upper sheath papery   *H. olivácea*
      (2) Stems .5-5 ft. high; upper sheath not
          papery   *H. palústris*
   b. Annuals with fibrous roots
      (1) Achenes black with a low tiny tubercle   *H. atropurpúrea*
      (2) Achenes brown, the large ovoid tubercle
          ¼ its length   *H. ováta*
2. Style 3-cleft; achenes 3-angled or swollen
   a. Stems 2-6 in. high; achenes ribbed and net-
      like   *H. aciculáris*
   b. Stems 8-15 in. high
      (1) Bristles 2-4 or wanting, shorter than the
          achene; achenes roughened   *H. ténuis*
      (2) Bristles 4-8, longer than the achene;
          achenes smooth   *H. rostelláta*

HEMICÁRPHA   Nees 1834
(Gr. *hemi*, half, *karphos*, chaff, from the single inner scale or sepal)

Spikelets solitary or in heads, terminal with an involucre of 1-3 leaves; flowers perfect, scales spirally imbricated; perianth a single sepal, bristles none, stamens 1-3, style 2-cleft; leaves and stems thread-like; tufted annual sedge.

Stems 1-5 in. high; spikelets 1-4, 2-3 mm. long   *H. micrántha*

Scírpus   Linné 1753   Bulrush, Club Rush
(Lat. name of the bulrush)
Pl. 44, fig. 16, 17.

Spikelets solitary or in umbels, spikes or heads, usually with a 1-several-leaved involucre; flowers perfect, scales spirally imbricated all around; perianth-bristles 1-6 or occasionally none, stamens 2-3, style 2-3-cleft; leaves long-linear or often reduced to sheaths; annual or perennial.

1. Spikelet solitary and terminal
    a. Stems 3-angled, grooved, 2-8 in. high; scales lanceolate, long-pointed; bristles 2-6, spiny; achenes gray, finely netted   *S. pauciflórus*
    b. Stems round, 4-15 in. high; scales ovate, obtuse; bristles 6, smooth; achenes brown, not netted   *S. caespitósus*
2. Spikelets more than 1 as a rule, usually several-many, often lateral
    a. Spikelets 1-12 in a dense, head-like cluster
      (1) Stems round; leaves channelled or revolute; bristles 1-3, not half as long as the achene   *S. nevadénsis*
      (2) Stems triangular
        (a) Involucral leaves of head 1
          x. Scales awned; leaves 1-3   *S. americánus*
          y. Scales short-pointed; leaves usually mere sheaths   *S. Ólneyi*
        (b) Involucral leaves 2-3
          x. Bristles usually 2, twice as long as the achene   *S. paludósus*
          y. Bristles 1-3, less than half as long as the achene, or none   *S. campéstris*
    b. Spikelets many, in panicles or umbels
      (1) Stems round, leafless; cluster lateral; spikelets 5-15 mm. long; bristles 4-6, barbed, as long or longer than the achene   *S. lacústris*
      (2) Stems triangular, leafy; cluster terminal
        (a) Spikelets 15-25 mm. long; scales with a long, curved awn
        (b) Spikelets 4-10 mm. long; scales without a curved awn   *S. fluviátilis*

x. Bristles downwardly barbed
  (x) Spikelets 4-10 mm. long; bristles us-
     ually 6; styles 3   *S. atrovírens*
  (y) Spikelets 3-4 mm. long; bristles 4;
     styles 2   *S. microcárpus*
y. Bristles smooth, 6; spikelets 6-10 mm.
  long; styles 3   *S. lineátus*

POÁCEAE GRASS FAMILY

Sepals and petals none, occasionally represented by bristles or scales, stamens 1-6, usually 3, styles usually 2, ovary 1-celled, fruit a seed-like grain; flowers perfect or sometimes monoecious or dioecious, or reduced to 1-2 scales, with 1-3 minute scales called lodicules, usually enclosed in 2 scales, the inner called the palet, the outer the lemma; spikelets 1-many-flowered, usually enclosed at the base by 2 scales or glumes, in racemes, panicles or spikes; leaves mostly long-linear, sheathing, the sheaths usually split to the base and bearing at the top a papery or thickened ring called a ligule; annual or perennial herbs.

1. Spikelets sessile in 2 rows in a one-sided or zig-
  zag spike
a. Spikelets in one-sided spikes
  (1) Spikelets dioecious, the staminate spikes
     one-sided, the pistillate ball-like   BULBILIS
  (2) Spikelets perfect, the spikes alike
    (a) Spikes long and narrow, thread-like
     x. Spikes in a raceme-like cluster   SCHEDONNARDUS
     y. Spikes in a digitate cluster   DIGITARIA
    (b) Spikes not long and thread-like
     x. Plains grasses with mostly horizontal or
      hanging spikes   BOUTELOUA
     y. Meadow or swamp grasses with erect
      or ascending spikes
      (x) Spikes long, the axis extending be-
        yond the spikelets   SPARTINA
      (y) Spikes short, the axis not extended BECKMANNIA
b. Spikelets alternating on opposite sides of a zig-
  zag, usually jointed axis
  (1) Spikelets usually single at each joint
    (a) Spikelets with the face toward the axis AGROPYRUM
    (b) Spikelets with the edge toward the axis LOLIUM
  (2) Spikelets usually 2-6 at each joint

(a) Spikelets 2-many-flowered, the glumes
   lanceolate   ELYMUS
(b) Spikelets 1-flowered, the glumes awl-
   shaped and in a row   HORDEUM
2. Spikelets not in 2 rows in a one-sided or zig-zag
   spike
   a. Spikelets 2-many-flowered
      (1) Lemma awned from the back
         (a) Spikelets less than 1 cm. long
            x. Lemma fringe-toothed or 2-toothed at
               tip   DESCHAMPSIA
            y. Lemma 2-cleft at tip, the teeth awn-
               pointed
               (x) Awn bent and twisted   TRISETUM
               (y) Awn straight or none   GRAPHEPHORUM
         (b) Spikelets more than 1 cm. long   AVENA
      (2) Lemma awned from the tip or awnless
         (a) Plants dioecious; lemma 3-awned   SCLEROPOGON
         (b) Plants not dioecious; lemma entire or
            2-lobed
            x. Hairs very long and enclosing the lem-
               ma; tall swamp grasses   PHRAGMITES
            y. Hairs none or shorter than the lemma
               (x) Spikelets in the axils of spiny
                  leaves; stems spreading, 1-4 in.
                  high   MUNROA
               (y) Spikelets not in the axils of spiny
                  leaves
                  m. Lemma 1-3-nerved
                     (m) Lateral nerves of the lemma
                        hairy
                        r. Spikelets appressed on the long
                           branches of a panicle   DIPLACIINE
                        s. Spikelets not appressed on long
                           branches   TRIODIA
                     (n) Lateral nerves not hairy
                        r. Lemma copiously long-hairy at
                           base   REDFIELDIA
                        s. Lemma not long-hairy at base
                           (r) Upper glume much broader
                              than the lower   EATONIA

(s) Upper glume similar to
   the lower
  h. Panicle cylindric and
    spike-like   Koeleria
  i. Panicle with spreading
    branches, not spike-like
    (h) Spikelets 2-flowered;
       water grasses   Catabrosa
    (i) Spikelets 4-20-flow-
       ered; land grasses Eragrostis
n. Lemma 5-11-nerved
  (m) Upper lemmas of the spikelet
    empty, broad and folded
    about each other   Melica
  (n) Upper lemmas not broad and
    folded together
   r. Stigmas arising from the tip of
    the ovary
    (r) Lemma flattened, keeled
     h. Lemma awn-pointed;
      spikelets in one-sided
      groups   Dactylis
     i. Lemma not awn-pointed
      (h) Glumes 1-3-nerved
       k. Axis of spikelet ex-
        tended into a hairy
        tip   Graphephorum
       l. Axis of spikelet not
        extended into a
        hairy tip   Poa
      (i) Glumes 5-7-nerved Distichlis
    (s) Lemma convex or rounded
     on the back
     h. Lemma awned or acute
      (h) Lemma 5-nerved; axis
       of spikelet smooth Festuca
      (i) Lemma 7-11-nerved;
       axis hairy   Danthonia
     i. Lemma obtuse and papery
      at tip

        (h) Lemma distinctly
            nerved; style pres-
            ent   PANICULARIA
        (i) Lemma faintly nerved;
            style none   PUCCINELLIA
     s. Stigmas arising below the tip
       of the ovary; spikelets large,
       usually awned   BROMUS
b. Spikelets 1-flowered, often with an extra or
   sterile lemma
(1) Spikelet with lemma and palet alone, the
       glumes none   HOMALOCENCHRUS
  (2) Spikelet with glumes as well as lemma and
      palet
   (a) Spikelets in pairs or threes, one stalked,
      the other stalkless
    x. Spikelets in spike-like clustered or
      panicled racemes   ANDROPOGON
    y. Spikelets in panicles
      (x) Stalked spikelet reduced to a pedi-
        cel   CHRYSOPOGON
      (y) Stalked spikelet present SORGHUM
   (b) Spikelets not in pairs
    x. Two extra glumes or hairy stalks be-
      tween the glumes and the lemma and
      palet
      (x) Spikelets with a perfect flower
        alone   PHALARIS
      (y) Spikelets with 1 perfect and 2 stam-
        inate flowers   HIEROCHLOE
    y. Spikelets without 2 extra glumes
      (x) Lemma and palet hyaline, thinner
        than the glumes
        m. Lemma awned at the tip, the awn
          usually long
          (m) Spikelets in pairs in a spike-
            like cluster   LYCURUS
         (n) Spikelets not in pairs
          r. Lemma thin and papery MUHLENBERGIA
          s. Lemma thick and hard
            (r) Awns 3-forked   ARISTIDA

(s) Awns simple

   h. Awns twisted, persistent STIPA

   i. Awns straight, falling off

     (h) Lemma with long
        silky hairs ERIOCOMA

     (i) Lemma smooth or
        finely hairy ORYZOPSIS

n. Lemma usually awnless or awned
  from the back

  (m) Spikelets in a single dense
     spike

   r. Spikelets falling from the axis;
     awn on the back ALOPECURUS

   s. Spikelets persistent; awn none
     or short PHLEUM

  (n) Spikelets in a panicle

   r. Lemma with a tuft of hairs at
     base

     (r) Lemma thin and papery CALAMAGROSTIS

     (s) Lemma hard and leathery CALAMOVILFA

   s. Lemma without a tuft of hairs

     (r) Lemma awned on the back

      h. Glumes awned POLYPOGON

      i. Glumes acute

       (h) Palet 1-nerved; sta-
         men 1 CINNA

       (i) Palet 2-nerved or
         none; stamens 3 AGROSTIS

     (s) Lemma not awned

      h. Grain permanently en-
        closed in lemma and
        pale. AGROSTIS

      i. Grain not permanently en-
        closed

       (h) Stamen 1; stigma at
         tip of glumes PHIPPSIA

       (i) Stamens 2-3; stigma at
         side of glumes SPOROBOLUS

(y) Lemma like the glumes, or thicker
  and firmer

m. Spikelets in 3's in a cylindric spike
　　with zig-zag axis; lemma and
　　palet like the glumes in texture Hilaria
n. Spikelets in panicles, or in spikes,
　　not in 3's; lemma thicker and
　　harder than the glumes
　　(m) Spikelets in a spiny bur-like
　　　　involucre　　　　　　　　Cenchrus
　　(n) Spikelets not in a bur
　　r. Spikelets in one-sided racemes
　　　　or spikes
　　　　(ɼ) Spikes 1-2　　　　　　Paspalum
　　　　(s) Spikes 3-10　　　　　Digitaria
　　s. Spikelets in a panicle or cylin-
　　　　dric spike
　　　　(r) Spikelets in a panicle
　　　　h. Spikelets solitary, not
　　　　　　awned　　　　　　　Panicum
　　　　i. Spikelets in spike-like
　　　　　　groups, awned　　　Echinochloa
　　　　(s) Spikelets in a cylindric
　　　　　　spike with an involucre
　　　　　　of bristles　　　　Chaetochloa

Agropýrum　Gaertner 1770　Wheat Grass, Quack Grass

(Gr. *agros*, field, *pyron,* wheat, from the habitat of the quack grass)

Pl. 46, fig. 26, 27.

Spikelets 3-many-flowered, in a terminal spike, sessile, and single at each joint of a more or less zig-zag axis, the face of the spikelet turned toward the axis; glumes 2, lanceolate or lance-linear, often awned; lemma rounded on the back, 5-7-nerved, acute or awned, palet 2-keeled, the keels often ciliate; annual or perennial.

1. Stems in bunches, without creeping rootstocks or
　　stolons
　　a. Awns 2-3 cm. long; stems spreading or pros-
　　　　trate; at 10-13000 ft.　　　　　　　*A. Scribneri*
　　b. Awns less than 2 cm. long; stems erect; at 4-
　　　　10000 ft.

(1) Spikelets much flattened; awns spreading,
1-2 cm. long   *A. spicátum*
(2) Spikelets cylindric or little flattened, awned
or awnless   *A. canínum*
2. Stems not in bunches from creeping rootstocks,
usually forming a turf
a. Spikelets much flattened, not densely hairy;
awned or awnless   *A. occidentále*
b. Spikelets nearly cylindric, or densely hairy
when somewhat flattened
(1) Spikelets cylindric, usually smooth, enclosed by the glumes or nearly so   *A. pseudorépens*
(2) Spikelets somewhat flattened, usually
densely hairy; glumes half as long as the
spikelets or less   *A. dasystáchyum*

Agróstis   Linné 1753   Redtop, Hair Grass
(Gr. *agros*, field, from the habitat)
Pl. 46, fig. 13.

Spikelets 1-flowered in panicles; glumes 2, keeled, acute or awned;
lemma obtuse, hyaline, occasionally with an awn on the back, palet shorter,
sometimes tiny or wanting; annual or perennial.
1. Axis of spikelet extending beyond the palet;
spikelets 2 mm. long   *A. thurberiána*
2. Axis of spikelet not extending beyond the palet
a. Palet distinct, 2-nerved
(1) Lemma shorter than the glumes
(a) Stems 1-3 ft. high; panicles open and
spreading; lemma without prickle on
the back   *A. álba*
(b) Stems 4-8 in. high; panicle narrow,
spike-like; lemma with a tiny prickle
on back below the tip   *A. depréssa*
(2) Lemma equalling the glumes; awnless   *A. húmilis*
b. Palet a tiny nerveless scale or none
(1) Panicle narrow, not spreading; spikelets
2-4 mm. long; glumes about equal; lem-
ma ½-¾ as long as the glumes   *A. exaráta*
(2) Panicle open and spreading; spikelets 1-2
mm. long; glumes equal; lemma a little
shorter or equalling the glumes   *A. hiemális*

Plate 46

GRASSES

Clusters and spikelets, the latter x3 except where indicated.

GRAMA GRASS TRIBE

1. Bulbilis dactyloides: Buffalo Grass; 1. staminate branch; a. pistillate branch; b. staminate flower x3.
2. Bouteloua oligostachya: Grama Grass; spikes; spikelet
3. Bouteloua curtipendula; spikes; spikelet x2
4. Spartina cynosuroides; Cord Grass, Slough Grass
5. Beckmannia eruciformis
6. Schedonnardus paniculatus; spikes; spikelets

OAT TRIBE

7. Danthonia Parryi: Oat Grass
8. Avena striata: Oat
9. Graphephorum muticum: cluster; spikelet x2
10. Deschampsia caespitosa: Hair Grass; cluster; spikelet
11. Trisetum subspicatum: False Oat; spike; spikelet

REDTOP TRIBE

12. Calamagrostis purpurascens: Reed Grass
13. Agrostis hiemalis: Hair Grass; cluster; spikelet
14. Sporobolus tricholepis; cluster; spikelet
15. Stipa comata: Spear Grass
16. Stipa viridula
17. Aristida purpurea: Wire Grass
18. Alopecurus geniculatus: Foxtail
19. Oryzopsis micrantha: Mountain Rice
20. Eriocoma cuspidata: Indian Millet
21. Muhlenbergia gracilis
22. Muhlenbergia gracillima
23. Phleum alpinum: Timothy

BARLEY TRIBE

24. Elymus sitanion
25. Hordeum jubatum: Squirreltail Grass
26. Agropyrum caninum: Wheat Grass, Quack Grass; spike; spikelet x1½
27. Agropyrum spicatum: spike; spikelet x1½

CANARY-GRASS TRIBE

28. Hierochloe odorata: Holy Grass
29. Phalaris arundinacea: Canary Grass

PANIC-GRASS TRIBE

30. Panicum capillare: Panic Grass; cluster; spikelet
31. Digitaria sanguinalis: Finger Grass

HILARIA TRIBE

32. Hilaria Jamesii: Black Bunch Grass

BLUESTEM TRIBE

33. Chrysopogon nutans: Golden Beard
34. Andropogon scoparius: Bluestem, Bunch Grass
35. Andropogon furcatus: pair of spikelets

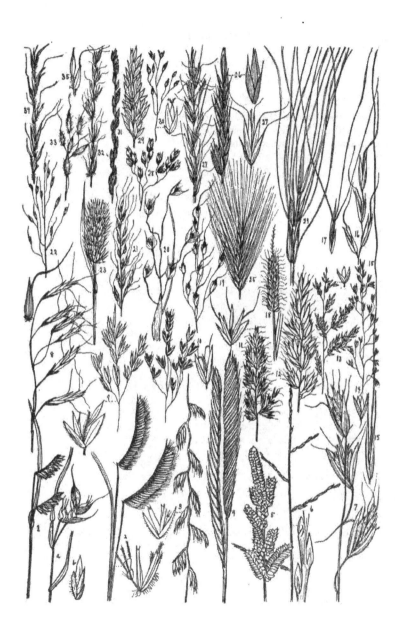

ALOPECÚRUS   Linné 1753   FOXTAIL

(Gr. *alopex,* fox, *oura,* tail, from the spike)

Pl. 46, fig. 18.

Spikelets 1-flowered, flattened, in a narrow spike; glumes acute or short-awned, flattened and keeled; lemma obtuse, 3-nerved, awned on the back, palet hyaline, acute or none; annual or perennial.

1. Spikes 1-4 in. long, 4-8 mm. wide   *A. geniculátus*
2. Spikes 1-1.5 in. long, 8-15 mm. wide   *A. alpínus*

ANDROPÓGON   Linné 1753   BLUESTEM, BUNCH GRASS

(Gr. *aner, andros,* man, *pogon,* beard, from the hairy axis)   ·

Pl. 46, fig. 34, 35.

Spikelets in pairs at each joint of the hairy axis of the terminal and axillary spikes, one spikelet sessile and perfect, with 2 glumes, 2 lemmas, the inner awned, and a palet; the other spikelet with a stalk, either staminate, empty, or represented by a single scale; tall perennials.

1. Spikes solitary, 1-2 in. long, distant; stems 2-4
   ft. high, usually densely clustered; awn of the
   glume 10-12 mm. long   *A. scopárius*
2. Spikes 2 or more in a cluster; stems 2-6 ft. high
   a. Spikes 2-5 together in an umbel-like cluster;
      stems 3-6 ft. high
      (1) Hairs as long as the stalk, or longer; awn
          4-10 mm. long or wanting   *A. Hállii*
      (2) Hairs less than half the length of the stalk;
          awn 10-15 mm. long   *A. furcátus*
   b. Spikes several in a short panicle; stems 1-4
      ft. high; awn 8-16 mm. long   *A. torreyánus*

ARÍSTIDA   Linné 1753   ARISTIDA, WIRE GRASS

(Lat. *arista,* awn)

Pl. 46, fig. 17.

Spikelets 1-flowered, in narrow panicles or spikes; glumes keeled; lemma stiff and folded, bearing 3 awns, sometimes united at base, the 2 lateral awns sometimes much reduced or wanting, palet 2-nerved; annual or perennial, often with needle-like leaves.

1. Glumes nearly equal, the upper with an awn 4-8
   mm. long   *A. oligántha*

2. Lower glume about ½ as long as the upper
   a. Central awn 1-3.5 in. long   *A. purpúrea*
   b. Central awn 8-15 mm. long   *A. fasciculáta*

AVÉNA Linné 1753 OAT

(Lat. name of the oat)

Pl. 46, fig. 8.

Spikelets 2-several-flowered, in panicles, the upper flower often staminate and imperfect; glumes more or less equal, persistent, often large and enclosing the spikelet; lemma rounded on the back, acute, usually awned on the back, the apex often 2-toothed, palet narrow, 2-toothed; annual or perennial.

1. Glumes 1-2 cm. long, enclosing the spikelet; annual   *A. fátua*
2. Glumes 4-7 mm. long, much shorter than the spikelet; perennial
   a. Lemma 6-8 mm. long; panicle open   *A. striáta*
   b. Lemma 12 mm. long; panicle spike-like   *A. mortoniána*

BECKMÁNNIA Host 1805

(Named for Beckmann, a Russian botanist)

Pl. 46, fig. 5.

Spikelets 1-2-flowered, globose, compressed, densely imbricated in 2 rows on one side of a continuous axis, in short 1-sided spikes; glumes sack-like; lemma narrow, papery, palet 2-keeled; perennial with erect spikes in a terminal panicle.

Stems 1.5-3 ft. high; spikes 10-12 mm. long; spikelets
2-3 mm. long   *B. erucifórmis*

BRÓMUS Linné 1753 .BROME GRASS, CHESS

(Gr. *bromos*, a kind of oats)

Pl. 45, fig. 18.

Spikelets 5-12-flowered, in terminal panicles; glumes unequal, acute; lemma rounded or keeled, 5-9-nerved, apex usually 2-toothed and with an awn just below the summit, palet shorter, 2-keeled; annual or perennial.

1. Annual weeds
   a. Lemma awned
      (1) Spikelets 5-8-flowered, hanging; lemma 8-12 mm. long, the awn 12-16 mm. long   *B. tectórum*

(2) Spikelets 6-10-flowered, ascending or
somewhat drooping; lemma 6-8 mm.
long; awn 6-8 mm. long   *B. secalínus*
b. Lemma not awned; spikelets 7-12-flowered, up
to 1 in. long   *B. brizifórmis*
2. Perennial, usually native
a. Lower glume 1-nerved; upper glume 3-nerved
(1) Leaves and sheaths smooth or nearly so;
spikelets 2-2.5 cm. long, usually awnless *B. inérmis*
(2) Leaves and sheaths hairy or rough   .
(a) Panicle erect; lemma 10-12 mm. long,
densely hairy, the awn 2-3 mm. long *B. pumpelliánus*
(b) Panicle drooping
x. Leaves more or less hairy on both sides;
lemma 8-12 mm. long, sparsely to
densely hairy, the awn 4-8 mm. long *B. ciliátus*
y. Leaves rough above, smooth beneath;
lemma 12-15 mm. long, hairy, awn 3-
5 mm. long   *B. Richardsónii*
b. Lower glume 3-nerved; upper glume 3-7-
nerved
(1) Panicle erect
(a) Leaves and sheaths hairy; spikelets 5-
10-flowered; lemma hairy   *B. marginátus*
(b) Leaves and sheaths usually smooth or
rough, not hairy; spikelets 7-11-flow-
ered; lemma not hairy   *B. polyánthus*
(2) Panicle drooping; glumes hairy; lemma
densely silky   *B. Pórteri*

BOUTELOÚA Lagasca 1805 GRAMA GRASS
(Named for Boutelou, a Spanish botanist)
Pl. 46, fig. 2, 3.

Spikelets 1-2-flowered, 2-rowed on the flat axis of a 1-sided spike; axis
of the spikelet extending beyond the base of the flower and bearing 1-3 awns
and 1-3 tiny scales; glumes acute, keeled; lemma broader 3-toothed, teeth
awned, palet entire or 2-toothed; annual or perennial.

1. Spikes 1-6, erect or spreading, 1-5 cm. long; stems
2-20 in. high
a. Glumes hairy

 (1) Leaves hairy, especially on the margins
  towards the base; axis of spikelet without a tuft of long hairs under the scales
  and awns   *B. hirsúta*

 (2) Leaves not hairy as a rule; axis with a tuft
  of hairs under the scales and awns *B. oligostáchya*

 b. Glumes smooth
  (1) Spikes 3-6; lemma 4-lobed   *B. polystáchya*
  (2) Spike usually solitary; lemma 3-lobed *B. prostráta*

2. Spikes many, hanging from the axis, 6-15 mm.
 long; stems 1-4 ft. tall   *B. curtipéndula*

BÚLBILIS Rafinesque 1819 BUFFALO GRASS
(Name of doubtful origin)
Pl. 46, fig. 1.

 Spikelets 2-3-flowered, staminate spikelets in 2 rows in 1-sided terminal spikes, pistillate spikelets in spike-like clusters of 2-3, mostly hidden in the sheaths, borne on short stems; glumes unequal, 1-nerved; lemma 3-nerved; glumes of the pistillate spikelets hardened; monoecious or apparently dioecious perennial spreading by stolons.

Stems with staminate flowers 4-12 in. high, with pistillate flowers .5-3 in. high; staminate spikes 2-3 in a
 group   *B. dactyloídes*

CALAMAGRÓSTIS Adanson 1763 REED GRASS
(Gr. *kalamos*, reed, *agrostis*, grass)
Pl. 46, fig. 12.

 Spikelets 1-flowered, in panicles, the axis usually extending beyond the flower and hairy; glumes keeled; lemma obtuse, usually long-hairy at base and with an awn on the back, palet shorter, 2-nerved; perennial.

1. Panicle open, the lower branches long and spreading
 a. Lemma 2-toothed, about the length of the awn *C. canadénsis*
 b. Lemma 4-toothed   *C. Scríbneri*

2. Panicle dense and spike-like, the branches short,
 ascending or erect
 a. Leaves more or less inrolled, at least above
  (1) Leaves erect, stiff and sharp-tipped
   (a) Leaves smooth; spikelets 3-4 mm. long *C. Suksdórfii*
   (b) Leaves very rough; spikelets 5-6 mm.
    long   *C. purpuráscens*

(2) Leaves loose and almost thread-like; spikelets 4 mm. long   *C. neglécta*
b. Leaves flat
(1) Leaf-sheaths smooth; lemma equalled by
the hairs   *C. hyperbórea*
(2) Leaf-sheaths rough; lemma longer than
the hairs   *C. scopulórum*

CALAMOVÍLFA Hackel 1890 REED GRASS
(Gr. *kalamos,* reed; Vilfa)

Spikelets 1-flowered, in a panicle, the axis not extending beyond the flower; glumes strongly unequal; lemma with a ring of hairs at the base, palet 2-keeled; perennial.

Stems 2-6 ft. high; spikelet 6-8 mm. long; lemma
twice as long as the hairs   *C. longifólia*

CATABRÓSA Beauvois 1812 WHORL GRASS
(Gr. *katabrosus,* eaten, from the fringed glumes)
Pl. 45, fig. 24.

Spikelets usually 2-flowered, in a panicle with whorled branches; glumes much shorter than the lemma, unequal, obtuse; lemma fringed or toothed, slightly longer than the palet; aquatic or swamp perennial.

Stems .5-2 ft. high; spikelets 2-3 mm. long; flowering
scales 3-nerved   *C. aquática*

CÉNCHRUS Linné 1753 SANDBUR
(Ancient Greek name of the millet)

Spikelets enclosed in spiny involucres, the latter in spikes; glumes 2 with a sterile lemma, the lemma and palet enclosing a perfect flower; annual.

Stems .5-2.5 ft. high; spikes 1-3 in. long; involucres
globose, spiny, 2-flowered   *C. tribuloídes*

CHAETÓCHLOA Scribner 1897 FOXTAIL
(Gr. *chaíte,* awn, *chloe,* grass)

Spikelets 1-flowered or rarely with a second staminate flower, in dense spike-like panicles, with bristles at the base; glumes 2 with a sterile lemma; true lemma and palet enclosing a perfect flower; annual or perennial.

1. Bristles at the base of each spikelet 1-4
a. Annual; spikes dense, not interrupted, 3-10 cm.
long   *C. víridis*

b. Perennial; panicle more or less interrupted, 5-
   16 cm. long   *C. compósita*
2. Bristles at the base of each spikelet 5-16   *C. glaúca*

CHRYSOPÓGON Trinius 1820 GOLDEN BEARD
(Gr. *chrysos*, golden, *pogon*, beard, from the golden-yellow hairs)
Pl. 46, fig. 33.

Spikelets in pairs or 3's, in terminal panicles, 1 spikelet sessile and perfect, with 2 hardened glumes, a sterile papery lemma and a lemma and palet
enclosing a perfect flower, palet sometimes wanting; the lateral spikelet
stalked, staminate empty or reduced to plumy stalks alone; perennial.

Stems 3-8 ft. high; panicle golden, 4-12 in. long; awn
1-2 cm. long   *C. avenáceus*

CÍNNA Linné 1753 INDIAN REED
(Origin and meaning uncertain)

Spikelets 1-flowered in nodding panicles; glumes 2, keeled, acute,
lemma keeled, often short-awned on the back, palet shorter, 1-nerved,
stamen 1; perennial.
1. Branches of the narrow panicle erect   *C. arundinácea*
2. Branches of the loose panicle drooping   *C. latifólia*

DÁCTYLIS Linné 1753 ORCHARD GRASS
(Gr. *daktylos*, finger, of little application)

Spikelets 3-5-flowered, in spike-like panicled clusters; glumes thin,
unequal, keeled, tipped; lemma larger than the glumes, 5-nerved, keeled,
the mid-nerve extended into a short awn, palet shorter, 2-keeled; perennial.

Stems 2-4 ft. high; panicle 3-8 in. long; lemma 4-6
mm. long   *D. glomeráta*

DANTHÓNIA DeCandolle 1805 OAT GRASS
(Named for Danthoine, a French botanist)
Pl. 46, fig. 7.

Spikelets 3-several-flowered, in closed or open panicles, the axis extending beyond the flower; glumes 2, keeled, acute, nearly equal, usually
enclosing the spikelet; lemma rounded, 2-toothed, the awn arising from
between the awned teeth, awn bent, flat and twisted, palet 2-keeled, obtuse
or 2-toothed; perennial.
1. Spikelets in a spike-like cluster with short, erect
   branches
   a. Empty glumes 15-20 mm. long   *D. serícea*
   b. Empty glumes 8-10 mm. long   *D. spicáta*

2. Spikelets in an open raceme or panicle, on spreading and somewhat drooping stalks   *D. califórnica*

DESCHÁMPSIA Beauvois 1812 HAIR GRASS
(Named for Deslongschamps, a French botanist)
Pl. 46, fig. 10.

Spikelets 2-flowered, in close or open panicles, the hairy axis extended beyond the flower; glumes 2, keeled, acute, sometimes enclosing the spikelet; lemma toothed, with an awn on the back, palet narrow, 2-nerved; perennial.

1. Glumes longer than and enclosing the spikelet; panicle narrow, 1-2 in. long   *D. atropurpúrea*
2. Glumes shorter than the spikelet and not enclosing it   *D. caespitósa*

DIGITÁRIA Scopoli 1772 FINGER GRASS
(Syntherisma Walter)
(Lat. *digitus*, finger, from the grouping of the spikes)
Pl. 46, fig. 31.

Spikelets 1-flowered, in pairs or in 3's on 1-sided spikes which are digitate and terminal; spikes often purplish; glumes 2, sterile lemma 2 or 1; lemma and palet enclosing a perfect flower; annual.

1. Spikelets 2-3 mm. long; lower glume tiny, usually present; upper glume about 1 mm. long   *D. sanguinális*
2. Spikelets about 2 mm. long; lower glume usually wanting; upper glume about 2 mm. long   *D. lineáris*

DIPLÁCHNE Beauvois 1812
(Gr. *diploos*, double, *achne*, bristle)

Spikelets 5-10-flowered, in an open panicle; glumes unequal, acute, keeled; lemma 2-toothed and short-awned between the teeth, 1-3 nerved, palet 2-nerved; perennial.

Stems 1-3 ft. high; panicle 4-12 in. long; spikelet 6-10 mm. long   *D. fasciculáris*

DISTÍCHLIS Rafinesque 1819 SALT GRASS
(Gr. *di*, two, *stichos*, rank, row)
Pl. 45, fig. 23.

Spikelets 6-16-flowered, in a spike-like panicle, dioecious, flattened; glumes narrow, acute, keeled; lemma broader than the glumes, acute, palet 2-keeled; perennial.

Stems .5-2 ft. high; panicle 1-3 in. long; spikelets 8-20 mm. long   *D. spicáta*

EATÓNIA   Rafinesque 1819   EATONIA
(Named for Eaton, an American botanist)
Pl. 45, fig. 30.

Spikelets 2-3-flowered, in narrow panicles, the axis extended beyond the flower; glumes unequal, the lower linear, acute, 1-nerved, the upper much broader, obtuse or rounded, 3-nerved, the edges papery; lemma lanceolate, usually obtuse, palet narrow, 2-nerved; perennial.

1. Panicle dense and spike-like, the branches 1-1.5
   in. long; upper glume obovate, almost truncate *E. obtusáta*
2. Panicle loose, the branches 1-2.5 in. long, upper
   glume oblanceolate, obtuse to acutish *E. pennsilvánica*

ECHINÓCHLOA   Beauvois 1812   BARNYARD GRASS
(Gr. *echinos*, hedge-hog, *chloe*, grass, from the spiny spikelets)

Spikelets 1-flowered, in 1-sided racemes which are again grouped in racemes or panicles; glumes 2, the upper awned or awn-pointed, a sterile awned lemma, the lemma and palet enclosing the perfect flower; broad-leaved annual.

Stems 1-4 ft. high; panicle of 5-15 branches; sterile
lemma with a long or short awn *E. crus-gálli*

ÉLYMUS   Linné 1753   WILD RYE
(Gr. *elymos*, rolled up, from the inrolled palet)
Pl. 46, fig. 24.

Spikelets 1-6-flowered, usually in pairs in a dense terminal spike, alternating on the joints of the axis, the glumes forming a sort of involucre for the cluster; glumes awl-shaped, acute or awned; lemma rounded, 5-nerved, usually awned, palet 2-keeled; perennial.

1. Awns spreading widely; joints of the axis separating from each other readily at maturity *E. sitánion*
2. Awns erect or ascending, or none; joints of the
   axis not separating readily at maturity
   a. Lemma conspicuously awned
      (1) Spikelets spreading from the axis of the
          broad spike; glumes with awns 16-32
          mm. long; awn of the lemma 2-5 cm.
          long *E. canadénsis*
      (2) Spikelets appressed to the axis of the nar-
          row spike; glumes 8-12 mm. long, short-
          awned or awn-pointed; awn of the lem-
          ma 1-2 cm. long, or less *E. sibíricus*

b. Lemma awn-pointed or merely acute
   (1) Stems 3-10 ft. tall; spikes 4-15 in. long,
      thick   .   *E. condensátus*
   (2) Stems 2-4 ft. high; spikes 2-4 in. long
     (a) Spike densely hairy; spikelets 2 at each
        joint   *E. innovátus*
     (b) Spike not hairy; spikelets usually 1 at
        some or all of the joints   *E. triticoídes*

ERAGRÓSTIS Beauvois 1812 ERAGROSTIS
(Gr. *er*, spring, *agrostis*, grass)
Pl. 45, fig. 26. •

Spikelets 2-35-flowered, flattened, in panicles; glumes more or less equal, keeled, 1 or 3-nerved; lemma longer than glumes, keeled, 3-nerved, palet shorter, 2-nerved or 2-keeled, usually persisting after the lemma falls; annual or perennial.

1. Spikelets 8-35-flowered, 5-16 mm. long, 3-4 mm.
   wide; lemma 3-4 mm. long   *E. májor*
2. Spikelets 5-15-flowered, 3-8 mm. long, 1-2 mm.
   wide; lemma less than 2 mm. long
   a. Stems .5-1.5 in. high; panicles 3-8 in. long, us-
     ually greenish   *E. Púrshii*
   b. Stems 1-3 ft. high; panicle 6-24 in. long, purple *E. pectinácea*

ERIOCÓMA Nuttall 1818 INDIAN MILLET
(Gr. *erion*, wool, *kome*, hair)
Pl. 46, fig. 20.

Spikelets 1-flowered, in panicles; glumes broad, awn-tipped; lemma firm, oval to elliptic, densely silky-hairy and with a terminal awn; perennial.
Stems 1-3 ft. high; panicle 6-12 in. long; spikelet 6-8
mm. long   *E. cuspidáta*

FESTÚCA Linné 1753 FESCUE
(The ancient Latin name)
Pl. 45, fig. 19.

Spikelets 2-13-flowered, in racemes or panicles; glumes more or less unequal, acute, keeled; lemma narrow, rounded on the back, 5-nerved, usually awned at the tip, palet little shorter; annual or perennial.

1. Spikelets 6-13-flowered; stamens 2; annual   *F. octofióra*
2. Spikelets 2-10-flowered; stamens 3; perennial
   a. Leaves inrolled, 1-2 mm. wide

(1) Stems densely tufted, without root-stalks
   or stolons
   (a) Stems 1-8 in. high; spikelets 2-4-flow-
      ered; lemma not twice as long as the
      lower glume, with an awn 1-2.5 mm.;
      long   *F. brachyphýlla*
   (b) Stems 8 in.-2.5 ft. high; lemma more
      than twice as long as the lower glume,
      with an awn 1-4 mm. long   *F. ovína*
(2) Stems with root-stalks or stolons   *F. rúbra*
b. Leaves flat, 2-5 mm. wide
   (1) Awn longer than the lemma   *F. Jónesii*
   (2) Awn 1-2 mm. long or none
    (a) Spikelets 5-9-flowered; upper glume 3-5-
       nerved   *F. elátior*
    (b) Spikelets 3-5-flowered; upper glume 1-
       nerved or 3-nerved at base
      x. Panicle open, spreading; leaves 2 mm.
         wide   *F. scabrélla*
      y. Panicle spike-like; leaves 2-4 mm. wide *F. confínis*

GRAPHÉPHORUM Desvaux 1810
(Gr. *graphe*, pencil, *phora*, bearing, from the tuft of hairs on the axis)
Pl. 46, fig. 9.

Spikelets 2-4-flowered, flattened, in a panicle, the axis hairy and extending beyond the flower; glumes acute, keeled; lemma longer than the
glumes, 3-5-nerved, entire, sometimes with a short awn below the apex,
palet narrow; perennial.
Stems 1-2.5 ft. high; panicle 2-6 in. long; spikelets 5-
  6 mm. long   *G. melicoídes*

HIEROCHLÓE Beauvois 1812 HOLY GRASS
(Gr. *hieros*, sacred, *chloe*, grass, from its use on saints' days)
Pl. 46, fig. 28.

Spikelets 3-flowered, in panicles, terminal flower perfect, the others
staminate; glumes nearly equal, acute; sterile lemma and lemma somewhat
shorter, obtuse, entire or 2-toothed, sometimes awned, palet hairy at the
tip; sweet-scented perennial.
Stems 1-2 ft. high; panicle 2-4 in. long; spikelets 4-6
  mm. long   ·   *H. odoráta*

HILÁRIA H. B. K. 1815 BLACK BUNCH GRASS
(Named for St. Hilaire, a French botanist)
Pl. 46, fig. 32.

Spikelets in groups of 3 at each joint of the zig-zag axis of the spikes,
the outer spikelets 2-3-flowered and staminate, inner spikelet 1-flowered,
pistillate; glumes unequal, 5-nerved, usually 2-lobed, the lower glume
awned; lemmas much narrower than the glumes; perennials with terminal,
solitary spikes.

Stems 1-2 ft. high; spikes 2-4 in. long; spikelets 8-10
  mm. long; awn of the lower glume longer than the
  spikelet   *H. Jámesii*

HOMALOCÉNCHRUS Meigen 1776 RICE, CUT GRASS
(Gr. *homalos*, like, *kenchros*, millet)

Spikelets 1-flowered, in panicles, strongly flattened; glumes 2, the lower
broad and folded, the inner much narrower; lemma and palet lacking;
marsh perennial.

Stems 1-4 ft. high; panicle 5-9 in. long; spikelets 4-5
  mm. long   *H. oryzoides*

HÓRDEUM Linné 1753 BARLEY, SQUIRRELTAIL GRASS
(The Latin name of the barley)
Pl. 46, fig. 25.

Spikelets 1-flowered, usually 3 at each joint of the axis of the terminal,
cylindric spike, lateral spikelets usually short-stalked and imperfect, the
axis produced beyond the flower; glumes usually awn-like and appearing
like the involucre around the spikelet; lemma rounded on the back, 5-
nerved, awned, palet nearly equal, 2-keeled; annual or perennial.

1. Spikes feathery with spreading awns; awn of the
    central lemma 1-3 in. long   *H. jubátum*
2. Spikes narrow, the awns short and erect
    a. Glumes needle-like, all alike
        (1) Lateral spikelets neutral   *H. nodósum*
        (2) Lateral spikelets with flowers   *H. boreále*
    b. Glumes of 2 sorts, those of the middle spikelet
        broad at base, lanceolate   *H. pusíllum*

KOELÉRIA Persoon 1805 KOELERIA
(Named for Koeler, a German botanist)
Pl. 45, fig. 28.

Spikelets 2-5-flowered, in a spike-like panicle; glumes unequal, narrow,
acute, keeled; lemma 3-5-nerved, palet 2-keeled; perennial.

Stems 1-3 ft. high; panicle 1-7 in. long; spikelets 4-6
mm. long, the keel rough-ciliate *K. cristáta*

LYCÚRUS H. B. K. 1815 TEXAN TIMOTHY
(Gr. *lykos*, wolf, *oura*, tail)

Spikelets 1-flowered, usually in pairs on spike-like terminal panicles;
glumes 2, 3-nerved, the nerves often extending into awns; lemma broader
and longer than the glumes, 2-nerved, palet smaller, 2-nerved, 2-toothed;
tufted perennial.

Stems 8-20 in. high; panicles 1-3 in. long; spikelets 4
mm. long, the lemma with an awn its own length *L. phleoídes*

LÓLIUM Linné 1753 DARNEL
(The Latin name)

Spikelets 4-10-flowered, solitary, sessile, and alternate in the notches
of the terminal spike, flattened, the edge of the spikelet turned toward the
axis; glumes 1 or 2; lemmas rounded on the back, 5-7-nerved, palet 2-
keeled; annual or perennial.

1. Glume shorter than the spikelet *L. perénne*
2. Glume equalling or exceeding the spikelet *L. temuléntum*

MÉLICA Linné 1753 MELIC GRASS
(A Greek name of the sorghum, probably from *mel*, honey)
Pl. 45, fig. 22.

Spikelets 2-5-flowered, in panicles, the axis extended beyond the flowers
and usually bearing 2-3 empty scales; glumes more or less unequal, 3-5-
nerved; lemma rounded on the back, 7-13-nerved, sometimes awned, palet
shorter than the lemma, 2-keeled; perennial.

1. Stems bulbous-thickened at the base; spikelets 5-8-
    flowered, 10-12 mm. long *M. bulbósa*
  2. Stems not bulbous-thickened at the base; spike-
    lets 2-5-flowered
    a. Spikelets nodding *M. parviflóra*
    b. Spikelets not nodding *M. Smíthii*

MUHLENBÉRGIA Schreber 1789 MUHLENBERGIA
(Named for Muhlenberg, an American botanist)
Pl. 46, fig. 21, 22.

Spikelets 1-flowered, in open or dense, spike-like panicles; glumes acute,
sometimes awned; lemma 3-5-nerved, obtuse, acute or awned, palet narrow;
annual or perennial.

1. Panicle narrow or spike-like, the short branches
    erect or ascending
    a. Lemma with an awn usually 1-2 cm. long
        (1) Panicle dense; lemma with a tuft of basal
            hairs its own lengtl.   *M. comáta*
        (2) Panicle narrow, not dense and spike-like;
            lemma without a tuft of basal hairs   *M. grácilis*
    b. Lemma with an awn 1-2 mm. long, or awnless
        (1) Stems with scaly root-stalks
            (a) Glumes about equal, much longer than
                the lemma   *M. racemósa*
            (b) Glumes somewhat unequal, the longer
                equalling the lemma   *M. mexicána*
        (2) Stems without scaly root-stalks
            (a) Panicles 1-2 in. long, upper glume 3-
                nerved   *M. filicúlmis*
            (b) Panicles 2-4 in. long; upper glume 1-
                nerved   *M. Wríghtii*
2. Panicle open, the branches spreading, often hori-
    zontal
    a. Lateral branches of the panicle panicle-like;
        spikelets 3 mm. long; awn 1-2 mm. long   *M. púngens*
    b. Lateral branches of the panicle raceme-like;
        spikelets 2 mm. long; awn 2-6 mm. long   *M. gracíllima*

MUNRÓA Torrey 1856 MUNROA
(Named for Munroe, an English botanist)
Pl. 45, fig. 25.

Spikelets 2-5-flowered, in clusters of 3-6 in the axils of the floral leaves;
glumes lanceolate, acute, 1-nerved; lemma larger, 3-nerved, 3-toothed at
apex with tufts of hairs near the middle, palet narrow, acute: low grass with
short spiny-tipped leaves.

Stems tufted, 2-8 in. high; leaves an inch long or less,
    spiny-tipped   *M. squarrósa*

ORYZÓPSIS Michaux 1803 MOUNTAIN RICE
(Gr. *oryza*, rice, *opsis*, likeness)
Pl. 46, fig. 19.

Spikelets 1-flowered, in panicles; glumes about equal, obtuse or pointed;
lemma broad with a terminal awn, palet narrow; perennial.

1. Spikelet, exclusive of awn, 2-5 mm. long
  a. Awn 1-2 mm. long, much shorter than the lem-
    ma; spikelets 3-4 mm. long   *O. júncea*
  b. Awn 4 mm. long; spikelets 4-5 mm. long   *O. exigua*
  c. Awn 6-8 mm. long; more than twice as long
    as the lemma; spikelets 2-2.5 mm. long   *O. micrántha*
2. Spikelets, exclusive of awn, 6-8 mm. long   *O. asperifólia*

PANICULÁRIA Fabricius 1763 MANNA GRASS

(Lat. *panicula*, panicle)

(Glyceria Robert Brown)

Pl. 45, fig. 20.

Spikelets 3-13-flowered, in panicles; glumes acute or obtuse, 1-3-nerved; lemma rounded on the back, 5-9-nerved, palet scarcely shorter, 2-keeled; perennial swamp or water grasses.

1. Spikelets ovate to oblong, 2-6 mm. long
  a. Panicle 3-8 in. long, nodding, at least above
    (1) Spikelets 2-4 mm. long; lemma 7-nerved *P. nerváta*
    (2) Spikelets 4-5 mm. long; lemma 5-nerved *P. pauciflóra*
  b. Panicle 8-15 in. long, erect or nodding   *P. grándis*
2. Spikelets linear, 1-2 cm. long   *P. flúitans*

PÁNICUM Linné 1753 PANIC GRASS

(The Latin name)

Pl. 46, fig. 30.

Spikelets 1-2-flowered in panicles, when 2-flowered the lower one staminate; glumes 2, sterile lemma sometimes with a staminate flower; lemma and palet enclosing the perfect flower; awns none; annual or perennial.

1. Spikelets pointed, lanceolate or lance-ovate
  a. Stems 1-2 ft. high; sheaths bristly-hairy; spike-
    lets 2-3 mm. long   *P. capilláre*
  b. Stems 3-5 ft. high; sheaths not hairy; spikelets
    4-5 mm. long   *P. virgátum*
2. Spikelets not pointed, obtuse or rounded, ovoid to
  obovoid, 2-3 mm. long   *P. scopárium*

PÁSPALUM Linné 1759 PASPALUM

(The Greek name of a grass)

Spikelets 1-flowered, oblong to round, plano-convex, in 2-4 rows on 1-sided spikes, the latter single, paired or panicled; glumes 2; lemma and palet with a perfect flower; perennial.

Stems 1-2 ft. high; spikes 1.5-4 in. long, mostly single;
spikelets 1.5-2 mm. long   *P. setáceum*

PHÁLARIS Linné 1753 CANARY GRASS
(Gr. *phalos*, shining, from the grain)
Pl. 46, fig. 29.

Spikelets 1-flowered, in spikes or spike-like panicles; glumes 2; sterile
lemmas 2, tiny or reduced to silky awns; lemma pointed, hairy, palet similar; annual or perennial.

1. Spikelets in a spike-like panicle; glumes not
   winged   *P. arundinácea*
2. Spikelets in an ovoid to cylindric spike; glumes
   broadly winged
   a. Spike ovoid to oblong, .5-1.5 in. long; spikelet
      6-8 mm. long; sterile lemmas small scales   *P. canariénsis*
   b. Spike cylindric, 1-4 in. long; spikelets 5 mm.
      long; sterile lemmas hairy-awned   *P. caroliniána*

PHÍPPSIA Trinius 1821
(Named for Phipps, an Arctic explorer)

Spikelets 1-flowered, in small panicles; glumes tiny, the lower often
wanting; lemma keeled, palet somewhat shorter, fringed-toothed, 2-keeled,
stamen usually 1; tufted alpine perennial.

Stems 1-4 in. high; panicles .5-3.5 cm. long; spikelets
1-1.5 mm. long   *P. álgida*

PHLÉUM Linné 1753 TIMOTHY
(The Greek name of a plant)
Pl. 46, fig. 23.

Spikelets 1-flowered, in spikes; glumes 2, flattened, keeled, mid-nerve
produced into an awn; lemma much shorter, broad, toothed at tip, palet narrow; annual or perennial.

1. Spike cylindric, 1.5-8 in. long, 5-8 mm. wide;
   stems 2-5 ft. tall   *P. praténse*
2. Spike ovoid to oblong, .5-2 in. long, 6-12 mm.
   wide; stems .5-1.5 ft. high   *P. alpínum*

PHRAGMÍTES Trinius 1820 REED GRASS
(Gr. *phragma*, hedge, from its dense growth)

Spikelets 3-several-flowered, in panicles, first flower often staminate,
axis jointed between the lemmas, long-hairy; glumes unequal, lanceolate,
acute, shorter than the spikelet; sterile lemma sometimes with a staminate

flower; lemma narrow, long-pointed, much exceeding the palet; reed-like swamp perennial.

Stems 5-15 ft. high; panicle .5-1.5 ft. long; flowering
  scales 10-12 mm. long   *P. commúnis*

PóA Linné 1753 BLUE GRASS
(Gr. *poa,* grass)
Pl. 45, fig. 21.

Spikelets 2-6-flowered, in panicles, flattened, flowers mostly perfect; glumes keeled, 1-3-nerved; lemma longer than the glumes, often cobwebby-hairy at base, 5-nerved, the nerves usually hairy; palets usually shorter, 2-nerved or 2-keeled; annual or perennial.

1. Stems annual, i. e., without rootstocks, tufted, 2-8
     in. high; lemma 5-nerved, not cobwebby at base *P. ánnua*
2. Stems perennial, with rootstocks
     a. Stems distinctly flattened and 2-edged   *P. compréssa*
     b. Stems round, not 2-edged
          (1) Lemma cobwebby at base
               (a) Panicle small, 2-4 cm. long   *P. láxa*
               (b) Panicle large, 5-15 cm. long
                    x. Branches of the panicle reflexed   *P. refléxa*
                    y. Branches not reflexed
                         (x) Lemmas acute or pointed   *P. praténsis*
                         (y) Lemmas obtuse   *P. fláva*
          (2) Lemma not cobwebby
               (a) Panicle 2-4 cm. long; leaves 2-4 cm.
                    long, 3-4 mm. wide   *P. alpína*
               (b) Panicle 4-15 cm. long; leaves 5-20 cm.
                    long, 1-3 mm. wide
                    x. Stems 1-8 in. high; at 11000-14500 ft.
                         (x) Stems 1-4 in. high; lemma smooth
                              or nearly so   *P. Lettermánnii*
                         (y) Stems 4-8 in. high; lemma very
                              hairy, especially the nerves   *P. Pattersónii*
                    y. Stems 1-4 ft. high, at 4-11000 ft.
                         (x) Spikelets distinctly flattened
                              m. Flowers perfect
                                   (m) Plants tufted, without root-
                                        stocks; panicle narrow,
                                        dense, green to purple;
                                        glumes more or less un-
                                        equal   *P. subaristáta*

    (n) Plants not tufted, with creep-
          ing rootstocks; panicles
          open; leaf-sheaths hairy to
          smooth   *P. Wheéleri*
    n. Flowers dioecious   *P. fendleriána*
  (y) Spikelets nearly round, little flat-
          tened
    m. Lemmas hairy, at least at base   *P. lúcida*
    n. Lemmas not hairy, finely rough-
          ened   *P. nevadénsis*

POLYPÓGON Desfontaines 1800 BEARD GRASS
(Gr. *poly*, many, *pogon*, beard)

Spikelets 1-flowered in spike-like panicles; glumes awned, lemma smaller, short-awned below the tip, palet shorter; annual.

Stems tufted, 4-20 in. high; panicle 1-4 in. long;
  glumes 2 mm. long, with a bent awn, 4-6 mm. long *P. monspeliénsis*

PUCCINÉLLIA Parlatore 1848 MEADOW GRASS
(Named for Puccinelli, an Italian botanist)

Spikelets usually 3-10-flowered, in panicles; glumes unequal, obtuse or
acute; lemma rounded on the back, obtuse or acute, 5-nerved, the nerves
faint, palet about equal; perennial.

Stems 1-4 ft. high; spikelets 3-6 mm. long; lemma 2
mm. long   ·   *P. airoídes*

REDFIÉLDIA Vasey 1887 REDFIELDIA
(Named for Redfield, an American botanist)
Pl. 45, fig. 29.

Spikelets 1-3-flowered, in panicles; glumes 2, equal, 1-nerved, shorter
than the spikelet; lemma 3-nerved with a tuft of hairs at base, palet shorter,
2-nerved; perennial.

Stems 1-4 ft. high; leaves 1-2 ft. long; panicle 8-20 in.
long; spikelets 6 mm. long   *R. flexuósa*

SCHEDONNÁRDUS Steudel 1855 SCHEDONNARDUS
(Gr. *schedon*, near; Nardus)
Pl. 46, fig. 6.

Spikelets 1-flowered, sessile and alternate on a zig-zag axis, in slender
spikes forming raceme-like clusters; glumes 2, narrow, awn-pointed; lemma
longer, palet narrow, shorter; annual.

Stems .5-1.5 ft. high; spikes 2-4 in. long; spikelets 2-
3 mm. long   *S. paniculátus*

SCLEROPÓGON   Philippi 1860
(Gr. *skleros*, stiff, *pogon*, beard)

Spikelets dissimilar, dioecious, in a narrow panicle, staminate spikelets
flattened, linear, 10-14-flowered, with lanceolate, acute glumes and a 3-
toothed lemma equalled by the palet; pistillate spikelets linear-oblong, 3-5-
flowered; glumes lanceolate, the upper larger; lemma cylindric, enclosing
the palet; joints of the axis, 5-nerved, the 3 main nerves ending in 3 long
twisted awns.

Stems tufted, 4-12 in. high; staminate spikelets 1-3 cm.
long, pistillate 1-2 cm. long   *S. karwinskiánus*

SÓRGHUM   Persoon 1805   JOHNSON GRASS
(The Indian name)

Spikelets in pairs at the joints, or in 3's at the ends of the branches of
terminal panicles; one spikelet, sessile and perfect, the lateral stalked, staminate or empty; glumes 2, the outer hard and shiny; sterile lemma present;
lemma awned, enclosing a small palet and perfect flower, or the palet sometimes lacking; annual or perennial.

Stems 3-5 ft. high; panicle .5-1.5 ft. long; sessile spike-
let 4-6 mm. long, the awn 8-15 mm. long   *S. halepénse*

SPARTÍNA   Schreber 1789   CORD GRASS, SLOUGH GRASS
(Gr. *spartinos*, cord-like, from the leaves of some species)
Pl. 46, fig. 4.

Spikelets 1-flowered, jointed with a pedicel below the glumes, in 2 rows
on the axis of 1-sided spikes, the latter in raceme-like clusters; glumes 2,
unequal, keeled; lemma keeled, palet often longer, 2-nerved; marsh perennial.

1. Lower glume equalling the lemma, upper glume
   awned; stems 3-6 ft. high; spikes 5-20, 2-5 in.
   long   *S. cynosuroídes*
2. Lower glume, acute, shorter than the lemma, up-
   per glume not awned; stems 1-3 ft. high;
   spikes 4-8, 1-2 in. long   *S. grácilis*

SPORÓBOLUS   Robert Brown 1810   RUSH GRASS
(Gr. *spora*, seed, *bolos*, thrown, from the deciduous grain)
Pl. 46, fig. 14.

Spikelets 1-flowered, in panicles; glumes 2, equal or unequal; lemma equalling or longer than the glumes, smooth or long-hairy, palet 2-nerved; perennial or annual.

1. Panicle narrow and spike-like
   a. Plants 1-2 in. high; spikelets 1 mm. long   *S. Wólfii*
   b. Plants 4-20 in. high
      (1) Spikelets 3-5 mm. long   *S. vaginiflórus*
      (2) Spikelets 1.5-3 mm. long
        (a) Spikelets 1.5-2 mm. long; panicles 1-2 cm. long   *S. simplex*
        (b) Spikelets 2.5-3 mm. long; panicles 1-7 cm. long   *S. brevifólius*
2. Panicle open, at least after flowering
   a. Lemma densely silky-hairy on the nerves; spikelets 2.5-3 mm. long   *S. trichólepis*
   b. Lemma not densely silky-hairy
      (1) Glumes about equal
        (a) Annual; leaves 1-1.5 mm. wide   *S. confúsus*
        (b) Perennial; leaves 2-3 mm. wide   *S. asperifólius*
      (2) Lower glume half the length of the upper
        (a) Spikelets 4-6 mm. long   *S. heterólepis*
        (b) Spikelets 1.5-2.5 mm. long
           x. Panicle 1.5-3 in. long; lower glume about ¼ the length of the upper   *S. argútus*
           y. Panicle 5-15 in. long
            (x) Panicle more or less included in the leaf-sheath; spikelets 2-2.5 mm. long; lower glume ⅓ the length of the upper   *S. cryptándrus*
            (y) Panicle usually exserted; spikelets 1.5-2 mm. long; lower glume about ½ as long as the upper   *S. airoídes*

STÍPA Linné 1753 STIPA, SPEAR GRASS
(Gr. *stypa*, tow, probably from the use of some species)
Pl. 46, fig. 15, 16.

Spikelets 1-flowered, long and narrow, in open or dense panicles; glumes narrow, acute or awn-pointed; lemma stiff, inrolled, with a hairy hard point at base, bearing a usually bent awn which is spiral at base, palet 2-nerved, included; tall perennial or annual.

1. Awn 1-5 cm. long
   a. Panicles open

(1) Awn long-plumy; glumes equal, 5 mm. long *S. mongólica*

(2) Awn rough, not plumy; glumes unequal,
the lower 9 mm. long *S. Richardsónii*

b. Panicles narrow and spike-like

  (1) Awn long-plumy, the hairs 1-6 mm. long

    (a) Glumes 10-12 mm. long; lemma sparsely
hairy, 5-6 mm. long *S. occidentális*

    (b) Glumes 16-18 mm. long; lemma silky,
10-12 mm. long *S. speciósa*

  (2) Awn not plumy, or at least the hairs less
than 1 mm. long

    (a) Lemma with a tuft of hairs at the tip *S. Scríbneri*

    (b) Lemma without a tuft of hairs at the
tip; stems 3-8 ft. high; sheaths smooth
or hairy; awns 2-4 cm. long *S. virídula*

2. Awn 3-7 in. long

a. Awn plumy; glumes 3-4 cm. long *S. neo-mexicána*

b. Awn not plumy, glumes 2-3.5 cm. long

  (1) Panicle usually partly included in the
sheath; glumes 18-27 mm. long; lemma
8-12 mm. long *S. comáta*

  (2) Panicle not enclosed at base; glumes 24-
36 mm. long; lemma 14-25 mm. long *S. spártea*

TRIÓDIA Robert Brown 1810 TRIODIA

(Gr. *tri-*, from the 3-pointed lemmas)

(Tricuspis, Triplasis Beauvois)

Pl. 45, fig. 27.

Spikelets 2-12-flowered, in racemes or panicles; glumes keeled, 1-3-nerved; lemma 3-nerved, lobed or toothed at tip, the nerves hairy and usually extending as short points between the teeth, palet broad, 2-keeled; perennial.

1. Spikelets loosely 2-5-flowered, 5-8 mm. long;
lemma 2-lobed at tip, the middle nerve becoming a short awn *T. purpúrea*

2. Spikelets 5-12-flowered

a. Lemma awnless, entire or 2-toothed *T. mútica*

b. Lemma awned

  (1) Spikelets 6-7-flowered *T. pulchélla*

  (2) Spikelets 8-12-flowered *T. acumináta*

Trisétum   Persoon 1805   False Oat
(Lat. *tri-*, three, *seta*, bristle)
Pl. 46, fig. 11.

Spikelets 2-4-flowered, in spike-like or open panicles; glumes 2, unequal, acute; lemma usually shorter than the glumes, 2-toothed, with an awn on the back, palet narrow, 2-toothed; perennial.

    1. Panicles dense and spike-like, 1-4 in. long; leaves
        1-4 in. long; lower glume 3-nerved   *T. subspicátum*
    2. Panicles loose but not spreading; leaves 5-10 in.
        long; lower glume 1-nerved   *T. montánum*

PINALES   PINE ORDER

PINACEAE   PINE FAMILY

Sepals and petals none, stamens scale-like, forming cones several-many in a cluster, pistils scale-like, bearing the ovules exposed on the surface, forming few-many-scaled cones, or berries, fruit a cone with few-many woody, papery or fleshy scales, sometimes a berry; flowers or cones usually · monoecious; trees or shrubs usually with scale-like or needle-like, evergreen leaves.

    1. Leaves alternate or in clusters
       a. Leaves alternate, scattered; cones fringed or
          with papery scales
          (1) Leaves square or 4-angled, inserted on
             raised bases; cones hanging, not fringed Picea
          (2) Leaves flat
            (a) Cones hanging, fringed with 3-lobed
               scales   Pseudotsuga
            (b) Cones erect in the top of the tree, not
               fringed   Abies
       b. Leaves in clusters or fascicles; cones with thick,
          woody scales   Pinus
    2. Leaves opposite or in whorls of 3; cones berry-
       like   Juniperus

Ábies   Jussieu 1789   Fir
(The Latin name)
Pl. 47, fig. 8, 9.

Staminate cones axillary, pistillate cones lateral, erect on the topmost branches of the trees, ovules 2 on each scale, the latter with a thin papery, pointed bract; fruiting cones oblong to cylindric, the scales falling away from the spine-like axis; leaves flat, linear, scattered, single, spreading and appearing 2-ranked; evergreen trees.

1. Cones 7-12 cm. long, 3-5 cm. wide; leaves 3.5-6 cm. long, widely spreading — *A. cóncolor*
2. Cones 5-7 cm. long, 2-3 cm. wide; leaves 2-3.5 cm. long, usually somewhat crowded — *A. lasiocárpa*

JUNÍPERUS Linné 1753 JUNIPER, CEDAR
(Lat. form of the Celtic name)
Pl. 47, fig. 11, 12.

Staminate cones oblong or ovoid, pistillate cones with the few scales opposite or rarely in 3's, fleshy, usually with a single ovule on each scale, fruiting cones roundish, berry-like, with 1-6 seeds; leaves sessile or whorled, awl-shaped or scale-like, usually of 2 kinds; flowers dioecious or sometimes monoecious; evergreen trees or shrubs.

1. Trees or tree-like, 10-40 ft. high
   a. Berry 1-seeded, 8-10 mm. wide
      (1) Berry with juicy, resinous flesh, 5-7 mm. wide — *J. monospérma*
      (2) Berry with dry, fibrous sweet flesh, 3-6 mm. long — *J. utahénsis*
   b. Berry 2-4-seeded, 4-5 mm. wide — *J. scopulórum*
2. Low shrubs, 1-5 ft. high, as a rule, forming dense patches
   a. Leaves all awl-shaped, prickly-pointed, 1-2 cm. long — *J. commúnis*
   b. Most of the leaves scale-like, appressed, in 4 rows — *J. sabína*

PÍCEA Link 1827 SPRUCE
(The Latin name, perhaps from *pix*, pitch)
Pl. 47, fig. 6, 7.

Staminate cones axillary, pistillate cones terminal, ovoid to oblong, ovules 2 on each scale, seeds winged, cones ovoid to oblong, hanging, the scales papery, persistent; leaves linear, 4-angled, scattered, single, on short bases; evergreen trees.

1. Cones 3-5 cm. long; twigs finely hairy; leaves only moderately stiff and sharp — *P. Engelmánnii*
2. Cones 5-10 cm. long; twigs usually smooth; leaves very stiff and spiny — *P. púngens*

Plate 47.

PINES-JOINT FIRS

PINE FAMILY

PINE

1. Pinus ponderosa: leaf cluster; cone x½
2. Pinus flexilis: leaf cluster; cone x½
3. Pinus edulis: leaf cluster; cone x½
4. Pinus aristata: leaf cluster; cone x½
5. Pinus murrayana: leaf cluster; cone x½

SPRUCE

6. Picea pungens: leaf and cone
7. Picea Engelmannii: leaf and cone

FIR

8. Abies lasiocarpa: leaf and cone
9. Abies concolor: leaf and cone

10. Pseudotsuga mucronata: leaf and cone
11. Juniperus sibirica: Juniper, Cedar
12. Juniperus scopulorum

JOINT FIR FAMILY

13. Ephedra trifurca: Joint Fir

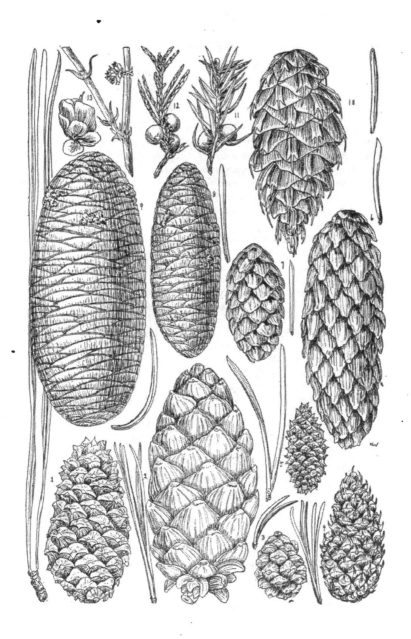

Pínus Linné 1753 Pine

(The Latin form of the Celtic name)

Pl. 47, fig. 1-5.

Staminate cones at the bases of new shoots, several-many in a cluster, pistillate cones solitary or few on year-old twigs, in the upper part of the tree, composed of scales with 2 ovules, borne on small bracts; cone woody, maturing the second autumn, seeds winged; leaves of 2 kinds, primary, linear or scale-like, deciduous, secondary, needle-like in clusters of 2-5, rarely single with a papery sheath at base; evergreen, monoecious trees.

1. Leaves 2-3 in a cluster, rarely single
   a. Leaves 1-3 in. long
      (1) Trunks 4-20 ft. high; leaves usually 2, sometimes 1, 1-2 in. long; cones 1-2 in. long; tips of the scales very broad and thick, without prickles   *P. edúlis*
      (2) Trunks 20-100 ft. high; leaves 2-3 in. long; cones 1-2 in. long; tips of the scales not broad and thick, prickly-pointed   *P. murrayána*
   b. Leaves 4-8 in. long, 2-3 in a cluster; cones 3-5 in. long; scales thickened, with a strong recurved prickle   *P. ponderósa*
2. Leaves 5 in a cluster
   a. Scales of the cone with a prickle; cones 2-4 in. long; leaves 2.5-4 cm. long; stems 10-40 ft. high   *P. aristáta*
   b. Scales of the cone without a prickle; cones 4-8 in. long; leaves 2-3 in. long; stems 20-60 ft. high   *P. fléxilis*

Pseudotsúga Carrière 1867 Douglas Fir

(Gr. *pseudes*, false, Japanese, *tsuga*, hemlock)

Pl. 47, fig. 10.

Staminate cones axillary, pistillate cones terminal or axillary, oblong-ovoid, ovules 2 on each scale, seeds winged, cones ovoid-oblong, hanging, scales papery with long, 2-pointed and awned projecting bracts; leaves flattish, scattered, single; evergreen trees.

Trunks 30-100 ft. high; cones 1.5-4 in. long, fringed by the bracts; leaves 2-4 cm. long   *P. mucronáta*

GNETÁCEAE JOINT FIR FAMILY

Staminate flowers in catkins with solitary or clustered stamens in a papery, 2-toothed perianth, pistillate flower an erect ovule with a projecting, style-like appendage, enclosed in a perianth which is hardened and often thickened in fruit; flowers dioecious with persistent bracts in axillary clusters; shrubs or small trees, mostly with jointed, opposite or clustered branches and opposite or whorled foliage-like or scale-like leaves.

EPHÉDRA Linné 1753 JOINT FIR
(Gr. *epi*, upon, *hedra*, seat)
Pl. 47, fig. 13.

Characters of the family.

1. Scales and branches opposite; bracts united; fruit
   5-6 mm. long   *E. antisyphilítica*
2. Scales and branches in 3's; bracts hardly united;
   fruit 7-12 mm. long
   a. Scales short, 2-3 mm. long; fruit rough, 7-8
      mm. long   *E. Torreyána*
   b. Scales long, 6-12 mm. long; fruit smooth, 12
      mm. long   *E. trifúrca*

ERRATA

Page

5. Read *scopulórum* for *scópulorum*

7. Omit *R. Purshii* in line (y)

12. Read *alpínum* for *álpinum*

14. Transpose 7 and 6, and insert "Fumitory Family" before the latter

22. Read *palustris* for *palustre*

28. Add (Gr. *thlaspi*, cress, from *thlao*, crush) under *Thlaspi*

39.º Under *Geranium,* transpose the phrases "typically in moist soil" and "typically in dry soil."

42. Insert after *Frankenia,* "Characters of the family."

54. Read *Silene Scouleri* under 1; *tamariscina* for *tamarischina* under 20.

78. Insert the following key under *Pirolaceae*

    1. Flower solitary   MONESES

    2. Flowers several to many

      a. Flowers in a raceme; leaves basal   PIROLA

      b. Flowers in a corymb; leaves on the stem CHIMAPHILA

79. Read "Leaves mottled with gray above" in line (1)

90. Read "Wintergreen Family" for "Heath Family," and insert the latter after 7.

114. Read *Hyoscýamus* for *Hyoscyámus*

119. Omit *Krynitzkia* after line (2) (a) y, and insert

        (x) Nutlets attached laterally; native KRYNITZKIA

        (y) Nutlets attached basally; introduced SYMPHYTUM

GLOSSARY

Accessory Additional

Achene A dry one-seeded fruit

Acute Sharp-pointed

Alpine Above timber-line as a rule

Alternate With a single leaf at each level of attachment

Amphibious Growing in water or on land, usually in mud

Annual Lasting only one growing season

Anther The upper part of the stamen containing the pollen

Apex Tip or upper end

Apical At the tip

Appendage An addition or projection

Appressed Lying close to or against another part

Aquatic Growing in the water

Arctic Far northern

Aromatic Spicy, fragrant

Attenuate Drawn out gradually into a point

Awl-shaped More or less spine-like

Awn A slender bristle-like structure

Axil The angle between leaf and stem

Axillary Borne in the axil of a leaf

Axis The part of a stem or branch which bears leaves, flowers or flower parts

Banner The largest petal of a pea flower

Barbed Curved like a fish-hook

Basal At the base or lower end

Beak An elongated tapering structure

Beaked Bearing a beak

Bearded With hairs restricted more or less to a definite area

Berry A fleshy fruit with a thin skin or soft rind, the seeds embedded in pulp

Biconvex Both surfaces rounded or convex

Biennial Living two seasons and flowering once

Bipinnate With two sets of leaflets, primary and secondary

Blade The flat part of a leaf

Bract A reduced leaf associated with a flower or flower cluster

Bristle A stiff hair or prickle

Bulb A short round stem with fleshy scales, usually below ground

Bulbil A small bulb, usually above ground

Bulbous Like a bulb; bearing bulbs

Calyx The cup- or saucer-shaped outer part of the flower, made up of sepals and usually green

Capitate Head-like

Capsule A dry fruit consisting of two or more carpels or pistils and splitting when ripe

Carpel A simple pistil or the unit part of a compound pistil

Catkin A narrow hanging cluster of sessile flowers

Caudex The erect perennial base of a stem

Cell The cavity or chamber of an ovary

Chaff Small papery colorless scales between the flowers of an aster head

Channel A groove

Claw The narrowed lower part of a petal

Cleft Cut about halfway to the middle

Coherent United or clinging together

Compound Consisting of two or more similar parts united

Compound leaf Consisting of two or more leaflets on a common axis, the whole falling off together as a rule

Compressed Flattened

Concave Hollowed or curved inwards

Cone An elongated axis bearing stamens or ovule-bearing scales, as in the pine

Constricted Narrowed or pinched

Convex Curved outwards

Convolute Rolled up lengthwise

Cordate Heart-shaped

Corm A solid bulb-like organ, as in the crocus

Corolla The brightly colored part of most flowers, just within the green calyx and made up of petals

Corymb A flat-topped or convex flower cluster, blooming first at the edge

Corymbose Corymb-like; arranged as in a corymb

Creeping Growing along the ground

Crenate Scalloped; with rounded shallow teeth

Crest A toothed or fringed appendage

Crested With a crest

Cross-wall Partition

Crown A crown-like structure in the center of the flowers of milkweeds

Cylindric Oblong and round in section

Cyme A flower cluster blooming from the apex or middle first, usually somewhat flat

Cymose In a cyme; cyme-like

Deciduous Falling off, usually at the close of the season

Declined Bent down

Deflexed Bent down

Dentate Toothed

Diffuse Spreading

Digitate Resembling the fingers of a hand

Dilated Broadened

Dioecious Bearing pistils and stamens on different plants

Disk The base of a flower to which the parts are attached

Disk flower One of the flowers in the central part of a head of flowers

Dissected Cut or divided into numerous parts

Divided Lobed nearly or quite to the base

Drupe A fleshy fruit with a pit or stone, such as the plum

Drupelet A small drupe

Eared With ear-like appendages

Ellipsoid Nearly elliptic

Elongated Long drawn-out

Entire Without teeth, lobes or divisions of any sort

Equitant Astride, as in the leaves of an Iris

Even-pinnate With all the leaflets paired

Exserted Projecting beyond the surrounding parts

Face The broader surface of spikelets, fruits, etc.

Fascicle A cluster, usually dense

Fascicled Borne in clusters

Felted With a dense felt-like coating of hairs

Fertile Bearing fruit; bearing pollen

Fibrous Consisting of fibres; woven in texture

Filament The stalk bearing the anther

Fleshy Thick and watery

Flower An axis bearing stamens or pistils or both, and usually also sepals and petals

Foliate With leaflets

Follicle A dry fruit of one carpel, splitting on one side only

Fruit A developing or ripened ovary; often also the axis containing the real fruits

Galea The hood-like upper lip of a corolla

Genus A group of related species, as the pine genus, the buttercup genus

Glabrous Without hairs

Gland A surface or structure which produces nectar, resin, oil, etc.; often a small appendage or projection

Glandular Bearing glands, or gland-like

Glaucous Covered with a bloom, a bluish or whitish wax coating

Globoid Nearly ball-like

Globose Ball-like

Glume One of the two small scales found at the base of the grass spikelet

Hastate Arrow-shaped but with the basal lobes diverging

Head A dense cluster of sessile flowers, such as that of the aster and sunflower

Herb A non-woody plant which dies annually, at least down to the ground

Herbaceous Herb-like, soft

Humus A rich vegetable mold

Hyaline Clear

Imbricated Overlapping like the shingles of a roof

Imperfect Referring to a flower which lacks either stamens or pistil

Included Not projecting beyond the other parts

Indehiscent Applied to fruits that do not split to let out the seeds

Inferior Applied to an organ situated below another one, especially to the ovary when below the other parts

Inflated Swollen

Inflexed Bent in

Interrupted Used of a flower cluster with large spaces between the parts

Intruded Grown inwards

Involucrate   With an involucre

Involucre   The group of leaves or scales just below a head of flowers, as in the sunflower, or sometimes below a single flower or cluster

Irregular   Applied to a flower in which the petals are unlike

Keel   The two fused lower petals of the flower of the pea family

Keeled   Ridged like the keel of a boat

Lance-linear   Narrowly lance-shaped

Lanceolate   Lance-shaped

Lance-ovate   Between lance-shaped and egg-shaped

Leaflet   The division of a compound leaf

Lemma   The outer and lower scale of a grass flower.

Ligule   A ribbon-shaped corolla, as in the rays of a sunflower head

Linear   Line-like, long and narrow, with the sides nearly parallel

Linear-oblong   Between line-like and oblong

Lip   The upper and lower halves of an irreguler corolla or calyx, as in the snapdragon; the irregular petal of an orchid

Lobe   A division of a simple leaf

Lobed   With the margin more or less cut or divided

Loment   A pea-pod deeply constricted between the seeds

Margined   With a flat border

Mealy   Covered with a white meal

Median   In the middle

Membranous   Membrane-like, papery

Monoecious   Bearing stamens and pistils in different flowers of the same plant

Mottled   With large irregular spots

Nectary   A pad of tissue, sack, spur or other structure producing or containing nectar

Nerve   One of the lines or ridges running through a leaf

Netted-veined   With veins running in various directions and connecting with each other

Neutral   Without stamens or pistil

Nut   A dry, one-seeded, non-splitting fruit with a stony shell or covering

Nutlet   A small nut

Ob-   A prefix meaning reversed or inverted

Obconic   Reversed cone-shaped

Oblanceolate   Reversed lance-shaped, with tip downward

Oblique   Slanting, uneven

Oblong   About twice as long as broad, the sides nearly parallel

Obovate   Reversed egg-shaped, the tip downward

Obovoid   More or less inverted egg-shaped

Obpyramidal   Reversed pyramid-shaped

Obtuse   Blunt

Odd-pinnate   With an odd or unpaired leaflet at the tip of a compound leaf

Opposite   Of leaves, directly across from each other; of flower parts, in front of

Orbicular   Round

Ovary The part of a pistil containing ovules or seeds

Ovate, ovoid Egg-shaped

Ovule The young unfertilized seed, as found in the flower

Palate The upper more or less swollen throat of an irregular corolla

Palet The upper and inner scale of a grass flower

Palmate Like the fingers of the hands

Panicle A compound flower cluster, the lower branches longer and blooming first

Panicled In panicles

Papilla, papule A minute projection on the surface

Pappus The bristles, hairs, awns, etc. found on the tips of fruits of dandelions, sunflowers, asters, etc.

Parasite A plant growing upon and getting its nourishment from some other plant

Parietal On the wall

Pedicel The stalk of a single flower

Peduncle The stalk of a flower cluster or a solitary flower

Perennial Lasting from year to year

Perfect A flower having both stamens and pistils

Perfoliate Applied to leaves which are united around the stem

Perianth The term applied to the calyx and corolla when they are similar

Perigynium, (pl. perigynia) The sack enclosing the ovary or fruit in the sedges

Persistent Remaining after blooming or fruiting

Petal The term applied to each part of a corolla

Petiole The stalk of a leaf

Pinnate With leaflets on both sides of a common stalk

Pinnatifid Pinnately cleft to the middle or beyond

Pistil The central part of the flower containing the young seeds and consisting of ovary, style and stigma, as a rule

Pistillate With pistils but without stamens

Plaited With two or more folds

Placenta (pl. placentae) Place of attachment for ovules

Plumose Plume-like or feathery

Pod A dry fruit of one carpel, splitting along two lines

Pollen The dust-like matter found in the anther

Pollinia Pollen-masses in orchids and milkweeds

Polygamo-monoecious The perfect and imperfect flowers on the same plant

Polygamous With both perfect and imperfect, staminate or pistillate flowers

Pome A fleshy fruit with a core, as the apple

Pore A small opening

Posterior At the back

Prickle A sharp needle-like outgrowth of the bark

Prickly With prickles

Prostrate Lying on the ground

Pungent Sharp

Pyramidal Shaped like a pyramid

Raceme A somewhat elongated axis bearing flowers with about equal pedicels

Racemose In a raceme

Ray One of the ribbon-like flowers of the composites or asters

Rayless Without rays

Receptacle The end of a flower stalk bearing the flower parts or in the asters bearing the flowers

Reflexed Bent down or back

Regular Having the members of each part alike in shape and size

Reniform Kidney-shaped

Resinous Bearing resin

Revolute With the margin rolled back

Rhomboid More or less diamond-shaped

Rootlet A small root

Rootstock, root-stalk An underground stem

Rosette One or more circles of leaves

Rudimentary Imperfect; beginning

Runner A slender stem lying on the ground and bearing one or more buds

Salver-form, salver-shaped With a slender tube, abruptly widened into a flat top

Samara A winged fruit, as in the maple

Saprophyte A plant living on dead matter and without green coloring

Segment A part or division

Sepal One of the outer circle of flower parts, usually green, a division of the calyx

Serrate With teeth as in a saw

Sessile Not stalked, seated

Sheath The part of a leaf or leaf base which clasps or encloses the stem

Shrub A woody plant, usually less than 20 feet tall

Simple Consisting of one part, not compound

Spadix A fleshy axis bearing sessile flowers

Spathe A leaf-like structure more or less enclosing a flower cluster

Spatulate Spoon-shaped, shaped like a spatula

Spike An elongated axis bearing sessile flowers

Spikelet A small few-flowered spike, the flower cluster of grasses and sedges

Spine A sharp woody outgrowth of the stem, a reduced leaf

Spur A hollow projection from a sepal or petal

Stamen The part of a flower which bears the pollen

Staminate With stamens but without pistils

Staminodium (pl. staminodia) An imperfect stamen

Stellate Star-shaped

Sterile Not producing seed; without pollen

Stigma The tip of the pistil which receives the pollen

Stipule A leaf-like part at the base of the stalk of the leaf

Stolon A stem which bends to the ground and takes root, or a runner

Strap-shaped Long and narrow in outline

Striate Marked with parallel lines

Style An extension of the pistil, bearing a stigma at its tip

Subglobose Nearly globose or head-like

Submersed, submerged Under water

Succulent Fleshy, watery

Superior Applied to a part placed above another part

Tendril A slender coiling holdfast

Terete Circular in cross-section

Terminal At the end

Ternate Of three leaflets

Ternately-compound The divisions in threes

Terrestrial On the ground, not water dwelling

Thallus A flat disk- or leaf-like body growing on the substratum

Throat Open upper portion of a united corolla

Trailing Creeping along the ground

Transversely Cross-wise

Truncate Cut off squarely

Tubercle Projection or wart

Tuberous With a tuber or with large swollen roots

Tubular Tube-like

Umbel A flower cluster with all the stalks arising from the same point

Utricle A one-seeded fruit splitting circularly

Valve One of the portions into which some dry fruits split

Verticillate Three or more in a circle

Whorl A group of three or more similar organs, as leaves, radiating from the place of attachment

Wing One of the two lateral petals of the pea flower

INDEX

The simple numbers refer to the page on which the description occurs, the grouped numbers to the page of the plate, and to the figures.

CPSIA information can be obtained
at www.ICGtesting.com
Printed in the USA
BVHW051015020821
613411BV00002B/129